CW01496400

Transition to Agro-Ecology

For a Food Secure World

Jelleke de Nooy van Tol

authorHOUSE®

AuthorHouse™ UK
1663 Liberty Drive
Bloomington, IN 47403 USA
www.authorhouse.co.uk
Phone: 0800.197.4150

Published by AuthorHouse 09/28/2016

ISBN: 978-1-5246-3336-3 (sc)
ISBN: 978-1-5246-3337-0 (hc)
ISBN: 978-1-5246-3383-7 (e)

Print information available on the last page.

First published in Dutch, November 2013, titled HEEL DE WERELD, by Jan van Arkel Publishing House, in collaboration with the Netwerk for Vital Agriculture and Food, NVLV, Netherlands.

Contact:
Issuu.com/jellekeforagroecology
www.jellekedenooy.nl
info@jellekedenooy.nl

This book is about Man's relationship with his most essential life support system: his food supply and the ecology that sustains it.

It is also about the due rehabilitation of this support system:
by restoring coherence in regional agro-ecological systems;
by restoring soils;
by learning from the future as it emerges;
being led by 'the *New Normal*'.

A call to Agroecology.

Contents

TRANSITIONING

EMERGING FUTURE

TO BE OR NOT TO BE

1. Que Sera? What Will Be?

"Between 2010 and 2020 we saved the world by changing to eco-agricultural practises, worldwide. That is what we will be saying in 2030, when we look back upon these times."[1]

Changing the way we observe, to create the world we want[2]:

---

[1]   John Ambler, Vice-President for Strategy, Oxfam America, in 2011.

[2]   After Frances Moor Ecomind

You are sitting in a plane, quite relaxed. The plane left on time and is heading in the right direction, or so you assume. Then suddenly you see that one of the airplane's wings is on fire. Alarmed, you call the stewardess who assures you that all is fine and guides you back to your seat. Yet you are too nervous to meekly stay in your seat so you don't agree and run to the cockpit to talk to the pilot. Then it appears no one is there behind the steering wheel...

Lesson learned: no one is in charge. Different people are responsible for different parts, but no one guides the *whole*.

This is how Joris Luyendijk[3] starts his book '*It can't be true*'. He interviewed many different people working in the financial heart of the world in London, about how the 2008 crash happened, wondering if it could happen again. In the course of his interviews it appears that it can happen again, since no one is in charge of the whole, no one oversees the consequences of what happens when one group of experts starts using the tools developed by others.

The same seems to be true for the world's agriculture and agro-food business.

No one is responsible for the whole. Industrial agriculture production systems have spun out of control.[4] Business, governments, farmers' associations, advisors, NGOs and financial donors each do their own thing to the best of their knowledge. But they work in silos, as the Americans say; each in its own silo, not aware of what the others are doing.

However, I am convinced that, since around 2005, we are moving to a worldwide tipping point, after which the world will push to produce in agro-ecological ways. Different groups, organisations, companies are making the turn to a sustainable solution for the world's agricultural production, being agro-ecology in all its forms and shapes. And this becomes a movement. Of course the frontrunners go faster than the others, but it is happening. And the tipping point may show up somewhere around 2019.

After showing you how industrial agricultural practices have spun out of control, this book will discuss 26 examples of people and organisations that have made the move to agro-ecological practises, worldwide. They are ground breaking frontrunners. You will get an overview of what is actually going on in agriculture and food production in different places in the world. And more: how it is changing. Transition is the word - structural changes are taking place and each of us can support those changes. Not by being

---

[3] For two years Joris Luyendijk was active on the Joris Luyendijk Banking blog for the Guardian in London, an experiment in long-tail journalism. His book (in Dutch) will soon be translated into Engish. http://www.jorisluyendijk.nl/english/

[4] See chapter 5 for examples of how systems have spun out of control.

innovative. By being a *follower.* Did you ever see that great 3-minutes Youtube film on leadership?[5] It is not the innovative and exceptional leader, but the first daring *followers,* who establish a group that, with the other then attracted followers, make a movement until there are more followers than people staying behind: the Tipping Point.

Towards the Tipping Point. The recent climate talks in Paris somehow showed us *sort of a tipping point.* All countries in the world agreed to take measures to decrease the warming of the earth to *only* 2,7 centigrade warmer than now. We know the magical number to survive is a maximum of 2-centigrade increase, so more efforts are still needed. But 2,7 is a fair result compared to the 5-7 centigrade we were talking about only 2 years ago. Obviously our politicians now realise climate change is serious! Just as serious as the near- catastrophe we experienced in 2008 in the financial world. That catastrophe can happen again, because no one is in the cockpit and the parts of the system take each other down in their fall like a domino game. So goes for the climate, so goes for agriculture and food. The *tipping point* of the climate made me realise that what is possible for the climate discourse (dragging more than 30 years, with the oil business fuelling climate sceptics), is also possible in the long lasting debate about intensive large scale agro- & food business versus organic and smallholder farming, enabling 9 billion people to live peacefully in 2050.

Now is the time! It is time to share with you the many magnificent examples of people, and organisations, all over the world, who make the change to growing good nutritious food, in a climate conscious way, for their own region, while taking care of the land. By paying attention. By following their heart. By understanding the soil-plant-food system. By applying agro-ecological practices. It is time to share with you how each of us plays a role in this transition. Time to share the interviews and case studies and views on this transition, which I published in Dutch, in 2013.

Peace, refugees, food and a healthy soil are related. Agriculture and food production are a hot item now: treating the root causes of the floods of refugees coming from Syria, Eritrea, Sudan and Iraq. Now of course people's mass movements have happened throughout all ages, in particular in 400 AD and between 1100 and 1300 AD. Just like in old times, these movements are occurring because those people need food and they cannot grow it in their own countries any more, due to political crises or climate change. They are now even called *climate refugees.* The changing climate is causing droughts and floods where they didn't occur before.

Resilience. So, if we could somehow arrange enough food and income from agricultural produce in their home-countries, the refugees may not even

---

[5]   http://tinyurl.com/utubetippingpoint

need to flee. Then we treat a *root cause*. Yes of course we need peace in those countries as well. Peace as a precondition for agriculture. But mind you, this is a *chicken and egg* discussion. Agriculture may be a precondition for peace. Amazingly, the resilience of people, to cope with threats to their existence, is directly related to the condition of the soil on which they live. The more eroded the soils, the less their resilience. This direct relationship was scientifically proven by my now deceased friend, Dr.Heleen van Haaften, through research in China and West Africa.[6] Whenever a region takes care of its soil and soil health, groundwater re-appears, livelihoods improve, self-confidence and trust in life return.

Sustainable production and consumption is the *New Normal*. What now still seems 'normal' - in our present turbulent times of food insecurity and hunger (in developing countries with smallholder farming), obesity and chain management (in so called 'developed' countries with industrial agriculture), oil and money crises - will be unbelievably old fashioned and unsustainable when we look back to this era, by the time it is 2030.

This book therefore lets you see:
1. How different *modern* agricultural systems have spun out of control, by lack of adequate feedback mechanisms.
2. How there are many farmers, organisations and programmes all over the world giving us the good examples of the *New Normal* and sustainable ways of agriculture and food production.
3. How we can learn from the latter group on how to let this transition happen.

What earlier seemed 'alternative' (organic agriculture, conservation agriculture and permaculture) will be the norm from 2019 onwards.

Agro-ecology (an umbrella for all those practices) is the application of ecological principles to the production of food, fuel, fiber, and pharmaceuticals, and to the management of agriculture, the growing of crops, as an ecological system; agroecological systems and agro-forestry including the social aspects. The term encompasses a broad range of approaches, and may be considered as a science, a movement, and/or a practice. Agro-ecological practices include, amongst others: organic soil and water management, restoration agriculture, conservation agriculture, closed-loop agriculture, family farming, climate conscious agriculture, holistic management and multi stakeholder certification of food. For Agro-ecologically produced food there are not such certification rules and regulations as for organic food. But there are labels![7] So as a consumer

---

[6] Dr. ir Heleen van Haaften †, 2004. Human resilience in a degrading environment.
[7] http://ec.europa.eu/environment/ecolabel/

you can support agro-ecological production, also in Africa, by critically purchasing[8] your food and flowers.

Making the difference. The *New Normal* approach is about recovering and restoring the connections and interactions between soil, water, plants, animals, food, health and us, which have been lost. We have each our own individual role in this restoration process. Because in food and agriculture, all our actions - as consumers, as employee, as a company, politician, decision maker, NGO or a financial donor to developing countries - have impact. The *New Normal* way of observing and thinking (in coherent systems and feedback mechanisms) and paying attention to how our food is being grown, helps us recreate a sustainable planet. It helps us in decision-making, as awareness helps us to recognise what actually is 'not done' any more. Just by looking at our world from a different perspective we can see and make the difference!

So what can we do to realise double harvests in a world where 90% of the farmers are smallholder farmers? No, not more chemical fertiliser, which is very often too expensive for a farmer to buy, and in the end depletes soils. No, not even more new technologies.
And yes, we must assist the smallholder farmers (both in the South and the North) in understanding and rehabilitating their soil-plant-food system, and share the existing knowledge on sustainable grazing, land management, intensive rice /root systems, traditional quality seed production, peer learning, push-pull technology, multi-cropping, conservation agriculture etc. We should assist smallholder farmers to get access to resources, not in the least the use of compost and carbon for their soils. Yes we should scale up existing good practises and appropriate technologies. And yes we should continue programmes for sustainable land management to eradicate soil erosion and continue to encourage financial capacity building for smallholder farming all over the world.

We should stop industries to sell – for only their own benefit - fertiliser and other expensive inputs (imported seeds) to relatively poor farmers. Because the result is that either the farmers do not buy as they cannot afford it and so have a very small harvest, or the farmers buy, subsequently cannot pay back the loans, or they pay back at the cost of their family's survival, or they disappear altogether.

Attention. Now how can we play a role in enhancing this change for the better? The answer is: by paying attention. By not letting your attention being drawn away by commercials, or by positive looking labels on unsustainably produced food. By not letting your attention being drawn

---

[8]   Sustainability labels on food products: Consumer motivation, understanding and use; http://www.sciencedirect.com/science/article/pii/S0306919213001796

to *fear* for more refugees and unrest, nor to the negative world news, nor to your smartphone. Because if you let that happen, then there is no space left in your brain for positive attention or for seeing new opportunities. No space to think clearly.

Instead we can pay attention to our worldview. That means asking yourself: am I (in the way I do my work or buy my groceries, or buy shares) exploiting natural resources, or just maintaining them? Or am I being part and parcel of the whole food producing system? Do I care how food is grown? And how then should I interact? This book gives you clues.

You could for example buy organic or sustainably produced food. We can pay attention to articles in newspapers that deal with exactly those issues. If you buy from a sustainably producing smallholder farmer (organic or fair trade if it is for tropical foods) then you directly support his or her farm, or business. If you buy the cheap meat or the cheap oil in the supermarket, you invest in the big agro-industrial complex, which can only survive on degrading animal welfare and the loss of bio-diversity. Your investment in the big agro-food complex (also if it is the government paying for research supporting industrial agriculture) is also detrimental to the survival of smallholders; another effect may be that your body may become undernourished (lack of essential minerals) or allergic (due to residues of pesticides or food preservatives).

Guts. Agriculture in Transition is an investigation amongst people and organisations, learning from them how - right now – agriculture, food production and consumption are in transition. We can read and see how all three are becoming more coherent and resilient again. The cases that follow show us how these changes take place. They show us which catalysts, which type of actions, which change of roles are needed; how personal development and 'having guts' make things happen. In this way, we will be able to live with 9 billion people on this planet in 2050.

Proud to be a farmer. There is one more thing I'd like you to know before we dive into this book. Most smallholder farmers are crafts (wo)men in the interface between man and Earth. Agriculture is about a wise use of natural resources (e.g. water, soil, fish, forests, land). Agri-culture is a culture: a set of rules and behaviour and decision-making that has grown during centuries and is related to the land and the people living there.

By farming a farmer interacts with nature all the time. Traditional and knowledgeable farmers play a crucial role in this interaction, having the skills and craftsmanship to manage the complex interactions between soil, water, soil life, plants and animals. They are the pharmacies of the future;

they can provide healthy food containing the necessary minerals and ingredients, as a result of good soil management. If they get the chance.

The good news is the establishment, just after the 2015 climate talks, of a new programme, called A.S.A.P. It is called so because we need to work on it *as soon as possible*. It stands for *Adaptation for Agriculture Smallholder Programme*. So maybe the smallholders will stand a chance.

The bad news is that our societies, worldwide, have changed the rules for farmers to farm in this knowledgeable way. The presently prevailing ideas about 'normal' agriculture are *entrepreneurial* and mostly to satisfy investors and shareholders. So making profits has changed policies, regulations and laws for dealing with land, with soil and with animals, even if it is detrimental in the long run. Those approaches have often overlooked other values. So let us see how changes are taking place.

Changing the Food Game. Lucas Simons, author of the recently published book with this title, states that the way we (the industrialised world) produce our food is *the cause* of exploitation, severe environmental pollution and loss of biodiversity. The UN also mentioned this in 2012. Lucas' contribution is his plea to change the rules of the game. That is the condition if we want to double food production within the next 30 years. Because right now, we still live in a world where *wrong behaviour* (that which is now regarded as 'normal') is being rewarded. Lucas also foresees a transition: in phases, step by step, by collaboration and involvement of local governments.

It is the highest time...

Go, go go, move on, move on, move on!
We are in an incredible haste
Make space, we are coming, make space as we are running really, really late,
We only have a few minutes to spare,
We have to run, jump, fly, dive, fall, get up and continue.
We can't stop now!
Go go go!
Make way, for agro-eco now![9]

---

[9]   After a famous Dutch song by Herman van Veen, translation and alterations by Author

2. Introduction

Imagine!

What will you do or say when, in 20 years from now, your children or grandchildren ask you:

"Tell us, you were a grownup in the time between 2010 and 2019. What did you do in that time of oil crises and financial crises, when people were still using chemicals in food production? What did you do when the oceans were being depleted of fish by unsustainable fisheries and plastic pollution? That time when half the western population suffered from obesity and ADHD as a result of unhealthy food and unhealthy eating habits? When people were still eating meat on a daily base, unimaginable!

What did you do at the time? Were you one of those who helped make the big transition? Were you one of the catalysts or early followers?"

This book is meant for you. Actually, it is written for anyone who is interested in what is going on in food production and consumption, related to our health, related to people in developing countries, related to climate change, soil and water, and how we can change it for the better. Each of us can do something, however small.

For frontrunners and trendsetters this is a *must read*, as it deals with the ways in which the transition takes place and how we can work together to accelerate reaching the tipping point. People working in agriculture and food production may find a practical overview about what is going on in the world at different scale levels, from local to global. We are at a crossroads really: do we continue to invest in large scale industrial agriculture, or do we take the road which supports sustainable climate smart, closed loop family farming? In this book we see that many individuals and organisations have already made the switch to the latter. However, the clue is that restoration of natural cycles in an agro-eco system is only possible when you are willing to look at agriculture from a systems perspective. That means: looking at the interactions between soil, water, plants, animals and the resilience of this complex system at different scales. Instead of looking only at the outcome: the products and profits.

Think globally, act locally! Policymakers, politicians and others who are involved in city food planning or world food programming may find this book enlightening as it gives many examples of the things that work and the things that don't work. But it does require you to dare look over the wall of your own sector, to come out of your *silo*, to go along with some out-of-the-box thinking. So if you have become curious now, read on!

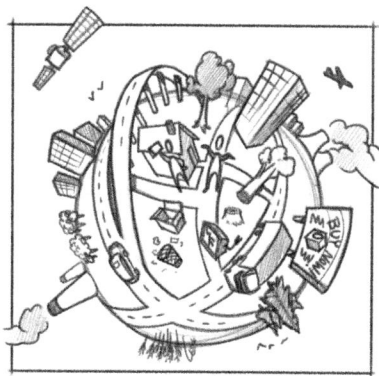

Fig. 1. Think globally, act locally

What will this book bring us?

In chapter 3 we are introduced to 3 perspectives, 3 ways of looking at agriculture and food. Chapter 4 then deals with the question *'To be or not to be?'* The world's food supply and the earth as an ecological system are at stake. Will we need three planet Earths to support us in 2050? If it weren't such a challenge we wouldn't need this book.

How *not* to do agriculture. Chapter 5 shows a varied range of examples of agricultural systems that have spun out of control, worldwide, often unintentionally. This makes us understand how it could happen and why we don't want such an unsustainable approach to agriculture any more. This is the WHY: we must change in order to prevent the worst-case scenario to happen.

Resilient agroecological systems. In chapters 6 and 7 we learn how we can create healthy agroeco systems and how important the role is of a healthy soil. About soil we can learn many things: that it is a complex adaptive system in itself with more biodiversity in a kilo of soil than in a hectare of rainforest; that it contributes to good nutritious food and that is gives resilience in climate change.

The *New Normal*: **Frontrunners in agriculture in transition!** Up to 26 individuals and organisations, that make a difference by understanding the agro-ecological interactions and adhering to them, are presented in chapters 8 to 13.
You can read what they do and why and how they make a change!

The change is made at all levels: individual farmers, regional associations, small and large projects, greening-the-desert initiatives and agribusiness turning green. Reading their views, their realistic approaches, the threats and opportunities they dealt with and their endogenous and experiential knowledge will give you unexpected insights.

How can we create change? In chapter 14 we read how we can collectively create the things we want. How can we co-create? How can we strengthen capacity? How can we work within a developing network to make the change to agro-ecology?

The emerging future is already here. In chapter 15 'To the Tipping Point', we will see how we can organise ourselves to make a difference. To catalise or facilitate the change. Which keys for change can we take up in our dialogues, in our projects, in our day-to-day life? In chapter 16 we look back from 2030 to see which roads we have taken to get to the eco-civilisation of 2030.

Catalysts. The people in the examples in this book are a catalyst in their own environment, their own business or organisation. A catalyst is the ingredient that is needed to trigger or accelerate, to speed up the process. Each of us can be such a catalyst or – just as important – a follower, helping to set the trend.

Yellow Pages. The Worldwide movement to the *New Normal* agro-ecology exists of many different organisations, books and debates. In a separate document 'Yellow Pages for Agro-Ecology' you will find an extensive overview of emerging movements, organisations and institutions and descriptions of what they do. All those emerging movements are mentioned as they may open up new ways for us. And you can choose to join or support them. Free download at issuu.com/jellekeforagroecology

3. Three Perspectives

This book uses three different ways of observing agriculture, three ways of looking at our real world. We use three differently coloured glasses, as it were, to understand agriculture, food production and consumption. They are the *Complex system* view, the *Culture, values and belief systems* glasses and the *Integral Landscape approach*.

Fig. 2. Three different perspectives

1. **The complex systems view.** I am still grateful to my dad (a physicist, now 96 years of age) for explaining to me as a child about his work in regulating complex systems. His example: in a regulated heating system we are used to feedback mechanisms; when it grows too hot in the room there is an automatic control that switches off or slows down the heating system, and the other way around.

    Now I know and recognise that in agro-ecological systems, and in social systems of people living together, there are feedback mechanisms too. A social feedback mechanism could be, for example, that you have taken too many cookies from a bowl. The feedback mechanism is that you get a frown, or worse, an upset stomach. The first (the frown) is an early warning signal; the second (upset stomach) probably makes you stop eating the cookies. So you act upon the warning. In agriculture, when plants have too little water they wilt (early warning sign) or die. The feedback is rather clear.

    However, an agro-ecological system is much more complicated than a heating system. It is comparable to a human body, which consists of a multitude of interactions and an incredible number of signals in order to maintain a healthy balance. In order to continue living, in order to remain healthy, such a complex system needs to build up resilience. It needs, therefore, understanding of balanced inputs, outputs, internal and external interaction and attentive, loving care.

2. **Culture, values, belief systems[10] and assumptions.** The 'culture' of a country, of an organisation, a people, a religion, a science or a family, dictates what we do and how we do it. This 'culture' is always a combination of economic considerations, short or long term advantages and values. Values are about individual, community or country policies, about what is 'done' and 'not done', about motivations, ambitions and how we view the world. It is about the assumptions we make about how things work, about what is right and wrong.

    So how do our culture and our belief system make us behave towards nature? Do we see nature as a subject, that we can rule, regulate and exploit, or as a partner in our living together on this planet? Are we part of nature, part of a whole that moves beyond our understanding, and do we behave as a responsible partner in this relationship?

    Agriculture is also a 'culture', with belief systems and assumptions about the ways we, as human beings, should be dealing with the earth, water, plants and animals in order to produce food and fibres. Through our culture we – often implicitly – know if it is good or not to use chemical pesticides, to treat animals well or to abuse them, to play music in a dairy shed to keep the cows healthy, to invest in healthy soil, or not. Agriculture is very much influenced by our values and our economic considerations, but we are rarely aware of that.

    The differences in culture of peoples explain the differences in agricultural systems between regions and countries. For example, lots of maize is grown in the Eastern part of the Netherlands while just across the border in Germany, under the same natural conditions and on the same type of soils, we find huge fields of wheat. Why? It is the culture (including economic arguments and either or not 'organic' belief systems) that precedes the decisions.

3. **Landscape as a revealing mirror.** Most of the beautiful landscapes of the world that we admire when travelling are manmade: they are agricultural landscapes. Examples are the Indonesian and Vietnamese rice fields; the Dutch polders; the French, Italian and

---

[10] A belief system is a set of mutually supportive beliefs. A belief is a proposition, or premise, an individual holds to be true.

German vineyards; the olive or almond covered slopes in Italy, Spain and Greece; the cork producing oak tree forests in Portugal and the nomad shaped Sahel regions. During the centuries, we, as different peoples with different cultures and values, have consciously and unconsciously created those landscapes, in order to provide food and materials. Everything is done for a reason. The location of a village (near a well, or near a forest for wood supply), the course of a road (on higher sandy land in the middle of a low lying clay area; or in the mountains following the river), the type of agriculture (beetroot and pig raising on poor soils, wheat, barley and teff on rich soils, potatoes in colder higher regions) and so on. We have done that by dealing with land, water and climate in the most optimal ways with the available techniques, as well as lots of manpower, ambitions and understanding!

Segmentation or integration. Looking on the scale of a region, the landscape often shows us different 'sectors', like nature reserves, agricultural fields, glass houses, roads and town extensions. The landscape 'mirrors' to us how we deal with nature. It shows us if we use her complexity in an integrated way, or if we segment her.

Looking through those 3 types of glasses, a landscape shows us very clearly what is important for us (as a culture, a civilisation, an organisation, a country), and what not. It shows in which type of activity we invest energy, money and thought. For types of food production and agriculture that we need, that sustain us, we invent regulations, watershed management bureaus and projects. Well drained and well protected lands in the Netherlands are an obvious feature. In other countries it may be erosion control or water conservation.

However, in the last 50 years, the focus (in our use of rural areas) has moved from the importance of a certain type of food and agriculture, to the type of business and profit that it generates. Where before we grew wheat, we now grow maize, which is feed for the cows. As mentioned before: the rules of the game have changed. And they must change again. And that change starts with our individual and collective view on the world, our 'culture' of doing agriculture, the way we observe how systems work and the daily decisions we make based on those views. All those decisions by individual people and organisations materialise in the real world in another way of working, eating, buying, and doing agriculture: *the New Normal*.

4. To Be or Not to Be

Our economy, i.e. our global and national 'households', are based on the 'myth'[11] of the individual, on our sense of separation from nature and on the belief that we can conquer it. By contrast, ecology teaches us about interdependence, abundance and co-creativity.

What if our economy, and thus our approach to agriculture and food production, were modelled on these concepts rather than on competition, scarcity and individualism?

Schumacher College, 2012

[11] Myth: a belief, an in our culture accepted value or assumption.

4.1 Why change to a more sustainable world?

Sustainability: it is in every annual working plan. But *why* do we want this, if we want it at all? Often the chapter about sustainability or social responsibility is written by one person in an organisation, and not part and parcel of the company's way of working. Why do we want sustainability? Not for the earth herself, usually, and not for the economy. No, it is for us, for our own survival. Because we want to continue living here in a healthy way, and we would also like our children and grandchildren to be able to live peacefully in this world, with enough food, clean water and clean air.

We cannot live without water and food. We cannot live without enough bees to pollinate our flowers in order to get sufficient fruits, seeds, grains and all those things we need to live. We need sufficient land with healthy soils, sufficient water and sufficient farmers who know how to take care of plants, animals, water systems and complex agricultural systems in order to produce healthy food and fibres (i.e. grass for feed, cotton, wool, flax, hemp, leather for clothes). This becomes more poignant with the rapidly changing climate.

We must make sure that sufficient quantities of healthy food can be grown, containing the right minerals and vitamins. And we have to make sure that all of this food is available for all of the peoples in the world. This is going to be difficult with an expected population of 9 billion in 2050, with the knowledge that now, in 2012, already half of the world's population is hungry. Unless the world population is destroyed by natural disasters, disease or wars (like it happened in other eras) we are facing a big challenge!

How can we have enough to eat and at the same time conserve the biodiversity of our planet? To be or not to be, that's what this is about. Without water and food, plants and animals, we as people cannot live. Our current situation can be described roughly as consisting of two separate and almost opposite mechanisms:

1. Exploitation as a result of the western economy and linked financial sytem. 'The North', including Australia and China, gets her food and the basic ingredients for food production from 'the South', being the developing countries and so called 'emerging economies'. As a consequence 'the South' suffers from:
   - A lack of water (through use of local water for agricultural export products)
   - Pollution with chemicals
   - A lower availability of land for their own food production. Not only due to food production, flowers or cotton for export, but also as a result of land grabbing by agribusiness

- Lack of food, e.g. fish is being fished away by huge on-sea fish factories; millions of hectares of maize and soy from 'the South' are being exported to 'the North' for animal feed and biofuel
- Lack of employment
- Missed opportunity for added value and therefore more national income, since bulk products (e.g. green coffee beans, cotton, maize, palm-oil, soy) are exported at a very low price. The refineries and food production plants that make - and earn - the 'added value' are in 'the North'.

2. Supporting 'the South'. A totally different (and separate) mechanism is represented by development aid. Its purpose is to ban hunger from the world, through organising regional food security, rehabilitation of irrigation systems and soil conservation. There is an enormous involvement of huge organisations, energy and money in this field of strengthening agriculture in 'the South'. To start with, there are the Asian and African Development Banks and the World Bank; the combined development efforts from individual countries, like EU, USAID, DFID (GB), GiZ (G), KFW, Danish, Swiss, Swedish, Norwegian Canadian, Dutch and French, Japanese and Australian development aid, usually spending 1-2 % of the national budget. Next to that there are many private foundations (amongst them the Bill and Melinda Gates Foundation, Clinton) and NGO's like Both Ends, Pro-Forest, FAIR TRADE, Oxfam, Farming Matters, etc...

It seems almost as if they try to counterbalance the negative impact of the 'industrial agriculture' on the agro-ecosystems and biodiversity in the world.

A third way? Only recently a third way has emerged. It is called sustainable business development. Businesses from 'the North,' wanting to work more sustainably and more socially responsible, are now also doing 'development work' as they say. In countries in 'the South', where they obtain their products, they now involve and teach the population to make the local production more sustainable. There are only some examples where we can speak of a real win-win situation. It is there where not only the global food chain benefits from the 'local production' but also the local food supply.

If things work out well, this approach benefits both the 'Northern' and the 'Southern' business development. But what we see up till now is mostly agribusinesses setting up large scale and intensified production (we cannot even call this farming any more, as it is an industry, not in relation to the environment), many times preceded by land grabbing, all to the detriment of the local people, of their self-sustaining possibilities and of their food sovereignty. The argument is that all those people who were poor farmers before now have an income, better than before, so their livelihood has increased. That is true. But the food (and often non-food products, like roses) that is being grown and the water used in the process are all exported and do not benefit the local population. Livelihood is not so much about money, as well as food and the ability to grow it/buy it in your own region, and respect for oneself.

4.2 How many people can the Earth carry? How many can she feed?

World grain prices during the last 10 years have been increasing. Global food demand will double during the next 40 years due to the increasing world population and the increasing welfare. However, global grain yields and agricultural productivity have decreased from 2-3% annually in the years 1961 to 1990, to about 1% in the years 1990 to 2007. Global meat demand is also going to double from 2015 till 2050 while almost 80% of all agricultural land is already devoted to livestock production. Livestock is the world's largest user of land resources, with pasture and land dedicated to the production of feed representing almost 80% of the total agricultural land.[12] The sector uses 3.4 billion hectares for grazing and one-third of global arable land to grow feed crops, accounting for more than 40% of world cereal production. 26% of the Earth's ice-free terrestrial surface is used for grazing. Therefore a structural change in how we produce and consume is critical to ensuring sufficient food for the world in the coming decades.

The so-called carrying capacity of the earth is often calculated by the number of (fertile) hectares that one person needs to live from. This includes all the land we need for growing food, feed, fibre and fodder and for providing the natural resources for living and transport. In 2012 this number varied from 9,8 ha per person per year in the United States to 5 in Great Britain and an average of 1,1 in Africa. However, if we look at the availability of fertile/useable land on this earth and divide it by the number of people, there is only 1.8 hectare per person available. 'The North' obviously uses too much of the available land and very ineffectively at that. You might even call it egotistical.

How to bring balance in the use of land? Scientists have calculated that – if all the people on earth should live at a 'Western' consumption level, needing an average of 7,5 ha per person - we will need three planet Earths to provide food, resources and space to live in 2050.

---

[12]   http://www.fao.org/docrep/016/ap106e/ap106e.pdf

Other scientists in favour of industrial agriculture tell us that we may be quite well able to feed the world in 2050 with only one planet, if only we make all agricultural production systems more intensive and of a larger scale with technical innovations and global chains, meanwhile improving transport (energy) and distribution systems. It means that *we*, the people in the industrialised world, will organise the food system and provide for the poorer countries, which will need to buy from us. I do not believe in this solution as we have seen the disastrous results of such industrial production methods, much to the detriment of peoples, ecological systems, water and the earth. Chapter 5 shows us how this happens, often unintendedly.

What surface of land do we actually use to produce our food? The ecological footprint below shows how many hectares are currently being used per person.

Continent	(ha)	Country	(ha)
North America	9,4	United Arab Emirates	11,9
European Union	4,8	United States	9,6
Europa (outside EU)	3,8	Belgium and Luxembourg	5,6
World	2,2	Netherlands	4,4
Middle East and Central Asia	2,2	Hungary	3,5
Latin America and Caribbean	2,0	Turkey	2,1
Asia (around the Pacific)	1,3	Brazil	2,1
Africa	1,1	Algeria	1,6
		China	1,6
Available bio-capacity per ha, p.p.	*1,8*	India	0,8

Table 1. The number of hectares being used per person for food

The ecological footprint[13] is a formula which calculates the area of fertile soil which is required to maintain a certain population. If all inhabitants of the world would be entitled to use the same area for food production and energy supply everybody could use an average of 1,8 hectares. The table above gives the average land use per person, per population group and way of living.[1]

So what is the solution? In fact, the question should be different in the first place. The question should be: how can we grow food in such a way that:
1. It is beneficial for people, socially and economically, from the point of view of food security, availability of food and contribution to health (nutrition). Since 75-80% of the food production in the

---

13   Look at 'ecological footprint by country' on the internet.

world is done by smallholder farmers[14], they need sufficient access to resources to double their harvests, which is possible.[2]

2. It is beneficial for the regenerative system of the earth and her ecosystems.

The greatest challenge for a worldwide adoption of agro-ecology and agro-eco approaches is not technical but social and political – said Olivier de Schutter[15] in 2010. "What we need is a transformation in the political, ethic and economic thinking of (favouring) the agribusiness, which continues to promote large scale industrial agriculture. The big crises[16], caused by the unsustainable approaches of industrial agriculture, are being masked by the continued and still growing stream of subsidies, also in the shape of scientific research, towards this type of food production."

Courage. A growing number of people, organisations, policymakers and scientists (as shown on World Food day October 17th, 2012) believe that we can manage with one Earth. If only we dare look at the mistakes we have made and repair them; and if we dare use integrated system approaches. That is, if we dare to step over to low external input agriculture and to agro-forestry systems and if we dare to listen to experiential knowledge; if we assist local projects in providing food, not merely for export, but also for the regionally necessary food supplies; if we dare change the rules of the game.

Courage is needed, since we will have to deviate from what is common, from what is the 'old normal' way of doing things. Courage is needed as we venture into such 'New Normal' and 'unknown' roads. And yet, they may be unknown to you, but many people and organisations in this world know them, as the examples in this book will show. Courage is needed since there are sometimes big financial and political interests that compel us not to change. So how will we manage the change? That is what this book is about.

---

[14] Eighty percent of the farmland in sub-Saharan Africa and Asia is managed by smallholders (working on up to 10 hectares). While 75 percent of the world's food is generated from only 12 plants and 5 animal species, making the global food system highly vulnerable to shocks, biodiversity is key to smallholder systems who keep many rustic and climate-resilient varieties and breeds alive. www.fao.org/.../Factsheet_**SMALLHOLDERS**.pdf

[15] Olivier de Schutter was appointed Special Rapporteur on the right to food at the United Nations Human Rights Council in 2008.

[16] The crises encompass hunger or the non- availability of food, food prices, water shortages, soil erosion, public health, obesity, droughts, environmental pollution in developing countries (as a result of our 'northern'food/ flower production, land grabbing, etc)

4.3 A breakthrough is needed[17]

Since World War II we have been trying to increase the food production and keep prices low in the Western world, as well as supporting people in developing countries to grow sufficient food. At first glance we have done well: since 1960 we have an increase of agricultural surface of 12% worldwide with an increased demand for food of 100% (doubled), so we have increased our yields tremendously with 75%.

Fig. 3. Sometimes we need to break through barriers – psychological or financial or practical - which keep us from doing what we really want to do.

Despite the appearance of success, we have failed. We are missing out on five other areas, resulting in 850 million inhabitants being hungry or malnourished. This is including seasonal hunger, when the harvest of last year is depleted and there is nothing else to eat (in 2015 in Ethiopia, 20 million people were without food due to this reason). Including people starving since their land has been 'grabbed' for palm oil, sugar or cotton plantations, so they have no land to grow their food on. Added to this is the inequity in access to food, resulting in deficits in vitamins A/D, Zinc and Magnesium. We are also faced with inadequate diets (in the industrialised countries); we get enough calories, but less resilience.

So where did we fail?
1. We have made food systems and agricultural policies that are not related to public health and health policies. For example, one third of the population of Mexico and the U.S. is obese.
2. Loss of biodiversity worldwide, due to a focus of agribusiness and agri-policies on only 7 crops: wheat, rice, maize, soy, potato, palm oil and cotton.
3. Greenhouse gas emissions resulting in climate change. 13,5% of the total greenhouse gas emissions is due to deforestation. 35% of the manmade greenhouse gas emission is caused by the energy needed in food production, mainly caused by meat production.

---

[17] This paragraph is based on the keynote speech of Olivier de Schutter on February 22, 2014

This includes the production of fertilizer and pesticides, transport and fossil fuels.

4. A wrong use of precious land. We (the so called 'developed' countries) converse high quality vegetal proteins (wheat, soy) into animal proteins (meat). For 1 kilo of meat we use 16 kilos of grain. We use 20 million hectares of land,[18] often by means of land grabbing. In the US an average 75 kilos of meat is eaten per person per year (that is including babies and elderly people, so the average for adult people is even higher); in South Africa it is 11 kilos per person per year, in India 5 kilos per person per year.

5. Global markets regularly dump large quantities of food and so spoil regional and local markets, both in developed and in developing countries.

As a consequence, in developing countries:

- Investments in local markets stopped and the produce for export grew
- More and more food needed to be imported
- Local farmers – being left without land and without work - went to the cities where public services are unable to satisfy rising demand, unless they continue to import subsidized food
- Nations face a growing inability to feed their own population
- Growth of inequality (rich people can afford the increasing prices)
- We create a lot of waste

How could this happen? The system we inherited from the 20th century has a number of in-built locks:

- Social-ethical: storage and transport have been developed for the food processing industries in the West
- Socio-economic: people have become highly dependent on the system, their jobs and their income
- Socio-cultural: we have developed a taste for highly processed food (sugar/ salt); we are used to spending little time on food buying and cooking
- Social-political: food production is dominated by a small network of influential actors. They veto any change. So there is no food democracy

There are solutions![19]

1. Move to **sustainable food production** systems (like agro-ecology) instead of sticking to the type of agriculture that depends on high

---

[18] http://www.fao.org/docrep/016/ap106e/ap106e.pdf

[19] This book is about the first of the four solutions mentioned here.

energy inputs, high fossil fuel that is detrimental to biodiversity, public health and social life. The high tech agricultural systems that we have now and that we even export – with all its negative effects - to developing countries, will make place for AgroEcology. In June 2016 food systems experts urge global shift towards agroecology[20] and leave industrial agriculture behind.

Agroecology is the answer. Agro-ecology is NOT 'going back' to traditional ways of farming. It is NOT organic farming. Is is farming with common sense, restoring complex resilient natural systems. It is family farming and cooperation. An important aspect of agro-ecology is the maintenance and improvement of soil health. We need to reduce our dependence on chemical fertilizer and pesticides. We need to change to agro-forestry and depend less on investments.

2. Move to sustainable **food consumption.** Our far too large ecological footprints depend on several things, including demographic growth, but this issue cannot be discussed. Lifestyles, choice of food and our policies have to be questioned:
   - Eat less meat or no meat at all, since its production has too high a demand on the land.
   - Stop producing biofuels in the South, so that the people there can use their land for food production.

3. More decisively address the issue of **waste**. 1.3 billion tonnes of food stuff is being thrown away, per year![21] We waste about half of the grains we produce - 95 kilos per person per year in Europe. Improve logistics in developing countries so that produce can be transported in the region. If not, the produce goes to waste and people will invest less effort in production.

4. **Change the rules of the game.** Reforms in the North (Trade, Investments) are related to what we do in the South and have impact on the South.

---

[20] These were the key messages from IPES-Food's first major report, released on June 2 during the 8th Trondheim Biodiversity Conference(Norway): 'From Uniformity to Diversity: A paradigm shift from industrial agriculture to diversified agroecological systems'.

[21] As much as half of all the food produced in the world – equivalent to 2bn tonnes – ends up as waste every year. The report, Global Food; Waste Not, Want Not, found that between 30% and 50% or 1.2-2bn tonnes of food produced around the world never makes it on to a plate. https://www.bsr.org/en/topics/reports/Food-Beverage-and-Agriculture

4.4 Toward transition – a mind-set

There is a growing awareness of cultural change taking place in our societies, worldwide. Our worldviews and attitudes are changing, and because of that our ways of organising life and work and our ways of dealing with problems are changing.

The Spiral Dynamics concept sketches how we are developing from a hierarchically top down organised society, scientific and materialistic (19-20th century), to a more process oriented society, communitarian-egalitarian (1990-2020), in which dialogue, systemic flow, integrated and participative approaches, are leading features. Meanwhile, from 2000 onwards, pioneering individuals and groups move already higher up in this spiral, into a more synthesis oriented society. Here an *organism* is the symbol for an integrative complex system, a more holistic collaboration and organisation.

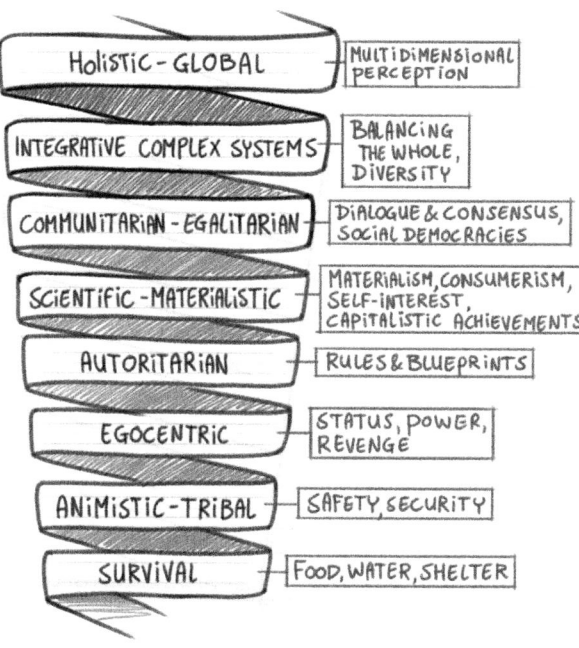

Fig. 4. Spiral dynamics approach of societal development

From this point of view, feeding the world in 2050 will be possible, as we will develop totally new patterns of behaviour. Food production will be concerned with regions everywhere in the world feeding themselves. *From I to WE* is already a well-known approach: we will consider the benefits (or negative impacts) for others and other parts of the world when deciding about individual or organisational moves.

With Otto Scharmers' *Theory U* we will learn how to put steps into the emerging future. So, we are already on our way to another way of being and living. And we can see the outlines of that *New Normal* taking shape in the work of pioneers and early adapters.

The change in the orientation of our value and belief systems will change the present control oriented and top down management mechanisms into process, synthesis, integrative and multi-stakeholder approaches. If you look around now, you can see the symptoms of this changing orientation everywhere. Individual people, producers, consumers, employees and CEOs - many have become aware of the fact that what one individual does will always have an impact on a bigger, related system: other people, other organisations, the earth, water, animals, plants and the climate. And so they are reconsidering their proposed actions and policies.

This phenomenon also works the other way around: being aware of the inter-relatedness of many things and actions offers new insights and new solutions. As Einstein said: *"one cannot solve the problems of today with the science and modes of thought that have led to these problems"*. In other words, one needs new ways of observing and thinking and knowing in order to find new ways of doing.

Our behaviour is our problem. How can we work in a more interrelated way? Now that the sustainability of our planet Earth is at stake, we face the question of how we can continue living *on* her and *with* her. If that is the case, why then do we talk *so little* about the ways we, as inhabitants, as peoples, as societies, should behave in order to safeguard and care for the continued existence of Earth?

Compare society with a human body. A human heart provides itself with blood (self care) and supplies cells with food, oxygen, light and energy (it cares for the bigger system it is connected and interrelated to). Just like the highly developed resilient system of a human body, a society where self-care and care for the whole system are integrated or combined (and not separate or antagonistic movements), shows a high degree of development and is resilient. Maybe our problem is not so much the Earth, but the fact that, as yet, we have not sufficiently understood what interrelated development means and how to give it shape, put it into action.

New concepts are available with regard to this pressing need for 'interrelated' or integral development. An interesting number of visions, concepts, theories and facilitating instruments have emerged. Many of the new practises are being taught in organisational development workshops and are written down in books as well. A few examples: *From I to We*[3], *The Conscious Business Model, Climate change is Social change, Mindfulness,*

Connecting Communication, The art of dialogue, Presencing and Theory U. In this era, we are looking for keys and principles that can help us to deal with organic wholes, combining our own goals and ambitions with those of bigger social and ecological systems.

Fig. 5. All our actions are related

Repairing natural cycles. My plea in this book is that we start working with such concepts and instruments. Interacting with bigger wholes, being aware of the connectedness of (up till now) separate actions that can repair local, regional and global natural cycles (closed loop) in agriculture and food production.

Using feedback mechanisms. We also need to work on the rehabilitation and monitoring of feedback mechanisms in the socio-economic and agro-ecological systems we deal with. It means that not just farmers, but also agribusiness, policy and politics and we as world inhabitants rub our eyes and observe with a new worldview, from new perspectives. We can see the interconnectedness of what we do as an individual (organisation) to the bigger whole of which it is a part. It helps to imagine such a bigger system as a holographic picture, in which each particle represents the whole. We will learn experientially where to pull or push in the whole system in order to improve a part of it. We need to learn how we can heal whole systems and how holistic management works.

Keys towards change. By reading through this book, we may find the keys towards change, towards restoring agro-ecosystems into more sustainable, resilient and coherent wholes. Will we be able to apply those keys in our own environment, in or own work? Will we be able to tell our children or grandchildren "Yes I was one of those people who helped creating the tipping point"?

Fig. 6 Keys to successful transition to agroecology

AGRO-ECOSYSTEMS

5. Agro-food systems spun out of control

Agrofood systems and agroecological farming are complex systems

"Beware The Complex System! The low-hanging fruit on the tree of knowledge has all been eaten. To make the next great leap forward we must wrangle complex systems."[22]

[22]   Posted by Graham Morehead on May 9, 2011, http://blogs.nature.com

After an introduction on the workings of complex systems, this chapter will take us along various agriculture and food production systems in the world that have deteriorated, fallen ill, irreversibly changed, or died.
You will find them in parts 5.1- 5.13.

Very often this derangement happened unintentionally. Mostly, people changed an agricultural system with the best intentions of improving harvests and providing more and cheaper food. The negative impacts were generally due to not understanding the bigger picture, the whole complex system, due to not understanding the interrelatedness of processes. When taking out or destroying one or more 'actors' or 'activities' in the system, the system loses essential feedback or ingredients.

The following thirteen cases will help us to discover how agro-ecosystems actually work in reality, how interrelatedness in complex systems works, how they deteriorate, and how we can become more aware of feedback signals to prevent mistakes.

Fig. 7. A complex system with interactions and feedback mechanisms

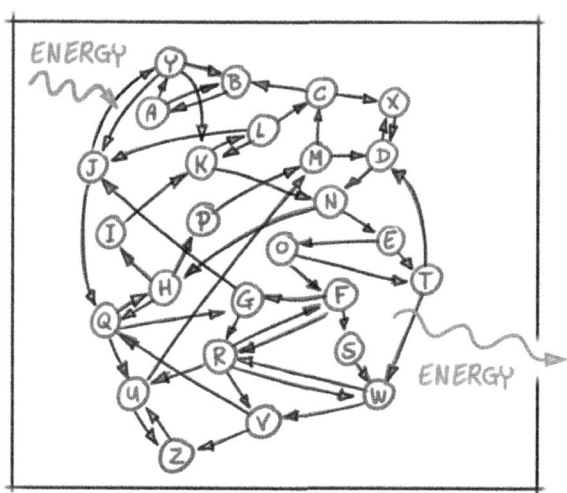

In the above oversimplified conceptual image of a complex system, we can see some 26 different parts, functions and relations, while in a full grown agro-eco system there are millions. Each part in this image could represent an ecosystem in itself, like a soil, a community of animals, a forest, or a pond. The arrows represent the flows of energy, which in essence come from the sun.

Within the system an enormous amount and variety of processes take place. They are interrelated and necessary: competition, collaboration, parasitism, symbiosis, feeding and composting, building up and breaking down, and – very important – information exchange! Some of the internal processes are unknown to us. We then speak of 'a black box'. It really is impossible to predict how a change from within or from outside will affect the whole system. Up to only recently soils were regarded as black boxes. Nowadays we know that soils are perfect complex interactive natural systems containing more than 120 million microorganisms per litre of soil, if the soil is healthy.

Experiential knowledge. If one cannot know the impact of interventions in such an agro-eco system, how can we ever manage complex agro-eco systems sustainably? Luckily, during centuries the knowledge of agriculture (remember it is a culture, a way of doing things) has been built up by trial and error, by passing on experiential knowledge from father to son and from mother to daughter. Knowledge builds up by watching closely, listening to and registering the signals that the system reveals. That could be, for example, the behaviour of animals, the death of plants or the way the soil looks. It still works that way. Ask a farmer in your neighbourhood, or look at the examples of positive change.

Farming is a craft, farming matters! Experiential learning has led to collective and integrated knowledge. Farming is a craft, fed by intuition and experience and the uniqueness of the location and the farmer. It is often not valuated as such by science. In many cases farmers' approaches, especially in the tropics, have been condemned as superstitious and indigenous and therefore backward and not useful. Sometimes experiential knowledge is seen more positively as 'farmers' wisdom'. It is good to know that in the last 10 years more attention is being paid to indigenous knowledge systems[23]. Another positive development since the 1980s is the organised exchange of knowledge from all over the world about Low Energy Input Agriculture (LEIA) and about local knowledge and ideas about farming systems. *Farming Matters!*[4], with its double meaning, is the name of both the website and magazine.

Farmer: peasant or entrepreneur? Professor Jan Douwe van der Ploeg (2006) made a distinction between peasants and entrepreneurs as to the different ways in which farmers deal with 'their' agro-eco system.
- → Peasants are craftsmen and craftswomen who aim to keep the balance in the complex agro-eco system they manage.
- → Entrepreneurs (in the conservative sense of the word) are only interested in increasing the harvests and their income while decreasing the costs of energy, money and labour. The last attitude takes their attention away from the necessary balance in the natural agro-eco system.

---

[23] Endogenous knowledge is the inherited, experiential and often spiritual knowledge inherent to the people in a region. From: COMPAS programme.

Almost anecdotal - if not so serious - are the observations by a farmer (peasant) from Wales, Joe Jenkins, when he travels in 1881 around Australia. He describes how incredibly unprofessional the English (not farmers originally, but convicts) deal with their land and agro-ecosystems: "They do not understand that manure is meant to feed the soil! Valuable manure and ashes about 6 ton, lay waste at the side or are being dumped in the rivers, while the pastures and fields are exhausted and yearn for organic matter."

Why the examples of deteriorating systems in this book? Because the examples show us - much more clearly and directly than a theoretical description would - what is meant by a coherent agro-eco system and what goes wrong when coherence is undermined.
In the examples, the original interrelations and feedback mechanisms have been disturbed in such a way that the agro-eco systems have deteriorated. With very negative impact on the environment (soil, water, sea, climate) and the health of plants, animals and human beings. The idea is that when we know which interactions have such bad effects we could prevent agro-eco systems to go to waste and we could design better ways of dealing with our agro-eco systems.

Always unexpected effects. Duncan Brown, in his fascinating book *Feed or Feedback*,[24] tells us that whatever well-intended intervention you make in an agro-ecosystem, there will always be an unexpected side effect. Usually we discover them much later or in another area: the time and space aspects of sustainable practice!

Treating the effect or the source of the problem? In our Western industrialized culture it is (still) common to do something about the *effect* and *not about its source*. An example. In Western Europe, previously quite compact and healthy manure of cattle has turned into a smelly slurry (in fact diarrhoea) as a result of a change in diet. We treat the effects (foul air, NH3 emissions) by injecting the slurry into the soil. Instead we should look at the whole cow (as a complex system) to discover that with her four stomachs she just can't cope with too much protein and too little fibre in her system. The diarrhoea weakens her and she becomes less resilient and needs antibiotics not to fall ill. So what is the lesson? We should carefully watch the side effects (feedback mechanisms) and look for their origins in the interrelated processes within the complex whole.

Well meant! Almost all interventions in industrial agricultural systems were well meant, mostly to increase food production, both in quality (high protein milk) or quantity (more litres or kilogrammes per ha).

---

[24]   Feed or Feedback: Agriculture, Population Dynamics and the State of the Planet, paperback, 2013. Duncan Brown.

Fig. 8. We send stuff to developing countries with good intentions. Good for whom?

But as mentioned before, such interventions were often carried out without awareness of the whole system and its balance. Sometimes interventions were not aimed at a healthy system at all. An example - the use of slaughter offal as animal feed, seemingly an efficient way to get rid of refuse and a cheap way to get animal feed. We all know the unexpected side effects it had: BSE in animals and the affliction of human health.

5.1 European legislation shatters century old agro-eco system

In Portugal in the 1970s, an age old agro-eco system was still in use. In the summer the sheep were brought to the higher areas in the mountains, where it was colder at that time. The manure of the sheep fertilised the soil and had as side effect that the soil would remain a few degrees warmer in winter and not freeze over. This was perfectly fitted for growing winter wheat in the rainy winter season. The wheat could ripen when the season became warmer and sunnier. After the harvest the goats and sheep could use and fertilize the area again.

However, at a certain time the European Union wanted to stimulate the growing of maize throughout the Union (a well meant intervention). For this purpose a subsidy was installed. The effect was that the villagers started growing maize instead of wheat, but with a big difference for the agro-eco system! The maize was planted in spring and harvested at the end of the summer.

This had many negative effects:
-   There was no space any more for the sheep

- There was no manure deposited any more, and the soil degraded quickly and required expensive chemical fertilizer
- The maize needed extra water (from the scarce resources there are) as there is no rain in the summer season
- The winter rain was lost for food production

5.2 Soil and society swept away

In the African savannahs south of the Sahara (Sahel) a subtle balance between nomads (pastoralists) and settlers (arable farmers) has developed over centuries of time. Nomads would take their cattle to places where enough water, herbs, grasses and leaves are available as fodder and so move from place to place, never overgrazing a certain area. The settled farmers grow staple foods (maize, millet, sorghum and cassava) and vegetables (mainly onions, tomatoes and pepper). They produce for their own subsistence, as well as a surplus to sell in the market and to brew beer from. They exchange this with the nomad families for dried manure, yoghurt and meat.

This regional cyclic agro-eco-food system was sustainable, socially and ecologically resilient. A clear feedback mechanism was in place: there were never too many cows as they would be paid as price for a bride, or sold as meat. This went well until the 1970s. At that time the nomad population grew; with them the number of cattle increased and the population in the villages grew. On top of that the seemingly 'unused' grazing area was diverted into arable land. As a consequence, the grazing area got reduced quite a bit so that too many people and too many heads of cattle were living in too tight an area.

Even though a savannah landscape seems quite an extended surface, the effective land use is restricted in *time* (one cannot graze too long in one spot or erosion will take away all the soil), in *season* (there isn't much growing in the dry season) and *distance* (one can only walk a certain distance in a day with a herd of cattle).

The result of this was that the vegetation disappeared altogether, the soil degraded and eroded badly. In the rainy season whatever top-soil remained was swept away and gullies now mark the old landscape. The cattle died, the nomads got ill or left.

5.3 Negative effects of cattle-feed on animal and public health

A logical and well-meant idea was to feed cows more protein (soy and maize) instead of grass, so that there would be more protein in the milk. There was an increasing demand in the Western world in the sixties and seventies due to a rapidly growing population. Dairy farmers started growing maize instead of wheat, as it was also subsidized. Soon cheaper soy and maize were being imported from Brazil and other developing countries. This led to an increase in large maize and soy farms in these countries and it became big (American and European) business. Additionally protein-rich grasses were developed and used as fodder. More and more cows were fed on protein instead of grasses. This had unexpected consequences.

Why? The four stomachs of a cow are made to digest and re-digest the long and tough fibres and woody elements in the fodder. If they don't get sufficient roughage and instead get too much protein (for which their stomachs are not equipped) the cows get a sort of diarrhoea. This stinks, since it contains too much nitrogen, it is acrid and not good for the soil at all, while the regular droppings are good manure.

Instead of taking notice of these signals as strong feedback, the Dutch government promoted to inject this rather fluid sludge into the soil. The soil is an interesting system in itself of interacting microbes, mycorrhiza and tiny animals, which together ensure that plants get enough food, air and water. The next side effect was that the life in the soil was poisoned by the sludge, making the soil structure collapse. The soil could no longer retain the rainwater, which went (literally) down the drains and ditches, washing out the excess nitrogen and polluting the ground water, which additionally has a bad impact on adjacent areas.

And the cows? As a result of the 'diarrhoea' and not feeling well, their resistance to diseases and their vitality decreases and they are therefore generally treated with antibiotics, residues of which collect in the urine and eventually reach the groundwater. Again we treat the effects instead of the source of the problem.[25]

---

[25] In the Netherlands a group of farmers, advisers and scientists, who didn't want to comply with this practice, started an association for coherent agriculture, promoting a return to the close-loop 'soil-plant-animal interaction system' www.netwerkvlv.nl. Organic farmers are by nature respecting the soil-plant-animal-interaction-system' and are not obliged to inject 'sludge' into the soil.

5.4 'Industrial' meat production destroys Brazilian rainforests

As a result of the increased demand for protein rich feed, man, represented here by the agro-business complex, is destroying nature on a large scale. Daily – while you read this - an area the size of a soccer field is being cut in the Amazon rainforests for the production of maize, soy beans and timber. Soy and maize are not grown for local consumption but serve as cattle feed for the rest of the world.

Fig. 9. European cattle feed uses an annual 9,3 million tonnes of Soy, for our daily meat.

9,3 Million TONS OF SOY FOR EUROPEAN CATTLE FODDER

An enormous trade is being conducted through the port of Rotterdam, where the Dutch economy profits from the transit of 90% of the bulk. Apart from the negative effects in developing countries, this trade is having a substantial negative ecological impact on the Western livestock and dairy cows, as well as on the West European citizen. In this context we have to conclude that this mechanism is oriented too much towards "I" (agribusiness' profit) and too little towards "WE", as if there is no relation between what we do here and what is happening over there.

Negative impacts are tremendous:

→ The impact on the ecosystems of the Amazonas are (1) a tremendous loss in biodiversity and (2) the loss of CO_2 storage capacity.

In addition water, minerals and trace elements - necessary for the maize production - are removed locally and will not benefit the local population while they also will not be returned to the soil, resulting in soil degradation and water shortages.

→ An undesirable socio-economical side effect is that small farmers have to make place for large agro-industrial complexes. They lose their land and cannot provide for their own food. At the same time national food self-sufficiency is an important point on the development agenda, which is counteracted by the disappearance of the small farmer. And this is just the result of the fact that food sovereignty is not on the agenda of the agribusiness.

An example: A steak in Europe of about one kilo requires about 10 kilos of protein rich feed, which could also have been used to feed people, as well as 200 litres of water. Add the transportation costs, and not to forget the loss of biodiversity, food, employment opportunities and the increase in social unrest in Brazil and you have an idea of the serious negative footprint that we leave behind. From the complex system point of view: we use the complete output of the system, unconcerned about the lack of input, and we do not take care of rehabilitation. On top of this we are not affected by the feedback signals from South America because we think that they are local problems and have nothing to do with our worldwide agro-production system. This can be considered as a lack of feedback in our systems and our way of looking really. It is clear that the 'overall view' of the complex system has been lost.

5.5 Disconnected urban growth leads from bad to worse

The unlimited growth of cities, worldwide, has an impact on the larger system of interaction between the city and the rural area and vice versa.

City development in the Middle Ages was only possible if an excess of food was produced in the surrounding rural areas and transported to the city. There was a balance between the city and the land as long as nutrients were returned to their origin (it is known from China and Amsterdam that in the 17th century *night soil* was brought back to the countryside) and farmers could supply enough food for the citizens. Interestingly, one of the first social geographers, Cristaller, based his theory on the dispersion of villages and cities in Europe on this interaction. Villages and cities in Western Europe still lay at a distance of a one-day walk, so accessibility of markets and food was the *regulating* factor. The distance between the cities with a regional market equalled a one day ride on horse back. In the ideal situation the city looked after the land and the land looked after the city. A beautiful representation of this principle can be found in the Frescoes in the town hall of Siena in Tuscany.[26]

---

[26]   The impact of bad Government on the Countryside and 'Good management of the countryside' (resulting in a flourishing city!) 1338-40, Fresco, Palazzo Pubblico, Siena

This *Allegory and Effects of Good and Bad Government* series was commissioned entirely by a civic group, the Council of Nine (the city council). The subject matter in this work is not religious like most artworks of the time, but civic. The Republic of Siena was one of the most powerful of the fourteenth century Italian city-states. It was an urban hub filled with bankers and merchants, with many international contacts. The fourteenth century was a turbulent time for politics in the Italian cities. There were constant violent party struggles; governments were overthrown and governments were reinstated. The frescoes painted by Lorenzetti promoted the morality of government and provided a constant reminder for the council to remain just leaders by showing comprehensive cause-and-effect situations of corrupt, tyrannical governing in comparison to those of virtuous governing. In the latter case, both city and countryside flourish!

No inbuilt break. When, at a certain moment, through an input from outside the system (fertilizer, irrigation, mechanisation), more food can be produced, a surplus is created, food prices drop and the city population will start growing. There is no break, no feedback that says 'stop, enough!' It is a self-re-enforcing process. Occasionally this vicious circle was broken, when there was a famine, a plague or a war, and the city population then became decimated. Presently, the walled cities of Tuscany have hardly any housing areas outside of the walls, as a result of the highly reduced population, which keeps a balance between the city (consumption) and the land (production).

The system is out of balance. Towards the middle of the 19th century this self-reinforcing process resulted in an increase of city populations by 100% and the system became out of balance.

Garbage accumulated in the cities and was no longer returned to the land, pests and diseases erupted, the air was foul, and the soils in the rural areas degraded through a lack of fertilisation. Splendid solutions were identified but they were - as usual - concentrating on the *effects* of the unbalanced system. Sanitation and drainage in the cities were improved so the city could become healthy again, but the garbage went into the rivers and the seas. The negative effects of this development were only identified after another century, in another place and another time, affecting a larger eco-system. To compensate for the lack of organic fertilizers, phosphate was mined (outside of the system) and guano, chicken manure, as well as burned cattle bones, were used.

With the invention of fertilizer[5] in Germany (around 1840), all of a sudden the problem seemed to be solved. Application of fertilizer resulted in increased production. The unexpected result was, however, that the city-countryside *system* got further out of balance. There was still no feedback.

As a result of the unbalanced application of nitrogen, potassium and phosphates, the rural soil system became unbalanced. Important elements for the soil, such as carbon and minerals, which are present in organic manure and compost, were lacking, resulting in a reduced resilience of the soil system. In this way the complex system of food production – city population – recycling of garbage – soil improvement, has run off the rails in the last two centuries. The figure below shows how food production, consumption and the use of manure are an essential cycle. This cycle also represents a complex system that has to be kept in balance.

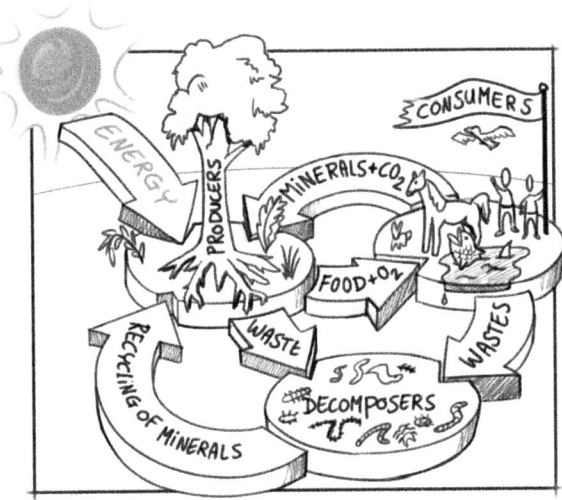

Fig. 10. The production, consumption and use of minerals form a key cycle. Also this cycle is a complex system which is to be kept in balance.

The problem remains unsolved. The city-countryside system in the Netherlands is still off the rails considering the newspaper article of June 24th 2012, which reports on the fact that, for the production of compost, garbage is imported from Milan. But if you would look at this system on a European level, you could get an entirely different impression. At the same time the 'surplus' of food - required for the unlimited growth of cities in the West and in China - is being produced all over the world, in increasing quantities especially since we are no longer dependent on the region for the transport of food. And so the unbalanced situation continues to reinforce itself.

5.6 Water is the restrictive factor worldwide

In the interaction between food production and the size of population, water is an even more restrictive factor than land. Water is necessary for domestic and industrial purposes as well as to grow food for man and animals. Water availability is a restrictive factor because: if it is finished it is finished! If more people need to be fed, more water is required or the other way round. If not enough water is available people will die from thirst and hunger.

To solve this problem there is a worldwide drive to build dams, although this does not increase the total available volume of water. It should be clear that the total volume of water that becomes available in a catchment area - as the result of rainfall and run-off - can never be increased through the construction of dams. If water is retained behind a dam, less water will be available for the downstream area, for its people, its agriculture and nature. This is valid for rivers and catchment areas, whether big or small.

It seems as if there is no notion about this relation, neither about the need to create a balance[6]. The following issue is at stake. People need water to live. If the population grows and the available water remains the same, the available water per person decreases. And as one cannot create more water we need a feedback mechanism in the system that says 'take care, out of balance, adjust your system: use less water or reduce your population'.

Uzbekistan is an interesting example. There are very fascinating wetlands in the middle of the steppe. It is being fed with water from the river Amu Daria. But since there is more water needed for the population and agriculture, the government decided (in 2012) that the water should be reverted to the irrigation canal. As a result the very biodiverse wetlands will dry out and die.

In 2000, the World Wildlife Fund carried out a research project to establish how much water is annually available in each of the world's largest river systems.[27] Next, they figured out how the water could be more sustainably used for agricultural practises (less water consuming species or approaches, returning to rain fed agriculture and, for example, no irrigated rice in dry seasons) in order that sufficient water would remain for nature.

Arjan Hoekstra, from the Dutch University of Twente developed the footprint for water. His book, the Water Footprint of Modern Consumer Society was published in April 2013. On the website we can find how much water is needed for the production of one kilo bread (1600 Litre), one kilo rice (2500 L.), the cotton needed for one pair of jeans (4000 L.), one kilo meat (15.400L.)

One can also find the water footprint by country,[28] telling us how much water we use in other countries than our own, for what we consume (food, flowers,

---

[27] Rivers such as the Nile, the Murry Darling, the Niger, see the Agwaterusefinalreport. pdf, file:///C:/Users/User/Downloads/agwaterusefinalreport%20(2).pdf

[28] http://www.waterfootprint.org/?page=files/NationalWaterFootprint

and clothes). The figure below gives an impression. While average household water use in the UK is around 150 litres per person per day, UK consumption of products from other countries means that each English citizen effectively soaks up a staggering 4,645 litres of the world's water every day. Even if this massive amount seems important in itself, the critical issue is where this virtual water comes from. In the case of the UK, about 62% of the total national water footprint is accounted for by water from other nations, whereas only 38% is used from domestic water resources. In other words, UK consumption of food and clothing has an impact on rivers and aquifers both globally and domestically and is inextricably linked to the continuing security and good management of water resources in other parts of the world.

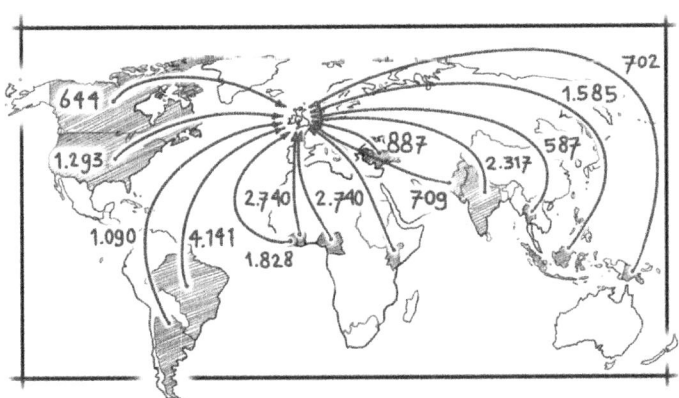

Fig. 11. The water footprint of the UK. Numbers are in cubic meters (1000 liter) per person per year.

It also has an impact on local communities who rely on the water and other services that are provided by such ecosystems. In order to address this, it is important to realise that, while reducing the UK's total water footprint might help, the best solutions will involve promoting good management of water in river basins. This includes more efficient farming practices and improved allocation of water between different water users.

5.7 The Aral Sea - ruin of a large and healthy agro-ecosystem

Large-scale irrigation in Uzbekistan and its impact on the Aral Sea show how an agro-ecosystem can be destroyed unintentionally. Two large rivers, the Amu Darya and the Syr Darya, originating in the Tian Shan Mountains, located towards the East of Uzbekistan, have been supplying water since time immemorial to the cities and villages in the steppe and desert, before discharging into the Aral Sea.

For centuries this sea was the centre of a complex and productive ecosystem. Its shores formed a rich habitat for birds and there were around 250,000 ha of forest and nomads were herding their cattle in the deltas of these rivers. The lake water was slightly saline and sustained a large fish population, with annual commercial catches up to 450,000 tonnes per year. Wheat and vegetable cultivation were possible with irrigation water from the rivers. In short, the system was in balance.

Between 1950 and 1960 the catchment areas of these two rivers were located in the USSR. Its flows were diverted to irrigate large-scale cotton plantations. The aim was to produce 1.5 million tonnes of cotton per year as the USSR wanted to be independent from other countries for its cotton supplies. As a result, the inflow of fresh water into the Aral Sea was reduced drastically between 1960 and 1990. Water levels dropped from 53 m. a.m.s.l.[29] in 1960 to 39 m a.m.s.l., a reduction of 20 percent in 30 years. In 1992 there was no inflow at all.

At the moment 30,000 km² of former seabed is now dry land; wind erosion is responsible for blowing away 108 tonnes of polluted dust and salts. The lake area is only one third of its size whilst its salinity has increased threefold. All higher animal species have disappeared including the fish in the lake. At the same time the river water, which is still being used for domestic purposes, is polluted by the chemicals used in the cotton production. This has a disastrous impact on the health condition of the local population.

Conclusion: a complex agro-ecosystem, based on a river basin, has been destroyed here by removing its most important element - water.

5.8 Grazing or overgrazing?

All over the world, for centuries, large areas have been used for pasture; for instance, the prairies in Northern America, the Sahel south of the Sahara and Eastern Europe. Grazing by animals serving human use (milk, yogurt, cheese, wool and meat) led to the development of complex social structures to keep the pasture land, herds and social systems in balance, as is still the case in Kyrgyzstan and Siberia.

The West, in its hurry to introduce the green revolution of the 20th century in these areas, ignored the local practices developed from tradition, sticking to a point of view that scientifically proven 'pasture management' with its related administrative procedures should result in well managed, productive areas. In South America this type of 'pasture management' is still being promoted, even after a hundred plus experiments over a period

---

[29]   a.m.s.l. meaning (meters) above mean sea level

of fifty years have proven that there is no increase in yield.[30] This shows something about the attitude of scientists, namely their idea that they know better, that they do not have to listen to experiential knowledge and can be conceited concerning these cultures. At the same time they are easily misled by simple and straightforward management solutions instead of trying to understand a complex socio-ecological cultural system.

Fig. 12. Steppes in Middle-Eastern Europe and China.

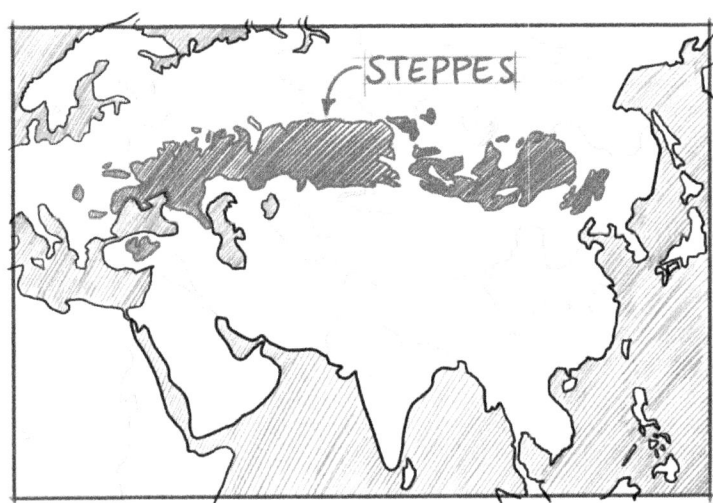

Different impacts (application of modern technologies, economical interests and droughts) on this subtle complex system have now resulted in overgrazing, erosion and the imminent extinction of nomadic pastoral societies. The picture above shows the extensive area covered by the prairies and the related pastoral communities.

We are lucky that the Savory Institute[31] provides worldwide training on sustainable grazing.

5.9 Roundup – a new 'input' with disruptive consequences

An apparently small scale 'improvement' can have a worldwide impact on a large scale. In the nineties of the last century a very effective herbicide, glyphosate, was developed and became well known under the name of 'Round Up'. By now you may have heard about it in your local newspaper as some shops take it out of their assortment now.

---

[30]   Gammon 1978, O'Common 1985.

[31]   http:/savoryinstitute.org

It is mainly applied in large-scale farming of, for instance, maize and soy bean, which have been genetically modified in order not to be affected by the herbicide. At the same time many people in the US and Western Europe use it for gardening.

Only later, between 2005 and 2010, Don Huber[7] discovered after many years of research the disturbing and negative effects glyphosate has on soil organisms, plants, animals and public health. That happens as glyphosate inhibits the necessary complex interactions in the soil to take place:
1. It reduces plant resistance to diseases, fungi and insects.
2. It disturbs soil systems and causes an increase in soil diseases
3. It increases the level of mycotoxins which are poisonous for soil improving organisms such as nitrogen fixers and fungi

Fig. 13. One missing ingredient (due to Glyphosaat), which organises the conversion from C to D, does irreversible damage to a whole pathway in the soil and plant cycle.

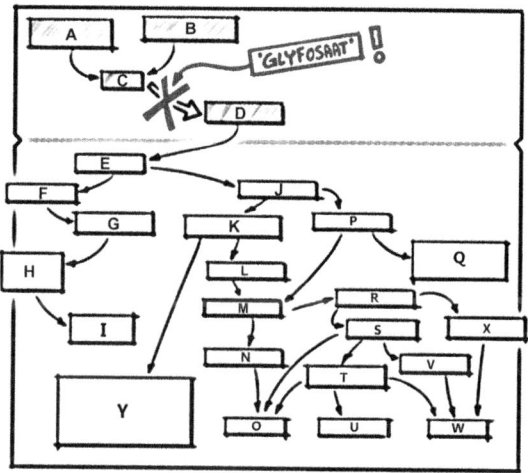

Deficiencies. As a result, an important lack of nutrients, minerals and trace elements develop in the food crops. In maize and soy beans grown while using Round Up, levels of Manganese, Copper, Iron, Zinc, Magnesia, Calcium and Potassium are reduced by 20 to 50 percent. These reductions, in combination with toxins, cause deficiencies in cattle. In the US, in some herds, over 50% of the calves were born dead due to a lack of Manganese. These deficiencies also result in infertility and allergic reactions with animals. Recent research work, done by Mae Wan Ho (I-sis institute, † 2016) and others show that the chance of getting breast cancer[8] is aggravated by small amounts of glyphosate in our bodies.

Human food chain. Because Round Up is also used for the production of vegetables, fruits and grains, the effects of its use can be traced in the human food chain. Don Huber shows that the lack of minerals, in combination with toxins, can be held responsible for the development of a number of new diseases like allergies, infertility, diabetes, Alzheimer disease and ADHD.

What has happened? As the result of an external element, all kinds of effective interactions, functions and feedback mechanisms in the soil system have been modified, changed or destroyed.

5.10 Birds victims of industrialised agriculture

Another unexpected side effect of industrial agriculture is the serious reduction in the numbers of farmland birds. A loss of approximately 50% of all bird species living on and around farmland areas is the result of a change in agricultural policies and farm management over the past 30 years. To increase productivity, hedges were uprooted, trees were cut, wetlands were drained, meadows were ploughed and pesticides and herbicides were applied, the effect of which only became clear at a later stage. Birds lost their nesting and feeding areas, their fertility was reduced and the eggshells became more fragile. The picture below shows how strongly the numbers of farmland birds have been reduced. According to research of the Pan-European Common Bird Monitoring Scheme in the UK in 2012 the number of Grey Partridge was reduced by 91% against a European average of 82%.

These tremendous losses are a serious indication that something is very wrong in agriculture's impact on nature. The most serious aspect is that this problem will probably increase in the future as the European Union is introducing the same large scale agricultural production systems in Bulgaria, Romania and other new member states where, until recently, small scale agriculture was practised and chemicals were rarely used.

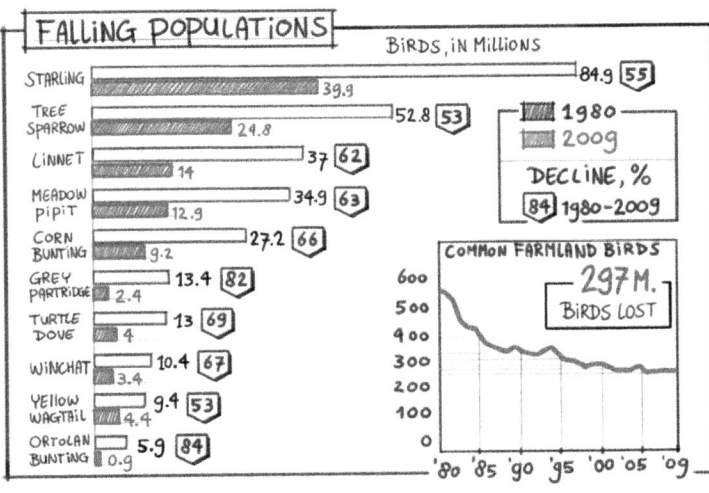

Fig.14. Reduction of bird populations in millions

"We need to introduce measures that consider the environmental impact of the agriculture policies we are implementing", is a statement made by many policy makers. In my opinion we should not only look at simple one-to-one impacts (as research often tries to do), but we must try to understand the coherence of the interaction of agricultural practises with nature and shift to coherent agro-eco farming systems.

5.11 Large scale industrial agriculture creates dead seas

Reduced soil fertility in large-scale agriculture results in water pollution and causes important losses in biodiversity in situ and elsewhere. Drive for six hours in Kansas and you will see nothing but maize and soy beans - mono cultures. Nothing else but these cash crops is growing there. Less than 0.1% of the original prairies remain.

This serious ecological and economic crisis exists since about 1990 and is the result of (1) a split in the production of grain and of cattle and (2) the intensification of these two monocultures, without taking the agro-ecosystem into account.

From an agro-eco point of view (using the landscape *perspective* and the complex system *glasses*) we see the following:

Energy. For 9 of the 12 months per year, in the major part of the American Midwest, the land is fallow; it is empty, not cultivated. This means that only during three months solar energy and carbon dioxide can be captured and converted: a serious loss and a miss of opportunities. In addition to this, a lot of fossil fuel energy is required to transport this feed to faraway cattle and hog farms.

Nutrients. The nutrients that were taken from the soil by the feed crops will now benefit some far off meat production enterprise and probably be exported in the shape of beef. That is a serious loss of minerals and nutrients for the region of origin. Alternatively, the grain could have been used to feed the human population in the region of origin. That would be a more efficient use of the natural resources; as for one kilogramme of beef about 5 kilogrammes of grain are required. Also, the nutrients – if used and eaten in the region - could be recycled after consumption and would so stay in the area of origin and replenish the soils.

Water. Nine months of fallow in the dry period result in a lowering of the groundwater table. In addition some 7.5 million tonnes of nitrogen are applied off which 50 – 60 per cent is absorbed by the crop, and the remaining 40 – 50 per cent is washed out into the groundwater. Part of this, 1.8 million tonnes, is being washed out into the Mississippi and Missouri rivers. Together with the eroded soil particles some 500 million tonnes. Over a large area in their estuaries the washed out nitrogen and the phosphates cause low levels of oxygen content, resulting in the dying off of shrimps and fishes. As a result of industrial agriculture hundreds of these kinds of polluted estuaries now exist all over the world.

Soil. In the soil, a number of minerals and trace elements exist that are important for our food as well as for the soil structure. As they improve the water retention capacity, the rooting depth also improves. As a result of the monocultures and the long fallow periods in particular, the organic matter, which was accumulated over centuries, is washed out, the soil structure has deteriorated and the availability of minerals and trace elements is strongly reduced. The impact of this process can be compared to the impact of cutting down the rainforests.

Animal species. A number of species (fishes and birds) have become extinct and others have been greatly reduced in numbers.

Social impact. In the US alone 11 million people suffer from hunger and 23 million have no food security. In addition a large number suffers from obesity and other symptoms, which are probably related to unilateral food, lacking of minerals and trace elements.

Losses and costs. The complexity of the original system is reduced by approximately 50%. The problem is that all the negative impacts (the costs of the loss of biodiversity, the loss of fish population, the costs of the rehabilitation of the biodiversity) are not included in the total economical results of the agribusiness. For this reason the production seems very cost-efficient and even cheap.

In 2004 the University of Iowa calculated the costs to society of the abuse of natural resources by this agribusiness system and came to the shocking result of about 20 billion dollar per year.

Of course the following questions come up:
1. What would the cost picture look like if we would change this type of agriculture into more integrated systems?
2. What would happen if these costs were included in the economic results of the agribusiness system? And thus be included in the sales prices.

Damage to:	Cost per year (M US$)
Water	419
Soil (costs per year: 2,243-13,395)	13,395
Air	450
Wildlife and ecosystems	1,160
Public health Pathogens	416
Public health Pesticides	1,090
Total (5.700-16,900)	16,200
Government costs (research and rehabilitation)	3,700
Total	20,000

Table 2. Tegtmeijer and Duffy, 2004

5.12 The giant food producer companies

To be or not to be? That is the question! The problems facing our food system are stark: 840 million people hungry, more than one billion overweight, climate change threatening crop yields and the supply of fresh water, competition for land and water leading to conflict and unrest.

Within this system, enormous influence rests in the hands of just a few giant brands, that have the power to help change the system for everyone. In a world with 7 billon food consumers and 1.5 billion food producers, no more than 500 companies control 70% of food choice. Just ten of those companies, the 'Big 10', Associated British Foods (ABF) Coca-Cola, Danone, General Mills, Kellogg, Mars, Mondelez International Nestle, PepsiCo and Unilever, together earn more than $1.1 billion per day. Their annual revenues of more than $450 billion are equivalent to the GDP of all of the world's low-income countries combined. Their supply chains are linked to every part of the system, from the farmers to consumers. Shifts in their business ripple throughout the world's food system.

Assessment. With this huge influence in mind, Oxfam conducted eighteen months of in-depth research on the policies and practices of the 'Big 10' to understand how they are wielding power on people in developing countries who supply the land, labour, water and commodities to make their products. The initial assessment, published in February 2013, was bleak, revealing the social and environmental policies of the world's ten biggest food and beverage giants were not fit for modern purpose and needed a major wake-up call.

One year later, the industry has made efforts to address some of its problems. The changes in policy amongst the 'Big 10' are slowly translating into practice, with agricultural producers and traders beginning to improve their practices to ensure they retain the business of the major brands. Ultimately this must lead to real change in the lives of people affected by the sourcing practices of these companies around the world.

Policy changes are the first step in that process. Vocal consumers and forward-looking investors have proved the most powerful force for change. There is evidence that organized and committed people can push companies towards more responsible policies and practices. The clearest examples of this are in improved company policies on land rights and women's equality, pushed through in response to Oxfam's campaigns on those issues. Supporters have taken nearly 400,000 actions; 31 major investment funds, representing nearly 1.5 trillion dollars of assets under management have joined our call on food industry giants to do more to reduce social and environmental risks in their supply chains. We can all accelerate this trend if more people mobilize to speak-out in urging companies to do things differently.

What's changed in a year? The ten biggest food and beverage companies in the world are slowly waking up to their responsibilities to help tackle some immense challenges facing the global food system. Thanks to pressure from hundreds of thousands of consumers and investors managing trillions of dollars in assets, leaders are emerging from the pack. We see evidence that companies are beginning to pursue more just and sustainable policies, which will better control the impact they have on farmers, workers, communities and the planet.

Hunger, poverty, women's rights, land grabs and climate change were the issues that companies were asked to address. Most change has occurred where consumers were organized and actively involved in calling on companies to address their failures. Nestle, Unilever and Coca-Cola have joined a race to the top on policies that help address those problems in their supply chains. They have shown measurable progress over the last year but have a long way to go before they can truly celebrate.

Associated British Foods and Kellogg have taken initial steps to catch up, but they are still among the lowest performers. Danone, Mars, Mondelez and PepsiCo were very slow improvers in 2013 while General Mills is the only company headed in the wrong direction.

Stuck! Overall, too many companies remain stuck in the mud with policies that fail to measure up to the threats facing their industry and consumer demand for transparent and responsible corporate citizenship. While the overall trend is pointed in the right direction, progress is far too slow. Even the leaders are only beginning to take the necessary steps to grapple with their influence on the lives of people living in hunger and poverty. To help build a world where everyone has enough to eat, more consumers will need to raise their voices to hold companies accountable for how they do business in developing countries.

Some Challenges Ahead for the Big 10

- Avoid catastrophe on climate change
- Pro-actively identify and address major problems in the supply chain
- Lift the 'veil of secrecy' that shrouds supply chains
- Pay a sustainable price for commodities
- Protect rights and give people a voice throughout the supply chain
- Make the change to agro-ecological practices throughout the chain

6. Towards Coherent Agro-Ecosystems

This chapter is an introduction to agro-ecosystems.

It covers how coherent agroecosystems work and how we can support the mechanisms of such complex systems.

6.1 The four elementary functions of the ecosystem

Even a simple ecosystem is very complex. It is complicated, interactive and cooperative. In order to understand and be able to work with agro-ecosystems we will have a look at four fundamental processes, valid for all ecosystems. These will provide us with tools that will enable us to check on the coherence or the vitality of an agro-ecosystem. A change in one of these processes will automatically change the other three as well because they are in fact all part of the larger coherent system.

The watercycle. Are plants and ground water fed by rainwater or does the water run off the land immediately and cause erosion? Are wells and streams perennial or only supplying water for part of the year?

The nutrient cycle: Are nutrients available for living organisms, are they fixed in dead plants or have they washed out below the root zone? Will nutrients become available elsewhere if plants are being burned or if the soil is washed away?

The energy balance: How much solar energy is absorbed by green leaves and is transformed into nourishment for the ecosystem? How much is being lost on fallow soil?

Dynamism in a society (plants and animals). Are there many species with a stable population of different ages? Or are there only a few species with strongly fluctuating numbers over time?

6.2 Interdependence and interaction

Imagine the four aspects above as four different windows through which you can observe the same room. Or imagine that they are the organs, blood, muscles and nerves of your body. You can't have healthy lungs without oxygen, but neither can you have a healthy liver if your lungs are not functioning. According to the same principles an ecosystem has to contain many different communities of organisms to dispose of effective water and nutrient cycles. Additionally, effective energy and water supplies are required to keep these communities alive, supported by a nutrient cycle, which supplies, removes and digests.

In a natural system there is a lot of interaction between the various components and mechanisms of this system. Each intrusion may have effects that could not have been predicted beforehand. In a vital system intrusions are dealt with without much disturbance of the system as a whole. Parts of the system take over if another part fails. Usually there is also an impact of the environment in which the intrusion takes place.

For instance, if liquid manure is injected in the soil when it is raining the negative impact is far lower than when this happens when the weather is dry. There may be effects 'later' in time and also 'elsewhere', outside the system, that one needs to be aware of.

Example of a poor, ill functioning ecosystem. The dry riverbed only carries water during a flash flood. The soil is bare and there is no vegetative cover. As a result the biological productivity is low and there is no soil development. Dry spells and erosive showers are the standard. The loss of biodiversity is substantial.

Example of a healthy ecosystem in the same region. The river carries water throughout the year as the vegetative cover of the soil ensures trapping of rain water, which keeps the groundwater level high. Biological productivity is much higher. Flash floods are less common as upstream rainwater is infiltrating the soil as well. There is a continuous increase of biodiversity.

6.3 Regularities in coherent, resilient agro-ecosystems

It is an established fact that all natural systems, including agro-ecosystems, demonstrate a number of inherent, internal rules, which can be recognised and have to be taken into account when one wants to interact with the system, or when one wants to take specific measures to change the system.

Feedback mechanisms. Every system in a 'positive'[32] feedback situation will destroy itself in the end, unless a limit can be put on to the energy input of

---

[32]   'Positive feedback' is not necessarily positive. The 'feedback signal' being positive means that with increased inputs the output will increase too, so that the process, whether negative or positive, is self-reinforcing.

this system. This limit we can register, it can be a warning signal, a timely feedback (if this, then no longer that) or a blocking mechanism.

Cycles. Farms as well as cities have to find a solution for the daily garbage, produced by men and animals. How this is done has a large impact on how the farms (which need the nutrients) are being supported. Over the centuries there are good and bad examples of the use of urban garbage to fertilize its surrounding rural area. Sewage systems already existed in 700 CE in old cities like Samarkand in Uzbekistan. In London and Amsterdam night soil was transported to the rural areas by boat. The most important point is that the import and export of nutrients should be in balance and that nutrients and water are returned where they have been taken away.

Resilience or stability assumes an internal balance in the system. This implies that reactions and events in a system are tuned into one another within the system. Another name for this phenomenon is compatibility and it assumes that complexity exists. If one factor changes, in a complex system this can be counteracted by the other elements or parts. If a system has been reduced to its most elementary interactions, even the smallest change or disturbance will put it off the rail. For instance, if a cow has been crossbred to improve its most important characteristic (a high milk production) while ignoring the strength of her bones or the vitality of her organs, she will get sick more easily or will have a reduced life expectation.

Holographic principle. In order to survive it is necessary for each individual species in the system that the vital processes necessary for that one species are coherent with the vital processes of the entire system. In other words, the nutrition required by your little finger is the same nutrition as required by your entire system. Or, the fungi in the soil need the same humidity and temperature as the plant roots and the soil organisms with which they interact.

6.4 How do we recognise a resilient complex system?

The facets, regularities and elementary functions of complex and coherent systems can be easily found. However, some training is required to see them and to recognise them as such.

The recognition of a coherent system resembles a little bit the old Sufi story about the blind men and the elephant: Once upon a time there was a city where all the inhabitants were blind. One day the king came to the town. He rode an elephant to impress the citizens. But of course the blind men and women couldn't see the elephant, so they touched the elephant to get an idea of what the animal would look like. The man who had touched the ear said, "it is big and soft, it resembles a carpet". The man who had touched the trunk said, "It is a straight hollow pipe, air is passing through it and it is scary". The one who had examined the leg said, "it is strong and sturdy, like a pillar or a tree trunk". Each of them had understood a part of the body of the elephant, but none of them had succeeded in getting the right picture of the whole animal. The same goes for complex systems.

Fig. 15. Recognising a complex system

The main task for the manager of a complex system (the farmer) is to see a problem in relation to all other aspects and processes in the system. He has to see what the relations and interactions are, which are necessary to let the whole system be what it is and to let it function as it has to. In order to do that he needs to understand these relations and interactions in the course of time, how they fluctuate and what causes the fluctuations. Farmers understand this often better than scientists and policy makers.

Finally one can recognise a healthy (farming) system from the healthy condition and radiance of all its components: soil, trees, animals and human beings, the water in the drains, its produce and the landscape. These are the external characteristics of the entire system. In fact, not much different from telling if a person is happy and healthy or not, just by the looks of them.

6.5 Complex systems require organic science

Breaking away from constraints of old-style scientific axioms allows us to explore an organic world that, until now, has been difficult to understand in overall terms. In such high-dimensional (multivalued) systems, reductionist thinking (in use by traditional science) proves inadequate; isolated single dimensional results do not predict real system behaviour. The co-evolutionary or epistatic nature of interrelated systems requires us to take a contextual approach, studying the dynamics of interactions rather than the static makeup of parts studied in more conventional science.

Contextual approaches recognise that systems do not exist in isolation, but are defined only in conjunction with other systems (including that of the observer). This co-evolutionary nature of multiple systems brings us to an ecosystem viewpoint and allows us to understand the irregular changes over time that characterise such systems. This viewpoint is not emphasised in the assumptions of our conventional sciences, which are based on static snapshots of what are non-static systems. In complex systems, solutions are always compromises, there is no single answer.

What we must do instead is to compare alternative answers or options in state space, using a plurality of techniques, with a view to identifying the best fit; the global optimum in the context of interest.

6.6 We don't need to start from zero: The Asilomar Declaration

The Asilomar Declaration for Sustainable Agriculture was formulated by the Committee For Sustainable Agriculture as early as the 25th January 1990[33]:

"Our current industrial agriculture has failed. We have produced abundant food and fiber, but the cost and the fragility of these successes are becoming more and more evident. Sustainable alternatives already prove their value. Not only are they more efficient in their use of energy, biological sources of fertility and pest management, they also enhance rural communities and encourage families to remain on the land.

We commit ourselves to hastening the broad adoption of agriculture that is environmentally sound, economically viable, fair, and humane. Sustainable agriculture that provides nourishing food, protects those who work the land, helps stabilize the earth's climate and safeguards soil and water depends on our ability to meet a number of challenges."

The Assilomar Declaration says we must address these challenges without delay:

1. Promote and sustain healthy rural communities. Healthy rural communities are attractive and equitable for farmers, farm workers, and their families.

---

[33] Developing a comprehensive vision of sustainable agriculture, http://casfs.ucsc.edu/documents/issue-papers/sust_in_balance_2.pdf

The continuation of traditional values and farming wisdom depends on a stable, multi-generational population. Absentee of corporate land ownership and the ever-increasing size of farms diminish rural life.

2. Expand opportunities for new and existing farmers to prosper using sustainable systems. We must devise ways to help people get started in sustainable farming, Reliable information on sustainable agriculture needs to be readily available to farmers, extension agents, bankers, and others. Training and apprenticeship programs should be provided for entry-level farmers and established conventional farmers interested in making the transition. Tax forgiveness or other incentives should be devised to ease the financial stress of new and transitional farmers.

3. Inspire the public to value safe and healthful food. The biological quality of food is known to affect the health and wellbeing of those who eat it. Food quality is a key factor in disease prevention. Approaches that are striving to be sustainable - such as organic farming - avoid hazardous pesticide use and maintain nutrient balance. Consumers' understanding of these facts will increase their willingness to pay prices that reflect the true costs of production.

4. Foster an ethic of land stewardship and humaneness in the treatment of farm animals. Sustainable agriculture recognizes that the gifts of nature upon which it depends - soil, water, plants, and animals, both wild and domestic - are to be treated with loving care and humility. The greatest calling of the farmer is to leave those gifts in better condition than when they were received. Such a responsible agriculture can only be achieved when nature is both mentor and model, and when natural systems are the standard against which success is measured. Farm animals often contribute to ecologically sound agricultural systems and they deserve humane care.

5. Expand knowledge and access to information about sustainable agriculture. American farmers are innovators. Given scientifically validated techniques, farmers will adopt sustainable agricultural practices. Seeing these practices in the field will speed adoption. We need demonstration farms, farmer-to-farmer field tours, and studies of successful alternative farms of all sizes. University teaching, research, and extension must be redirected toward understanding the whole farm ecology and away from chemical dependence in farm management.

6. Reform the relationship among government, industry, and agriculture. Governments must use resources such as subsidies, grants, and loans to convert significant portions of industrial agriculture to a sustainable system. Undue rewards to concentrated corporate interest should be replaces with fair returns to farmers who sustainable provide food and fiber.

7. Redefine the role of industrial agriculture in the global community. The present global agriculture trade is placing unnecessary pressure on the sustainability of the earth's resource base. The western industrialised agribusiness has a unique opportunity to change that situation. The people of many countries look to industrialised countries' for agricultural leadership. Those industrialised countries and their agribusiness can honor that respect by restricting their trade in dangerous substances. We can encourage the Agency for International Development, The World Bank, and international research institutions to convert to sustainable programs. The international programs of universities can become centers of sustainability training and research.

6.7 What keeps us from progressing?

Why do we (politicians, governments and advisors) wait such a long time (namely until 'science' has proven that things go wrong), before we believe that things go wrong, when we see it happening in front of our own eyes? And why do we take so long (until proven to be true by scientists again) to appreciate farmer-invented technologies that do work and to apply them in projects and programmes? SRI, the very sustainable System of Rice Intensification[34], invented and practised by farmers, is such an example. It took ages before 'science' and therefore governments and development policies recognised it as such.

There are several reasons why we are reluctant to change:
1. The advertisements of the large international agribusiness enterprises that want to make us believe that there are no problems. This is achieved with romantic pictures of 19th century farmhouses, happy animals and butterflies on the and with self-developed health certificates and hallmarks.
2. The publication 'Food Politics, how the food industry influences nutrition and health' by Marion Nestlé[35] shows that American nutrition specialists and scientist are strongly advised, if not put under pressure, by the agribusiness and food industry not to mention a number of issues and not to research them.
3. The relationship between education and reality. Lectures are often given by experts from the business. If 80% of the maize export, 80% of the maize processing and 80% of the processing and packaging of meat is with four large corporations, it is very likely that lobbying will occur and that the existing system will be continued.

---

[34] Please refer to http://sri.cals.cornell.edu/
[35] http://www.foodpolitics.com/food-politics-how-the-food-industry-influences-nutrition-and-health/

4. Our optimistic idea that the earth will be there forever. This idea leads us to manage our natural resources inefficiently and disregard natural systems. In Australia with its poor soils and vast desert areas people have become more aware of the fact that they have to be careful with their natural resources.
5. Wrong investments. A lot of natural and human energy is used for wrong ideas, because we do not see the larger relationships.
6. The interests of the multinationals and their impact on policies. After Rio 20+ (in 2012) Gro Harlem Brundtland said[9] "corporate power was one reason for lack of progress".

7. A healthy soil is a nourished world, forever

Why do we treat our soils so badly? She is our mother. She nourishes us!

In Amharic, the official language of Ethiopia, the word for soil is Afer. A slightly different word is Safer, meaning guilt.

During the Ethiopian Soil Campaign[36] a scientist from the Holeta Research Institute read a personally made poem, wondering how the Amharic words Safer (*guilt*) and Afer (*soil*) could be so closely related. The poem was wonderful and touched all of the participants.

His interpretation: we feel guilty because we treat our soils so badly.

Soils are just as complex and intriguing as an organisation. And to get some guidance about your personal choice of food, you might as well know a bit more about the virtue of good soil management and its immediate effect on good food and personal health.

A fertile, resilient soil is the base for healthy (agro) ecosystems and, as such, the basis for sustained life on earth. Organic farmers have known this for a long time. Experts are rediscovering this, with the result that increasing attention is being given to restoration of soils. In April 2013 the UN declared 2015 the year of the Soil[37]. In many countries around the world campaigns were organised to raise awareness about the importance of soil.

This chapter is a short introduction on the importance of soils and the relationship between soils, food and human health. It tells us all about soils and what you can do to help restore them. We will see how soils can be rehabilitated, in order to become fertile organic systems again, so that they can feed plants, animals and mankind, and retain and filter water.

---

[36]　http://agriprofocus.com/ethiopian-soil-campaign

[37]　On 24 April 2013 at the 146 FAO Council, FAO member Countries endorsed the request from the Kingdom of Thailand in the framework of the GSP for the proclamation of the International Year of Soils 2015. The IYS will serve as a platform for raising awareness on the importance of sustainable soil management as the basis for food systems, fuel and fibre production, essential ecosystem functions and better adaptation to climate change for present and future generations. http://www.fao.org/globalsoilpartnership/highlights/detail/en/c/175190/

7.1 Soil is the starting point for healthy agriculture

For the production of healthy food, we need healthy agro-ecosystems and they in turn need healthy soil. Soil is a fundamental requirement. For a healthy soil, the provision and availability of organic material (old leaves, green waste, compost, manure) is a must. The reason? Organic material is fundamental for the development of soil *life*[38] which, in turn, is a key factor in the development of humus. And humus is what plants and crops need to feed on and which they turn into nutritious food for us.

When a soil contains enough humus, there are many positive effects: it will become more fertile, it will be disease-resistant over a longer period, its water-retaining capacity increases, while it will contribute to a reduction of greenhouse gases as it will fix CO_2 as carbon. Plants will suffer less from diseases and will be provided with all the minerals they need. The minerals in the plant will enter the human food cycle and this will in turn keep us healthy.

The current agricultural legislation in Europe requires farmers to calculate the inputs and outputs of the minerals Nitrogen (ammonia), Potassium (urine) and Phosphate in the soil. But actually, we should focus on Carbon (manure, vegetable waste, compost, ashes) instead, as that will help turn our soils into healthy soils, worldwide![39]

7.2 How to get coherent, fertile and resilient soils

If organic material dies, it will end up on top of or in the soil, where it will be digested by soil organisms and turned into humus - a complex composition of stable, organic carbon compounds, proteins and trace elements. We know that soil, flora and fauna intensively exchange nutrients as a result of complex interactions over millions of years. Optimal development of this exchange between soil, soil organisms and plants depends on the availability of sufficient fuel (carbon) and the correct balance between minerals and trace elements. Therefore we want to:

1. **Focus on carbon!** Carbon has an impact on a number of soil characteristics, such as water retention, the volume of soil life (contributing to biodiversity) and the dynamism of water and nutrient cycles[40]. Carbon - which has been incorporated into the soil by plants and soil organisms - is a major contributor to proper functioning of the soil and its fertility. Farmers who aim for optimal

---

[38] Soil life or soil-web: a wide range of larger and smaller animals, organisms and fungi that interact.

[39] The World Bank issued a report in 2012, *Carbon sequestration in agricultural soils*, with exactly this plea: focus on carbon. Report nr. 67395-GLB.

[40] Nutrients including minerals

organic carbon content in their soils will experience higher yields, as the soil becomes an important production factor.

2. **Focus on trace elements.** Focussing on carbon does not make sense if trace elements like Zn, Fe, Mn, Cu, Co, Cr, Mo, Se, B, Si, Ni, Na, Al and Cl are not monitored. Trace elements are crucial in the development of sustainable soil fertility. They serve as a catalyst for special metabolic processes, without being absorbed. For instance, cattle need about one picogramme (10^{-12} grams) of cobalt per day. A quantity one can fit on the point of a needle. However, if they do not take this in through their food, they will become vulnerable to various diseases like Bush sickness, Coast disease and Salt sick[41], which have an effect on public health and on the economy.

3. **Focus on improved interaction between plant roots and the soil.** Soil life actually works like well-oiled machinery. The pictures show better than any explanation how that works.

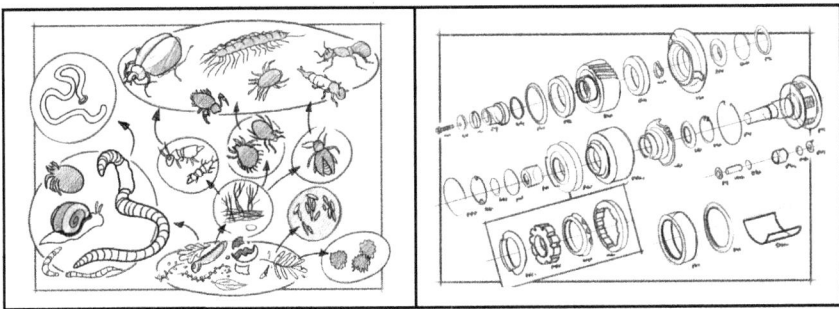

Fig. 16. Soil life (left) works as well-oiled machinery (right)

Production of humus is the result of the action of soil life (microbes, worms, fungi and algae) around the hair roots, the thin hairs on the roots. Soil life wants to exchange nutrients with active hair roots (very fine hair like roots) and vice versa. Hair-roots exude chemicals, which attract the nutrients they need to grow[42].

---

[41] Cobalt is an important building block in vitamin B. The cobalt deficiency shows by the legs of the animal pointing outward; also they suffer from listlessness, anaemia (lack of red blood cells), poor appetite, reduced growth, condition and production; calves are weak. If animals show these features, their vitamin B12 has been totally depleted since weeks or months before.

[42] Film fragments from the film 'LIFE IN THE SOIL' of the International Research Center for Nature Farming in Japan show how this actually happens. Film rights are with EM Agriton BV. You can order the film for 15 euro by sending an email to info@hortinova.nl asking for DVD 'Life in the soil'. Other short films on roots and micro-organisms, look at https://www.youtube.com/results?search_query=life+in+the+soil

4. **Focus on humus,**[43] **an absolute necessity for soil fertility**
   The volume of humus is the basis for maintaining a productive soil. Humus is organic material which has been digested and converted by soil life and has been deposited as skins around the mineral components of the soil. At least 4% of the mineral dry matter content is necessary to provide for enough nutrition for soil life and crops.

   Humus possesses some unique characteristics, which are essential for healthy crop development: humus regulates soil humidity; it is a stock of readily available organic plant nutrition; humus glues. In sandy soils humus glues soil particles together, reducing soil erodibility, improving soil structure and thus water retention. Roots can better penetrate the soil; humus has electro-magnetic characteristics, which is the reason that dew in the air is being adsorbed by the soil; frost damage is less and recuperation after drought is faster and better. Humus increases vitality and resistance of plants; CO_2 (a climate terror) is fixed by humus.

Due to these characteristics, humus has several positive effects on crop production:

- Increased efficiency in nutrient uptake by the crop, resulting in an increase in crop production with higher levels of trace elements and enzymes;
- improvement of quality and conservation period of food products;
- improvement of soil structure and water retention capacity, reduction of erodibility;
- reduced loss of nitrogen and minerals from leaching (see example in chapter 3.11 pg 55);
- lower need to apply pesticides as the crop is more resistant against diseases and pests; and
- improved health of the animals grazing on the improved meadows.

7.3 What goes wrong without humus?

There are a few but very serious effects when a soil doesn't have any humus:

1. Without humus you will get dead soils with a never-ending need for more fertilizer. Over the centuries, in the East of the Netherlands,

---

[43] Humus: the organic component of soil, formed by the decomposition of leaves and other plant material by soil microorganisms. Humus refers to any <u>organic matter</u> that has reached a point of stability, where it will break down no further and might, if conditions do not change, remain as it is for centuries, if not millennia. Humus significantly influences the bulk density of soil and contributes to moisture and nutrient retention.

soils with rich organic top soil have developed by a continuous application of manure and normal ploughing conditions. However, when after 1980 it became common to increase the depth of cultivation, the humus became mineralised in no time and lost its nutritious characteristics for the plants. Thus, in 40 years the humus content was reduced from 12 to about 2% of the total soil mass. Below 2%, agriculture is no longer possible. This is the simple explanation of the relation between deeper ploughing and the never-ending need for more fertilizer.

2. Unbalanced nutrition for plants. Without trace elements the plant is no longer capable of synthesizing proteins, which reduces crop vitality and increases the risk of infection. Crop and soil protection techniques (pesticides) now become necessary. Without trace elements human and animal food are no longer balanced either and both men and animals will suffer from disease.

3. Obesity is an example of a deficiency disease resulting from the consumption of unbalanced food, which is lacking certain essential components, such as lysine[44]. This deficiency is caused by the use of chemical fertilizer on soils with low humus content.

7.4 How then can we increase humus content?

There are a number of measures that can be taken by farmers, which they will do once they see the advantages:

Interventions directly applied to soil

1. **Provide sufficient organic nutrients.** Soil life has to be supplied with sufficient organic nutrients in oxygen-rich surroundings to stimulate root activity. The organic nutrients are provided by[45] compost, green manure, nitrogen fixing crops (legumes, pulses), stone meal or rock dust.[46]
2. **Mulching, or keeping the soil covered,** preferably with useful vegetation, or, if this is not an option, with a mulch which contains enough nutrients to promote soil life at the surface.
3. **Solid animal manure** is a better agent to increase the humus content than liquid manure, as the former contains no urine.

---

[44]   See the explanation about the effects of lack of lysine on human health on page 77

[45]   More detailed description of these tools in *Restoring Soils for a food secure 2050*

[46]   Re-mineralize the earth: better soil, better food, better planet. http://remineralize.org/a-rock-dust-primer. Regenerative farming combines organic amendments with soil improvement measures: http://rockinsoils.com/

4. **Apply secondary materials,** such as waste that contains nutrients. Of course there is a risk of an overdose of nitrogen and phosphate or pollution with micro-bacterial elements, heavy metals, antibiotics and dioxins. In his book *'4000 years of agro-eco agriculture'*[10], F.H. King describes how pre-fermented material (canal silt) after drying may be mixed with decomposing vegetative materials to continue the decomposing process. During this process, strong natural antibiotics will develop, which can kill dangerous pathogens like anthrax. An experiment at the former Institute for Humus and Compost has shown that 18 of the most dangerous pathogens will be killed by aerobic composting.
5. **A one-off dressing of trace minerals.** On the condition that sufficient humus is present to adsorb the minerals and prevent leaching, and cycles will be closed. Trace elements have the function of catalysts and are hardly used during the metabolic processes in the soil.

Interventions through more sustainable farming practises

1. **Crop rotation and change of crops.** This will stop the build-up of diseases as a result of monocultures and create a more diversified utilisation of the available nutrients. Farmers can change to a wider range of cereals (instead of maize) and cut them, in time, to be used as green manure. Sowing of the next crop can take place almost immediately in the residue. Frequent use of green manure crops is a very good practice to remedy soil exhaustion. No more use of maize for silage. In cattle farms a change must be realised to the use of Alfalfa (a legume) and grain maize, instead of silage.
2. **Convert farmland into meadows.** Meadows are one of the most efficient types of land use to increase humus. As this process mainly takes place in the rooting zone, the use of deep rooting grass varieties is preferred.
3. **No tillage.** By reducing the depth of soil cultivation or stopping this practice altogether, soil life is less disturbed and humus content in the top layer of the soil will increase. Worldwide, various 'no tillage' and 'minimum tillage' networks promote[47] this technique[11].
4. **Orient farming systems towards soil fertility instead of to highest yields.** Organic agriculture, biodynamic agriculture, permaculture[12] and the so-called agro-eco agriculture[13] are all aiming for the exclusion of fertilizer and chemicals while promoting the use of organic manure.

---

[47] The South Australian No-Till Farmers Association (SANTFA) is a non-profit farmer driven organisation. SANTFA has, over its seven years of growth, successfully promoted the benefits of no-till farming systems and conservation farming in general and now has over 1000 financial members across South Australia. http://www.santfa.com.au/about-us

5. **Mixed cropping versus monocultures.** To achieve a high level of activity in the soil it is necessary that a continuous, intensive exchange between hair roots and soil life exists throughout the year. This condition cannot be achieved under monocultures. A maize crop, for example, not only exudes an excess of sugars during a relatively short time, but in addition the composition of the discharge is rather limited and does not provide for the wide range of soil life. Another reason to grow several crops at the same time, each exuding its own composition of sugars over a longer period.

7.5 What about chemical fertilizer? Is there anything wrong?

Application of fertilizer is not wrong, but should always take place in combination with a source of organic material, like compost, seaweed, seaweed extracts or rock dust/stone meal. It is interesting to note that, by adding 5% organic material to the fertilizer, the original dressing can be reduced by two thirds without losing its efficiency. In addition, this combination of fertilizer/organic matter is 20 times more effective, whilst leaching of minerals is also reduced.

An example of a counterproductive activity is the application of fertilizer to compensate for the ever-decreasing soil fertility, which is a result of ploughing. At first, application of fertilizer seemed to be the find of the century: one applies some fertilizer and the crop shoots up. But on closer inspection this is, once again, fighting a symptom and not the source of the problem. The negative effect of ploughing (being a loss of minerals) is remedied for the short term, but fertilizer results in an inefficient uptake of nutrients, it is damaging to soil life and does not stop the accelerated mineralization of humus through oxygenation as a result of ploughing.

7.6 Less known negative effects of (chemical) fertilizer application

1. **Nutrient uptake is reduced drastically** upon the introduction of fertilizer. The plant is provided with a solution of nutrients in an unbalanced composition and does not develop optimally. As the plants are thirsty, they will still take up the solution and thus the nutrients. The balance between the various minerals is lost; some are absorbed in excess, others in too low quantities. This disturbs the normal metabolic processes. The plant has to use extra energy to take up nutrients that are not necessary, while having to use energy to get rid of the same excess of nutrients in the shape of ammonia (NH_3). This has two negative effects: the plant cannot

use its energy on healthy growth so plant production is reduced and there is an increase of greenhouse gasses.

2. **Lysine shortages:** Animals and people depend on plants for the production of lysine - an amino acid essential for our digestion. The shortages discussed above also have an impact on the production of lysine. There will be less lysine available per gramme product. As a result, the consumer, whether animal or man, will eat three times as much of the food concerned. The body contains a kind of tracker counting the units of lysine. A crop containing less lysine has to be consumed in larger quantities until a feeling of satisfaction is reached. The consumer continues eating, as long as he hasn't got the required quantity of lysine. As a result he grows fat. More simply put: you stop eating when your stomach is full, but you haven't got the required amount of lysine yet, and so you become malnourished.

3. **Extra pests in the crops.** The imbalanced supply of minerals causes the occurrence of pests and diseases. Evaporation of ammonia or alcohol by an unhealthy crop is a signal for insects that this plant needs to be eliminated. Insects can detect diseased plants with an infrared gas detection system, which allows them to identify the sick plant.[14] This almost automatically forces the farmer to use insecticides. Instead of tackling the symptom, it would be better to solve the problem at root level by restoring soil life, which produces humus in order to get the optimal plant nutrition.

4. **Destruction of soil life.** Salts in fertilizer and liquid manure are deathly for soil life in concentrations of more than 2%.

7.7 Healthy soils result in healthy people and healthy animals

Healthy soils solve problems of the welfare state. From the information above it is obvious that improved soil management will help in solving a lot of the challenges of the 21st century.

Improved soil management results in:

1. **Soil related improvements**
   - Reduction of the use of antibiotics, fertilizer and chemicals.
   - Reduction of welfare diseases. Because in a living soil, sufficient trace elements and nutrients will become available to the plant and they will also become available to people who eat those crops. The result will be a reduction of welfare diseases caused by lack of trace elements and nutrients - like obesity, cancer, cardiovascular diseases, high cholesterol levels, autism, ADHD, influenza, rheumatism, arthritis and resistant micro-organisms,

etc. In this way, healthy soils contribute to lower costs of public health care.

- Reduction of the dependence on minerals and oil for the production of fertiliser, bulk chemicals, fertilizer, pesticides and pharmaceutical products. A soil with enough humus will produce enough N, P and K as well as minerals.
- Targets - realisation of (political) environmental targets. A living soil acts as a filter, less N and P is washed out, and ground and surface water will become cleaner.
- Reduction of carbon dioxide emissions and increased absorption of carbon dioxide in plants and the soil.

2. **Integrated regional development.**

   Apart from the production of food, good soil management contributes a lot to the landscape, biodiversity, nature and clean water. This can only be realised if we leave the sector approach behind us and look at landscape, nature and biodiversity as integrated with agriculture. In our western society we have started to look at eco-services or ecosystem-services as activities that are separate from the agricultural production process; instead, an agricultural landscape with agro-ecology will provide an integrated entity. Sustainable land use is the result of healthy agricultural practices of individual farmers and enterprises in this landscape.

7.8 Policies for soil regeneration and focus on carbon

Flanders, Belgium has established limits for organic carbon content in the soil. For each soil type there are optimal levels of organic carbon, which are laid down in the Code for Good Practice on Soil Protection, 2009.[48] Furthermore a carbon simulation programme has been developed that will help farmers calculate the C/N levels, when they enter their cropping plans. Through this method, farmers are assisted in the optimisation of organic matter content in the soil.

The European Strategy for Soils acknowledges the threat to soil fertility, but does not propose regulations or values. Through the cross compliance regulations[15] of the European Community's agriculture policies, good soil management is enforced. The word 'Compliance' is used in the European Union for the requirements and regulations that farmers need to adhere to in order to get a subsidy for the maintenance and improvement of

---

[48] The soil conservation policies of 10 European countries (Belgium, Denmark, etc.) The measures are selected from the book 'Code of Good Practice – Erosion Control'.

agro-ecosystems, the so called ecosystem services. However, no specific regulations are identified for soil fertility.[49]

FAO - the Food and Agriculture organisation of the UN[50] - is promoting a transformation to 'Climate Smart Agriculture', starting from August 2012. This type of agriculture aims to increase productivity in a sustainable manner, reducing the level of greenhouse gases (by fixing CO_2 in the soil) and contributing to regional food security. The opportunity for realizing this type of agriculture is for 70% located in the developing countries.[51]

The year of the soil (2015) has been promoted by FAO and was very successful in raising awareness worldwide. There are many videos and activities on the internet[52] to stress the need of carbon sequestration and a healthy soil to allow for increased food production.

IASS - since 2012, the Institute for Advanced Sustainability Studies organises an annual International Soil week, where professionals in soil fertility from government to NGOs, companies and knowledge institutes, get together to discuss what we need to do to rescue and rehabilitate soils worldwide. In 2015's Berlin Soil Week there was a significant difference between industrialised countries and developing countries. The former pleaded for more organic agriculture, carbon sequestration; the latter focused on more and better fertiliser use.

The World Bank – not a soil policy or agricultural policy making institute, but with a strong international influence - stresses the need for carbon sequestration in agricultural soils. The focus lies on mitigating climate change; better harvests and food security are a secondary benefit. They state that sustainable land management practices *reverse* soil carbon losses! The measures they advise to be taken are, in increasing effectiveness: rotation; residue management; mulches; rotation diversification; no tillage; cover crops; manure; terracing; soil amendments; pasture improvement; water harvesting; intercropping; cross slope barriers; including trees in the field; tree crop farming; afforestation; alley farming (restoration farming); and improved fallow, Biochar.[53]

---

[49] May 2012, 'Thirty questions and answers about soil fertility,' Rene Schils, WUR

[50] Sequester carbon! Support World Soil Day and the International Year of Soils 2015: http://www.youtube.com/watch?v=TqGKwWo60yE;

[51] http://www.fao.org/climatechange/climatesmart/en/

[52] http://www.fao.org/soils-2015/en/

[53] Biochar is a name for charcoal when it is used as a soil amendment. Biochar is under investigation as an approach to carbon sequestration by which it can help mitigate climate change. Biochar can increase soil fertility, increase agricultural productivity and provide protection against some foliar and soil borne diseases. It can endure in soil for thousands of years. Report nr. 67395 GLB, 2012R

7.9 Individuals and organisations for soil health improvement

There are quite a number of individual farmers and organisations that are just *doing* it: working towards a healthy soil, focusing on carbon, increasing humus and restoring coherent agro-landscape systems. More can be found in the document Yellow Pages for Agroecology, for a food secure world, at issuu.com/jellekeforagroecology.

- All national organisations for **Bio-dynamic agriculture**.
- **IFOAM**, the umbrella organisation for the worldwide movement of organic agriculture and trade. Currently there are 750 member organisations distributed over 116 countries. Organic production and trade are growing fast in the entire world. The increase of organic production shows that it is moving from a niche situation to mainstream.[54]
- **CAAANZ**, Conservation Agriculture Alliance of Australia and New Zealand, was founded in 2005 for 'conservation farmers' (who maintain the agricultural landscape as an integrated entity) to facilitate an exchange of knowledge and information. Its members are involved with all types of management aiming for a fertile soil, ranging from research to physical carbon fixation and no-tillage systems.
- The worldwide **No Till Association** - a federation of organisations promoting no-tillage. At the GCARD2 conference of November 2012, Ivo Mello of Brazil presented an overview of their activities, which aim to increase food production with increased carbon fixation and a reduction of eutrophication.
- **The Soil Association in UK**. A large nationwide organisation promoting healthy ecological agriculture, especially organic agriculture and sustainable land use, based on a healthy soil.
- **Advisory services** that promote natural approaches to soil management. In the Netherlands there are a.o. Agriton BV, Van Iersel Compost[55], Rockinsoils, Soil&More. In the United States the association ACRES is guiding, worldwide, ILEIA with its magazine and website 'farming matters' works on the cutting edge for family farming, better soils and low energy input agriculture.
- The programme **'Landscapes for people, food and nature'** includes action research and knowledge sharing on the Internet about integrated, soil and social development augmenting projects.

---

[54] According to the FAO, of the total area of cropland of 1,475 million hectares in 2012, 26 million hectares are under organic management.

[55] http://www.soiltech.nl/pages/en/home.php?lang=EN;

FRONTRUNNERS

8. Restoration of Closed Loop Cycles in Farming Enterprises

"Agro-ecology is the structural answer for future agriculture."[56]

We are lucky to have many groundbreaking frontrunner farmers, project initiaters and organisations that are now our role models.

Case studies of twenty-six of them are assembled here

Chapters 8-13 present a number of impressive, innovative examples on how *The New Normal* - restoration of closed loop cycle agriculture and coherence in agro-ecosystems - is being realised. Starting from small scale, individual enterprises at local level, we read about big changes toward urban agriculture and restoration of regional cycles, in both the developed and developing world.

Examples of transition that give us clues for transition in our own work and life.

These examples are only a small selection of the fast-growing number of beautiful developments in this world. This book is not trying to present an exhaustive selection. The main purpose of the examples in this book is for us to discover the keys for change, the clues on how to act when you want to make, or contribute to, the transition to a healthier world.

I expect that the initiatives presented here are a revelation and I hope that they provide sufficient inspiration to change your own perspective or approach to work, or even to change your decision-making and lifestyle.

---

[56] This statement was made by the IAASTD, the International Assessment of Agricultural Science and Technology for Development, in its report *Agriculture at a Crossroads, 2007,* based on all the investigations carried out all over the world by this group of well-known scientists.

In this chapter, four innovative farmers present their revolutionary activities. They have a dream or a vision, and they use their own qualities and skills to materialize it. Like the ability to see the agro-ecosystem as a whole; they dare to learn experientially, they are courageous, they trust and they persevere.

They are:

- De Groote Voort, a holistic dairy farm
- Pure Graze, a natural approach for dairy farming in Denmark/Netherlands
- De Hooilanden, a dairy farm that practices Pure Graze
- Manfred Wenz, a farmer who made the transition to organic arable farming in Germany

8.1 De Groote Voort (The Big Ford)

Jan Dirk and Irene van der Voort run an organic dairy farm and cheese factory called Remeker in the province of Gelderland, the Netherlands. On their farm they have restored the balance between soil, crops, animals and men. They are now running a coherent[57] system, which is balanced, interactive and organic. At the moment five and a half families get a living off 90 milk cows!

How did they achieve that? By looking, listening and feeling in an empathic way to what the components of the system (the farm, the soil, the animals and the plants) were telling them; by always inquiring on the feedback they got from the system; and by paying attention to signals. If things were not going well, the challenge was to adjust the management of the farm (the feed of the cows, the disease prevention, pest management, soil treatment) in the most natural way.

Innovation. Jan Dirk and Irene are *pioneers*[58] with their self-developed, consistently implemented farming philosophy. The results are a healthy soil, animals free of antibiotics, and cheeses and meat of outstanding quality and of very good taste. This is acknowledged by the Ekoland Innovation reward, which they got in 2011 and the fact that the Remeker cheese now sells very well in New York City. Let us have a look which factors of the complex system are so important and how Irene and Jan Dirk interact with them:

- **The soil:** eight meadows are part of De Groote Voort and spread over 30 hectares. Jan Dirk explains: "The soil is the foundation, the first living organism on our farm, which we cherish with all our heart. The soil is so old, she has to be respected. At the same time we are responsible for her. If we invest in the soil by applying fermented deep litter manure of ¾ years old, soil life will prosper, the humus[59] content will increase, rooting depth and carrying capacity will increase and we can harvest grass in abundance."

- **Grass and clover!** In the meadows a mixture of grass and clover has been planted. Clover is the basis for organic and agro-eco agriculture. The grass is tasty and liked by the cows. Apart from

---

57 A *coherent* system is a healthy, vital complex system in which the interrelationships are well organised, so that the natural system is resilient.

58 A pioneer is a front-runner, someone who invents new ways, and will therefore naturally have to deal with all the unknown obstacles, like finding adequate advisors, like dealing with regulations that do not support his new solutions, like learning from experience. More information about the role of *pioneers, first followers, early adapters* in a transition process in chapter 14.3 of this book.

59 A thorough explanation about the important role of humus can be found in chapter 7 of this book.

grass the cows are fed with freshly crushed grains, which Jan Dirk and Irene obtain from outside. They would love to have more land in order to grow the grain themselves.

- **The cows.** The farm has Jersey cows – a beautiful brown beast that requires little feed and still produces substantial quantities of milk, a characteristic that makes her quite suitable for organic agriculture. Also her milk is quite special - it has higher carotene content than the milk of other breeds and thus is more yellow, with a higher calcium content. The right protein for cheese production is also more present in Jersey milk. This causes a good curdling of the milk, only making use of acids and rennet. Just right for Remeker cheese!

- **Healthy cows produce healthy manure.** The cows look healthy and are not subjected to a diet, but are supplied with ample feed to adjust independently to changes in feed supply and the weather. Only a few cows need to be replaced, as there are hardly any sick animals. The milk production is good and the milk is very tasty. Also the manure produced by the cows is good, well digested, smells nice and is good for the soil!

- **The horns of the cows are important;** they are an essential component of the whole system. Horns are hollow and are in connection with the other hollow spaces in the head. If a cow loses her horns, you can see clearly that about 65% of the horn consists of living tissue, which contains blood. The horn acts as a store for minerals. Enzymes In the saliva of the cow use the minerals stored in the horns. These enzymes are important as they generate sodium bicarbonate, which a cow needs to stabilize her intestines. This is necessary if the feed they eat contains little fibre. The cow also uses the minerals from her horns when she gives birth to a calf, over a certain period of time. After a cow has been slaughtered we can see her age from the rings in her horns, comparable to rings in the stem of a tree.

- **When cows are ruminating,** an exchange of minerals in the horns takes place through the blood tissue, the horns then contain more blood and their temperature increases. The horns also have an important function in the regulation of beneficial and non-beneficial bacteria in the milk. Jan Dirk noticed that cows with horns could better stand the changes in the weather and the related change in composition of the grass (sugar, protein, fibre content).

> **A near miraculous ability of cows to make milk form cellulose.**[60]
> The central role of cows in human affairs derives, of course, from the near miraculous ability to transform grass and similar 'low quality recalcitrant plant sources' (consisting of mostly indigestible cellulose) into their flesh and blood and – that most astonishing of all fluids – milk. With its mix of creamy fat globules, energy rich sugars, body-building proteins, salts (sodium, potassium, magnesium and calcium) protective immunoglobulins and the full range of vitamins, milk is the most 'complete' of any food. The chemistry involved is staggeringly complex but also highly efficient as the cow, in a single day, transforms ten square yards of grass (about 10m2) into thirty pints of milk (about 14 liters)

- **Raw milk's cheese:** eventually the health of the farming system appears in the taste of the cheese. On *De Groote Voort* only raw milk, no preservatives and only very little unrefined sea salt are used. If the cheese has enough time to mature, a nice, well-developed taste will be the result. The cheese is well liked and has a high price, which is a certain disadvantage during an economic crisis.

- **The stable.** Through the construction of a spacious new stable, with a large rounded-off section, the cows have enough space. De Groote Voort keeps a herd of horned and hornless cows in one stable without injuries, which is unique for the Netherlands.

- **Natural feed from the region.** Apart from grass the cows are supplied with fresh feed that suits their digestive system.[61] This feed consists of grains that are crushed every morning in order to improve the enzyme uptake by the animals. As a result of this optimal diet and an open stable the cows are healthy.

- **No antibiotics.** Since 2004 antibiotics have not been used on the farm. A few years later de-worming and vaccination were no longer applied. Natural herbs which are currently added to the diet build up the cows' resistance and prevent them getting sick.

- **Calves.** To ensure that the new-born calves have a good start they stay with their mother for three weeks. This *New Normal* natural approach results in best resistance against diseases, according to Jan Dirk and Irene.

---

[60] By James Le Fanu, The Oldie, may 2014.

[61] Cows have 4 compartments in their extended stomach. They are made for the digestion of grasses, fibers actually, the longer the better. Therefore fodder needs to contain fibers, it should have *structure*. The protein rich feed (mais, soy) that cows usually get nowadays, is just the opposite and doesn't suit them.

Success factors? What has helped you to work in this way and get these results?

1. **The farm as a mirror.** According to Jan Dirk all the components on the farm - the soil, the grass, the cows, the manure, the milk and the cheese - interact and thus reflect the quality of the farm. If something goes wrong, he and his wife start looking for a natural process to solve the problem. In this way one gets a sense of the relations between the components, and the outcome will be a well-balanced total, reflected in the taste of the cheese.

2. **Observation and adaptation to nature**! Not using anti-biotics requires sharp observation. We know our animals, our land, and the feed composition thoroughly and can adjust for a single component or the total system, if required. With the assistance of Dirk Zaaijer[62] a feed composition was developed which is entirely digested in the cow's stomachs.

3. **Inspiration and personal development**. Jan Dirk: "There were several sources of inspiration, such as other farmers working along with the Platform PMOV,[63] the training course Ecotherapy,[64] Emotional Bodywork, and Yoga for Cows.[65] In this way I developed empathy and learned to think out of the box. This personal development taught me that I am the only one responsible for my actions and that everything that happens is the result of my actions. Only after this realisation it started working, I just did it. No revelations, no advice.
   - ✓ Sometimes there are specialists on one specific topic, like herbs or the functioning of the cow's stomachs; people who are working a bit outside the established order. Together with us, one plus one made three.
   - ✓ Always work from nature, in tight contact with nature, by feeling, listening, watching and communicating. When everything starts functioning, new problems will develop for

---

[62] Zaaijer († 31-12-2011) was an innovative veterinary doctor in the East of the Netherlands. He became well known when he set up practice as an independent specialist on health of cattle, with very outspoken ideas on fertility and animal feed.

[63] A platform for exchange of information for dairy farmers who started looking at their farms as complex unities, founded by Dr.ir Jaap van Bruchem (WUR). In 2008 the PMOV joined the Network for Vital Agriculture and Food, http://english.netwerkvlv.nl/

[64] Eco-therapy is a method to improve the vitality and auto-organisation of eco- and farming systems in cooperation with their manager. The method can be applied worldwide on small and larger scale levels. Generally remarkable results were realised. http://www.ecointention.com/index_e.htm

[65] Yoga for Cows, a course on mindfulness for farmers.

which a solution has to be found. Old issues will come up again as well and also need a solution. Nature has a solution for everything and will rebalance the system.

✓ Interest and curiosity. Discover more and more how the complex interactive system functions, this gives energy to continue.

✓ "I explain our working methods to groups that visit us. This reflection on what we are doing helps me to understand it better and helps me on. Our farming system is an open process, by the way, no secrets or patents."

✓ Confidence that it will work out, but this is a very lonely road to walk.

✓ The tremendous support and consideration of my wife. She wrote an interesting booklet on our development[66].

✓ The encouragement that we receive from all sides, now that we are doing well. This is also the reason why we receive people, show them around and explain what we are doing. It is important to us to know what other people think."

Dealing with setbacks. Which setbacks did we experience, which disappointments? Was there opposition? And how did we solve this? Jan Dirk explains: "There are as many setbacks as there are successes. We often had to go very deep.

- Stopping with antibiotics doesn't mean that the problems are over. It is only the start. We found ending vaccination much more troublesome than stopping the use of antibiotics! We had so many dead calves because of the rota corona virus,[67] that we had problems to keep our herd well stocked. In the end we found a solution by applying herbs, which was until that time an unknown phenomenon.

- For the cheese it is the same. By stopping all supporting processes, like pasteurisation, thermisation (heating), pickling and coating as well as the use of preservatives, we did take and are still taking tremendous risks. Nobody goes as far as we do. It has cost us a lot of money as well, because these additions are there for a reason. Your enterprise will only start working as a mirror when you dare to stop using all antibiotics

---

[66] *The farmer's wife explains.* This book (in Dutch) is written by Irene van der Voort. It is a frank story with interesting views and a lot of information on a modern farmer's life. "A farm is the world on a small scale. Even the cows raise their eyebrows when we introduce new approaches." Irene van der Voort tells that as a farmer's wife she had to look for the original, the natural and the unconditional in her own yard.

[67] Rota- and coronavirus is an intestinal infection that causes diarrhea with young calves of one to three weeks old. The virus is passed on through the mouth.

and other supportive actions. And when everything, soil-plant-animal-manure-milk-cheese is in balance.

- As we had little financial reserves, we have developed the farm step by step. We borrowed money from family members and increased the price of cheese steeply to be able to pay for all our efforts. This situation has not changed. If you are working the way we do, with a lot of attention and following an organic approach, you either have to have a lot of money of your own or you have to earn a sizeable amount, otherwise it is not possible. So what you get in return in healthy soils and animals does not cover the expense. It can be seen as our own contribution to public health and agro-biodiversity, both important agenda items of our governments' policy. They only do not acknowledge this 'sustainable agriculture' - way of contribution towards their goals.

- We have only been able to do this by following our feelings, by getting over our fears and by trusting that things would work out."

8.2 Pure Graze – a widely applicable healthy dairy farming system

Pure Graze is the enterprise of Karoline and Ado Bloemendal. They have developed the farming system *The Natural Way* (Natuurlijk Werken©) by themselves, based on the Pure Graze approach in Denmark. They added a couple of different techniques and adjusted the approach to the farming conditions of North-Western Europe. *The Natural Way* - or Pure Graze - returns to the basics of a dairy farm: cows and grass. The cows do not use a stable; they are outside most of the year as that originally is their natural habitat. When there is grass, from spring to autumn, the cows get calves and give milk; in the winter they don't. By fine-tuning the cow's natural rhythm and the grass season to one another, the balance is restored in the farming operation and it lowers milk production costs. So, healthy farm management becomes within reach of all dairy farms.

Healthy foods, healthy cows, agro-biodiversity and healthy soils. The goal of Pure Graze® is to contribute to a maximisation of the grazing period and to produce healthy and honest regional food products, reducing costs. Research of Wageningen UR[68] shows that an increase in income of 57% can be realised, apart from the priceless contribution to agro-biodiversity and healthy food through a more ecological soil management.

---

[68] This report is in Dutch only: http://www.puregraze.com/Overzicht2LKr2U 202011.pdf

How was the transition made? In 2001 the family was affected by a life threatening disease - cancer. As a result, Karoline and Ado investigated the inner quality[69] of the food they ate and what the impact of animal feed was on this quality. "This experience taught us that it is not self-evident that we are alive. Now, every day is a gift. If the sun rises for me for the last time it is important to know that I have made an impact, for myself, my family and my fellow men!"

As a reaction to their investigations, Ado and Karoline founded *Pure Graze®* in 2003. "With this concept of working The Natural Way, we want to show that it is possible to produce meat and milk in the Netherlands in a sustainable way, resulting in substantial benefits for the health of men, animal and the environment. Of course we do this in cooperation with the farmers involved. In 2013 some 40 farmers (cattle and dairy) use the concept on their farms. The next step will be to make the products of these farms available to the greater public. With the Pure Graze label people can see what they buy and then know that they are investing in their own health and in a better world."

A different way of observing and thinking: Pure Graze does not require large investments but commitment of the farmers to a different way of thinking. "Observe your cows and listen to them; you are what you eat; consider the entire coherent system. Try to reduce production costs instead of increasing production volume and enlarging your enterprise; many farmers are of the opinion that this is the only way to survive. Rely on yourself and your animals!"

What were the starting points for the change to Pure Graze®?
- ✓ The need for better health made us reinvent our approach.
- ✓ The conviction that you can make a difference, if you really want to. What we did was miles apart from the usual dairy farming systems approach, where the cows are kept inside all year round in order to use the grassland for hay (and not for foraging) and the other land for maize (feed). The start of "Pure Graze®" was therefore like a stone thrown in a pond.[70]

What are the success factors?
- ✓ Elimination of costs is much more efficient than reduction of costs. Independence from the bank and low variable costs, such as labour, veterinary consultations, concentrate and fertilizer, result in very low production costs. Several practitioners of the system have reduced their production cost of milk by 6 to 8 (Euro) cents a litre in 2012.

---

[69] In biodynamic agriculture, derived from Rudolf Steiner's anthroposophy, people observe an inner quality of food and plants, related to nature and nurture.

[70] As short a time ago as 2006, outside grazing was being re-introduced and promoted by the government and the bigger cooperatives in the Netherlands with incentive to upgrade the image of dairy farming. "Consumers need to see the cows in the meadow."

- ✓ Apart from lower production costs and a higher return on investment, *Pure Graze* provides for a more relaxed style of living, as work pressure is reduced.
- ✓ Craftsmanship. Finding the balance for a coherent system is not easy; it is an art or a craft. And how does that work? Pure Graze® returns to the basics of the cattle farm: soil, grass and cows. By fine-tuning the relation between these components, the balance will return to the farm.
- ✓ Turning to nature. Grass, in a natural herd system, is not for silage but for milk production; one of the principles of Pure Graze® is to let the cows feed autonomously. In summer that will be no problem, but in winter grass doesn't grow and the meadows are too wet to enter. The solution of Pure Graze® is to let the cows calve in spring, like sheep. In the period after birth until the moment that the cow has the highest milk production (100 days after delivery) and subsequently the highest demand for grass, there is enough fresh grass in the meadows.
- ✓ Follow the season - after reaching a maximum, milk production will gradually decline. At the same time less grass will become available in the meadow as the summer is advancing. At the moment that milking is stopped, the meadows are too wet to be grazed. When the cows do not produce milk they need less grass or hay, so the farmer does not have to store large volumes of hay, with the result that in summer time he has less mowing to do.
- ✓ Adjust - the system seems simple but it requires quite some adjustment and effort on the side of the farmer. It takes about three years before all cows have adjusted to the new time schedule. In this period the cows will be outside as much as possible, but the farmer also has to produce feed for the winter period and thus has to manage his meadows very carefully. This can be achieved by giving the cows a new section of meadow every three hours. The cows will learn that they have to graze the maximum before they lie down as the allocation of new grassland is limited. And then a new section is opened up and the procedure is repeated.

What lies ahead?

A next step is to develop Pure Graze® grass, in order that cattle can graze in rich meadows again. Grasslands that contain clover, herbs etcetera allow the animals to stay healthy. Eventually their healthy meat makes people healthier too. You are what you eat.

Another step forward is to have the meat of Pure Graze cows for sale in supermarkets, with its own label, so that the consumer can make a choice for healthy meat and for an environmentally healthy production process. By buying this meat the consumer eventually invests in a beautiful and ecologically sound landscape.

8.3 Farm De Hooilanden

The farm 'De Hooilanden'[71] is a good example of a Pure Graze® enterprise This farm is owned by Lodewijk Pool[72] and his wife. He explains how they experience *The Natural Way*:

"For various reasons we have the Blaarkop, or Blister Head cow at De Hooilanden. This sort of cow fits nicely with the management approach of The Natural Way. It will stay healthy at natural feed levels and still produce a good quantity of milk. The black and white Holstein cow (known worldwide as The Dutch cow) is capable of producing a lot of milk, some 50 litres a day, but requires a very balanced diet to do so. Under less well provided conditions, the Holstein will continue to produce milk, but her health will deteriorate, she will lose weight, become less resistant and fall ill more easily.[73]"

"The meadows of 'De Hooilanden are located at the lower levels of the peat soil area of the Gelre Valley. Low meadows are generally prone to suffer from wetness. Lighter cows can stay in the meadow for a longer period, and as the Blister Head cows are relatively small and light they are very suitable for this type of soil."

"Blister Head cows are a dual purpose type of cow. They can be used both for milk production (60%) and for meat production (40%). This is related to the aim of the farming enterprise. From health perspective Blister Head cows are much appreciated because they have no leg problems, strong black hooves and a pleasant quiet character."

Farmer Lodewijk Pool shares some important views with us:

Nutritional value of the milk: It has been known for over 10 years that a cow will always produce the same quantity of Vitamin A per milking, regardless of the total volume of milk produced. So if you take food to feed your body, which type of milk would you prefer? Milk from a 5,000 litre cow or milk from a 10,000 litre cow, which contains only half the quantity of vitamin A? From a public health perspective, maximising milk production per cow reduces the milk quality. Once a cow has had concentrates,[74] the quantity

---

[71]   Farm de Hooilanden, Bennekom. http://www.dehooilanden.nl/hl25/

[72]   Lodewijk Pool and Floor de Kanter are the farm managers of de Hooilanden after having obtained a degree at Wageningen University.

[73]   That is why efforts to export the Dutch cow to Africa (in order to boost milk production) do not work – the circumstances are too rough for her. Remark by the author from her experience in Ethiopia

[74]   Concentrates or pellets are the pressed nutrients and proteins that cows receive as daily food. They lack the necessary fibres, which come with grass or hay.

of Omega 3 in the milk will never again reach the level that is realized by a cow that *never* had concentrates.

Cross breeding has nothing to do with resistance. According to Lodewijk Pool the following equation can be applied: Genotype (or *nature*, 30%) + Environment (or *nurture*, 70%) = Phenotype (100%). "In my opinion the importance of cross breeding (to get a better genotype) is greatly exaggerated. The environment is decisive for the health of our animals. I can see it in our free-range pigs[75]. They are 'regular' pigs with an intensive farming origin. We have been warned by all kind of experts that it wouldn't work, but it is going really well. Resistance against diseases is important but can be achieved by taking care of the needs of the animals in line with their requirements, instead of breeding a resistant race that lacks other necessary qualities."

Success factors when changing into a Pure Graze® enterprise

✓ **The pleasure we have doing our work is the most important factor.** Working with animals in a natural setting, being outdoors, the space and the views together make our work a pleasure.

✓ **Observe and listen to your cows.** Register the signals that indicate that the cow/calf/herd has a special need or requirement. A herd in which all cows deliver in spring has a very tight relationship and a fixed social structure. This is the result of being in a herd situation during the entire year (as opposed to presently 'normal' farming enterprises). The herd will set out to graze as a group and will lie down to chew their cud at the same time. They even know the concept of babysitting, where some cows watch all the calves while the mothers forage. When the herd stands up, they indicate that it is time for a new stretch of meadow and the wire should be repositioned. The farmer is very much service-oriented towards his herd.

✓ **Start with the strength of the enterprise - the soil.** The soil should be the decisive factor for the type of enterprise. Some enterprises are more suitable for sheep raising or for small cows. Beef cattle should be kept on high grounds, while fattening of beef cattle is best done on low-lying grounds. High grounds that are rich in humus contain more minerals and proteins, while low grounds have more energy.

✓ **Observe the whole unit.** *The Natural Way* of working forces people to observe the nature of the enterprise and to consider it in its totality. Grazing also implies that you have to feed your soil life, even more than your cows, as the natural soil fertility is the critical factor for your production capacity.

---

[75]   Also see the example 'Natural Hogs' in chapter 11.4 on page 156

✓ **Think about your animal feed!** Many farmers are not aware of concentrate being *food* for their animals. They just follow the general trend and are not aware of the impact of the concentrate composition on the digestive system of their cows, and the consequences for milk, manure and animal resistance. With *The Natural Way*, fibre-rich grass is the basic feed. The four compartments of the cattle's stomach[76] are meant to digest that in order to produce health for the cow itself, healthy milk and well-balanced manure.

✓ **The concept of integrated sustainability, soil management, public health and regional development become directive.** According to Lodewijk Pool, the Peak Oil theory will force us to change our approach to work and way of thinking. We have to return to a regional economy. Agriculture is the second most oil consuming activity in the world, after transport. At this moment in history we cannot afford any longer to use natural oil resources for making chemical fertilizer. This is outdated. The next step will also go further than to narrowmindedly choose for clover and English ryegrass as the best grass for fodder. In *the New Normal* era a method will be developed to manage the soil and the soil life in such a manner that production will equal or be better than production with the aid of fertilizer.

✓ **The conviction that agriculture can and must provide for healthy food.** In the national discussions in the Netherlands about agriculture, and about food quality as a separate issue, the impact of low quality food on the ever-increasing costs of health care is consequently ignored. The recession, the aging, the allergies and increase of deficiency-related diseases, will force us to include the public health aspect - of the ways in which food is being produced - in our considerations. Isn't it ridiculous that products that are bad for our health are allowed to enter the market?

✓ **Follow nature's rhythm.** "In order to have a healthy balance in your bank account it is not necessary to work the whole year round." This sounds a bit awkward in our culture of monthly paid employees. But if you farm in *The Natural Way*, the same volume of milk is produced at a lower cost price during the summer; in the winter you can return to yourself, incubate ideas, do repairs and decide on your strategies.

✓ **Saving on the vet:** Pure Graze farmers report independently that the levels of antibiotic use on their farms stands at 20% of the

---

[76] The common misconception is that cattle have four stomachs, when the truth is it has one stomach with four compartments. This type of digestive system allows cattle to digest forage as their primary food sources, unlike us who only have a limited cellulose digestion capacity in our colon. Want to know more? http://fyi.uwex.edu/wbic/2012/01/18/back-to-basics-ruminant-digestive-system/

average of their vet's practice. Why is this lower? As a result of the natural production methods, the low quantities - or absence - of use of concentrate and fertilizer. But the most important reasons are that the animals live without stress and the pluriformity of feed and environment, especially the wide range of plant species.

✓ **Direct money.** The change to Pure Graze immediately resulted in savings for us as farmers. In the first year the savings were 2 to 4 cents per liter of milk, in the second year 4 to 6 cents and after the third year the maximum of 6 till 8 cents was realized.

Useful assistance by Pure Graze. This transition concerns the reorganisation of an enterprise. Critical factors for success appear to be:

1. Changing fast. Reorganisations which take more than three years will not be successful. The faster the change the more successful it will be.
2. A good business plan. It is important to decide on the opportunities for the enterprise and stick to the implementation schedule that was developed.
3. A sparring partner for the farmer, in this case Ado Bloemendal and other Pure Graze farmers. This is necessary support on the basis of knowledge and tested approaches. Just like in other networks it is important to learn from one another, as this is the most efficient way for knowledge transfer.

Failure and how to prevent this.

Obstruction can happen in the direct environment of the farmer. Like fathers who stick to the old ways and want security, so they resist the new development; or agricultural advisors and the bank, since they have other interests. In these cases it is important to take the people along, check whether they understand what you are doing and remove possible obstacles.

8.4 Transition to a coherent farming enterprise in Germany

Manfred Wenz bought his farm in Schwanau in Southern Germany in 1954 and was a pioneer for chemical farming until 1971: he performed well in arable farming, getting high yields, using fertilizers, pesticides and hybrid seed. In 1971 he changed his farm management in a fundamental way when his son was very ill. Manfred related this illness to the decreasing amount of humus in his soils and the negative effects on his yields. The cooperation with his son Friedrich is a prime example of how father and son can complement each other in restoring the production capacity of the fifties, a period without mechanisation at a small-scale level.

The transition. Manfred learned from a botanist that there is a direct relationship between the deterioration of the soil and the appearance of weeds that grow in semi-arid areas that were previously unknown in the area. He then realised that he had noticed this already several times in Southern Germany. In his own field an Amaranth from the Mediterranean areas was growing. In the same period his son Friedrich was ill for an extended period. He then decided to change his management style completely and became an organic farmer. He became one of the founders of the German agricultural society Bioland. This has grown by now into the largest ecological farming association in Germany, with 5717 members, who operate according to the guidelines of the Association. The total area they cover is 277.093 ha in 2013. The economy of organic farms is based on a circular economy, or closed-loop system, that doesn't use synthetic pesticides and synthetic chemical nitrogen fertilizer. Animals are humanely kept. The guidelines of organic farming are more stringent than the EU-Eco regulation.

As he had no experience, he started his transition with the abolition of the use of fertilizers, pesticides and herbicides, with disastrous results. Weed infestation was enormous and even ploughing and milling did not help much. Ten years of experiments followed. In 1981 Manfred started using the ridge cultivation[77] system as developed by Hans Kemink. The results appear to be a tremendous improvement. In 1995 Friedrich took over the management of the farm which has been renamed Eco-Din, but Manfred remains involved.

Sharing *The New Normal* knowledge. For a number of years Friedrich Wenz has opened his farm to visitors in the month of June. In the morning he gives a lecture and in the afternoon he and his father show the fields to the visitors. He starts his lecture with a citation of Hans Peter Ruisch, one of the originators of the scientific foundation of organic agriculture, after which he continues with his ideas leading to a different and more holistic farm management. There is an item about Manfred and Friedrich Wenz in the very worthwhile documentary 'Crops of the Future'.[16]

Essentials of the transition

1. **Soil fertility.** Friedrich compares the fertility of the soil with the fertility of cattle. The big difference is that, where a farmer immediately notices infertile animals, the reduction of soil fertility is a slow process that can only be detected over a period of

---

[77] The Kemink system was developed by the German farmer and inventor Hans Kemink (Fütterling 1984). It is characterized by ridging, frequent sub-soiling and controlled traffic. All field operations are performed using a special frame on which different implements for sub-soiling, ridging, seedbed preparation and mechanical weed control can be mounted. http://icrofs.dk/en/ Danish centre for organic farming.

time. The detection is even more difficult in regular agriculture, as the reduction of soil fertility (organic content and soil life) is 'covered up' by ploughing, fertilizer and pesticides. Since, in organic agriculture, chemical inputs are limited, this facilitates the discovery of the deterioration of soil fertility at an earlier stage.

2. **Loss of humus is a serious matter.** With pictures of soil profiles Manfred shows how the thick organic top layer has been reduced from 40cm in the fifties to less than 10cm in the seventies. By then the humus had been completely decomposed and there is a severe deterioration of soil structure.[78] He also recalls that over this period the soil became lighter and paler. His observations correspond with events in other parts of Germany where agriculture is practiced on mountainous slopes, and large volumes of topsoil were washed away as the combined result of the deterioration of the soil structure (due to a loss of humus) and the increased rainfall intensity as experienced over the last years.

3. **Adapted mechanisation.** When Friedrich Wenz took over the farm in 1995 he found the ridge cultivation too intensive a system. He changed to superficial composting without ridges in order to be able to cultivate a larger area. However, there was no mechanization system that met his requirements. Friedrich wants to carry out shallow soil cultivation, because cultivation at deeper levels disturbs soil life and causes an explosion of weed growth. He also wants to carry out precision operations while still covering larger areas, as the farm now covers some 33 hectares and is spread out over a rather large area. The available cultivation methods are only suitable for conventional agricultural practices.

So Friedrich started to design his own machines. He shows us some pictures of his *knife roller* and the *precision seed drill* Eco-Dyn. This machine is capable of sowing up to 4 different crops at different depths, plus an additional pre- and post-activity during the same pass. Every year the machine is adjusted to new ideas that Friedrich developed.

4. **Crop Management.** As a result of the mechanisation, mixed cultures can be compressed in time, which shortens the cropping period

---

[78] In the Netherlands there is an similar infamous example of deteriorating soils, as an effect of the use of chemical fertilizer. In the East of the Netherlands, for ages farmers brought manure and organic compost onto their poor (sandy) fields, thus adding 0.1 cm of soil each year. After 100 years this had grown to 10 cm at least. There are soils of up to 0.8 meters thick, which also make an interesting landscape. However, after growing maize on those soils (for cow feed) instead of the regular mixed cropping system, the organic soil content has decreased from 12% to 2%. Agriculture is not possible on a soil with an organic soil content below 2%. The soil then doesn't contain life any more, cannot drain water any more etc. It can only be used as a substrate.

and opens the possibility for an additional crop in the same year. Furthermore, Friedrich is in close contact with a Brazilian, Pereira,[79] who is one of the pioneers in the field of *no-till* land preparation and direct sowing in the stubble. At the beginning the mixed cultivation approach was quite difficult as Friedrich assumed that there was little growth in winter. Only later he realized that sowing in autumn would result in a very early start in spring. He then started to experiment with sowing wheat in clover, direct sowing of winter beans in maize stubble in October, or sowing soy beans in rye which was harvested with the knife roller.

5. **Mixed cultivation.** Incorporating the various crops into the overall cropping plan is not an easy thing to do. This requires a lot of experimentation and gives different results for different farms. There are so many factors that play a role. For example, when sowing wheat in clover it is important that the clover is 'disturbed' for at least 50% of the coverage as it will otherwise become too competitive for the wheat. After harvesting the winter wheat, clover will continue to grow and be mowed twice, with all the green matter remaining on the field. Finally clover seed is harvested (60 - 100 kg/ha).

   Another example of mixed cultivation is the combination of sunflower, clover and buckwheat. This will result in three crop levels. The buckwheat will cover the soil quite fast, after which the sunflowers will grow over the buckwheat, while the clover will remain a low cover crop. The first crop to be harvested is the sunflower, with the buckwheat second. Although the buckwheat will only yield about 400kg per hectare, at the same time it assures that no weed control has to be carried out. The success of the crop depends on very little things. Maize seed for instance cannot stand competition, while soy beans can easily be sown into a stand of clover.

6. **Crop rotation.** On the farm a crop rotation period of five years is maintained. This implies that the same crop will return to a field after approximately five years. But there is some flexibility. Below follows the detailed cropping plan. There is continuous experimentation on the composition of the cover crops and the intercropping.
   ### The crop rotation system:
   - In the first year, white clover is sown to keep the soil healthy. There are no restrictions on crop growth. When the clover is in flower it is mowed. This is repeated several

[79] Henrique M Perreira is Professor of Biodiversity Conservation, in Leipzig, Germany. He is renowned for his work on biodiversity such as *Scenarios for global biodiversity in the 21st century*, 2010.

times. Then in autumn, winter wheat (usually *Triticum aestivum*) is sown into the clover.

- In the second year the grain crop will grow, but the clover encourages a further development of the soil. You must know that wheat (grasses) and clover are allies, they stimulate each other's development. After this crop, shallow soil cultivation is carried out, which will be repeated if necessary. As a result of this shallow cultivation, weeds get the opportunity to germinate quickly.
- In the third year wheat will be sown in combination with Camelina[80]. This crop germinates fast, so no weeding or tillage is needed. It doesn't need much water. When it grows on poor dry soils it improves the soil and prevents weeds growing.
- In year 4 winter beans/ pulses (legumes) are planted.
- And in year five rye, spelled wheat or sunflowers will be grown, depending on the market.

7. **Be kind to the soil!** Friedrich's message is that one has to feed the soil sufficiently and that one has to be kind to the soil. To avoid compaction is a good example of the latter. By squeezing air out of the soil, aerobic processes will stop, soil life will die, root penetration is hampered and anaerobic processes (rot) will gain the upper hand – an ideal situation for pathogens.

8. **Manuring.** At the moment, Friedrich Wenz cultivates 33 ha of agricultural land and is completely independent in the field of energy input and manure. For 15 years he has not applied any manure or compost to his fields. The exception is pellets, which he has pressed from fermented plant materials; they can be saved in this condition for some time. The pellets are suitable to include in the sowing as a 'booster' for the newly germinating crop. It is not a matter of routine though, as plant materials which can be fermented should be available. The distribution of a biodynamic solution of cow horns dissolved in water is a standard practice.

9. **Stop our technical way of thinking, better support nature!** The fertility of the soil (i.e. the production of humus by soil life) is maintained by the combined action of plants (nitrogen fixation and green manure) and plant remains. The aim is to accumulate as much organic matter on top of the soil as possible. Worms alone already digest up to 6 tonnes of organic matter per hectare per year.

---

[80] Camelina sativa belongs to the plant family Brassicaceae. In the 19th century this crop was used a lot to produce lamp oil. The dry stems of the plant were used as brushes. There is a renewed interest in Camelina, since it grows well on poor soils, doesn't need fertilizer and produces a good oil.

10. **Never to leave the soil uncovered for extended periods!** Ten days being the maximum. This can be achieved by planting an intercrop, in which at a later moment a commercial crop can be sown. Friedrich Wenz uses his savings on work and inputs for extension activities, to spread the message that we have to stop our technical way of thinking and that we better support nature. In addition to this, a better understanding of soil life will help you to find broader solutions.

11. **Maintain soil life for a healthy soil.** Friedrich shows us how – on a plot that is ready for cultivation - one can see very small heaps of organic material that were produced by worms that incorporate this material into the soil. He states that in 0,8 m³ of soil some 1kg of soil life exists, of which less than half is visible (e.g. worms). Soil life activity is a good indicator for soil health. See table next page.

12. **Energy consumption.** Energy consumption is low. As a result of shallow cultivation and adapted mechanisation, Friedrich uses around 50 litres of diesel per hectare. In 2007 he used only 1,340 litres. Although he only needs a tractor for some 200 hours per year, he still has his own tractor to ensure that he can carry out his precision activities at exactly the right moment. Recently he started employing a contractor, to have more time for extension and consultancy.

13. **Viability of family farming.** According to Friedrich, this system of mixed cultivation could be a solution to keep family smallholdings viable, even without subsidies, on condition that one considers the entire system: crop rotation, mixed cropping and the ensuing savings in labour.

Success factors:

- ✓ Perseverance in improving the soil-plant-climate interaction over a period of 40 years.
- ✓ To consult with fellow farmers and scientists to gain understanding on how it all works.
- ✓ Knowledge of soil degradation processes.

Obstacles and impediments

Not knowing how to continue (1971-1981) and still persevering, because he believed that it could be done.

INVISIBLE SOIL LIFE

	number in millions	biomass in grammes
Bacteria	10.000.000,00	160
Fungi (actinomycetes)	120.000,00	380
Algae	1.000,00	90
Protozoans 600	600,00	115
Eelworms 1,8	1,80	4
Total invisible soil life		749

VISIBLE SOIL LIFE

species	number	biomass
Springtails	26000	11
Mites	18000	10
Polychaete worms	10000	2
Beetles and larvae	800	8
Centipedes	550	20
Ants	320	2
Millipedes	300	4
Fly larvae	240	26
Spiders	230	2
Worms	130	145
Snails	50	25
total		255

Fig 17. Biomass on 1m² of healthy meadow up to 0.8m depth, totalling 1kg.

9. Conservation Agriculture

Conservation agriculture is agriculture as a means to restore and develop nature, bio-diversity and landscape. The idea, of course, is to do this without subsidies, like we saw in the examples in the previous chapter. But subsidies or private investments are often necessary at the start of a new initiative, as margins in farming are very low and do not allow for extras, nor for taking private and personal risks.

With *conservation* agriculture and *restoration* agriculture we contribute to integrated forms of agriculture, food production, social life and regional economies. 'Food is not merchandise but an essential part of the complex regional mode of life and the regional economy.'[81] Therefore the following two concepts agree with and involve *conservation* agricultural practices.

Return to agricultural landscapes. An agricultural landscape - and which landscape in the world cannot be described as such? – should provide fibre, food and water, meet the requirements of nature and biodiversity and support sustainable professions of people who live in the landscape (and not somewhere else).

Landscapes for People, Food and Nature is a collaborative Initiative to foster cross-sectoral dialogue, learning and action. The partners involved aim to understand and support integrated agricultural landscape approaches to simultaneously meet goals for food production, ecosystem health and human wellbeing.

The examples in this chapter are:

9.1 Natural Fields

9.2 Natural Dairy

9.3 Farming for Nature

9.4 Closed-loop dairy farming

---

[81] From: The transition to sustainable food, in: *Terra Reversa*, Peter Tom Jones and Vicky de Meyere

9.1 Natural Fields: combination of nature management and agriculture

Over 100 farmers in the East of the province of Groningen (Netherlands) support nature development by the creation of so called 'nature fields'[82]. They are assisted by the Agricultural Nature Society of East Groningen. Nature management and agriculture go together quite well. Nature development used to be an integral part of farming in the past. Now it has become a farmers' activity once more. Only now it involves bridging the gap between the policy fields 'nature' and 'agriculture' and so represents a new type of collaboration.

Natural Fields are a new phenomenon in the Netherlands. It concerns farming where exploitation is not principally geared towards commercial production, but aims at the conservation of traditional farmland flora and fauna. In Natural Field farming, emphasis is laid on nature development and not on large-scale exploitation or the realisation of maximum yields. A Natural Field approach results in a diverse agricultural area, with various crops and rich in flowers. Winter wheat, rye, oats, fallow land and meadows with grass, clover, chicory, poppies, parsnip, cornflowers, marguerites, sweet peas and alfalfa will ensure flowers from the start of May till the end of September.

The fields require a different crop rotation; more grain crops, less fertilizer and less weed control than in conventional agriculture. In addition some animal and plants species are depending on one particular crop. By mixing different crops and land use practices a diverse ecological system can be developed. As a result, farmland birds such as the yellow and grey grouse, the yellow wagtail, the linnet, the quail, the partridge and skylark will be attracted. In fact, all the bird species that are now disappearing, due to industrialised agriculture (see Figure 13) are coming back. In addition we see various species of butterflies, bees and other insects.

The farmland area also develops into suitable hunting grounds for bats, owls and other birds of prey, like the grey hen harrier. The short eared owl, featuring on the red list of protected birds, can be found again in East Groningen, thanks to the nature fields. On top of this we have created'a beautiful stretch of nature, with a lot of forgotten flowers, which were rarely seen over the past 40 years and for which we now like to make a detour.

Farmers are compensated for the crops they can no longer grow. The project is subsidized by the national government and is a huge success in East Groningen. The next step should be in how this type of conservation farming can become an economically viable enterprise once again.

---

[82]   Westerwolde Actueel, Ocober 2012, Westerwoldeactueel.nl

9.2 Natural Dairy - dairy farming and nature management combined

In many nature reservation areas in Europe, large herbivores[83] are imported from undisturbed natural areas in Poland and Scotland, for the grazing management of nature areas and National Parks. This grazing management is needed to prevent open spaces turning into forests and to maintain specific natural conditions and biotopes, all necessary to achieve the nature management *targets*. This is quite costly, needs specific management and brings risks of diseases and dying animals, for which the regulations are different than for farmers' animals. All this is being paid for through taxes and Nature Conservation Associations members' contributions, and is not economically viable.

Some innovative farmers had the idea to use regular dairy cows to do the same job: graze the natural areas in an economically viable way. It is good for the cows to get a more diversified diet and good for the nature conservation organisations, as they could save money. But it appeared to be not so easy, due to all sorts of strict regulations and the difference between laws for farming and for nature conservation.

The Veld & Beek approach. Jan Wieringa started 'Veld en Beek'[84] in the Wageningen (NL) region in 1991 as a real pioneer: everything had to be invented, tried out and regulations had to be adjusted. He obtained permission from the conservation organisations in the neighbourhood to graze his Dutch Belted cows in their nature reserves, and he combined this natural dairy approach with dairy product retailing. Milk, cheese and beef are distributed to the consumers' association in an innovative way. Members of the Veld & Beek association receive a key enabling them to enter the cooled vans, which are stationed in three different locations. All the products are available in the van 24 hours a day; the members collect their weekly order at a time convenient for them.

This cooperation with nature and nature conservation managers and consumers is a system innovation in itself. It necessitated knowledge development, experimenting and exchange of experience in various fields. Collaboration, trust and perseverance were essential.

---

[83]   Like Heck's oxen, Galloways, Scottisch Highland bovines, Konik horses.

[84]   http://www.veldenbeek.nl/

9.3 Farming with Nature

Farming with Nature is the name of a project that started in 2003. An innovative farmer, Jan Duindam (Netherlands), started this project, supported by some very motivated action researchers from Alterra Research Institute. His grandfather started his farm in the Polder of Biesland (Pipingland) in 1910. The low-lying land is mostly peat, which is only suitable for grass and has therefore always been used for dairy farming.

How the transition was begun. The farm lies within a triangle, made up by the highway and 2 cities (the Hague and Delft) encroaching on the farmland. In order to survive and from his own idealism, Jan envisioned a farm that would provide dairy products as well as a beautiful recreational landscape to the nearby citizens. He wanted to lower parts of his meadows in order to create wetlands that would attract birdlife. At the same time he needed to change his herd into a more robust type of cow. His business-plan was calculated for 30 years. But the European subsidies for such 'eco-services' were only given on the basis of 6 year agrarian nature management contracts. It would be a disaster if, after 6 years, the subsidy was not continued. But Jan took the risk, assuming that 50% of the cost could be covered by income from consumers from the nearby cities, for recreation and for the natural products he would deliver.

Now, because of close cooperation with the civilian association for agrarian nature management, and the educational facilities at his farm and the high quality dairy products that he sells off farm, his farm has become very successful and an example for many. Jan involves consumers in how closed-loop farming works, what nature is and how meaningful it is to us.

Success factors:

✓ The involvement of two researchers for two years made the project well known with the government and opened some doors to discuss regulations for ecosystem services with Brussels.

✓ The set-up of a regional fund was the solution. This fund was filled in a one-time action, by various civilian organisations, the national and local governments. The eco-services of this farm are being paid for by the annual interest of the fund

✓ The vision and perseverance of the farmer and his wife.

9.4 Closed-loop farming

From 2002 till 2006, about 130 dairy farmers have been developing a more sustainable way of dairy-farm management, called closed-loop farming in the project Bedreven Bedrijven (Well Working Farms) in the Netherlands. They put emphasis on good soil management and introduced the *Natural Cycle Approach* or *closed-loop farming* on their farms.

One of the goals was to reduce nitrogen excess on the farm to 50 mg/l – below the EU standard. This is especially important as these farms are located near oligotrophic[85] lakes in nature reserves, which are threatened by the excess of nitrate. As an output of the project, the provincial government wanted to have the pollution of the groundwater (caused by minerals of agricultural origin) reduced. In this project therefore, the soil was to be restored to resume its function as a filter to generate a clean oligotrophic surface and groundwater. The farmers and the local authorities decided upon a *closed-loop* or *natural cycle* approach, as well as the introduction of a monitoring system for management aspects.

The Natural Cycle Approach (NCA - also called closed loop farming) requires some clarification. It is a holistic approach[86] in which farmers observe the interactions between soil-water-crop-animal-milk-manure-soil as a 'complex system'. This NCA was developed by a group of innovative farmers, who were not interested in organic farming as such, but nevertheless felt that a healthy soil is the basis for the whole farming system. A lecturer of Wageningen University, Jaap van Bruchem, supported them. His students took the idea further and did some supportive research on this approach. The approach is reflected in the picture below.

Fig 18. The natural cycle approach; picture to be 'read' starting from the soil, at the bottom

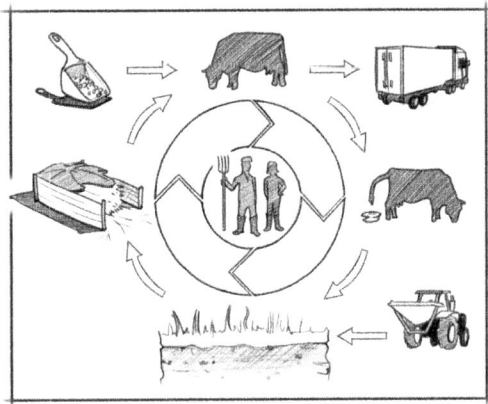

---

[85]   Oligotrophic- relatively poor in nutrients and containing abundant oxygen in deeper parts

[86]   Holistic as opposed to reductionist, the latter being the common approach in observing, researching and solving problems in present day agricultural science.

The Natural Cycle Approach explained:

First of all, from a healthy soil you get healthy (long-fibre) grass and hay, which is good for the cow. Then you want to reduce the amount of additional concentrates (in the upper left corner, containing too many nitrates). The output of the cow is double: high quality milk and good, fertile and old-fashioned, strong manure. You don't want the manure mixed with the urine, as that again contains high concentrates of nitrate. The manure will support a healthy soil. Inputs of fertilizer are to be reduced as much as possible; compost is advised.

The project *Well Working Farms* started in 2001 with 40 dairy farmers, inspired by a very motivated consultant. Two years later there were one hundred participants. Eleven farmer study groups were searching for a management approach that would bring benefits for farm management and the environment. The focal point was improved management of the cattle's feed through an integrated approach of the entire management system. From 2009-2012 a follow up was organised, called *Sustainable Farmers*. This time 116 farmers took part in study groups to make the transition. Due to the positive effects on water quality the *Support innovation in Closed-Loop Farming*[87] programme was set up by three provinces in 2014.

On a number of participating farms, the nitrate concentration in the groundwater was measured over a period of twelve years. The same system was used as the provincial water quality monitoring system. It was found that the nitrate levels of the participating farms are structurally below the provincial average and, for 8 out of 12 years, even below the European nitrate standard[88]. So it appears that, by closing their nutrient cycle, the farms acquire higher nutrient use efficiency (NUE) and lower emissions to the groundwater.

Results:

- A social contribution in reducing sources of water and nature pollution, and climate change mitigation. When all the participating 1100 farmers achieve the same good results as the top 20% farmers have done, the surplus of Nitrate in the soil (10,540 tonnes) in the province of Drenthe (68.000 Ha2) will be lowered by 4,200 tonnes. The phosphate surplus in the soil (over 1.400 tonnes) will decrease by over 1,000 tonnes. The annual emission

---

[87] The Dutch names of these projects are respectively *Bedreven Bedrijven Drenthe* or *Duurzaam Boer Blijven* and Programma *Steunpunt European Innovation Partnership Noord Nederland Kringlooplandbouw*, set up by the Provinces of Drenthe, Groningen and Friesland.

[88] For more information: www.boerenverstand.nl; www.bedrevenbedrijven.nl; www.duurzaamboerblijven.nl.

of ammoniac (NH3), now 3,800 tonnes, will be lowered by 500 tonnes nitrogen (N).

- A contribution to ecology and biodiversity. An important aim of the project was to restore soil life and soil health (as a means to get cleaner water, lower nutrient emissions and higher biodiversity). This has been successful, as was established in a scientific report[89].
- The three northern provinces in the Netherlands will place the Natural Cycle Approach at the centre of their agricultural development policies in the 7 years from 2014 onwards. This is an important signal to national politicians, to research institutions and to agricultural advisors.
- In a 2014 presentation of the province of Drenthe to international visitors, the following overall results of 10 years policy period have been presented: lower emission ammonia (20%), decreased use of fertilizer (25%), decreased nitrogen surplus (12%), decreased nitrate content in groundwater < 50mg/l, decreased vet costs (6%), increased percentage of soil organic matter (climate!), decreased emission of CO2 (10%)(climate!), decreased costs of feed, higher income, a more positive image for dairy farming, more job satisfaction!

Success factors:

- ✓ "Participating in a study group has accelerated my attentiveness. Through 'Bedreven Bedrijven' one gets in touch with good ideas that are not very well known yet. For example, the presentation on fibre-rich feed was an eye-opener for me. My lecture fees could be quickly recovered through the economies I make on my farm".
- ✓ As long as farmers are not rewarded though a market mechanism (i.e. lower costs or people/milk factories paying more for sustainably produced milk), it is important that farmers get a reward in kind. For example, if they contribute land to cleaner water through healthy soil management they get extra 'development space' for their farm elsewhere.
- ✓ In the scaling-up of the project, various farming advisors were invited to join. This appeared to be a very important step as the milk collectors, agricultural cooperative bank, feed distributors, fertilizer salesmen are all very influential since they each have their own supply driven advise to farmers. As soon as they recognised the advantages of this approach they started spreading the word. Even two veterinary doctors included the NCA in their own advice;

---

[89] Effects of close loop farming on biodiversity and ecosystem services; the potential of a cooperative effort in Nordlyke Fryske Walden. SKB, Wageningen University, 2012.

they upgraded their vision on animal health inter-relationship from cow+feed to cow+feed+soil.

✓ The introduction of a prize for the best farmers was a very good instrument as it involved the RABO bank (the bank that invests most in agricultural development) and made the project and its success more visible, on the radio and in magazines.

✓ Without the investment of the Province of Drenthe, this development would not have been possible. They invested 2 million euros in 10 years, say 200,000 annually, which is comparable to the gross costs of one senior employee.

Obstacles and impediments. Of course this process didn't go smoothly. A transition doesn't happen without problems. Here are some of the impediments and how they were overcome:

- Farmers and their advisors were initially sceptical. The conventional advice of the farming advisory services (feed industries, milk factories, banks and vets) was opposed to the *Natural Cycle Approach*. Only by showing the successes of a few pioneer farmers and, more importantly, by backing-up the practical experience with scientific data, could advisors be convinced.

- Farmers' contributions to society (i.e. biodiversity, nature reserves and clean water) are not being rewarded economically yet. This prevents many farmers from making the change to the *Natural Cycle Approach* - still at the moment of writing. Therefore it is important to make clear what the reduction in costs will be for the farmer, when he joins this approach.

- Pioneer status. Since the approach is not widely accepted and not so well known yet farmers are reluctant to talk in public about the change they made, as they fear to be laughed at by their peers. This relatively new approach is far ahead of the conservative 'industrial development' conviction that is dictated by the classical farmers' organisations and agribusiness. Only since 2012 has the Farmers Union realised that this *Natural Cycle Approach* may be an instrument to gain confidence from consumers again, the 'green light for agribusiness' they badly need. Also some milk/cheese factories have lately become interested in paying a little more for *Natural Cycle Milk*.

- The curricula of the formal Agricultural Schools are still very much based on last century's 'green revolution' belief systems. This is due to the teachers not changing along with new movements such as this Natural Cycle Approach, but also that the Ministry's policy, and therefore research, is still focussed on industrial agriculture and boosting agribusiness. To assist the schools in making the change, the project *Staying a Sustainable Farmer* produced DVDs with all the information about this approach. In 2012, five teachers together adjusted their teaching material.

10. Towards regional economies

The IAASTD report calls for another agricultural revolution – and this is in 2008! It calls for investments by governments in a new type of agriculture, one that is less dependent on fossil fuel, and one that relies on a family situation, agro-ecological agriculture and local inputs. It calls for agriculture with a regional economy that provides local job opportunities, generates local income and food security, while at the same time reducing transportation costs and environmental impact, through less pesticides and herbicides, less water and energy consumption.

In this chapter, several examples of the re-establishment of such regional cycles and a more integrated approach in agriculture, food supply and environment in regions are presented, including co-operation between entrepreneurs.

A visit is paid to LEAF, an organisation of farmers and citizens in Great Britain (Linking Ecology Agriculture and Food); there is an interview with Oregional, a cooperation between food producers (supply), restaurants and nursing homes (demand) in the Nimwegen region; Willem&Drees is an innovative initiative of two idealistic entrepreneurs who organise the direct transfer of regional products to local supermarkets; ECOVIDA is a cooperative in Brasil, where quality of products and production process is peer reviewed.

Furthermore we will see how *Farming at Sea* works on an integrated food production cycle, winning back phosphates. The integrated *Blue Drop Green Crop* project in South Africa shows us how they realise sustainable regional food production (horticulture) with a limited availability of water, at the same time improving degraded soils and creating employment opportunities.

10.1 Introduction: focus on the region!

"In urbanised countries, the region is the optimal level to realise sustainable development of the community and its environment. A lopsided perspective (urban or rural) or a sectoral approach[90] does not work out very well. We have to leave behind the idea that cities and rural areas are separate entities or that the rural area is lagging behind in development[91]." And this goes not only for Western Europe!

Regionalisation is a movement that opposes globalisation. The latter is - up to now - the prevailing development tendency. Globalisation has had quite a number of negative impacts on regional communities and regional economies, both in developed and in developing countries. For instance, production and consumption of goods and services have become detached (see Figure 24 in chapter 11.1). The relationship between the quality and characteristics of products and services on the one hand, and the region of origin on the other hand, has dissolved. Production of various goods and services (far away from where we live) and supply have become disconnected and are now regarded as separate activities in different sectors (disengagement).

Urban Food Policies. There are several examples in the world that show that *the region* is becoming more and more important for sustainable development, for the regional economy and for society. Cities such as London, Copenhagen, Rome, Bologna, Amsterdam and Rotterdam are getting actively involved in food production in tandem with the rural development of the sub-urban areas. This process is called urban food policy and *regional agriculture* is increasingly becoming a source of wellbeing.

Regional, ecological multipurpose agriculture is becoming the source of wellbeing.

1. As a result of urban food policies and consumer supported farming, the position of agriculture is changing. In the past 30 years, the main aim of North Atlantic agriculture used to be the contribution to national revenues, through the export of agricultural produce, with focus on the economy.[92] Agriculture is now increasing its

---

[90] A sectoral approach: focussing merely on agriculture, *or* on nature, *or* water *or* urbanisation next to the other sectors, as is habitual in Rural Planning.

[91] This was stated by Prof.Dr.Ir. Han Wiskerke when he accepted the title professor of rural sociology at Wageningen University, in November 2007

[92] In the Netherlands, the Ministry of Agriculture has become incorporated in the Ministry of Economic Affairs and Innovation, Min.EZI, in 2012. This ministry decided to get rid of the word *agriculture* in its name, as agriculture is seen as a purely economic sector (not related to food, health, biodiversity, nature management).

contribution to the improvement of the quality of life (promotion of well being) in fields like care, relaxation, sports, education, recycling, increase of biodiversity and the production of healthy, local food, clean water and pleasant surroundings.

2. The demand on the consumers' side is changing as well. Consumers are becoming less materialistic and more aware of the processes behind food production, the quality of the food they eat and its origin. A farmer is no longer appreciated because of the volume of his produce, but because of his attitude, in the way he looks after nature, soil and landscape, the quality and means of production, and whether he cares for his fellow citizens.

10.2 Linking Environment And Farming (LEAF) in Great Britain

LEAF[93] aims to link the environment and agriculture. It is an organisation of farmers and citizens, which assists farmers to produce in a more sustainable way. To promote a better understanding of the agro-ecological or integrated approach in the UK, LEAF has started a national network of demonstration farms. With an annual audit system, all aspects of sustainability on the farm are checked, as well as the entire farm system. This audit was developed by the LEAF farmers themselves, with support of the organisation's secretariat, so the criteria were not imposed by the government or a supermarket chain. This resulted in a wide acceptance of the approach and improved willingness amongst farmers to participate. The focus lies on regional sustainablility and regional food supply.

Brand. In 20 years LEAF has developed into a brand and LEAF products are available in the supermarket. A recent development (2011) is that Unilever is interested in using LEAF products to increase the sustainability of their production chain.

Audit system. This well-developed audit system, for what is essentially sustainable multifunctional agriculture, is very well applicable in other European countries. For each aspect (soil management, use of fertilizers, water use and management, animal health, stabling system, energy consumption, human resources management, environmental protection, footpaths, retail systems and farm economy) criteria have been developed. A score of 7.5 out of 10 has to be achieved for each aspect if the farmer wants to remain in the organisation. Social control and mutual exchanges promote the quality and the sense of unity.

---

[93] Based on an interview in 2010 with Caroline Drummond, Chief Executive Director of the Association. http://www.leafuk.org/leaf/home.web

As an organisation, LEAF is involved in the following activities:

- Development and promotion of integrated farming systems in the UK.
- Demonstration of IFM (Integrated Farm Management) to farmers and citizens.
- Management of 40 LEAF demonstration farms.
- Provision of assistance to farmers to change to IFM.
- Policy formulation.
- International cooperation with the European Initiative for Sustainable Agriculture (EISA).

10.3 Oregional

Oregional is a co-operative of farmers in the Nimwegen/Arnhem region of the Netherlands. These farmers and horticulturists are proud of their products and of their region; together they provide a wide selection of fresh produce, which is not necessarily organic, but ecologically sustainable. The products of the cooperative are sold directly to consumers in the region, making a short producer-consumer chain. They mostly supply catering business, nursing homes and shops.

Oregional cooperates with a diverse group of farmers and horticulturists to be able to provide a wide variety of products. All producers work within a distance of 50 kilometres from Nimwegen. Sustainability is a leading principle for the suppliers, and quality and crispness come first.

Transition to a circular economy. The idea to better organise food from the region had existed already quite some time in Gerard Titulaer's mind. From 1996 till 2006 he was the inspiration and coordinator of the foundation, *Friends of the Countryside,* in which he tried to involve consumers in agriculture and make them aware of the important role of agriculture for a pretty countryside. But he wanted more than that. His aim was for consumers to invest in their own region by buying from farmers who produce, next to food, a nice and sustainable landscape. So he took the initiative, first to establish the foundation Landwaard (LandLord) to organise support, and secondly to create a cooperation of farmers who supported his idea, now called Oregional. To get the right farmers together was one thing. Much more difficult was to involve consumers. Somehow the notion doesn't exist yet that buying products from your own region means that you invest in your own region and that you so allow farmers to work on and contribute to a sustainable landscape.

A healthy food supply appeared to be the right approach. From the very start of Gerard's initiative, the man responsible for food procurement in St. Maarten's Hospital was interested. He recognised the value of healthy food from the region for his rehabilitating patients and people living in the care home. His board of directors consented with his plan to source food from various local suppliers, instead of from the regular catering business. This was groundbreaking, as most institutions (like hospitals, municipalities and businesses) try to save money on food and therefore get their supplies from the bigger wholesale companies or involve a catering company. In the case of St.Maarten's hospital and care home, they got a lot of positive publicity and more people on the waiting list to come and live there.

The outcome. The experience of St.Maarten's hospital is that they save money by this initiative, annually tens of thousands of euros, while it was expected that buying regionally would be more costly. Also, since this initiative is still relatively new, it is an example for many. Both the foundation and the cooperation are asked to give presentations or interviews by municipalities and schools for professional education. In 2013 collaboration was started between Wageningen University, Arnhem-Nijmegen College, Nijmegen University and a chain of vocational training schools in order to further study and develop this concept.

Success factors:

- ✓ The vison, ambition, good contacts and networking abilities of the initiator were outstanding and necessary to succeed. And just as important were the efforts of the pioneer in the St Maarten's clinic to make his board agree with the regional economy and good food plan.
- ✓ Without the idealism and the work of the farmers participating in the cooperation, this whole project wouldn't work.
- ✓ The subsidies from the municipalities, the province and the Ministry of Agriculture were indispensable.
- ✓ The LandLord Foundation promotes the work of the cooperation Oregional tremendously in various ways. By giving lectures and workshops about the concept, by organising visits to the participating famers in the region and inspiring schools to make school-gardens where food is grown.

Challenges and solutions:

- Many care homes and hospitals try to save money on food and subsequently turn to a national catering business, which is not, per se, cheaper or better. That really is a mistake when you know that only 1-1.5% of the total budget is for food and management, while maintenance of the building and personnel consume the rest. If institutions would work more integratedly, if they would overlook the interests of individual departments and look at the picture as a whole, they would realise that keeping their patients and inhabitants healthier would save enormously in the fields of extra care and medicine. Various scientific studies have shown that people stay healthier with fresh healthy food.

- In many countries the government requires a *sustainable purchasing policy* for public institutions. One would assume that this would lead to buying food regionally, but nothing is less true. The bigger national food catering companies advertise being sustainable, but buy their food cheaply from all over the world. Purchasing officials just choose the easy way and keep thinking that buying food regionally is a hassle and more expensive. In order to support the purchase of regionally grown food, the foundation LandLord has written an advisory paper (2013, in Dutch), discussing the pros and cons of sustainable sourcing of food by institutions.

- For the cooperative, the demand has to be sufficiently large in order to cover the costs of supply and transport. Since in recent years the demand was only slowly developing, the cooperative now also focuses on individual consumers. Since 2012, consumers can purchase directly from the cooperative through Internet orders. Since February 2013, there has been a fresh food corner in Nimwegen centre selling products from Oregional.

10.4 Willem&Drees - regional products in the local supermarket

Willem&Drees[94] started in 2009 in the Netherlands by investigating the possibility - in the region Amersfoort - to make the vegetables and fruit of local farmers available in local supermarkets. "We thought it would be possible, although most people said that it would be a no-go, as supermarkets want to manage their own supply chains."

An initiative similar to Oregional, Willem & Drees successfully tried to break the 'business as usual' supply chain of supermarkets, who get their food worldwide paying the cheapest rates and often for 'dump prices', exploiting farmers.

The questions Willem&Drees started with were:

- Would supermarkets be interested in selling fruit and vegetables of local farmers?
- Can we collect directly from the farmer and deliver to the supermarket?
- Can we support the consumer by having the local produce in the supermarket, saving the consumer a weekly errand to collect a bag of vegetables at the farm?

---

[94] Willem&Drees, info@willemendrees.nl

- Can we find the best farmers?
- And most important: will the consumer buy the product? "It all turned out to be feasible", said Drees in 2013. "The strawberries are wonderful, the cherries are delicious. While we were still in the try-out phase, supermarkets asked us to continue and so we did. We will expand region by region."

Credibility. They work according to principles instead of regulations. Ten principles guide their daily work:
1. Local, within a range of 40 km
2. Seasonal
3. Better quality, fresher - it shows in the taste
4. The farmer gets a face - each product represents a person
5. Respect for the environment: more biodiversity and sustainable cultivation
6. Less transportation
7. Lasting relationships
8. Our idealism: entrepreneurship and long-term idealism
9. Transparency
10. Fun: adventures and experiments

Our growers. "We look for growers close to the supermarkets, so the products are regional. We want to 'click' with the grower. So first of all we meet the grower and assess whether his approach matches ours. You can recognise a professional by the way he talks about his enterprise and by the vegetables and fruits that he is growing. The growers also know who is the best in their particular line of business. And this will bring you from one grower to the other. Furthermore, research at Wageningen University has shown that growers who are good also use more sustainable ways of production."

Why this move toward transition? The initiative came from Willem who loves setting up new, innovative projects. He is an expert in putting new brands onto the market. Working within a big company he felt he couldn't contribute to societal sustainability as much as he wanted; he really wanted his work to help change the world. And he was really upset by some developments in food production systems. The increasingly growing distance between farmers and consumers, with sometimes half the globe in between them, worried him. So he left and invested his personal savings to work on this concept with Drees as business partner.

Why is this a real transition, a system's change?
1. "Because until about the 1970s, it was 'normal' to eat from the region. It was 'normal' to eat a variety of food, depending on the season. Nowadays, our global food system offers us any food in

any season, like strawberries at Christmas and green beans in January. This is made possible by mostly unsustainable or unfair production methods in developing countries *and* by food processing and transport, which use a lot of fossil fuels. Is that what we really want? People are in need of reconnection with their food. Local and regional initiatives are witness to that. We think that, as Willem & Drees, we contribute to the transition to the *New Normal*, where consumers know the producers of their food and the way it is produced, if only to be able to make the choice for healthy food."

2. "It is a transition, since this is a systems change, in which, for the first time, a relation is made between small, local farmers and the big supermarkets. Until now *big* was collaborating with *big*, and *small* was collaborating with *small*. It is difficult too, because the partners initially do not trust each other, as they come from different backgrounds and have different worldviews."

3. We actually follow up on the transition that has been set in by consumers. They are 'en masse' becoming aware of the fact that they themselves are part of the problems like overconsumption, obesity, hunger in developing countries, land degradation, land grabbing and water shortages in the South and climate change. They now discover that they can contribute to solutions by the choices they make. So people now question themselves if they still want to invest in pension funds that invest in the wrong projects, or if they want instead to put their money in banks that invest in sustainable businesses. The only problem is that people often do not know where to start. Going to an organic farmer in the neighbourhood is often too complicated, too time consuming and expensive. By offering regional products in the supermarket, we seduce, as it were, the consumer to make a first move towards regionalising production and consumption, which brings awareness and next steps.

4. We have a *New Normal* way of working. Instead of the 'accepted' way of following rules, regulations and restrictions, we work on the base of principles, the foundation for trust.

What outlook for the future? Willem&Drees believe that their approach may have quite an impact on consumers and their purchasing behaviour in the coming years. And with that, there will be quite an effect on the regionalisation of production. In the Netherlands, that is a challenge. In 2013 about 70% of the Dutch vegetables and fruit are exported, only 2.5% (potatoes and tomatoes) ends up in a supermarket. Willem&Drees do not source even 1% of their products from the very big producers. It just means that once there are sufficient consumers who choose regional products (say 30%) then the tipping point is there.

Success factors:

✓ The most important factor is the motivation of the initiators of Willem&Drees. They have a dream and motivating reasons, giving them the energy to do this. The very accessible brand name works well - people can relate to them. Furthermore, they chose a strategy of seduction instead of patronizing: this is about appetizing food, 'good for you and your health!'. Because of their well-established networks they easily could attract funding for the starting up of this initiative.

Impediments and solutions:

- Operating between *big* and *small* is difficult, since people on both sides are not used to that, so initially there is no trust in the other party.
- It was also difficult in the first 3 years of starting up, that we had to work on a minimal budget. We are still (2013) depending on investors and as yet make no profit.
- Holding on to the dream and not giving up when things do not turn out as expected and developments are disappointing slowly. For example, they worked top down, starting with the director of a supermarket chain, who was interested and pointed out which stores would be interested to start this innovation. Now it appears that for some supermarket chains it is not interesting enough if only 10 out of 400 of their stores participate. So they may have to start from the bottom up and see which supermarket franchisees are interested.

10.5 Ecovida – cooperation for certification

In three provinces in Brazil - Paraná, Santa Catarina and Rio Grande do Sul - a Participatory Guarantee System (PGS) has been developed and established by the farmers, to guarantee the quality of their products. Bianca Martin did research into this approach developed by the ECOVIDA network at the Centre Ecologia in Rio Grande.

The situation:

Out of a total of 37 million farmers in the world who work ecologically, almost a quarter (23%) lives and works in Latin America. The costs of an official certification are usually far too high for them. The bureaucracy makes it even more difficult to obtain certification. Therefore the farmers in the ECOVIDA network took the initiative to improve the quality of their products and to monitor the production processes themselves. With a self-developed system of technical and social controls, they established a good working certification system.

Generally speaking there are three types of certification systems in the world, according to Bianca. Most of them are organised top-down: government regulations or those of agribusinesses are determinitive and usually not adapted to the region, or to the technical and social conditions. The PGS system however is organised horizontally. Fig.19 gives the comparison.

Type 1	Type 2	Type 3
Vertical organisation. Top-down. For the farmer, this is an individual, expensive process. He/she adheres to rules and learns nothing.	Organised by paid advisory services. Here, the farmer is being trained individually and is personally involved in the development of his farm.	Horizontal organisation. Peer reviews, 'inter-collegial feedback' Here, the farmers learn from each other and with each other. There is empowerment of people and of the region.

Fig. 19 Certification systems

The PGS system is a 'Type 3' certification system. It works as follows. As soon as a farmer has applied for membership of the association, he gets a peer visit. That means that a farmer from the neighbourhood, also a member, will judge how the farmer can participate and what is required. Then follows regsistration. The farmer starts documenting the activities on his farm, in order to get a better view on the integrality and the quality of the process. This is the start of the transition. Because, by writing down what you do, you discover how things can be done better or differently. Eight to twelve farmers' families make a group in which they support each other, reflect and give feed back. A few technical advisors (at the regional coordination cente) can give advice. Once a year there is an evaluation visit, an audit so to say, done by a farmer from a neighbouring area, to assure neutrality. This also stimulates exchange of experience, mutual learning and connection.

The collaboration within the association is bottom-up. The picture below shows how that works out.

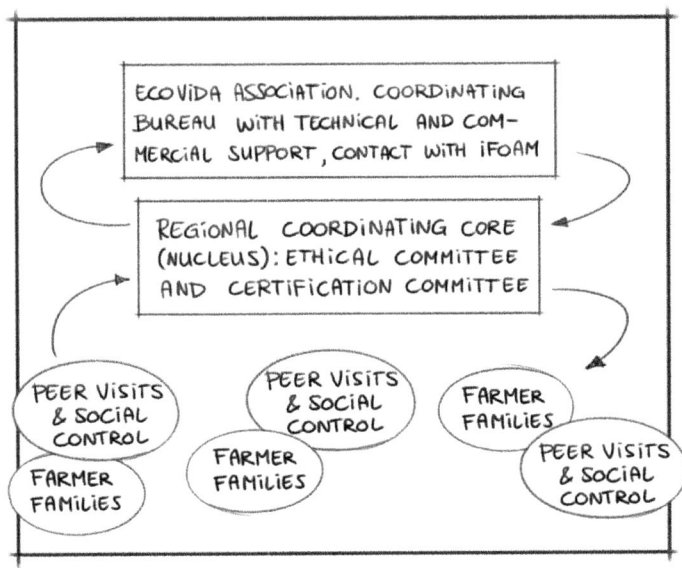

Fig. 20 Ecovida's bottom-up organisational structure

The advantages of such a certification system are:

✓ There is an evaluation of the production process, more than only the evaluation of the products.

✓ The evaluation of the production process is done in relation to the farmers' family's health, social life, water and soil conditions, etc.

✓ It is a farmer-to-farmer approach that creates reciprocity, mutual respect and learning.

✓ A farmers' group also becomes a social group, which strengthens social life and the socio-economic power of the region.

✓ There is a high level of responsibility, autonomy and decision-making.

✓ The advisor has a *facilitating* role, with technical knowledge and social information. The relationship is horizontal, not top down; the farmer is not obliged to follow the advice.

✓ A common responsibility develops. Members feel responsible for the commons.

✓ Social values are high.

Qualification of the production process. ECOVIDA certification is based on the quality of the agro-ecological production processes. It is important therefore, to know the difference between the institutionalised *organic* production process and the *agro-ecological* approach. This is captured in the figure below.

Impediments and how to deal with them

- Of course there are farmers that predominate socially. Then others cannot develop as much as they would. Here, the advisor is important; he needs to be a personal coach/facilitator for the development of the group and the support of mutual feedback.
- A lot of effort is being asked of the participating farmers, not only in their learning process, but also in developing a network in the region, visiting others. The advantage is that this system is not expensive and there is no bureaucracy.

Organic	Agro-ecological
Without chemicals/ herbicides	Integral and holistic approaches. As little chemicals as possible
Certified according to top-down institutionalised criteria. The criteria are not any more – as was the original organic approach – derived from restoring the natural closed-loop farming cycle	Low Input Agriculture, use of homegrown, locally available and locally crossbred seeds, contributing to agro-biodiversity Horizontal knowledge exchange
Internationally commercialised with worldwide trade, which requires globally identical certification standards	For the local and regional market; low energy and transport costst

Fig.21. Differences between organic and agro-ecological production processes

Challenges for the future

This validation and certification system and the resulting quality label are recognised within Brazil, so the products are available and recognisable in the market and supermarkets, comparable to the LEAF hallmark in Great Britain. It would be a step up if international certification standards would recognise those regionally developed labels for *sound* agro-ecologically grown products.

10.6 Farming at Sea

In Jules Verne's *20,000 Leagues Under the Sea* (1870), the iconic Captain Nemo announced that, *"In the depths of the ocean, there are mines of zinc, iron, silver and gold that would be quite easy to exploit"*[17] while predicting that the abundance of marine resources could satisfy human need.

Farming at Sea is an innovative idea, developed by Willem Brandenburg, Wageningen University and Research Centre. The idea is that seaweed is grown and harvested as a new protein-rich crop for our growing food demand.

Fig. 22. Farming at Sea

Seaweed instead of meat?

This is his line of thought. If, by 2050, we have to live on this earth with 9 billion people and the Earth's surface doesn't have enough space any more, then, we should start thinking about new crops and totally different ways of producing and consuming. Those new ways have to be sustainable and should preferably use a *Cradle2Cradle* principle.

For food security we need proteins. Presently we consume too much meat from animals as a protein source. And the production of this meat costs too much vegetable protein, actually 3 times the quantity of animal protein that we so generate.[95] Additionally, the global meat production chain causes a lot of ecologic and social problems, so there is a good reason to look for other sources of protein.

---

[95] Those vegetable proteins could even be put to better use if they were directly eaten by the people that grow them, mostly in developing countries, but that is beside this issue about growing seaweed.

Seaweed seems a good alternative to meat, since the proteins in seaweed consist of a combination of amino acids that is positive for our human digestion system. We actually need less seaweed protein than meat protein to feed ourselves healthily. Additionally, seaweed contains a lot of healthy minerals. It has been scientifically proven that the Japanese are healthier, due to their seafood eating habits.

Sustainable seaweed plantations, would that be possible? The next question indeed was whether it is possible to grow and harvest seaweed on a large scale, and in an economic and sustainable way. The purpose of the *Farming at Sea* project is just that: finding out how feasible it is.

Aspects of this transition:

- Seaweed as *food* is very normal in Japan and China. Laver bread is a traditional Welsh dish from seaweed and is delicious. In Australia and the U.S., seaweed as food is becoming more accepted since eating *sushi* has become very fashionable there. Of course it is quite possible to eat fresh seaweed, but it requires a mindshift from the consumer.
- Using seaweed as *feed* is another option. Since seaweed contains high value proteins, it could be used as a base ingredient for the production of processed human and animal food. In animal feed it could for example replace the soya and maize from South America, possibly reducing the speed with which rainforests are being cleared. In human food, seaweed is used as a binding agent.
- A change in eating habits. There have been a variety of initiatives in which seaweed has been used to make attractive healthy food. In 2013 in Amsterdam, a *weedburger*[96] was introduced by Lizette Kraysler. Her motivation was as follows: "If we like to eat fish, but we do not want to empty the oceans of fish by the overfishing we are presently making ourselves guilty of, why not eat seaweed instead? It has the same taste!"
- Ecologically sustainable. Production of food that is based on seaweed would generate a much smaller ecological footstep. At the same time it would contribute to a much-needed increase of food protein in the world. However, there is one big challenge here: not to make the same mistake as we do in land-based agriculture, exchanging nature for industrial processes and thereby depleting natural resources! Of course it is the algae and micro algae in the oceans that produce the food. If we exhaust those rich resources, we would be wrong. So we will re-use the mineral waste, like Nitrogen (N) and Phosphate (Ph), that washes out from the land into the sea by rivers and pumping stations. Imagine, 70% of the

---

[96] Taste the Change! That was the slogan used to convince people to contribute to a better world and one's own health in times of crises by eating the seaweed burger. Dutchweedburger.com.

Earth's surface is sea and all those minerals are brought to the seas. And there should be sufficient space on sea.

- There is a good chance that in between the seaweed fields a new ecosystem develops, of fish and shrimps
- Seaweed cultivation produces more biomass per hectare than agriculture on land, since seaweed grows in three storeys. Why is that? There are different types of seaweed that require different depths to grow, as they use another part of the spectrum of sunlight.
- This project recovers phosphate, which is important as the global stocks are getting rapidly depleted and this could become a global catastrophe (see box). Presently, more phosphate (as an ingredient of chemical fertilizer) is rinsed away through rivers than we are mining. By cultivating seaweed, we recover the phosphate and micronutrients from the rivers. Otherwise said: we recycle.

Phosphates are essential for life. Both animals and humans need phosphates to live. Phosphates are a compound of phosphorus and oxygen. Phosphate compounds are essential elements in human DNA and provide our energy to live, work, think and act. People and animals get their phosphate through food. Plants and crops take their phosphate from the soil. That is why phosphate is an important ingredient in fertilizer. Phosphate is also used in the pharmaceutical industry and in washing powders and liquids.

The phosphate crisis. Only a few countries in the world have phosphate mines. In Europe it is only Finland that owns phosphate mine. Worldwide, the U.S., China and Morocco are the biggest phosphate producers. Because of the growing world population, their increasing consumption of meat and the increasing biomass production for bio-fuel, the demand for phosphate is increasing rapidly. Experts have calculated that with the present stocks we will be able to just manage until about 3000. After that, there is no more phosphate, at all. Which means that we will all die. So we need to find a way to bring phosphate back into the production cycles, stop wasting it and find other phosphate resources, like manure, human and animal urine.

Meanwhile, most European countries, the Netherlands in particular, have a surplus of phosphate in their soils and surface water. The cause: eutrophication by topdressing the soil with too high quantities of mixed animal manure and urine.

Winning back of phosphates. Fifteen percent (15%) of the phosphate imoported in the Netherlands ends up in the sewerage system. By fertilizing more efficiently and by recycling phosphates, every country could become less dependent on (the import of) phosphate ore and reduce the impoverishment of it. Winning back phosphates from sewage systems has proven to be an environmentally friendly process. There are 3 locations to do this actually:

1. In or next to the toilet by separation of urine and faeces (decentralised sanitation);

2. At the sewage treatment plants, by making phosphate precipitate as struvite (Mg (NH_4) PO_4 · 6 (H_2O)), magnesium ammonium phosphate. Struvite is a very good, slow releasing fertilizer; and

3. At silt incinerators, by winning back phosphate from the silt ash.

How can we realise this transition? There are many issues to be dealt with. To start with, the sea is not user friendly at all. Even if you don't go far off the coast, it can be very cold and waves can be 6- 10 metres high. In 2012 and 2013 the first *near shore* experiments were done. Later, experiments are foreseen with the help of *off shore* technologies. Because seaweed is a fresh food, and there will be a lot of biomass, the logistics of harvesting and transporting are important. Another question is how to do that sustainably, without emissions and without contributing more to the already far too extensive plastic belt, see box.

The plastic belt is a thick 'carpet' of plastic, drifting in the Pacific Ocean that is twice as large as the United States, with a thickness of about 30 metres. This plastic waste is built up of bigger and smaller and micro plastics, including the microscopic plastic particles that make our lotions and creams softer (so look what you buy next time!). This phenomenon also occurs in smaller seas and rivers. In 2013, the volume of plastic in the oceans was bigger than the volume of protozoans, the essential source of life in the ocean. Via fish the toxic plastic ends up in our foodsystem.

Source: Marine geologist Marc de Batist, University of Ghent, Belgium

Environmentally friendly cultivation and crop protection. Seaweed is a wild plant, so starting seaweed cultivation, as a process, is comparable to the start of arable farming about 10,000 years ago, but we have more knowledge now. Also in seaweed there are predators, bacteria and fungi that attack vulnerable plants. How do we treat them in an ecologically sound way? From our experience with the present industrialised agriculture, we have learnt that monocultures do not work and have negative effects on the environment. So how will we do the cultivation at all?

Paradigm shift. This paradigm shift calls for another one. If, for example, seaweed is not acceptable for consumption, it might be used for other purposes, such as building materials. A lot of surplus CO_2 is being stored in seaweed, so we contribute to decreasing climate change.

Success factors:

- ✓ A highly motivated initiator, with enthusiasm, vision and the ability to engage others.
- ✓ Subsidies - without subsidies the experiments and project would not have been possible. The province of Zeeland (NL) invested 88.000 euro. On a national level people have become interested, too.
- ✓ Scientific attention and promotion remains very important. This project Farming at Sea (De Zeeboerderij) is one of the Food for Thought projects of the Wageningen University Fund.
- ✓ A location to carry out this experiment was obviously an important condition for the project; it was assigned in April 2011. With investments by the private enterprise Hortimare and the Economic Impulse Subsidy, it was possible to build a raft of 600 square meters and to do some experiments. This gave us the base for the development of more fundamental knowhow.
- ✓ Sharing knowledge with other educational institutes, and cocreation by involving students, leads to new and better ideas and prolongation of the research.

Impediments and solutions:

- It is difficult to get research funds. Decision makers are scared of putting their heads above the parapet for something innovative that has not yet been proven to work. Because this is interdisciplinary work, it is difficult if not impossible to gain kudos in prestigious scientific magazines, which is often a prerequisite for sponsorship or fundraising. Because of this, the project loses a lot of time in acquiring small amounts of money to help them make further steps.
- Seaweed farming is actually primary production, like potato, onion, rice, soy and milk production. That means that the price for the raw material will be low. That means that production costs have to be low as well. How are we going to do that? Especially when starting up, that is not possible.
- There is a growing notion in the European Union that we actually need some sort of regional planning instrument for the seas, because of the increase of different uses. Apart from fisheries and this new seaweed farming idea, there is solar and wind energy, oil drilling platforms, the increasing exploitation of mangenese nodules, and pipes for gas and oil and communication. There are no regulations yet so it is difficult to get permission.

10.7 Sustainable regional food production in South Africa

In cooperation with the partners Aqua Terra Nova, For Elements and the South African NGO Living Lands, Soil & More[97] developed a model for storing water and composting organic waste.

The project is called *Metropolitan Food Cluster, Blue Drop, Green Crop*. It aims to sustainably re-cycle water and waste from horticultural enterprises, in order to develop horticultural production without exhausting natural resources.

The situation. Population growth and urbanisation require more food and clean water at short notice. To meet the increasing demand for safe food, South Africa wants to develop horticulture in spite of insufficient water resources due to the rainfall distribution. Efficient water use and water distribution have not been well developed yet. Other challenges include countering land degradation (due to cutting down of natural vegetation) and preserving soil fertility, which is deteriorating as a result of unsustainable practices and high applications of fertilizer.

What is this transition about? The idea is to develop horticulture, save water and increase soil fertility. The *Cradle2Cradle* (C2C) concept 'waste = food' is applied here. Waste and waste water are recycled for use in horticulture. For the re-use of waste water, a water purification system has been developed that requires little investment and maintenance. To improve soil fertility, organic waste is converted into high quality compost. Regular applications of compost improve soil structure and thus the water retention capacity of the soil. As a result, irrigation frequency can be reduced and less water seeps out of the rooting zone. The water footprint of horticulture is reduced in this way. At the same time yields increase and it is expected that in the future more jobs will be created. So this development, starting with the improvement of the soil, will create more job opportunities in horticulture as well as related products and services such as water purification, food processing and transportation. It is anticipated that this will be extended to other regions.

Success factors:

- ✓ There is vision, nerve and necessary perseverance with all parties involved.
- ✓ The supply of waste water and organic waste from the urban area is guaranteed year round.

---

[97] Miriam Bogatzki, Soil & More, January 2012. http://www.soilandmore.com/

- ✓ The interdisciplinary collaboration by the different partners works well.
- ✓ This project and its 'business development' approach in South Africa is supported by the Royal Netherlands Embassy and the NWP - Netherlands Water Partnership.
- ✓ The modular set-up of the project allows for additional projects.

Impediments and problems and how they were solved

- With this innovative concept it took a long time to convince the different parties involved that it would work better and be more sustainable than the conventional approaches. In particular the people responsible are scared to embark on a new idea.
- The sectoral departments involved (for water, agriculture and waste management) were not used to collaborate or communicate, which is the case in many countries. This made a collaborative solution quite difficult. The project therefore made an effort to entice and involve the different parties in order to have them experience how cooperation in a multi-stakeholder process can lead to unexpected integrative solutions.

11. Consumer Supported Agriculture

Fig. 23. Consumer
supported agriculture

After an introduction, four examples of consumer supported food production and agriculture follow: The Community Supported Agriculture concept (CSA), Lazuur Food Community Wageningen, the London Food-Link project and Transition Towns.

11.1 Introduction

'Be aware of what you eat' – this is an increasingly important aspect when we choose our food. *What* do we buy and *where* do we buy it, in the supermarket or from a local farmer?

Where does it come from, *how* has it been produced, with *what effect* on the environment and at *what social costs*? And *what* does it contain?

More and more people are realising that, for our present food supply, we are depending on fossil fuels, which are getting scarcer every day. Transition Towns[98] is one example of a direct civil reaction to this fossil fuel consuming production system. At the same time, more information - about the negative impact of large-scale food production on the environment, on animals and on our health - is becoming available.

What has happened? What is going on? Most of all, the connections and feedback within the producer-consumer system have deteriorated. The figure below shows how an ever-increasing number of steps were introduced in the production and trade process. As a result of that the consumer became increasingly removed from what is actually happening in the production and processing of the food. The consumer has no idea what she is buying in a shop as she doesn't know what happened during the various steps in processing, packaging, trading. Neither can she give feedback to the processors involved.

The two figures below show the difference between the situation about 50 years ago and now.

In *Situation 1*, the connection between producer and farmer exists and feedback is taking place through social controls. The farmer sells his produce on the market and receives money as well as comments on the quality, questions and suggestions. The consumer is able to observe how the farmer treats his cattle, crop or farm, as it is in the neighbourhood, so he can base his decision on this information. This situation was quite normal 100 years ago in Europe and still is very normal in rural areas in developing countries.

In *Situation 2*, in the picture below, the producer lives far away. How he manages his production, and under what conditions, is not clear. How much money he earns is not clear either, because of all the steps involved in brokering and transportation. The international 'big five' food producing companies[99] now speak about this range of steps as improving the value-chain. The result: even in a small country such as the Netherlands, so many steps are involved that a farmer will receive *only 1%* (1 eurocent) of the

---

[98]   Transition Towns, an initiative to counteract PeakOil.

[99]   The Big Five: Unilever, The Coco Cola Company, Associated British Foods, Groupe Danone S.A., General Mills Inc., Kelloggs Inc. http://247wallst.com/special-report/2014/08/15/companies-that-control-the-worlds-food/

price for which a kilo of his onions is sold in the supermarket (1 euro). If the consumer complains about some product, an investigation is carried out to identify which step or which farmer was involved and the supermarket may decide to drop the company or the farmer. Neither does the consumer have information on the production process. It is not clear whether the farmer maintains a coherent agro-ecological system or if he has done some landgrabbing, if he erodes the soil or if he uses all the available water in a dry African or South American country. The consumer is only directed by the label and the goodlooking and convincing hallmarks of the supermarket.

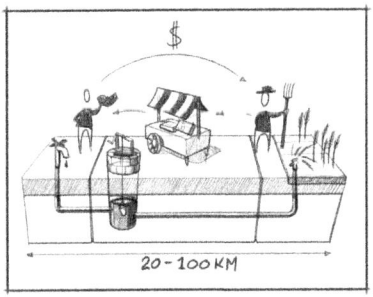 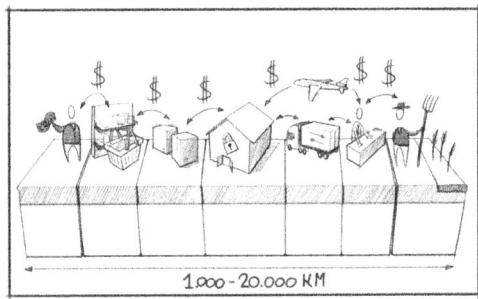

Situation 1 - in Europe around 1900   Situation 2 - in the world around 2010

Fig.24. The changed producer-consumer relations

Conclusion: the customer is supposed to be king, but generally he does not use his power. By making your choice as a consumer you actually have an important impact on what appears on the shelves and who will be the producer. You can decide, by your conscious purchasing, which company and which farmer, wherever in the world they may be, will earn an income: a farmer in England of whom you know that he produces sustainably, a global agribusiness concern that grows green beans in Tanzania or green asparagus in Peru. In each of the latter two cases it is hard to find out whether the produce is sustainably grown or not.

Let us look at regional food production and consumption: who will benefit?

- Where will the *greengrocer* get his benefits? Will he earn more money from a tomato that has travelled half the world, or from a tomato from a greenhouse around the corner? Does he want to share the profits with the grower, the dealer, the transporters, the airlines, the bank and the auction house? Or can he share the profits with the grower only?
- What is beneficial for *the consumer*? Seasonal food has a better nutritional value and contributes to his overall health. Lots of supermarkets and food chains 'pimp' their out of season vegetables

and fruit to make them shine. This reduces the natural nutrition level. This foodstuff is often high in pesticides, waxes (to make them shine), preservatives and other chemicals to make them look fresher than they actually are. Food from around the corner? By consuming fresh seasonal products your menu changes with the seasons, which prevents the possible development of allergies. At the same time a varied diet helps in the detoxification of the body in a natural way.

- What will benefit *local agriculture*? A larger diversification in production generally makes enterprises more stable as they will become less dependent on the fluctuations in a single sector. In this way the development of an ever-increasing scale of production can be interrupted. In the end, more small-scale enterprises will also provide more job opportunities, but this will make their products quite expensive. More crops in the crop rotation, also in winter, will result in improved soil condition, as well as a more interesting landscape.
- What will benefit *the local economy*? If you spend one euro at a local enterprise, three times that amount will remain in the region than if you spend this amount at an international chain. If you add the economic value of the local production, the result will be even more important.
- What will benefit *the environment*? Crop rotation and winter crops will result in a healthier soil, which will supply more minerals and trace elements to the crop and thus to your food. As less transport is involved, less energy is required, which will contribute to climate change mitigation. The environment elsewhere will also improve. Because if we eat meat from cows that have been fed with local feed, then there is less need to cut down rainforests in South America (at the rate of one soccer field per day) for soy and maize plantations, for exports as cattlefeed.

How can I contribute to more sustainable food production worldwide? By being more conscious when shopping. By making sure that the produce comes from healthy, coherent agro-eco systems where biodiversity is maintained, wherever in the world, and preferably from the region. This is being complicated by all kind of hallmarks, also issued by the supermarkets themselves, which indicate that a product has been grown in a sustainable way, while we have no clue about the methods that were used.

How to go about it? We would like to have a feedback mechanism that ensures that we, as consumers, can buy produce from the region, produced in a sustainable way and delivered in time. It is also important to ensure that whatever is produced by the regional producers is made available to local consumers. It shouldn't be impossible as it is often the case now; many people cannot afford the time to go to all the different selling points for vegetables, bread, fruit, honey, cheese, etc, in addition to having a job, a family and a household.

In this chapter we will see many developing communities of people, both producers and consumers, who take responsibility for their own sustainable food production. This is a movement for food sovereignty that is getting more and more important, as can be seen from the following examples.

11.2 Community Supported Agriculture (CSA)

The idea behind CSA is that a group of consumers supports the farmer (or enterprise) by investing in the production *before* the growing season starts. With this money, the farmer can buy his inputs - such as seeds and compost - and he receives part of his annual income in advance. During the year, the 'investors' will receive vegetables, fruit, eggs, meat, milk and other farm products in return. In some cases the customers share ownership of the farm, or buy land. For example in the Dutch village of Lunteren, a landscape fund was set up, which issued shares on a hectare basis, in order to safeguard an old small scale farming area for farming activities and to prevent urbanisation.

Typical for a CSA is:

- Reciprocity and support; a win-win situation. Both parties will benefit from their investments (money, energy and labour). In Flanders they say CSA = power and courage to be interdependent.
- Openness and honesty; the farmer is open and informs the consumer on his farm management and is willing to modify this after consultation with the consumer.
- Active involvement of consumers with heart, head and hands. Through their participation a real community will develop.

How does it work? The participants of CSA pay in advance for a share in the harvest and will be paid back, in kind, throughout the year. They normally pay for a fixed period, annually, quarterly or monthly, which will exempt the farmer from taking a costly loan from the bank. This will reflect in the price of the product. This price will be calculated by the establishment of the annual amount, which includes all costs of inputs and labour.

CSA's are not new at all! Rudolf Steiner developed the first idea of CSAs around 1920, as part of his ideas on a worldwide economy. His idea was that consumers and producers are linked by a common interest: healthy food! These ideas were only realised after World War II. The author of *Small is Beautiful*, E.F. Schumacher (1970s) added the idea of a local economy where all that is consumed is produced locally. This approach is still considered as too alternative by government and scientists. Meanwhile, the *ecological footprint* has been developed, and this 'measurement instrument' shows us also that buying locally often reduces your ecological footprint.

Community gardens dating back to 1970. In Japan and Chile this kind of 'community garden' projects started in the 1970s. In Japan the CSA Teikei was started by a group of women who were concerned about pesticide levels in common vegetables. In Chile the CSA was started as a cooperative movement during the government of Salvador Allende. In the United States the number of CSAs is increasing tremendously. The first wave took place from 1986 till 1990. One of the publications from that time is *Basic formula to Create a Community Supported Agriculture* by Robyn van En. In 1992 the CSANA, CSA North America, was founded, a clearing house for CSA development and training. In 2010 there were some 1800 CSAs, some of which covered around 10 hectares with over 1000 participants. Since 2010 we have seen an increasing number of CSAs in Europe, not least stimulated by the film of Farmer John[100].

Agriculture for a sustainable future!

CSAs are considered to be a sustainable solution for the following reasons:
- It has the potential to return vitality to thousands of locations from towns to suburbs and rural areas (the vegetable garden on the land of the White House supports this fact).
- It is not a new marketing method. It concerns necessary innovation and transformation of agricultural production through a healthy link with society, people and their values.
- This resilient 'agricultural production close to home' will be very useful in case an oil crisis[101], or other crises that may materialise, which is not unthinkable at all. More about Peak Oil in the endnotes.[18]
- In 2006 the United Nations stated in a report on worldwide economics, that there is convincing proof that the so-called efficient (industrial) agriculture is not only depleting natural resources but also has an unacceptable impact on the environment, which harms mankind.
- CSA is an ecological, social, and economical alternative, with new types of communal property, cooperation and economy, which are becoming more and more acceptable.
- Consumers are losing confidence in the food industry.

---

[100] to be found on YouTube.
[101] See Peak Oil at http://en.wikipedia.org/wiki/Peak_oil

Success factors:

- ✓ The connectedness of the consumer with the farmer and the community.
- ✓ The sense of contributing to sustainability, and of being involved.
- ✓ The consumer is getting value for money. The farmer is getting more appreciation for his work and is more financially rewarded, than when he sells to a supermarket chain.
- ✓ The farmer receives feedback on his production methods and is accountable.
- ✓ The farmer and consumer share the risks of the production process (pests, crop failure and weather, etc).

Pitfalls and impediments and how to solve these.

- If the harvest turns out to be lower than expected, the consumer needs to be flexible and accept a lower return. As he is involved in the whole process he will be able to understand this, but it is not easy to accept for everyone.
- Communication between farmer and consumer is complicated and takes a lot of time. As a result, farming operations may be delayed. A solution might be if an intermediary (volunteer) will take responsibility for this activity. In both cases we face hidden costs.

11.3 Lazuur food community, Wageningen, 2012

Starting points for this community of producers and consumers were:

- Restoration of the producer-consumer feedback system. Initially the baker produced bread to provide the customers with bread. This has changed to 'produce bread to earn money', without feedback of the client to the baker on whether the bread is good quality and tasty or whether it could be improved.
- The shopkeeper is the link and service provider between *the consumers* (who decide together on the acceptable sustainability levels) and the *producers (*who provide what the consumers ask for).
- *Investment* instead of *procurement*. Money paid for a product by the consumer is considered as a means to enable a process. The shopkeeper, as the representative of the consumer, can buy, initiate production and provide what is required. The consumer invests beforehand instead of paying afterwards.
- The consumers, by having a voice, take responsibility. Their wish list for products they want to see in the shop is not non-committal.
- A commitment is created with the producers and agreements are formulated.

How do I envisage this stakeholders' economy?

Responsibility of the consumer. The customers are member of the consumers' organisation. Their contribution is the investment to finance the stock. The consumers' organisation has a role in the procurement policy and indicates in which direction production methods should develop. Their active participation and guidance assures sustainability.

The 'value chains' in the conventional food production and agribusinesses link the producers in various parts of the world to the supermarket, but do not include the consumer. Presently supermarkets are involved in creating social sustainability in the countries of origin, by e.g. supporting coffee and cocoa farmers, and rightly so. But they cannot hand over responsibility to the consumer. At the same time they lure the consumer to go for cheap shopping. The customer in the supermarket can hardly oversee the consequences of his purchasing behaviour; he can see the origin of a product, but has no idea under what conditions it has been produced; 'green' products are no guarantee at all.

Fair share. In the Lazuur food community the customer is part of the food production–consumption chain and thus carries responsibility. The customers observe their position in the context of the chain. The customer has an idea about cultivation, the region, climate impact and the personal situation of the grower. A Lazuur member will get discount on her purchases and in this way recover part of her investment over the year.

The producers in the region are informally organised in a producers' cooperative where they agree mutually on who will provide which product. Together they organise the logistics and agree upon the quality criteria for their products. The cooperation exists in different ways. Transport of manure from the peat area, where the meadows are located, to the higher situated loamy sand areas, is one. Tourist cycle and footpaths have been laid out along the participating farms. In this way a new type of 'estate' has been developed. Instead of a Manor, now the farmers coordinate jointly the sustainable land use of the area in a kind of *virtual* Estate. In the ideal situation, the entire consolidated area would be managed in this way.

How was this transition realised? It started with a cooperation of concerned consumers in 1974. They founded a shop and organic restaurant, *Yokari*. The shop was separated from the restaurant as an independent enterprise in 1982. Involvement of the customers continued through funding of the stock. The managers were responsible for the daily overall management. The next step was a consumer-based procurement. So the shopkeeper became informed on his clients wishes, and thus advised the producers on how to diversify and improve the quality of their produce (1986 – 2006).

Round table. In 2012, consumers and farmers met at a round table to discuss production and distribution methods. The concept *'Healthy food, good for everyone, while taking care of the Earth'* overrides individual interests. Actual alignment with the overall interest is the guiding principle for everyone's actions, which is also determined by the individual capabilities. One for all, all for one. The shopkeeper, comparable to the man at the market stall in figure24 in chapter 11.1, remains responsible for the daily overall management and directs the policy, for consumers and producers. This innovative and interactive way of shop keeping needs continuous improvement and is developing all the time.

Success factors:

- ✓ Vision and enthusiasm - the capacity to both identify the opportunities *and* implement them, as well as the perseverance of the shopkeepers.
- ✓ The existence of a large community of highly educated customers in Wageningen who are supportive of sustainable development.
- ✓ Financial support from the Innovation Network to realise the ideas.
- ✓ Between 2010 and 2011 the percentage of products that did *not* come from the region reduced from 90% to 81%. This 9% increase of products from the region was caused by a change in attitude and willingness from local farmers to grow agro-ecologically or organic, and supply locally.

Pitfalls and impediments and how they were overcome.

- To start a food community is a process which cannot be laid down in a model. It is the participants who work together, with ups and downs. They do not always understand each other and it needs faith and trust and enthusiasm to survive and go through all the ups and downs.
- The skilled maintainance of deliberations has to be kept up, because every moment something new develops. If one party forces something upon another party, the situation gets out of balance and needs adjustment.

11.4 Outdoor Hogs

Outdoor Hogs[102] aims at a sustainable and natural production of tasty pork - more than just free range pigs. Throughout the year the pigs remain outdoors in forests, on meadows and farmland, where they can freely move around, graze and grub. The breeds raised in this enterprise are *Gasconne* and *Pied Bentheimer*.

How did this transition start? Outdoor Hogs originated in Twente, a region in the East of the Netherlands. Pecus developed the concept and implements it together with three other farmers. "Together we have the drive to keep pigs in a different way, outdoors, therefore the name Outdoor Hogs. It is not obvious that we will succeed, but we try. Instead of farming on an ever-increasing scale, in an anonymous way, for exceptionally low profits, we want to produce in a diversified way, tastier, on a small scale. We are sure that there is a market for our products, based on the enthusiast reactions of consumers and restaurants. The plan was born in Portugal. When we were on an excursion there, we had very good meat in a restaurant. This turned out to be pork, the most expensive item on the menu. Good, animal friendly and tasty meat. When we toured the countryside we saw the pigs grazing under the cork trees. Some research taught us that nobody in the Netherlands had yet begun such an approach, so we decided to do it and started Outdoor Hogs."

A Breakthrough. Outdoor Hogs wants to create a breakthrough in pig farming. A breakthrough in that it is tasty, healthy, sustainable, regional, transparent and honest. We were looking for CSA investors to support us and had a target for the first year (2011) of 1000 consumers to support our agriculture. This target was met and in 2013 when we had 2000 investors.

Fig.25. Here are Ben and Cas. Ben is a Pied Bentheimer and Cas is a Gasconne pig. Ben lives in a meadow and Cas in a forest nearby. Together they live an adventurous life.

---

[102] The websites are in Dutch only: http://www.buitengewonevarkens.nl/; Willem. rienks@rom3d.nl

Crowdfunding or Community Supported Agriculture? This is how the initiative is being presented: "With your assistance, a pig in a forest or on farmland will be as normal as a cow in a meadow. For an investment of 100 euro we will return meat products at a value of 150 euro. An interesting return on your investment, better than the stock market. We can achieve this result as we skip a number of steps in the retail chain. Through your contribution you ensure that the pigs have a good life, whilst also contributing to a diversified landscape, that the farmers have a good income and that the connection between farmer and consumer is short and clear. We are working with local butchers[103] who are allowed to slaughter and butcher outside of the slaughterhouse. Such skills have become scarce recently."

Fair for animal, farmer and consumer. "By fair we mean that our hogs have a good life, they stay outside during their entire life and have sufficient space to behave in a natural way. They live in family groups in forests or farmland. They sleep in a pigloo with lots of straw. Our farmers have a good income. We pay them an honest price for the feed they produce and the work they do. If there are profits in the production chain we will share these with them. The consumer will pay a fair price for the product. The price will not be as low as the action prices in the supermarket, but because we can keep the supply chains short and clear, skip a number of steps, we can offer exclusive meat for a fair price."

Success factors:

- ✓ "In the meantime we have 12 areas where the hogs are running free. For 2014 we have been offered 10 additional areas. So there are quite a number of landowners who like the idea and make their land available."
- ✓ "We get a lot of free publicity in the local press. This contributes to our visibility and creates interest with crowdfunders. The public sees how we keep our animals and when they like that they will contact us or use the Internet to become a crowdfunder. In this way we were able to generate a substantial starting fund, necessary to build the cabins, buy good feed and pay the farmers who look after our pigs. The cost precedes the benefit."
- ✓ "An important success factor is that we do not yet depend on this enterprise. We have scheduled a period of three years to start the business and will then evaluate whether we generate enough income to continue."

---

[103] Butchers G. ter Weele & Zn. and Kastelein, artisanal butchers who produce their own sausages.

Pitfalls and impediments and how did we overcome them?

"When you start you make a business plan. We really thought it over thoroughly, but you run into issues which you cannot envisage before. In one of the forest lots our hogs were affected by poisonous plants and it took us some time to figure out why they had health problems. Knowledge about wild vegetation and hogs has obviously disappeared since over the past 40 years the animals were only kept inside."

"In addition we have tried to give good value to all our products. Not only do we produce good pork chops, we also want to create good value for the lower quality meat by making sausages, pate and soup. This will increase the profit we make and renders the enterprise just that bit more profitable. We have experienced that the regulations on pig farming all take it for granted that the animals are kept in a stable. We follow an entirely different concept which occasionally creates problems as it doesn't follow the regulations. This requires more labour where manure and transport are involved, but we manage. The logistical part is still a headache. We have 1200 crowdfunders and have to keep in touch with them. We also have to distribute 1200 parcels; this requires a lot of time but is fun to do."

11.5 The London Food-Link Project

The aim of this two year project was to procure about 10% of the catered food in four London hospitals locally and/or organically. The hospitals involved were Ealing General, the Lambeth Hospital in Stockwell (mental health care), St. George's in Tooting, and the Royal Brompton in Chelsea (heart and lung diseases) - all four part of the National Health Service, the NHS. Annually the NHS spends some 500 million pounds (700 million euro) on food to cater for 300 million meals in 1200 hospitals. And although nobody expects a 4 star chef in the kitchen, as a patient one wants good food, in order to get better and as something to look forward to. In cooperation with the *Soil Association*, the British Association for organic agriculture, this project aimed at increasing the share of good and healthy food supplied in London hospitals.

The project started after an encouraging outcome of research, conducted by the *Soil Association* in 2002 and 2003 in cooperation with the *Foundation for Local Food Initiatives*. This research concerned the feasibility of the use of organic products in the catering procedures of St. George's Hospital, Tooting. The project was funded by the *Ministry of Environment, Food and Rural Areas* (DEFRA) in the framework of the *Rural Enterprise Scheme*, a programme for rural development, and by the *The King's Fund*.

There is now widespread consensus amongst public, private and voluntary associations as well as NGOs, at regional, national and European level, that food production, supply, processing and preparation should and can be done in a more sustainable way. Food produced under more sustainable conditions will result in better quality for the consumer, will bring more profit for the grower and retailer and would cost less for the governmental institutions and be thus more beneficial for the taxpayer. It will also be beneficial for the environment and reduce the risk of environment related illnesses, such as allergies and probably Alzheimer's.

Strategy for sustainable food production. In the UK, the government has agreed upon a strategy for sustainable food production and sustainable food, following the recommendations of the *Curry Report*[104]. The aim is to create a sustainable future for farmers *and* the food industry by the introduction of a number of improvements:
1. The economy – the support of efficient producers, strengthening of income and reduction of taxes.
2. The environment – conservation and management of natural resources, maintenance of biodiversity and protective measures for climate conservation.
3. The community – improvement of public and animal health and strengthening of rural communities.

The Food Initiative (*The Government's Public Sector Food Procurement Initiative*, PSFPI)[19], wants to implement this strategy by:
1. Increasing and improving the production and processing standards.
2. Promoting the inclusion of local medium and small-scale enterprises.
3. Increasing the consumption of healthy and nutritious food.
4. Reducing the environmental impact of food production, at farm level as well as in the processing and supply phases.
5. Strengthening of the capacities of small regional suppliers to meet demand.

Results:

By changing their food procurement policy, NHS succeeded to reduce the region of origin of their food supply from 'the entire world' to the South of England.

---

[104] 2002, Great Britain; Farming & Food, Report of the Policy Commission on the Future of Farming and Food

12. Greening the Desert

Greening the Desert is about the restoration of agro-eco systems on a regional scale. In this chapter we see five examples where impoverished and severely degraded soils have been restored for food production in regions where hunger and poverty are widespread.

They are:

12.1 Restoration of mangrove agro-ecosystem in Eritrea

12.2 Permaculture in Jordan and Ethiopia

12.3 Territorial regeneration in the Sahel

12.4 The Sekem project in Egypt

12.5 The Loess Plateau in China

12.1 Restoration of mangrove agro-ecosystem in Eritrea

Along the almost empty desert coast of the Red Sea, a miracle has happened. Green mangrove forests, almost resembling a jungle, stretch over a length of seven kilometres with a width of around a hundred metres. It is a well-functioning ecosystem and serves as a nursery for fish, crabs and oysters.

The innovation. Some fifteen years ago this beautiful green mangrove forest was re-established on the coast of Zula Bay, once the centre of the lost Punt civilization. An exceptional feat, as this was done in the middle of thousands of hectares of desert. Now it is an estuary that provides food for men (fish and shrimps) and animals. Mangrove leaves and seeds are providing an almost complete diet for goats, sheep and camels, which in their turn supply meat and milk to the local people. Together with fish, this has been their sustenance of life for ages.

A coherent system has been restored in one of the hottest and least inhabited areas on earth, where temperatures can reach over forty degrees Celsius, while annual rainfall is less than twenty millimetres. For comparison, the average annual rainfall in Spain varies between 160 millimetres in the North West to 50 millimetres in Barcelona and 40 millimetres in Madrid. The annual rainfall in the Netherlands varies between 740 and 830 millimetres.

What made this transition possible? An American of Japanese origin, Dr. Gordon Sato, used his private means to transform these sandy beaches. Since the main problem there was a lack of water, he added nutrients like iron, nitrogen and phosphate to the locally available seawater to create suitable conditions for plant growth. The nutrients were buried in plastic bags at a depth of sixty centimetres and punctured with two little holes, through which the nutrients were released in low doses. His idea is that one could pump seawater into the desert to grow halophytic salt-loving crops like samphire[105] and thus contribute to a greening of the desert.

A new agri-culture for the world's coastal zones! In cooperation with a team of the Eritrean Ministry of Fisheries they discovered that mangroves could also grow in areas where they were not present before. This creates possibilities to grow food in areas where this was not possible before. Mangrove forests, which used to be considered as a source of pests

---

[105] Samphire: Salicornia europaea. Also known as glasswort, sea asparagus and sea pickle, Marsh Samphire traditionally grows along the coast. Once described as poor man's Asparagus, this is now fast becoming a trendy garnish in many gourmet restaurants. That said, this is a fantastic vegetable in its own right or can be made into a wonderful pickled vegetable. Once only available in season from market stalls, it is now widely available on fish counters in the U.K. and the Netherlands.

and disease, are now a key element in the greening of the desert, the prevention of coastal erosion and the increase of the fish population. Therefore, Sato is convinced that this simple approach can also be used elsewhere to counter the worldwide impact of deforestation and produce food in areas like Somalia, Djibouti, Mexico and Peru. Africa's coastline used to be covered with mangroves, which can be easily restored. In Bangladesh restoration is taking place on a large scale.

A new agricultural culture! An interesting aspect of this project is the socio-cultural development. Cooperation, learning together and the re-development of the area caused people to interact amongst themselves and with the land in a new way. They regained their confidence and self-esteem as they had an important role in the renewal and management of their natural resources.

Success factors:

- ✓ Dr. Sato's personal motives, his vision, enthusiasm and perseverance.
- ✓ Investments, the use of private means and environmental awards from the Rolex and the Ashi foundations.
- ✓ Practical innovations, like the use of mangrove seeds and leaves as feed for sheep and goats.
- ✓ Cooperation with the Eritrean Ministry.

What were the pitfalls and impediments and how were these overcome?

- Disbelief - both the established order and science did not believe this could be a solution, so they did not want to cooperate.
- Sato named the project Manzanar, the concentration camp where he and his family were held during World War II, which did not help to generate funds in the US, or the support of American aid organisations.
- By his perseverance and the commitment to invest his private fortune, Sato was able to prove that it was really possible to re-establish a healthy ecosystem.

12.2 Greening the desert with permaculture in Jordan and Ethiopia

In Jordan a complex system was re-established through permaculture and the rehabilitation of the water system.[106] Permaculture covers two concepts of Latin origin, *permanens* (permanent) and *cultura* (household). It may be a contraction of Permanent Agriculture or Permanent Culture. The concept was developed in the seventies at the University of Tasmania (Australia) by Bill Mollison and David Holmgren. They wanted a solution for the large amount of problems occurring from industrial monoculture agriculture. In Australia these were large-scale desertification and soil erosion, groundwater pollution as a result of excess use of fertilizer and pesticides, and the high incidence of diseases in monoculture products.

Mankind can turn the desert green again, it is possible! There is no more topsoil, no shade, the sun is burning and temperatures reach fifty degrees Celsius. This country is completely dependent on external supply of goods and services on which you have no impact at all. This area used to be *The Fertile Crescent*. The present desert is the result of thousands of years of abuse of the ecological services[107] once rendered by the area. The ecosystem was over-exploited, and we can still see this happening elsewhere. This project shows that we can change the situation, even when it is very serious.

Ho.w was the transition made?
- Mulching: all erosion gullies and small riverbeds were filled up and covered with organic material, dead branches, straw and leaves.
- By digging ditches, filling them with organic material, so reducing evaporation.(here four times higher than rainfall), and so saving water.

Inversion of desertification → greening! As a result of the mulching, plants started to grow again on the covered areas. These plants adsorb water to their roots and prevent seepage after a rain shower. The deeper the roots went down, the more water was retained. After some time the green area in the erosion gullies and riverbeds spread out over the adjacent fields. As a result of the increased vegetation, rain will fall more frequently in the area.

---

[106] On the website you can watch a video by Geoff Lawton on this process.http://www.nakedcapitalism.com/2012/05/greening-the-desert.html

[107] Ecosystem services is the description of the 'services' that natural resources render to a population, next to making agriculture possible. The term ecosystem services could only develop after the uncoupling (around 1960) of 'industrial agriculture' (as a non-natural mechanism) on one side and nature, landscape, environment and biodiversity on the other side.

After six years a number of species is doing quite well. The soil is 'growing', meaning that the water-retaining layer, which contains the organic matter, is growing as a result of the water-conserving impact of the ditches.

Using the same approach In Algeria, from 2005 till 2008, the groundwater level went up from sixty metres depth until two metres and rainfall increased, in an area with a diameter of five hundred kilometres.

Success factors

- ✓ As a result of the cooperative action, people started to feel responsible for their area again and became proud of themselves and their area.
- ✓ There are more successful examples in Eritrea and Namibia, which help convince others of the reliability of this approach. They will be used in future for educational projects and excursions.
- ✓ Vision, initiative, personal confidence and perseverance of the people to make a change.

Pitfalls and impediments and how these were overcome

- The project ran into conventional ideas, like the necessity of *sweet* water for plant growth. It is true that in the beginning only halophytic plants would grow. Salinity *is* a big problem in many areas in the world, e.g. the West Australian Wheat Belt and Uzbekistan. But halophytic plants and crops can be grown; they will attract rainwater in the end as well. Groundwater depth only needs to be at a few feet in order to keep a permaculture system alive.
- The habit of burning organic materials (also for cooking when there is a lack of wood) instead of using it for mulching. Burning organic material is a common thing in many countries and hard to un-learn. That is why it is also important to introduce solar energy and solar cooking methods to those areas.
- This *Greening the Desert* approach is not yet accepted worldwide. Probably because of the 'not invented here' syndrome; it is not yet scientifically proven and not promoted by well-known agricultural institutions.
- Especially government and development banks, consider such low profile NGO approaches as too small-scale, not relevant and not suitable for larger projects. Politically it may be less interesting as a government cannot 'score' with big investments or high economic results. The very positive ecological, social and health results are usually not counted.
- Since over the past six years the *Greening the Desert* project has hardly received any outside financial support, little attention has been paid to the results. 'Official' projects get a lot of attention

as they are obliged to make annual reports and organise a final conference showing the results.

12.3 Territorial regeneration in Niger

One of the most successful projects in the world for regeneration of a whole district is the *Farmer Managed Natural Regeneration* (FMNR) project, which started in the 1980s. Three million hectares of seared Sahelian land turned green again, biodiversity of flora and fauna returned, humus in the soil increased as did water retention capacity, and the microclimate improved. As a result, health and resilience of the local population also improved. This method is now also applied in Chad, Burkina Faso, Ethiopia and Mali. It has also received a lot of publicity e.g. in *The New York Times.*

Fig. 26. Wood for cooking is often hauled from kilometres far away, on foot.

How was the transition done? [20]

Fifty years ago the trees and shrubs in the agricultural areas in Niger were almost completely destroyed, with disastrous results. As a result of the lack of vegetation, the impact of the regularly returning droughts, the wind and the high temperatures increased. The soil lost its fertility and pests broke out in cattle and crops. In combination with rapid population growth and poverty, hunger and famine became chronic. In 1981 the entire country was completely degraded, almost a desert. The population experienced severe stress and suffered a lot from disease. Wood for the kitchen (a responsibility of the women and girls) and for construction had to be transported over ever-increasing distances. As dung was used for cooking and construction as well, minerals were not returned to the soil. Without the protection of the trees and without water, the crops did not want to grow and were suffering from pests. Birds, reptiles and other insects, which would normally carry out pest control, had disappeared with the trees. Conventional approaches for reforestation had all failed.

The FMNR approach solved the problems, like migration and hunger, by reinforcing one element of the agro-ecosystem, which restored the coherence; not water this time, but the still existing underground forest root-system. People were instructed to select the stumps of felled trees and make a deliberate decision - which shoots to cut and which to leave - instead of robbing the natural resources they had at hand. The 'permanent' shoots developed into trunks and resumed their protective function, while supplying leaves (fodder) and organic matter for humus production and creating a habitat for pest-predators.[108] If a large trunk was harvested, it was obligatory to select a small shoot to let it develop into a trunk again.

Impacts. The crops benefited directly as the microclimate improved. There was more organic matter, less wind, lower temperatures, higher humidity and higher rainwater infiltration. Because of that, cattle remained in the shade of the trees for a longer period and left more manure. The environment got a boost from the increased biodiversity, because natural cycles resumed their function. The availability of leaves and nuts to feed the cattle increased. Food production increased by 100%, soil fertility increased and enough fuel wood was available. For over 30 years now, this region has been in use according to these principles and continues to function well. Previous stresses in men, animals and soil disappeared. Even the stress between agriculturalists and pastoralists has been reduced. As the yields have increased there is a tendency to leave more organic matter in the field, which is grazed by cattle in the dry season. The cattle droppings increase the soil fertility and another cycle has been restored.

Success factors

- ✓ The idea and the conviction of the team leader/initiator that the forest system still existed on a subterranean level, and his perseverance not to give up despite many impediments.
- ✓ The opportunity to use the *Food for Work* programme in Maradi. This helped to convince the inhabitants of 95 villages to test the method.
- ✓ Seeing is believing - many people were surprised that the crops grew better under the trees. They all benefited from the extra wood for their household and were able to sell off the surplus. When the advantages of the FMNR became clear, the farmers themselves became the strongest promoters. By word of mouth, the project turned into accepted practice.

---

[108] Pest predators are smaller or bigger animals and insects that eat the pest-causing bacteries, fungi and animals on the plants and in the soil.

- ✓ The project staff in the villages supported the farmers and gained their trust, even when wood was stolen and quarrels had to be solved. This was very important at the beginning of the project when there was still a lot of resistance against the FMNR.
- ✓ When the project started doing well, model farmers were nominated for regional and national awards, which gained status for the project.
- ✓ Active lobbying by USAID to change the law, so farmers could become the owners of the trees. This was only realised in 2004.
- ✓ Consensus and support from the village and district heads to protect private property.
- ✓ Farmers' motivation grew when they saw that trees were no obnoxious weeds, but a cash crop.
- ✓ Farmers discovered that they themselves could manage their natural resources, not depending on foreign aid any more. No need any more to buy expensive inputs like fertilizer and seeds.
- ✓ The simplicity and accessibility for even the poorest farmer.

Pitfalls and impediments and how they were solved

- The population in Niger normally consider the trees as competitors for their crops.
- The absence of traditional communal property rights, like 'the Commons' in UK.
- Inconvenient rules and regulations. The national forestry law of Niger in those days expropriated the trees and thus took away the responsibility (and care) for the trees.
- Acceptance at the start was slow; the few farmers who cooperated were laughed at, as is usually the case with pioneers. In addition their young shoots were stolen, as wood was scarce.
- The fact that trees had no other value than utility wood. The word for tree in Hausa is the same as 'fuelwood'" in the same way as small animals are called 'small meat'.
- The lack of appreciation for NGO solutions. The fact that this project is successful in one of the poorest countries in the world and requires little financial support should make it a model project for other Sahelian countries. But as long as the UN or FAO do not promote this approach, and no major donors are involved, governments are hesitant or not interested to follow up.

12.4 The Sekem project

SEKEM was founded in 1977 by Dr. Abouleish in the North Eastern desert of Egypt. His idea was to combine the production of healthy food with rural and community development. Dr. Abouleish wanted to realise this through a three-way approach, by contributing to:

1. The development of the community;
2. Human dignity;
3. The healing of the earth.

This is the basis for this inspiring project that has developed into a holding with various branches. Dr Abouleish found his inspiration for education and development, craftsmanship, creativity and economic development in Islam. It all started with the development of seventy hectares of desert by the use of organic practices.[109]

After thirty-five years the main goals are still:

-   To heal the soil and the landscape by the use of organic practices. This will improve the agro-biodiversity without excessive waste. All products can be re-cycled or re-used, thus contributing to a sustainable process.
-   Production is demand driven instead of supply driven.

The transition: a change from desert project to business. In 35 years SEKEM has developed into an impressive business with a religious background, which could serve as a role model for other (Islamic) countries. In 2012 SEKEM consists of 3 main departments:

1. The SEKEM Holding, consisting of 6 companies, each responsible for the realisation of one of SEKEM's value-based business plan. They are:

    ATOS - production/ marketing of phyto-pharmaceuticals and health products;
    LIBRA – farmers' cooperation for organic fresh fruits, vegetables, spices;
    HATOR - packaging the fresh LIBRA products; CONYTEX - production of organic textiles for the local market; ISIS - production of fresh organic food; and
    LOTUS - processing organic herbs and spices from biodynamically grown plants.

---

[109] Bio-dynamic agriculture is based an anthroposophic philosophy, developed by Rudolf Steiner(1920), in which the agricultural enterprise is considered as an organic entity. A bio-dynamic farm focuses on soil fertility and the strengthening of natural growth, takes cosmic influence into consideration and aims for diversification of crops and cattle.

2. The Society for Cultural Development (SCD), supporting an integrated development of Egyptian society. The Society consists of a hospital, a special teaching programme for disadvantaged children and an academy for vocational education to develop and extend knowledge on medicines, herbs, biodynamic agriculture, art and social development in Egypt.
3. The Cooperation of Employees (CSE), responsible for Human Resources Development.

What has this project achieved?

✓ The realisation of a local and international cooperative network. A strategic step to extend the application of organic practices in Egypt; SEKEM contributed knowledge to the Egyptian Biodynamic Association (EBDA), founded as an NGO in 1990, to carry out research and development in bio-dynamic agriculture and train farmers in the use of BD practices.

✓ SEKEM supported the foundation of the Centre for Organic Agriculture in Egypt (COAE), responsible for the regulation and certification in line with the directives of DEMETER and the European regulations for organic agriculture.

✓ These two organisations promoted *chemical-free agriculture* in a large number of Egyptian villages.

✓ In cooperation with the Ministry of Agriculture, SEKEM has developed a new approach for the protection of cotton, which reduces the use of chemicals to less than ten per cent of the original volume.

Success factors

✓ The vision of Dr. Abouleish, his strong belief in himself, his 'just get started' approach and his perseverance.

✓ The son of Dr. Abouleish, Helmy Abouleish, who follows in his father's footsteps and continues the development of the project with the same energy. He is now the managing director.

✓ Four years after the start of the biodynamic agricultural activities, SEKEM could export its first shipment of medical herbs and food to the USA. This made the project convincing and economically feasible.

✓ In the world economy one has to be competitive, but in the long run it is people and individual capacities that count. For this reason training of the employees was concentrated on social awareness, personal and emotional development. Encouragement of creative skills, social responsibility and the realisation of an ethical approach were important elements in the development of the holding into its present day shape.

- ✓ By cooperating with sister organisations in Germany and the Netherlands, SEKEM could get support from the *European Commission*, the *Ford Foundation, USAID* and the *Acumen Fund*.
- ✓ Work on publicity to create visibility and thus generate recognition. In 1997 SEKEM obtained the ISO 9001 certificate and was selected as a *World Wide Project* at the *Hanover EXPO 2000*. In 2004 SEKEM was nominated as the outstanding social enterprise of the year by the *Schwab Foundation*. Subsequently SEKEM was the first economic enterprise to win the alternative Nobel Price, also known as the *Right Livelihood Award*.

Pitfalls and impediments and how they were overcome.

- At the start it was very difficult to convince others of the advantages, the realistic approach and the consistency of the project.
- The idea of environmental management and custody of the earth and the environment was not widely accepted.
- Government officials were not familiar with organic agriculture and were suspicious.
- There was no skilled labour for organic agriculture. So all training had to be conducted right from the start, which led Dr. Abouleish to start the desert project as a multifunctional development project with a 'learning by doing' approach.

Sekem's Vision on Agriculture, 2011.[110] SEKEM is convinced that only sustainable methods[21] such as organic, biodynamic and agro-ecology will be able to supply sufficient food in the next fifty years.

To realize our Vision for Sustainable Development in Egypt...

- We establish biodynamic agriculture as the competitive solution for the environmental, social and food security challenges of the 21st century.
- We support individual development through holistic education and medical care.
- We create workplaces reflecting human dignity and supporting employee development.
- We build successful business models in accordance with ecological and ethical principles.
- We innovate for sustainable development through research in natural and social sciences.
- We locally and globally advocate for a holistic approach to sustainable development.

---

[110] Vision on agriculture is downloadable on www.sekem.com

Today's prevailing agricultural paradigms need to be transformed. In the developed world, industrial agriculture achieved high productivity levels, primarily through the extensive use of chemical fertilizers, pesticides and herbicides, of water and of transportation fuels. Traditional agriculture, mostly in developing countries, often results in deforestation and the excessive extraction of soil nutrients.

The only solution is agroecology. Sustainable modes of agricultural production represent the only solution that can provide sufficient quantities of affordable and nutritious food for our growing global population. In these times of change, as we have recently experienced in Egypt, the window is open for renewed and intensified efforts to promote sustainable solutions to the great challenges that we face.

SEKEM's vision on food security[111]

In 2050, mankind will have to produce enough food for nine billion people. The availability of, the access to, and the affordability of sufficient nutrients are the defining criteria of food security that have to be taken into consideration when choosing the farming system of tomorrow:

Availability: Contradicting the long-established belief that external inputs such as chemical fertilizers are necessary in order to substantially increase food production, an increasing number of scientists, policy panels, and experts, such as Olivier de Schutter, the United Nations' Special Rapporteur on the Right to Food, are now claiming that resource-conserving, low external input techniques have a proven potential to significantly improve yields. In traditional farming systems in developing countries, and in regions where soils are degraded, yields can be increased up to 200%.

Access and affordability: The rural areas where the greatest yield increases could be achieved through eco-intensification methods, such as agro-forestry, are often the same regions where poverty and hunger are widespread. Increased yields would therefore directly tackle access to food, and nourish the farming population. As sustainable farming systems are more labour intensive, a substantial number of jobs would be created which, in turn, would enable many more people to buy foodstuffs for their families.

---

[111] Find the complete text in *"Farming for the future" (Helmy Abouleish)*; article in the UNIDO magazine "Making It – Industry for Development", 2nd quarter 2011 [link leads to PDF]

12.5 The Loess Plateau in China

The Huang Tu plateau, better known as *The Loess Plateau*, is a huge elevated area of about 640.000 kms2 (about 5 times the size of England), in the headwaters of the Yellow River in China. Loess is a type of soil, built up from very fine particles, that is very fertile but also quite susceptible to wind and water erosion. To get an idea of the enormous surface of the Loessplateau, please look at the picture below.

Fig. 27.
The Loess Plateau

The plateau used to be very fertile and was the cradle of Chinese civilisation. Centuries of deforestation and overgrazing have resulted in almost dead ecosystems, desertification and a poor population.

In 1994 the World Bank started the *Loess Plateau Watershed Rehabilitation Project*, to prevent further desertification and regain some of the land for agriculture. This project covers with 16,000 km2 about one fortieth of the plateau. That area is now (20 years later) green again, covered with forests and sustainable agriculture.

The transition. The focus of the project was the introduction of integral (holistic if you wish) approaches in agriculture and horticulture, with the aim of increasing food production, food security and higher incomes in at least part of the plateau. Therefore, on the erosion-prone slopes, agriculture was forbidden. Erosion control measures were put in place, next to land and water conservation measures. The slopes were re-planted with trees, shrubs and grasses, first of all for the stabilisation of the soil, but also to provide fodder, fuel and building wood.

One important demand of the Chinese government was that *less* loess would flow into the Yellow River. Loess is a big problem as it congests the dams, which pushes up the water level on the upper side of the dams and so causes flooding. To take the loess away from behind the dams costs a lot of money. The total costs of this loess project were US$252 million for the first phase and US$103 million, for the second.

The outcome of this project. At least 2.5 million people from the 4 poorest provinces – Shanyi, Shaanxi, Gansu and the autonomous region of Inner Mongolia – have come out of poverty. Their land has become fertile again; there is sustainable production of crops and food security has improved tremendously. During the second phase of the project, the harvest of grain increased from 365 kilo per head to 591 kilo per head. Meanwhile this approach has been copied in other areas. In 2013 it was estimated that about 20 million people in China have profited from this approach.

Lessons for the future. This project – like the ones we saw in the chapters before - proves that is is possible to turn deserts into green and fertile areas again, with food security for the population. We should copy this approach in many other places.

- However, the re-structuring and management of watershed areas is not possible without a well-integrated package of social and technical measures that generate income for the local population. In this project the package existed of re-afforestation, erosion control measures like terracing, and the introduction of sustainable grazing methods.
- Ownership of the problem (and thus the responsibility) was divided over different levels. Ownership was both with the farmers (for their own future) and the local government (for the area under their jurisdiction), as well as the national government (for the dams and because of the problem of an increasingly poor and hungry population). The villages developed their own plans and the inhabitants made the terasses by hand.
- The support by the government was indispensable. They organised highly qualified technical, financial and management personnel to support the project. Of course, since this project made a huge contribution to solving the problems in the Yellow River Basin, the government was very positive towards its progress.
- Good project management was important. The recruitment of locally available employees, their capacities and the quality of work all helped to make the project successful. A transparent and robust monitoring system is absolutely necessary.
- You must always start with a pilot project. Learn form the mistakes made and the successes and then roll out for a bigger area.
- The continuous presence of a consistent team, which was accepted and appreciated by local and regional governments, was a prerequisite for success.

13. Sustainable Chain Management

'Sustainable Chain Management' and 'Value Chain Development' are the latest trends in development cooperation. A value chain is the chain of activities from first inputs (seed and resources), by a farmer, a firm or a set of stakeholders, to the delivery of a valuable product (food and fodder) for the market.

The concept comes from business management and was first described and popularized by Michael Porter in his 1985 best seller, *Competitive Advantage: Creating and Sustaining Superior Performance.*

The idea of the value chain is based on the process view of organisations, the idea of seeing a manufacturing (or service) organisation as a system, made up of subsystems each with inputs, transformation processes and outputs. Inputs, transformation processes, and outputs involve the acquisition and consumption of resources - money, labour, materials, equipment, buildings, land, administration and management.

How value chain activities are carried out determines quality and costs, and affects profits. The idea is that every step in the production chain should be sustainable, preferably including the last link in the chain (consumption) and the first (the use of natural resources as land, water, soil and energy). And if it is difficult to make them ecologically *and* socially *and* economically sustainable, than they should at least be socially accounted for.

Sustainable chain management and Value Chain development could be considered as a follow-up on the calculation of the *Ecological Footprint*. Because, once you know what the (negative) impact is of a particular step in the production process, you can aim at rendering each step sustainable, so that the whole chain becomes sustainable.

Via the value chain you can even promote a *positive* ecological footprint! In such a case, the production of goods in 'the South' for 'the North' will contribute to the improvement of the local environment, water and soil, quality of life and food security in 'the South'.

In this chapter we will see some interesting examples of attempts to make the chain more sustainable. We visit a food processing chain in Sri Lanka, a dairy chain in the Netherlands and the worldwide flower production and consumer chain. The latter received quite some attention in 2012 from HIVOS, a Dutch NGO in Amsterdam, about the social and ecological costs of the production of roses for Valentine's Day.

13.1 A sustainable chain consists of sustainable links

This example[112] is based on a sustainable production and consumption project in Sri Lanka. The aim is that the local food processing industry will take up a more sustainable way of working, in particular to reduce the environmental impact of the local medium and small-scale enterprises. This link in the chain is preceded by the agricultural production link and the transport-to-the-food-processing-industry link. The project deals with the production of bread, dried coconut, tea, dairy products, poultry, fruit and fruit juices and food products, such as jam.

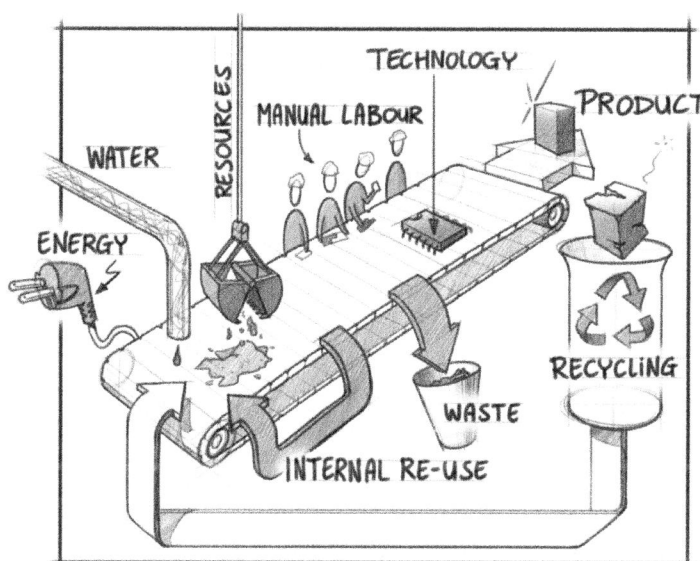

Fig.28. A sustainable production chain

How was the transition established? How does one assess a production cycle if you want to make it sustainable? Inputs and outputs as seeds and planting material, use of water and energy, social conditions (as labour situation and labour availability) and environmental impacts are all evaluated on how they can be put to work in a cleaner and more sustainable way. This so-called eco-efficiency approach always starts by looking at, and solving, the sources of pollution in each step of the chain. Then, if you are able to increase the sustainability of certain elements of the production process, this may affect the product, its presentation or its packaging. So one has to investigate how the product (*the output*) may be adapted without having a negative impact on its quality.

You also have to assess whether the *input* can be improved. In Sri Lanka it was found that it was better to use a fuel that was 50% more expensive,

---

112   Based on an interview with Ckees van Oijen, IVAM UvA BV, Amsterdam.

as it improved the quality of the product so it could be sold for double the price. It also makes sense to investigate how you can use local products.

The enterprise benefits and the region profits as well. It makes sense to assess local products found in your region. This will reduce the cost per production input and thus reduce the overall costs. This will also reduce waste production, as waste can be recycled in the production process of your company, or by companies in the region. The environment is less heavily taxed, or, less environmental levies have to be paid. However, there are opportunities and limitations, for instance in the supply of basic inputs. Of course you can formulate your requirements at this step or start a discussion with the people at the source. Creation of a sustainable chain is only possible if all personnel are involved and all suppliers cooperate. This requires a lot of motivation and it is necessary to provide the driving force for this. Supporting policies will help a lot!

Participative approach. The best way to create a sustainable chain is to cooperate with all stakeholders, in an interdisciplinary fashion, and to discuss all potential solutions. It usually turns out that improvements have been identified a long time ago, but nobody ever asked for solutions. On average some twenty to twenty-five solutions are identified. They differ:
- The cheap solutions have already been applied.
- The larger technological changes have been identified but require investments for which generally no funds are available.
- Often solutions are available to reduce inputs or substitute them with more sustainable inputs.
- Good housekeeping, or the more economical use of inputs, often results in the reduction of emissions.

Guarantee continuity. There are a number of support measures to help ensure that a chain will continue to work in a sustainable way. They are:
- Demonstrate how the investments are linked to the economic results.
- Create change by introducing observation studies or internships for students.
- Foundation of 'green business clubs' or organisations in the region.
- Formation of study groups for the various steps in the chain, where information and knowledge can be exchanged to improve implementation.

Pitfalls and impediments and how were they solved?
- If people are deprived of their right to be heard, their self-esteem or economic opportunities, this will cause confrontation and obstruction at a later stage. So it is important to use a multi

stakeholder approach right from the start. And listen to what craftsmen have to say!
- If people cannot imagine a different reference framework, they often do not understand the advantages of change. To force them to accept change does not help. The best thing is to create conditions where doing it the right way is easier than doing it the wrong way. Ask them what the advantages are for them to do it right and then introduce these advantages at the workplace.

What support can the Government in Sri Lanka (and elsewhere) give?
- Link the issue of permits to environmental impact assessments.
- Reduce taxes for sustainable production chains.
- Make information on sustainable production available to enterprises and consumers.
- Set a good example by buying sustainable products and thus promote sustainable production.

Governments can promote sustainable production and consumption in three ways:
1. Stimulate enterprises to produce in a sustainable way by e.g. the creation of eco labels (which gives a lead in the market), sustainable procurement, creation of business clubs.
2. Give subsidies to promote local production of inputs. E.g. for inputs such as compost and rockdust (stone meal) which support the sustainable production processes, or for regionally produced fodder and animal feed to replace (soy) imports from elsewhere.
3. Entice consumers to buy sustainable products, by setting the example and create improved sales opportunities for sustainable enterprises.

Promising initiatives. From a consultation of policy makers and market parties, a number of promising initiatives have been identified:
- Make more subsidies and support available for organic and stonemeal manure, or transfer the subsidies for chemical fertilizer to subsidies for organic manure.
- Link the annual sustainability reporting (and the monitoring criteria) to licences.
- Formulation of a communal industrial code of conduct.
- Reform of taxes and levies to promote sustainable production.
- Introduce loans for entrepreneurs who want to make their enterprise more sustainable.
- Funding of research to create and develop sustainability.
- Introduction of environmental management accounting.
- Introduce a classification for environmental business certification.

Are we heading in the right direction? As there is little experience with the inclusion of partners in the sector to formulate and evaluate policies, there is still a long way to go. Local and international initiatives and trends can stimulate governments, enterprises and consumers to look for a direction towards sustainable development.

Pitfall! At the moment, the main problem with sustainable products of large international companies is that their corporate communication creates certain consumer expectations about their sustainability. An example is the palm oil used by Unilever for the production of margarine and other foodstuff. To ensure sufficient production of palm oil, plantations continue to be established at the expense of tropical rainforest. A round table, organised by the WWF, resulted in a covenant, signed by all participants, to produce sustainable palm oil. This sounds very responsible and Unilever gets credit for this. However, the sustainability criteria, which the producers have to meet, are very low and can be easily met. Some criteria have been left out, like landgrabbing issues. So without a major effort, thirty per cent of the palm oil production qualifies as sustainable. It is a start, but there is still a long way to go.

Cat and Mouse game. For years, environmental and fair trade organisations, NGOs and social organisations have been the watchdogs where sustainability is concerned. In 2012, however, this has deteriorated into a situation where they criticise the large industrial companies, who in their turn throw them out as being too ideological and not realistic. In the Netherlands and other European countries, NGOs are often subsidised to take on this 'thorn in the side' position. The big multinationals therefore do pay attention to and cooperate with these NGOs (Greenpeace, Oxfam and WWF e.g.) as they represent the public opinion, which should not be turned against them.

In countries outside of Europe, civil society organisations will often not receive subsidies (Iran, and the –Stan countries). They are less present and cannot realise much. Even an organisation like the WWF can be kicked out of the country for interference in internal affairs. Government policy in these countries often depends on administrative and political interests. As a result, in many countries, multinationals can often go ahead without receiving too much criticism.

How can we get out of this trap? The Internet, the new media and organisations like *Avaaz* (in the UK 38 *degrees*, at https://home.38degrees.org.uk/) that expose abuses, and put on exhibitions such as *Reset the Future*, are all new opportunities to inform people about the relations, opportunities and motions to realise change. This book also aims at raising awareness.

13.2 FoqusPlanet - a roadmap to sustainable production

This case is at *FrieslandCampina* (FC),[113] a big Netherlands-based international business in dairy products.

How did FC realise sustainable production? It is important to know that FC is a cooperative. That means that farmers are not only shareholders but also owners of the company. They choose representatives to form the board of directors. The main office thus has to implement what the farmers think is important.

In 2009, when the Friesland Foods and Campina cooperatives merged, Jan Willem, as strategic advisor, wanted to introduce sustainable production in the company, but was a bit ahead of time. In those days sustainability was *not done* and not business like; it was still too alternative for the company. With some like-minded colleagues however, support could be created for the introduction of a sustainability strategy, which was developed by committees and working groups. Within the cooperation, farmers were asked whether they were interested in participating in sustainable production. As 10% of the 14,400 farmers/members were in favour, the directors of the cooperative decided to follow up. Since 2012, the sustainability programme *Route 2020* is the basis of the Corporate Social Responsibility programme. This sounds very serious, but in fact deals with *creation of value*[114] for the farmer and for the cooperative, as well as for the society in which we are working.

How was this innovative programme realised? Through a multi-stakeholders approach! For a full year, workshops were organised with interested farmers. They were asked what they considered important factors in sustainable management. The result covered subjects such as economies on energy, outdoor grazing, animal health, milk quality and the health of the cow. Subsequently, 140 workshops were organised with 6,000 farmers on how to realise sustainability on these subjects. Based on the outcome of the workshops, fourteen approaches were identified. These were then tested in five groups, consisting of thirty farmers each. They met three times for a full day to discuss the experiences with these approaches and the outcome.

---

[113] An interview with Jan Willem Straatsma, 2013

[114] Creation of Value: the performance of actions that increase the worth of goods, services or even a business. Many business operators now focus on value creation, both in the context of creating better value for customers purchasing their products and services, as well as for shareholders in the business who want to see their stake appreciate in value. So there will be extra benefits: the value added to the intrinsic value (of the environment or the product, or the health of a person) is being expressed and given a new shape, usually making money in the process.

Roadmap. These preparatory activities have resulted in a *roadmap* FoqusPlanet. It presents the options to improve quality, food security and sustainability. Every farmer can make a choice for the options he wants to realise on his farm. Some are obligatory, such as the farm's animal health plan and the vaccination programme. 78% of the farmers think it is a sensible approach. Workshops are organised where farmers can learn from other farmers' experiences and exchange information. As an incentive, the farmers who get high quality milk by this approach are less controlled and get an extra cent per litre of milk. This is based on points that are awarded as bonuses for the extra efforts the farmer has to undertake when realising the roadmap: 6 points equal excellent, 4 is good and 2 equals acceptable.

Restoration of agro-ecosystems and humus content. When I asked Jan Willem whether the roadmap also envisages possibilities to restore agro-ecosystems and to concentrate on humus content of the soil, as is currently done by a number of pioneering organisations as NetwerkVLV, VVBM, *Duurzaam Boer Blijven* in the Netherlands and WERVEL in Belgium, I was informed that this is still in the pipeline. The problem is that solutions that are still in a pioneering phase are not readily accepted by conventional farmers and are not generally accepted within FC. However, if farmers have heard from colleagues that the approach is effective, more will follow. Discussions on how to stimulate and reward an increase in humus content have started in 2012. In 2013 a so-called '*agro-eco pointer*' has been introduced. This is a guide for farmers in dealing with nitrate, carbon dioxide, environmental monitoring. Developments in the right direction go fast!

I asked Jan how he realised the project, and what problems he encountered in this substantial transition?

- "In 2009, only two out of a hundred staff members of the cooperation office were involved with sustainability. First of all I had to ensure full cooperation of all parties involved.
- I told my story on sustainability to the Young Farmers' Council, 23 members in all, and explained why I think it is important. It appeared that three out of five were already working with more sustainable approaches, and that made the change acceptable to the directorate.
- While preparing the strategic vision for 2020, we put forward the question: How will consumers and NGOs think about dairy and dairy farming by that time? What do they expect from the products, from us, from the farmers, from the farming process? And will they have different conditions? What will their demand be? Another change will be that the milk quota, compulsory for the EU, will have been abandoned by that time. That will create lot of change for the farmers. What can we do to support change towards sustainable milk production?

- Outdoor grazing, or grass fed cows, is very important for the Dutch government as well as for the citizens. It is the perception of the landscape, the image of Holland and the idea that cows are happier outdoors that make outdoor grazing important. Farmers receive half a cent more per litre of outdoor milk, an investment of 45 million euros for the cooperation. The Ministry of Agriculture gives substantial financial support for research on the subject of sustainable dairy farming and food production. The foundation *Nature and Environment* and the *Society for the Protection of Animals* support the idea of more outdoor grazing, for different reasons, but that is important for our consumer support.
- To keep 'advanced' farmers involved, the *'agro-eco pointer'* was developed, which will give an additional point to successful farmers in the sustainability programme.
- The strategy is not to invest in the rearguard but to create incentives for the 'early adapters'.
- It required guts to present a clear and courageous long-term vision for large groups of conventional farmers and cooperation members. Not a blueprint but clear targets. Like in 2020 a 30% reduction in carbon dioxide emission, as compared to 2012, and a reduction of the use of antibiotics to the level of 1999. This is also required by the market. Unilever, Danone and Kraft, dairy purchasers, attach great value to sustainable production.
- Apart from having the right intentions, it also requires taking meaningful steps. How clear is the vision or the dream, how effective the interaction/dialogue? How much support is given?
- To be the leader in a change process is not an easy job. It requires the capacity to absorb fear, to give confirmation, to be a role model, to create safety, to guard reality and be consistent in behaviour."

13.3 Fair Flowers Fair Plants

This section is about the 'greening' of the production and consumption chain of cut flowers. This cut flower chain is relatively simple, less complex than a food chain and thus easier to grasp. It will help us understand the issues and discussions that are part of rendering a production chain sustainable.

Fair Flowers Fair Plants is an independent foundation, established in 1999 to work towards a globally accepted social and environmental norm[115] for flowers and plants. Meanwhile, FFFP has become an international quality mark for plants and flowers that measure up to the highest norms. The criteria for this certification lie in the areas of environment, working circumstances, hygiene and security.

The current cut flower industry is a worldwide, dynamic business, which has shown tremendous growth over the past twenty years, not only in volume, but also in economic importance. We are now talking about countries that only *produce* flowers like Kenya and Ethiopia, countries that only *consume* like Moldova and countries that do *both* like the Netherlands. The worldwide consumption of cut flowers is estimated at thirty billion euro a year. The Dutch flower trade holds 60% of the market.

Since the nineties, flower cultivation has changed from the Northern countries to locations with a better climate, where labour is cheaper and where environmental regulations are less strict or even non-existent. As a result, the new cut flower production centres are located in countries such as Kenya, Ethiopia, Sri Lanka, Costa Rica, Colombia and Ecuador.

Sustainable? The immediate question is of course whether it makes sense to grow flowers and potted plants in such far-off locations. Especially as, for transportation to the North, transportation costs will be high and a lot of carbon dioxide will be emitted, which is bad for the climate! Research has shown, however, that growing the same plants in glass houses in the North would require a lot more energy than under the current situation.

The unsustainable character of flower cultivation lies in the chemicals used (resulting in the pollution of surface water), the enormous amounts of water used (and that in dry areas where water for local agriculture and household use is scarce) and labour. This resulted in a lot of criticism throughout Europe on employment conditions and the substantial negative environmental impact.

---

[115] In 1999, the international federation of the wholesale flower trade, Union Fleurs, took the initiative for one global social and environmental norm. In 2001, the first negotiations for a consumer based hallmark took place.

Socially sustainable? In 2013, just before Valentine's day, the negative social aspects of the rose-growing industry were highlighted on televison in the Netherlands. For the timely delivery of the roses, women in Ethiopia and Kenya worked up to 16 hours a day, without babysitters, sometimes badly mutilated on hands and faces by the chemicals used. They tolerate regular sexual abuse in order to keep their jobs and the necessary income. Already a week after HIVOS started its campaign, *Power of the Fair Trade Flower*, important steps were taken on the road to sustainable flower production. On November 10, 2013, the Volkskrant reported that the cooperative for the flower production sector is developing a hallmark for Fair Trade flowers and that the PLUS supermarket chain will in future only sell roses with the Fair Trade hallmark. This is very good news for the women working in the flower industry in Africa. HIVOS supports these initiatives and will follow the development of an international hallmark for Fair Trade flowers attentively.

Environmentally sustainable? In Kenya, for instance, the lakeshore of lake Navaisha is almost entirely used for flower cultivation. Have a look on the Internet[116] and you will be astounded at the surface covered by the flower industry. Wildlife currently has almost no access to Lake Naivasha to drink. Substantial use of water from the lake and the pollution of the lake are very serious, as they affect the drinking water supply and the health of the local population.

Fig. 29. The water footprint[117] of one rose is about 10 litres of clean water

---

[116] http://makewealthhistory.org/2009/02/13/the-price-of-kenyan-roses-and-the-tragedy-of-lake-naivasha/

[117] See also waterfootprint in Figure 10, chapter 5.6

The water footprint. About 16 million m3 (about 14.2 billion gallons) of water per year is being pumped out of Lake Navaisha in Kenya for the flower industry alone. In comparison[118], that is about the quantity 10 to 11 million American households use annually, and almost 1.5 times the quantity used by the entire population of New York in 2014 (8 million).

If we look at the type of water used, then it appears that cut flowers use 22% of the available rainwater, 45% of the surface and groundwater and 33% *grey* water. The *grey* water footprint stands for the polluted waste water and the amount of clean water that is needed to cleanse it (Hoekstra and Champaign 2007/8). In lake Navaisha the surface of natural papyrus vegetation (a natutal cleansing agent and habitat for waterfowl) has decreased by 90% from 50 square km to 5 square km.[119]

Certification. To counter criticism, a lot of different 'standards' have been developed. They meet various combinations of sustainability criteria, both social and environmental. They have been formulated both by the producing countries as well as the growers. These standards show a wide differentiation in origin, contents, application and monitoring procedures. The aims, scope and area of application are quite diverse. There exist many business-to-business (B2B) standards, which will never be read by the consumer. There are also consumer-oriented labels such as *Max Havelaar/ Fair Trade, Fair Flowers Fair Plants* (FFP) and the *Flower Label Programme* (FLP).

Making the flower production-consumption chain more sustainable. It is not clear whether the consumer is interested at all in the origin of her bouquet, its environmental impact or the social conditions under which the flowers have been produced. And yet, change can only start with the consumer asking the florist or supermarket where the flowers come from, if they are certified and with what label, because entrepreneurs will not invest or take extra efforts unless the market demands it.

The world bouquet. If you buy a bouquet in a flower shop or petrol station, it generally consists of a combination of flowers. It is quite possible that each flower will come from a different country. Flowers from all over the world are brought to the auction house, where they will be mixed and exported again - a so-called *world bouquet*. Thus, the sustainability of a bouquet can only be measured by the combination of production (socially and environmentally fair), trade and transport from flowers from different countries and different growers. That is not easy at all! Let's look at the various aspects of sustainability.

---

[118]   Americans use large quantities of water inside their homes. The average family of four can use 400 gallons (1500 litres or 1.5 m3) of water every day. On average, approximately 70 percent of that water is used indoors.

[119]   Everard et al.

Economic sustainability. The responsibility for this aspect lies currently with the flower industry and NGOs (Oxfam Novib, WWF, Fair Trade etc). The countries where flowers are being produced are generally not yet involved. Local production conditions are usually taken into consideration, as is Fair Trade. Employment is considered a big plus.

But the more important sustainability questions are generally not addressed:

- Is it a positive development in a country like Ethiopia, with little water and little food supplies, to grow flowers and generate income instead of growing food?
- 50% of the investments of the Dutch flower growers in Ethiopia have been paid from the Dutch Development Aid budget. Is this the kind of assistance one should give to Ethiopia? It leads us to ask "Who has been 'aided' here?"
- How important is this contribution to the local economy and the development of the country? It is interesting to see that the contribution of the flower industry to the GNP of Kenya was more than the total of *all development assistance* that was given in that year. The question also is whether the GNP is a measure for development. More valuable criteria can be formulated, such as income for everyone, sufficient food for everybody, employment opportunities.

Social sustainability. Human rights and land use rights (i.e. to prevent landgrabbing) are generally not included in the quality standards; only the FFP label checks on this aspect of sustainability as part of their certification process. Fair Trade is currently organised as a separate market to ensure that profits will flow back to the producers. This is very good and has had a worldwide impact for coffee, bananas and chocolate.

The question now is how we can render existing markets and trade more sustainable and fair, in other words mainstreaming of the concept. Or would there be possibilities to merge conventional trade with Fair Trade? Dutch auction houses handle about 80-90% of the Dutch flower production and 60% of all imported flowers from everywhere in the world. Auction houses have the largest impact on world trade as they set the prices. Next to all conventional products three standards are mentioned on the auction clock: MPS-ABC, FFP and Florimark. At the moment, however, it is not required for flower growers to have been certified if they want to send flowers to the auction.

Nowadays (2013) at an auction, there are only three *visible* business-to-business standards: MPS-ABC, FFFP and Florimark, next to the day-to-day flowers without a mark. MPS-ABC works as a measuring rod. It shows with A,B and C the measure of *environmentally friendly* management. Florimark is a quality mark for Corporate Social Responsibility. They have a number of conditions concerning environment, social aspects, quality and tracking and tracing, developed by the MPS foundation for producers and traders in plants and flowers.

Ecological sustainability. The impact on the environment (water use and water footprint, pollution, application of chemicals and carbon dioxide emissions) is also not included in the certification. Only the FFP labelling has criteria for these aspects. Another aspect is the use of fossil fuels. It would seem that this whole system of worldwide production for mostly Western markets would be doomed if there were an oil shortage, as transport by air would become either too expensive or extinct. If flowers need to be transported by sea and road however, they can, amazingly, be brought into 'sleeping condition' like in a coma, from which they can be revived after the longer duration transport. So, what is the issue here? We would still need oil for the transport!

Transition is required: the road to really sustainable flower chains. During an international FFP conference in August 2010, the conclusion was that sufficient demand should exist if sufficient sustainable flowers and pot plants were to be produced. And today this demand does not (yet) exist, not with the consumers and not with the retailers, while at the same moment, the production cannot meet an eventual demand either, as it is still too low.

A big change, a transition of the system, should take place, but how to begin? A good solution would be if the Dutch auction houses would set an example by having the courage to *only* trade certified flowers and pot plants. This will force all producers to adopt sustainable systems, as they will otherwise not be able to sell their products. As there would be no exception to the rule, there would be no advantage in not accepting this change.

Mainstreaming of certified flowers. In December 2010, FFP organised a follow-up meeting with all captains of the flower industry, representatives of the auction houses, trade and labour organisations and the flower growers, from Kenya, Ethiopia, the Netherlands and Sweden. The discussion went as follows:

1. Do we want a sustainable flower and pot plant production and consumption chain? The answer was yes!
2. Is FFP a suitable method to carry out certification and auditing? The answer was yes!
3. Are the large companies prepared to pay 50% of the investments required to establish a worldwide certification system? The other 50% would be made available by the RABO Bank, NL. The answer was negative, as the Dutch were considered to be untrustworthy.

They have a too colonial mentality. *"They are good at doing business, but not at collaboration".*

The Floricultural Sustainable Initiative (FSI). Eventually in 2013, this neutral platform was established. A platform in which all stakeholders, even the NGOs, participate and have voting rights to agree on the strategies to be followed and the regulations to be applied. Some companies and trade organisations are hesitant concerning the participation of the NGOs in view of the impact they might have. A neutral party, *New Foresight*, has been employed to ensure mutual harmony.

The agenda of this platform should be:
1. The development of a sector-wide vision on sustainable flower production and trade, using a multi-stakeholder approach.
2. The establishment of pre-competitive standards as bases for labelling and certification.
3. A more in-depth certification system that sets criteria for water use and water footprint, pollution, application of chemicals and carbon dioxide emissions.
4. Inform consumers.
5. A concerted action to make sure that auction houses deal with certified plants and flowers only.

Which enabling context is necessary to make sure that the platform can have an impact? Sustainabilty in the chain can only be realised if power and leverage are shared. Are the big players (the Netherlands, Kenya and Colombia) prepared to reduce their control of the world market and use their power as a lever for sustainability? Who feels responsible for the process and its outcomes? Can this be made a communal item? Will the stakeholders in the platform have the courage to go for sustainability?

Impediments. What are the impediments, the threats and weaknesses in this process?
- The conventional flower trade considered FFP as a threat to their own label B2B. So instead of accelerating the process, FFP turned out to be an impediment for the development of sustainable production.
- The power and the colonial attitude of the Dutch in general and the Dutch flower trade in particular are a strong handicap in the process.
- Sustainability in the flower production and trade can only be accomplished when power and influence are shared. The question remains if the big players (Netherlands, Kenya and Colombia) are willing to use their influence and control upon the world market as a lever for a more sustainable production chain.

TRANSITIONING

14. Transition – How can we make it happen?

14.1 Lessons learned from the frontrunners

The frontrunners in chapters 8-13 in this book show us that transition becomes effective through many different factors, but mainly through personal leadership and individual action. Transition is personal. What lessons did we learn?

Pioneers. There is always one, or a few, pioneers who start something new. They have a dream, or an image of the *New Normal* and what it looks like. The examples in chapters 8 to 13 show us that such a person always combines a vison with a practical, hands on approach. These people persevere when there are setbacks. They are also naturals in getting people and organisations involved in their plans. Intuition and collaboration are prerequisites.

For what reason is transition being started? We learn from the 26 examples[120] that pioneers were disappointed or angry about the regular approaches in agriculture and food production, but always combined with a clear concept or dream for a solution. Often it was a shocking experience in their life or work that triggered the transition.

Market economies. The transition to another, more sustainable way of producing is often brought about by the demand in the market. International food suppliers demand from their contract farmers that they deliver products that are produced in a more sustainable/socially responsible way. Sometimes consumers choose 'en masse' a certain product, e.g. mothers now buy *only organic* baby food.

Personal leadership. People who start and manage the transition are powerful in that they organise an enabling environment in order to get the change done. It is not only about pursuing a personal dream; they must also listen to what others want and be open to opportunities when they present themselves (the emerging future).

Institutional support. Financial and social support systems are necessary conditions for success. Facilitation of the transition process, a sparring partner and a good plan are essential. Attention and promotion by others are also supportive. But this support only comes when:

1. Potential supporters see chances for success. They shouldn't be 'way-laid' by following their own agendas, which *prevent* change.
2. Pioneers can present their plans or ambitions in a convincing way, with a story, enthusiasm, arguments and a business plan.
3. There is room for budgetary or organisational experiment.

---

[120] See the 26 cases by frontrunners in chapters 8 to 13 in this book.

4. When the criteria for supporting 'change-projects' are open; that is, criteria should not be based on a predetermined concept of the shape of the change.

Room for experiment. We must allow ourselves to learn from mistakes, from our own experiences and the experiences of others. We need room for experiment, participative action research and learning networks. Experiments show us direct results. Principles such as 'seeing is believing' and 'good example attracts followers' do work.

14.2 The transition is already here!

So here we are, in the middle of a worldwide transition. Even if you hadn't noticed yet, a change towards different ways of living and producing has set in. This change may have been triggered by concern about deteriorating ecosystems, or imminent water shortages, or climate change or hunger. At the same time a change is going on globally in personal and organisational development, towards other worldviews and perceptions. We are also changing, worldwide, from conventional industrial agriculture to agro-ecology, restoration agriculture, permaculture, family farming, integrated regional development and local cooperation. During the World Cultural Forum conference in China,[121] it was stated "that we experience a *systems change*, from the economy, GNP and profit-dominated era, into a time of promoting Ecological Civilization Construction, based on equal exchanges".[22]

From a distance, and when we look back on history, a *transition* seems a continuous process, in which the character of a civilisation gradually undergoes a structural change. You could compare such a transition to a caterpillar changing into a chrysalis and a chrysalis changing into a butterfly. But if you find yourself in the middle of such a change, the transition appears to happen more jerkily, as a sudden manifest effect of a process that has been going on for a while. Such a process starts quite unnoticed, as members of a group, an organisation or population changing their minds, their focus and their decision-making. After a while, some sort of collective consciousness develops, which makes earlier conventional ideas and approaches obsolete. All of a sudden, in a group or at organisational level, people recognise in each other the new, changed approaches; the penny drops, collectively. That is *the Turning Point*. A paradigm shift has taken place, we now look different at things and processes; this expresses itself in our (new) ways of living and working. The new approach has become the mainstream, the *New Normal*.

---

[121] China, the World Cultural Forum, May 2013. Yu Zhengsheng: Strengthen International Cooperation for Ecological Civilization. http://www.thffc.com/tcf_en/nianhui-article.php?id=91

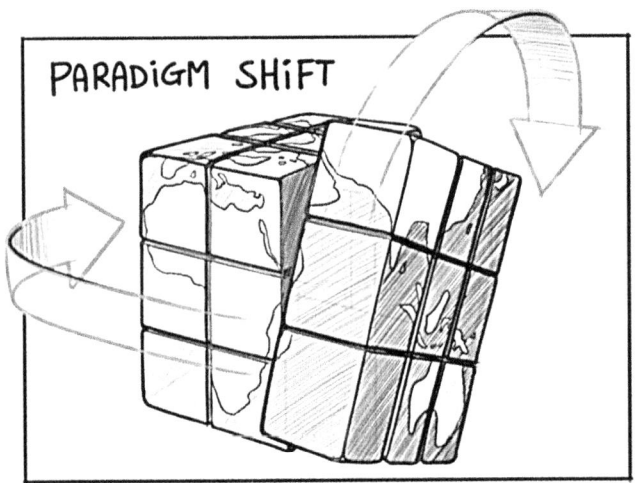

Fig. 30.
Paradigm shift

PARADiGM SHiFT

14.3 Time for the followers

In each process of change there are *frontrunners* (or *pioneers), quick adapters, followers* and *latecomers*[122]. The latter group doesn't like change or is scared of change; usually they stick to conventional views and ways of doing things. Often, in their anxiety, they plead for more control and enforcement measures, as those seem to offer a (fake) sense of security in times of insecurity.

Pioneers are usually eyed with suspicion. They are regarded as 'alternative' and 'naive'. Generally they are not taken seriously, like the environmentalists of the first hour. And that is only caused by them behaving differently, in new ways; they may put across 'out of the box' views and try out inventions that we don't know yet. Many pioneers' views and practices are not trusted, since we live in a western knowledge-system culture that only approves of something after it has scientifically been proven to be true. Many sensible practices[123] by farmers, based on experiential knowledge, are not accepted as long as scientific experts deny them.

Inventions by pioneers are picked up by so-called *early adapters* - the ones who see opportunity in such an invention and make it an innovation. They create an environment in which the idea can be put into use under real life conditions. Those *early adapters* still have problems getting subsidies

---

[122] Frontrunners, early adapters, followers and latecomers. The Innovation curve by Rogers.

[123] Like permaculture, soil health improvements with stone meal or copper wire, homeopathic treatment of animals, use of salt water, natural cycle management, etc.

or investments,[124] as the criteria for investments are often based on conventional agendas and views.

But we do see changes! Between 2013 and 2015 in Ethiopia, the Fund for Sustainable Rural Entrepreneurship (FSRE) invested in such innovations[125] in order to scale up innovative practices in agriculture. In 2014 and 2015 the fund Securing Water For Food (SWFF) invested in innovators to scale up.

Followers are the people who really want the change, but cannot, or dare not, make the first step. Followers need to let go of preconceptions and prejudices. They only *adopt* an innovation if the risks are clear and can be dealt with, when the necessary (social and financial) resources are in place; when it leads to more income; when it is socially acceptable; or when more people are doing it. For followers, the good examples in the neighbourhood are important. Therefore, it should be encouraged to nominate more demonstration farms and model farmers in every region.

The frontrunner examples in chapters 8 to 13 are all *pioneers* or *early adapters*. They should be convincing enough for large groups of potential *followers* to make the change to better soil management, agro-ecology, other certification systems, regional cooperation, etc.

How can we get potential followers to follow? *Pioneers* have attempted to push latecomers (governments) to make or support the change, but that doesn't work.
For the transition to the *New Normal* we very much need – and need to support – the *quick adapters* and the *followers*. By assuring an enabling environment, in which the risks are clear, the social and financial resources are put into place and the innovation is made socially acceptable. Throughout the period 2010- 2019 the *followers* are the ones that will make the good examples of the *pioneers* into successes.

14.4 Towards knowledge systems that support transition

To make the transition, we cannot wait any longer for the established science and technology. Because for the most part, they are employed by the incumbent powers that are tightly knit to industrial agriculture and monoculture production systems. There are three main obstacles that make it hard for scientists to really make the change:

---

[124] As we have seen in the example of sea weed production and regional food for hospital kitchens.
[125] http://www.agriprofocus.com/fsre-fund

1. The traditional belief that science should objectively state the truth, by means of technological and methodological analyses, to the smallest details of a system (thus not seeing the integrated whole). This is combined with a strong belief in technological progress and the economy (profit, production at marginal financial costs) as the steering wheel. For agri-*culture* as a coherent culture of soil management, food production, social life, personal development and health, that is an outdated approach.
2. The way in which scientific research is organised - with PhD's focussing on details of systems, competition for financing, the need to publish in high quality scientific journals that only allow disciplinary (and not holistic, integrated and interdisciplinary) studies – prevents self-reflection and interdisciplinary systems approaches. Thus it is difficult for a scientist to open up to new ways of looking at the world and to other scientific approaches.
3. The unilateral focus of *institutions* that finance scientific research (like ministries of agriculture, large funding agencies like banks, agribusiness and food production multinationals) prevents scientists from focusing on holistic systems and integrated approaches.

Agricultural Research for Development (ARD) requires new thinking if it is to be relevant in the rapidly changing global context. Because agriculture's role is undergoing rapid change. Agriculture is now seen as a key cause, and potential mitigator, of anthropogenic climate change; a producer not only of food, fibre and fuel, but also of vital ecosystem services (such as access to fresh water); and a key factor in poverty reduction and food security. Key recent international reports have not only called for renewed attention to agriculture, but have also emphasised that business as usual is not an option.[126]

Agriculture is multi-functional. Its function is not only to produce food, fibre and fuel, but also to deliver other ecological services, including water, climate change mitigation, and biodiversity, which are vital for regenerating the troposphere.

Smallholder farming. The underused potential of the millions of hectares of smallholder farming, with its productivity of typically one tonne per ha, holds the best promise for dealing with the current global food and sustainability crisis, and for addressing persistent rural poverty in Sub-Saharan Africa; African smallholders are dynamic and innovative and will eagerly exploit opportunities offered to them.

Institutional change. The development of smallholder farming requires both realistic and remunerative opportunities through institutional change, and

---

[126] IAASTD 2008; World Bank 2008; IPCC 2007; Millennium EA 2006; and IAC 2004.

raising yields through new technolog. Institutional and technical change can be addressed through an Innovation Systems (IS) approach, i.e. facilitating the concentrated action of relevant development actors, assembled around perceived opportunities for smallholder innovation.

Exploration and participative approaches. Development activities that are appropriate and effective in creating realistic opportunities for smallholders cannot be designed beforehand on the basis of expertise. CoS1 taught us that pre-analytic choices cause path-dependency before you know where you need to be going. We require an incremental process that features exploration of opportunities and constraints, participatory identification of 'impact points' and negotiated concertation among development actors.[127]

A new 'frame of mind' for science. It is therefore time that the 150 year old existing 'social contract' between society and western science (delivering 'objective' knowledge) changes to 'supporting socio-eco-technical development'. In the old contract it was about 'knowing better'. In the new contract it is about 'facilitating change', by offering knowledge exchange methods that are effective in the different contexts.

14.5 Science that supports transition

Such science is already available and can be profiled in various ways:

1. Offering insights and knowledge on the processes that are needed in **system innovation,** like multi stakeholder approaches and social learning. Emphasis lies on societal management of sustainable development. Such research needs to be done in collaboration with social partners, in open processes of innovation. It is the study of 'transition' and how it works as a means for sustainable development towards an ecological society. The institute DRIFT in the Netherlands is an example of such an approach. The purpose of CoS-SIS[128] is to carry out inter-disciplinary policy experiments with a view to elaborate, apply and assess an approach to sustainable rural poverty alleviation and food security, based on Innovation System (IS) thinking.

---

[127] Says Jim Woodhill: 'Dealing with the complex means investing in multiple 'experiments' and scaling up what works –an evolutionary design approach to development intervention'. At the start of CoS-SIS, the only thing we know is that we don't know.

[128] Convergence of Sciences, Strengthening Agricultural Innovation Systems. http://thepolicypractice.com/projects/mid-term-evaluation-convergence-of-sciences-strengthening-agricultural-innovation-systems-in-benin-ghana-and-mali-cossis/

2. **Process management** and **process facilitation for collective learning** is another field of study. In 2010, professor Jan Jonker took an out of the box initiative in this field.[129] He called it a *crowdsourcing* project. Everyone in the country was invited to take part in 30 thematic brainstorm groups to work on the *'Our Common Future'* Report 2.0. This resulted in something like a 'current', made up by maybe 1% of the population; it catalysed thinking and talking about the problems and the solutions in the networks of all participants. The soil campaigns of 2015 generated a similar joint focus and awareness within many different organisations. The effect is comparable to what Avaaz and other such Internet based communities do when they take responsibility for a certain issue or development and so institute a *stream of thought*. Such approaches have already become another new way of knowledge development, working towards the necessary transition.

3. Offering a **platform** for reflection and knowledge development on the interconnectivity between the different facets of sustainability, e.g. by generating knowledge and insight with the different stakeholders together, like businesses, government, social partners, NGO's and knowledge centres. The International Institute for Environment and Development (IIED, London) focuses[23] on exactly that. The same thing goes for the Institute for Advanced Sustainability Studies (IASS, Germany). AgriProFocus (NL) provides facilitation for platforms on topics in agriculture that are in transition (on a national scale) in ten developing countries. It is not only about generating knowledge, but also about applying it in policy agendas. New concepts can be tried out as an experiment, which are then closely monitored by scientists on their Strengths, Weaknesses, Opportunities and Threats. CoS-SIS[130] is making headway in unleashing very interesting dynamics. It seems that bringing together key actors on multi-stakeholder platforms, around some issue, sets in motion a trajectory of self-propelled development that does not need injections of non-replicable special resources. Such dynamics suggest the existence of mechanisms that have barely been recognised.

4. **Supporting governments in choosing the right policies and practices.** Between 2014 and 2019 IIED[131] supports governments and advocacy partners to put international agreements into practice at national and local levels, using practical evidence we've

---

[129] Jan Jonker, professor at Nijmegen University, NL. His books (in Dutch) are about strategic sustainable management: entice, connect and anchor!.

[130] Convergence of Sciences, Strengthening Agricultural Innovation Systems.

[131] International Institute for Environment and Development, London. http://www.iied.org/

collected together to inform and influence decision-making, linking local issues to global debates.

5. **Reflexive monitoring.** This means just monitoring without a predefined set of indicators to which they should adhere. Monitoring what frontrunners and quick adapters do. The focus should be on how their approaches work: personal ideas, inter-linkages, feedback mechanisms, inputs, outputs and impact. It is scientifically interesting to find out *why* such experiments work, *what mechanisms* make them work and what conditions are needed.

6. **Finding the steps** that make transition happen. It is, scientifically speaking, very interesting to find out how and why people and organisations make the change to agro-ecology, restoration farming, permaculture, supporting family farming or integrated farming in developing countries, including learning about successes and failures, as well as the factors that are stopping people from changing. Once we know this, institutional support can focus on strengthening the success factors, and remedying the fail factors by creating an enabling environment.

7. **(Participative) research** into how regulations and legislation and policy agendas can contribute to an overall change to agro-ecology and agro-forestry and integrated regional development. A good example is the CoP-SIS programme, Convergence of Sciences[132] - Strengthening Agricultural Innovation Systems; Promoting African Smallholder Agricultural production systems through Institutional Innovation.[24] "We concentrate on facilitating Innovation. We have identified the following major hurdles and challenges" (Hounkonnou et al, 2012):
   1. Institutional change is threatening interest and creating enemies due to conflicting interests of stakeholders.
   2. Who sustains local multi-stakeholder innovation systems, if research projects (or facilitation) end?
   3. Progress depends on whether decision makers believe in smallholders as a path to food security.

8. **Scientific support and development of endogenous knowledge systems.** The focus is on dis-covering (N.B. the original focus of science: un-covering hidden mechanisms!) local experiential knowledge and culture- or group related knowledge. Biodynamic farming, Vedic agriculture, permaculture and closed-loop farming can also be regarded as culture- related knowledge.

9. **Substantiate that agro-ecology works.** Agro-ecology comes in various shapes, depending on the physical and cultural properties of the region. Action research, supported by experiential learning

---

[132] Proceedings of the CoS-SIS International Workshop Elmina Ghana 2012

in existing farming practises, will support the expansion of such approaches. Landscapes for People, Food and Nature is actually doing that. http://landscapes.ecoagriculture.org/

10. Research into the approaches for, and effects and impact of, **shared and community learning** and participatory certification systems. In Ethiopia, ICCO has a special fund only for this purpose: the money is used solely for exchanges on experiential knowledge between innovative sustainable farmers. It is important to have the Lessons Learnt documented.

14.6 Obstacles for transition

Which obstacles and blockades do we meet when working on transition? When we look at societal change from a complex systems' view, taking into account the powers that play a role, the interconnections between people and organisations, the patterns that occur, then it is effective to know which *activities, interventions* and *contexts* oppose and block transition. Because, once you are aware of them, when you know the causes, then you can overcome them. Here are[133] a few blockades and counteractive mechanisms:

Wrong choices. Very often an important, powerful or influential player in the field (government, policymaker, lobby group, business) stimulates the wrong development. Not uncommonly as a result of personal interest or profit. A 'wrong' decision could also be an investment with the purpose of *getting a certain intended outcome*; we know that the uncontrollable dynamics of the reality of multi-stakeholder processes always lead to other than expected results.

The one-sided description or interpretation of a problem and also the narrowly focused beliefs in one-sided solutions, preventing 'out of the box' innovations. It would be much better to do some participative back casting exercises, to get a broad view of opportunities.

Negative and counteractive **personal qualities** of decision makers, such as a 'wait and see' attitude; indecisiveness; lack of trust; unwillingness; and ego-driven decision-making.

Lack of personal leadership. Personal leadership is required in all layers of an organisation, not only with the formal leaders or managing directors. People that have personal leadership will not bow to pressure, they will

---

[133] From the essay 'Klompen in the machinerie' (Sand in the machine; conscious and unconscious sabotage of the transition to sustainable energy) by Jan Paul van Soest, environmental expert, 2010. http://www.gemeynt.nl/en

listen to their own conscience and will choose what is good for the whole organisation, or country, or region.

The power of **a small but influential group.** They are sometimes called 'dressed up stakeholders'. We talk about lobbyists for a certain important *individual* goal, who pretend to be objective and independent advisors. Even though you would not suspect it, at times this happens to be the case within highly recommended, formal government-advising institutes.

'Framing' of the debate. Framing means that a discussion about pros and cons will be conducted within a previously designed 'frame'. This *frame* describes the problem as it is perceived by an influential group, and it gives a number of previously conceived and well calculated solutions, probably not including all possible solutions or any 'out of the box' opportunities. Arguments and facts from outside this frame are not taken into account; they are usually dismissed as *non- realistic* (i.e. not fitting the frame). If the *frame* should appear to be ill fitting, then most often the real problems in the real world are not addressed, instead of the frame being adjusted to a broader scope of the more complex reality.

14.7 Breaking through the barriers?

Blockades and the way to deal with them have been described in Terra Reversa[134], a book about the transition we are presently making towards a *liveable* sustainable world. Peter Tom Jones & Vicky de Meyere show us the blockades at the *consumer* and the *producer* side of a food production process. Terra Reversa turns to Ken Wilber's[135] model for ways of solving the blockades. Wilber argues that transition is only possible if four parallel societal changes take place, while supporting each other[iv].

We are to instigate those social changes in the areas of Attitude (norms and values - what people find acceptable or taboo), Behaviour (what we see people do around us and the materialisation of their attitide), Culture (world views and belief systems) and Structures (organisations, regulations, laws, taxes, subsidies and the materialisation of the culture).

In Ken Wilber's integral approach (Fig. 31) we see that all necessary changes in the four social areas (attitude, behaviour, culture, structures)

---

134 Terra Reversa, transition to fair sustainability, 2009. If we want the generations after us to inherit a liveable world, we must change our ways substantially. In this book, Peter Tom Jones &Vicky de Meyere elaborate on suitable transition paths that need to be taken by governments, businesses and entrepreneurs.

135 Ken Wilber is regarded by some as one of the most influential contemporary thinkers in transpersonal psychology, philosophy and spirituality.

are established in interaction with each other. ***The internal sphere*** refers to the non- visible attitudes, worldviews, dreams and culture (within a person, an organisation or region). They become visible in the ***external sphere*** through actual behaviour; externally we see the manifestation of dreams and actions into the physical reality and the environment. ***Individual*** and ***collective*** attitudes, stakes and ambitions influence each other.

Fig. 31. Ken Wilber's integral approach about societal change

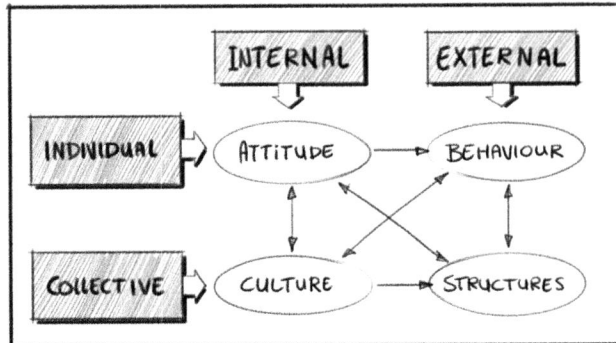

The necessary, parallel, societal changes in attitude and behaviour at one hand, and in culture and structure at the other, are best explained with an example from Terra Reversa. See endnotes.[25]

14.8 The 4 E's – effective strategies for behavioural change

Behavioural change is one of the four aspects of transition as we saw in Ken Wilber's analysis.[136] DEFRA, the Department for Rural Affairs and Agriculture in Great Britain, has designed the 4 E's[137] approach. The 4 E's are instruments for change in behaviour, but they must be used at the same time, supporting each other. The four E's represent ***Enable, Encourage, Exemplify*** and ***Engage.***

1. Enable

For sustainable behaviour to occur, conditions have to be in place. Conditions that enable consumers to easily employ sustainable behaviours. It must be easier for consumers to buy sustainably produced products. This can be done by labelling, so that the products are more easily recognised, by advertisement and by price incentives.

---

[136] See figure 31 in chapter 14.7
[137] Stevenson and Keehn, 2006

In enabling sustainable production and consumption, governments play an important role, if they take the role, that is. A government can facilitate economic conditions that allow frontrunners to create innovative solutions. Alternatively, governments can mainstream such new developments. It means supporting such innovations by putting them on the agenda and making sure that the 'alternative' becomes the *New Normal*.

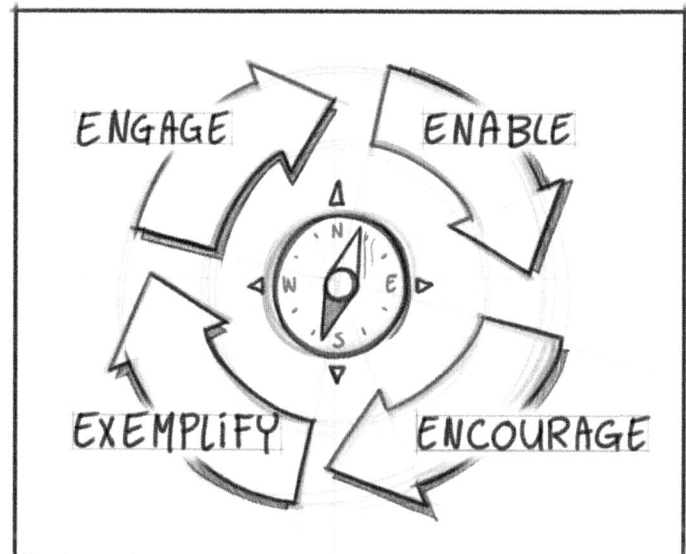

Fig. 32. The 4 Es

2.   Encourage

How can we encourage consumers to buy sustainably produced products? Presently, we are mostly discouraged to buy sustainably because of pricing. For example, a ticket for a seat on a sustainable high-speed train from Brussels to the South of France may be three times the price of a ticket for an (unsustainable) air flight and organic products are still much more expensive than regular food. Meanwhile, the very low prices of meat (chicken, pork and beef) do not correspond with the actual high costs of their production and the subsequent environmental damage and public health problems.

Including such costs in the price would be more transparent and make clear to consumers what the hidden costs are. It would also allure them into buying the relatively cheaper, sustainably produced food. Encouraging is possible by giving sustainable producers a tax advantage, since they contribute to lower public health costs and lesser investments in water sanitation and soil repairs.

A few possible *encouragement* measures (used by National, European, North American and Australian governments) are:

- Revoke government support for unsustainable farming systems and agribusiness, including the funding of scientific research into its development, as well as abolishing the support of colleges that teach such approaches.
- Internalisation of so called 'external costs' (environmental damage and public health care) in the costs of the products. Such 'external costs' are now being paid from tax money.
- VAT regulations. The VAT for unsustainable products should be higher than for sustainably produced food. Governments could also consider a zero VAT for agro-ecological produce.

'Nudging' is also a form of encouragement. 'Nudging' is a recent phenomenon and simply means giving a little push in the desired direction. Supermarket chains and the larger international food groups use *nudging* when they put preferred sales items at eyelevel in the supermarkets. Some people find that 'nudging' is misleading consumers. The positive aspect of nudging is that it could support the purchase of sustainably produced goods.

3.   Exemplify

In other words: be the good example and practice what you preach. Here, too, the government has an important role. In the Netherlands in 2008, the Government enforced organic catering in all her departments at national level. All government institutes, also at provincial and municipality level, promised to have 100% sustainable procurement by 2012, not only for food, but also for paper and electronic equipment. In catering, a target of 40% sustainable products was agreed upon.

Also business can give the example. In Europe there is the Social Venture Network[138] of both small and large businesses. The members make an effort to produce more sustainably and they share their experiences amongst each other, through peer learning!

4.   Engage

To bombard people with information about what is good for them and the environment doesn't work. We have seen over the past 40 years that it is not effective. What *does* work is the engagement of communities in which people know each other, or have the feeling that they are a group with a common interest, even on the Internet.

---

[138] http://svn.org/who-we-are/about-svn. Social Venture Network Europe is a network of entrepreneurs, business leaders, corporate catalysts for change and non-governmental organisations dedicated to changing the way we and the world do business. creating a more just, humane and sustainable world.

An interesting example is the 'Thursday Veggie Day' in Belgium, initiated by Ethical Vegetarian Alternative (EVA)[139] responding to the demand for nice, healthy and fashionable vegetarian food. Municipalities that wanted to work on food policy quickly adopted the campaign and it then spilled over to the Netherlands.

Another example of community change projects is the multitude of *urban farming* initiatives that we see nowadays in most countries in Europe. There, people in an urban area, work together to make vegetable gardens in spaces that lie wasted. Apart from producing their own vegetables, there is a huge social impact since people get to know each other across cultural borders.

14.9 From *regular* policy making to *transition* policy

To support transition, governments would do best to change from their regular way of policy making into transition policies. The difference between the two is made clear in Table 3, which gives a comparison of approaches:

Regular policy making	Transition policy making
Short-term planning (4-8 years ahead);	Long term horizon (20-50 years);
Sectoral approach - each sector plans without thinking of the impact on other sectors;	Integral systems approach, getting al impacts in view and relating the external structure and effects to the internal aims and attitudes;
A few actors who have the lead;	Multi-actor approach, participatory;
System optimisation;	Sustainable systems innovation;
Customary management systems, based on control;	Old and new management principles, inviting for opportunities;
Complexity and insecurity are a problem;	Complexity and suspense are the base;
Regular steering committee meetings; and	For decision making: use of transition arena's, networks of people that make the change together;
Linear knowledge development.	Participative experimenting, learning and exchanging insights.

Table 3. Comparison of regular and transition policies

---

[139]   Ethical Vegetarian Alternative, website only in Dutch: http://www. evavzw.be/

14.10 Transition management

Now of course the question comes up as to whether or not we can 'manage' transition at all? Manage, as in directed steering and guiding of the transition process towards an envisaged outcome, is difficult. Because transition – a process that transforms regular ways of doing into new and unknown ways of doing – has, qualitate qua, an unknown outcome. However, the DRIFT[140] institute introduced a transition management model[141] to support transition processes. That model was developed for the energy transition in the Netherlands and the transition towards sustainable house building in Flanders, Belgium.

The 'management' of a transition consists of a few consecutive steps:

- The first step is to bring together some enthusiast and influential frontrunners, not necessarily in management or leading positions; this is called the transition ARENA. They describe and discuss the complex situation. Together, they analyse the existing different views, the underlying attitudes and values. Together they decide what is necessary to come to a shared view of the future. Visionary and challenging images of the future play an important role. The jointly accepted image of the future situation works as an inspiring beacon. It is so exciting and alluring that it surmounts the anguish for the unknown and unsecure.
- Next, the group decides about the 'transition-path'. This path consists of specific steps towards the realisation of the future situation. Such steps become clear only when the stakeholders in the 'arena' dare to look back (from the imagined future situation) onto the road taken to get there. Such a process yields not only the steps, but also the necessary conditions and support that are needed.
- Transition experiments, financed by governments or by funds, give space to try out innovations of which the outcome is uncertain; especially important for individual entrepreneurs who cannot afford the experiment themselves. Another way of putting it is sponsoring the pioneers and the early adapters, whilst knowing that about 40% will be successful.

---

[140] Dutch Research Institute for Transition, Erasmus University Rotterdam, the Netherlands

[141] Transition management as a model for managing processes of co-evolution towards sustainable development. René Kemp, Derk Loorbach and Jan Rotmans; UNU-MERIT, Maastricht, The Netherlands

14.11 The course of a transition process

Transition is not an automatic or easy process. Real change can happen only when individual people change, according to Ken Wilber (page 194, fig. 31). And this only happens when circumstances are right. Of course we can influence the existence of 'good circumstances' also called 'enabling environment'.

Interaction. According to prof. Barbara van Mierlo,[142] the whole transition process is about interaction between individual and group processes. She actually takes us along in the process that occurs when you follow Ken Wilber's concept: people change individually and learn together in a spiralled process, depicted in the figure below. New insights and knowledge lead to new structures and even new institutions. The arrows in this figure represent the course of change.

Fig. 33.
The course transition takes. After dr. Barbara van Mierlo 21-11-2011

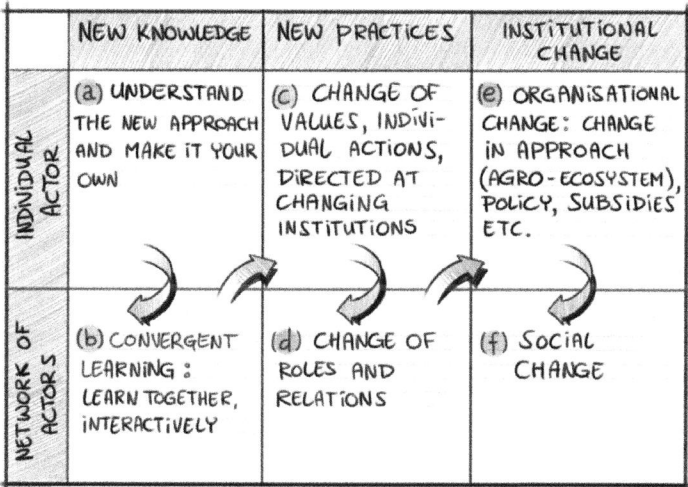

The spiral development process for transition. When we look at the picture below we see that, on an individual level, you get introduced to and get interested in a new approach: (a) first you make that your own approach; (b) in a network of similarly interested individuals/stakeholders, you exchange ideas about this approach; you learn together, in an interactive way; then (c) on a practical level, you experiment and/or exchange experiences and/or you look at how others are already doing this new thing. When you apply this new approach, this change, you behave differently; and even your role in your network changes; (d) because of you and other people behaving differently, the role of institutions start changing; and (f) as a result of that, social change is imminent.

---

142 Barbara van Mierlo, Assistant Professor Knowledge, Technology and Innovation Group Wageningen University

Empowerment. The figure above also shows that in all aspects from (a) until (d) of a transition process, 'empowerment' is necessary. Empowerment is the increase of personal capacity to take responsible action. The question of course is: how can we support people to be aware of opportunities, to have self-confidence, to be powerful and to feel responsible? Usually 'capacity building' is the solution to this question. Interesting to know is that all of the frontrunners' in the chapters 8 to 13 are self-confident, aware of opportunities, they trust their intuition experience and have personal leadership.

14.12 Transition requires us to learn from the emerging future

Otto Scharmer's model of the U-shaped transition process[143] shows us necessary phases. He stresses that, through the acts of co-creation(a combination of inner leadership and collaboration based on a shared goal) social change can happen.

Learning is not based on what we know from the past. Because we have judgements about what is good and bad. *Now, we learn from the emerging future.* We need to develop sensitivity for new developments and new situations in the future that announce themselves already now, but are not always easy to recognise. It is in fact the art of *recognising signals* that allow for new development. This art is called presencing[144], a combination of 'presence' (being present, alert, mindful in the here and now) and 'sensing' (feeling, listening, connecting). For presencing you need to be able to listen in different ways to others: *collecting information* from what you hear, *focused* listening, *involved* listening, *generative* listening or listening to hear/see opportunities in order to create.

---

[143]   http://www.ottoscharmer.com/. Otto Scharmer is the well known author of Theory U. He works at MIT (U.S.A.) in action research, creating innovations in learning and leadership.

[144]   The word presencing is coined by Peter Senge, MIT, in his theories about organisation development and change. Presence is the title of his book (2009).

EMERGING FUTURE

15. To the Tipping Point

When will all these innovative movements reach the Tipping Point? The Tipping Point is the visible materialisation of a sustainable society, the so desired ecological civilisation. When will the 'New Normal' become our normal way of life?

Fig 34. The Tipping Point

15.1 How we can reach the Tipping Point to worldwide agroecology.

On our way to a world which already exists! All over the world, in many countries, regions and groups of people experience what excellent impact these *New Normal* approaches to production and consumption have on us. We are moving into *a future that has already started*. In 'The Food paradox'[145] the contours are presented of a new world, which is not only possible but *actually exists already*[146]. In other words the world of ever increasing movements to agro-ecological agriculture and good food is already there and we can participate in it. We only need to see and recognise this world and then join it. Why don't we simply do it?

To the Tipping Point. According to Malcolm Gladwell[26], the Tipping Point is reached when the critical mass, necessary for the transformation to the *New Normal* into a mainstream movement, has been reached. That happens when a critical mass of some 10-15% of a society is supporting a movement so that it becomes the 'New Normal'.

The question is of course how, with so many global transitions and obstructions, can we realise this Tipping Point? The answer is: just do it! A very informative YouTube movie[27] shows us how a Tipping Point can be reached through courage, leadership, enthusiasm and followers: http://tinyurl.com/utubetippingpoint

The three important factors that stimulate such growing movements are according to Gladwell (1) the law of the few, (2) the stickiness factor and (3) the power of context. All factors have to coincide to turn a trend (e.g. buying energy efficient cars and substituting meat) into a widely accepted movement. Let's have a look at these factors.

Factor 1. The law of the few

Before an idea is widely supported it must be 'lived' by a few exemplary people. President Obama's wife is such a person who simply lives the *New Normal* by starting urban gardening. According to Gladwell there are three types of people involved: *Connectors, Mavens and Salesmen*. If these people confirm the new idea and promote it, there is a strong possibility for success and there is a big chance of realising the Tipping Point.

---

[145] This book sketches the paradox in our present world where hunger is enormous (one out of four people are hungry or severely malnourished) and at the same time more than enough food is available, even for a growing world population.

[146] The food paradox describes the contours of another world which is not only feasible but already exists.

Connectors are people with large networks. They usually know people across an array of social, cultural, professional, and economic circles, and make a habit of introducing people to others who work or live in different circles or arenas[147]. They are bridge builders who connect and ensure crosspollination, which would not take place if they were not there. By their connecting activities, organisations adopt new visions.

Mavens are naturals in communication; people who have a talent for facilitating well informed decision-making. They are writers of articles and books, advisors for transition processes, personal coaches who keep asking what is important for you, and enthusing (team) leaders.

Salesmen are people who use their uncharacteristic charisma to convince people to change their behaviour, their way of thinking, their perception and their consumer behaviour.

Factor 2. The stickiness factor

This is the characteristic of a product or a concept or a way of doing something, which causes people to continue to return to it. Whether a product has a stickiness factor also depends on the context. *Stickiness* develops unexpectedly, it is unconventional and opposite to logic. In Copenhagen in 2008, a weekly crate of vegetables delivered to your door all of a sudden turned out to be very attractive; everybody wanted to have such a crate; you belonged to a fashionable group if you had one. It looks as if permaculture is developing a similar attractiveness, but agro-eco and agro-forestry could do with a little support.

Factor 3. The power of context

This is often more important than is generally expected. The context (ideas, social behaviour, movies, important events, world policy and awareness) creates a situation in which a phenomenon can change to popular and generally accepted behaviour. Even a small change in a social setting (the neighbourhood, a social group, a section of the population or a political party) can be an important flywheel, to reach the Tipping Point.

In order to become the *New Normal,* all emerging movements in agroecology still need *connectors, inspiring experts* and *salespersons.* Are you interested to use your skills in one of these fields? The possibility is there and the challenge as well. You will need courage and leadership before everything else to realise your dream.

---

[147] An Arena is an area of attention or subject matter, like poverty control, climate change, trade, sustainable energy or food supply. It is called an Arena, because a game is being played around the solutions for the problem by various actors. Wat happens outside the Arena is generally not considered and will not be included in the game.

15.2 Courage, leadership and cooperation

We're actually not so far away anymore, from the *New Normal*. We have seen how the Tipping Point can be reached. It is mainly a question of changing our behaviour, together. Courage, leadership and cooperation are more important than the individual case. Your drive is the motor for the movement to the tipping point. But how do you realise that?

The philosopher Ken Wilber helps us to understand the process through his *integral quadrant*. This shows us how changes first have to be realised inside us, in our awareness and our attitude, before we can start implementation. Or as Engbert Breuker[148] formulates it; *"If your heart feels, and your head thinks along, your hands will automatically start doing the right things".*

In **Ken Wilber's** quadrant (see figure below), the upper row represents the individual level, the lower one the collective level. The left column represents the invisible inner world of man, and is subjective. The right column is the tangible manifestation of the inner world; this column is measurable and objective. In the right column, the tangible reality, the *New Normal* becomes visible.

Internal I and WE	External materialisations
'I' Inspiration; personal values; motivation; and attitudes towards nature and awareness.	'It' Factual individual behaviour; projects; initiatives; books; and presentations.
'We' Culture – the way things are done in a region/country; how people treat nature; regulations; collaboration and social responsibility.	'The Collective' System perspectives; organisational structures; physical changes in building and materials, decision making; sustainable value chains; integrated approaches in land management and agriculture.

Fig. 35. Quadrant of Ken Wilber. Source: the X-factor in spatial development

The changes in our personal awareness (the 'I' - top left in the quadrant) manifest themselves in the Individual 'It' - in what we create and in what we do, outside and inside the tangible reality. This change becomes visible in

---

[148] Engbert Breuker; champion of human oriented entrepreneurship and chairman of Social Venture Network Nederland

farmers who change their production methods; citizens, who change their consumption and shopping patterns; as an employee or a director who changes the approach of a company; as writers and film producers who show different concepts and ideas; and in new projects, citizens' initiatives and foundations.

Changes also become visible in 'The Collective'. This also happens through tangible matters, like actions that start up movements; new forms of organisations; multi sectoral integrated projects; a more integrated regulatory system; a sustainable countryside, multi cropping systems in agriculture; mountain slopes show terracing instead of erosion gullies, natural springs have returned at the feet of slopes.

15.3 How can we do that, make the collective change?

Learning and cooperation have changed. To create new ways of thinking and to make new choices, essential learning abilities are required which depend on three skills at the same time:

1. Perception of systems (your company in the larger context);
2. Transboundary cooperation (transgressing the boundaries of departments, sectors and structures);
3. Creation of a desired future.

Listening has become important: listening to others, being open to opportunities and sharing dreams. It is essential to link what is important to the individual to what is important for the world as a whole. So no longer work along the lines of task organisations or silos (e.g. agriculture next to nature, next to catering), but go for value creation through co-creation; no longer top down, but together.

The 'initiative spiral'[28] can guide us through the different phases of the change process:

The first step is the *inspirational phase*. During this phase the key persons will increase the number of campaigners, educate them and prepare them so that the existing regime will have to take the movement seriously. These key persons and campaigners can be found not only in the periphery or at the bottom, but they are also present amongst directors and managers.

The next step is the *discussion* (by the key persons) with the people who keep the existing system in place, e.g. the managers who have to ensure continuity and security. However, they are also the people who have the power to change the situation. The aim is to create an open dialogue and to conduct experiments to find new solutions. To change everything at one time is not an option; you can't go from the cellar to the attic without passing the floors in between. In the dialogue it can help to identify which solution was provided by the old way of thinking. Is another solution possible if you take a different approach? How could the old way of thinking and acting continue for such a long time whilst everybody could see that we were going in the wrong direction? Which mechanisms support the old ways and is it possible to modify these progressively?

What has to happen to reduce the resistance against change? Will improved alternatives and the emerging movements that develop in the niches reduce the resistance? Is it possible to take a top down approach to stop undesirable behaviour? How can we declare a social ban on the old way of behaving? That is what the discussions on the new approaches are about.

15.4 How do others do it? Real life examples

The start of change

- Start from your own power and initiative. Check if this new move fits your business'character and ideals (Unica).
- Follow your heart (Bavaria).
- Follow your own beliefs, otherwise you will not succeed (Eneco).
- Try to pro-actively provide solutions to social issues. This way a company can keep as much control of its own context as possible (Tata Steel).

The role of the leader

- Start leadership at an individual level (FrieslandCampina).
- The directors play a key role in the wider acceptance of the sustainability policy; you need to have a good presentation (Harbour Rotterdam).
- Sustainable management has everthing to do with the universal laws of organisational development: consistent behaviour and leadership (BAM).
- The message has to be consisistent and repeated time after time (Van Gansewinkel).
- Read Braungart's book and reform your enterprise according to 'Cradle to Cradle' (Desso).
- Patience; let go, you can't take everybody along at the same time. The pitfall is to be so excited, that you think everybody will become excited, but that is not the case (KLM).

Organise

- Do not consider socially responsible enrepreneurship as a secondary activity. Do not treat intiatives as incidents (Rabobank).

- Organise at a small scale, related to sections of the enterprise, and have coordination meetings (NS).
- Organise sustainable production internally and bottom-up (Philips).
- Analyse your organisation with the help of the *conscious business approach*. It shows the attitudes in your team, priorities in internal and external management and how you are connected to the inspirational source of the enterprise and to the world. But most of all it makes clear to all participants how they relate to each other and what that means for the future of the organisation.
- Be open to, and trust, new ways of collaboration; a collective of entrepreneurs can give new inspiration.

Employees
- Conduct frank discussions with employees to start the way to the tipping point (Siemens).
- Let people do what they like to do (Albron).
- Organise the drive/passion (PGGM).
- Involve empoyees by having them experience the difference you can make as a company, brand or person. In the end it is people who realise the change (Unilever).

16. Steps into the unfolding future

The unfolding future

"In the world of 2050, healthy food is abundant and politicians view a sustainable agricultural system as non-negotiable. Looking back, it's clear that institutional reform was the key to success in the realms of innovation, production, and consumption. Somewhere between 2010 and 2015 we have saved the world by a worldwide change to agro-ecological practices."

John Ambler, Vice-President for Strategy, Oxfam America, 2011

......and we can say with certainty that people in these future agricultural and food production systems, their values and regulations, their organisations, technologies and practices, will all be completely different from the present.

International Assessment of Agricultural Knowledge, Science and Technology for Development, IAASTD report 2008

16.1 Observe and act from the future

The future that we desire invites us to take the required steps to realise it. But how do we do this? How do we identify these steps, this road to the future? Joseph Jaworski,[149] the formulator of the first Shell scenarios,[150] says "At a level that cannot be observed by us, there is an unfractured wholeness, an implicit order[151] from where seemingly independent events originate. All human beings are part of this unfractured wholeness, which continuously expands. One of our responsibilities in life is to be open for this expansion, which in time will enable us to perceive and implement these new realities." Scenarios can be used to give a positive turn to the future, to make the world a safer place for diversity.

16.2 Facing the challenge

The future challenges us. Face it and accept the challenge. Start working from possibilities and opportunities, from your position in the world connected to the world. We apply the lessons learned. The lessons of the derailed agricultural systems, for instance, have taught us that we should look at agriculture from a complex systems point of view. The new knowledge has taugt us how we can be aware of other attitudes to nature. Which steps will we take when we start using the 'keys', the examples that have been handed to us by the pioneers?

At every position in society, you can use your drive to contribute to the emerging future; starting from the 'I' position in Ken Wilber's quadrant, making the change visible in the 'It' and in 'The Collective'. You can contribute as a citizen or a consumer, as an individual farmer, as a farmers' cooperative, as a policy officer in an organisation, the government, or as a politician, you name it.

Looking back from 2030 we see what happened and which major actions we needed to undertake:

- **Restore soil fertility** and concentrate on carbon instead of nitrogen. This is the *New Normal* for farmers, in industry, in the international agribusiness, with governments and NGO's.

- **At farm level** we promoted restoration of production cycles and complex natural agro-ecological systems. We changed to

---

[149] J. Jaworski (2000) 'Synchronicity, the inner path to leadership'

[150] "The Shell approach is an important basis for transforming scenario planning" according to Adam Kahane, Associate Fellow, Saïd Business School, Oxford University.

[151] An implicit orderliness similar to the quantum vision of the University as described by Bohm

integrated or holistic management, all over the world, also in the international agribusiness.

- **Industries and governments** changed their policies in order to reduce land use and water consumption per unit of product.
- Between 2016 and 2019, **the financial crisis intensified**. New value systems[152] developed as well as regional money. Existing cooperation networks and institutions modified their organisations in a much more drastic manner than we could have imagined, in say 2008. This institutional transformation was the key to the successes in 2030.
- Around 2018, there was a **re-organisation of the world market for food**. Especially in Africa and South America, more food was produced for local consumption.
- **Citizens** started buying with greater awareness; they have an impact on the production methods by their choices for socially and ecologically grown, regionally produced food.
- There is more **regional food production** and regional self-sufficiency in food products by changing to mixed farming.
- **Internationally**, development assistance and the international agribusiness started to work together, agribusiness supporting local and regional food self-sufficiency in the South.
- **All over the world** we called a stop to desertification. Through intensified sustainable land management programmes and watershed management; through permaculture, agro-forestry and other agro-ecological approaches. This was done in a participative manner, with the farmers as stakeholders in the development of projects. The World Bank and other major international donors and NGOs supported this approach.
- Policy making strongly supported sustainable agro-ecological principles. The choice for this type of agriculture is permanent and cannot be turned back again. Agro-ecology fits well with the (economic) regional cluster approach and the integrated landscape approaches that are being advertised since 2010.

16.3 How did we manage this?

Personal leadership appeared to be the basis for all structural change: we supported what is really important, we engaged people, we supported and we became *followers* of the *New Normal* movement.

---

[152] A value system is an entity of values, opinions, standards - in a society or community – which is expressed in a way of living.

From 'I' to 'We'. We linked individual and business interests to work for the greater whole and for the world. This was only possible as a result of value driven leadership; by a change in regulations (the rules of the game!); by long term planning based on ecological principles and a circular economy; and by increased awareness with consumers, employers, employees, politicians and law givers. All were inspired by their individual drives and examples of others.

Smallholders in Africa, Asia and South America made a direct transition to sustainable types of eco-agriculture, *climate conscious* and conservation-based agricultural practises. Of course they were supported worldwide to change to more sustainable practices by practice-oriented research, by lots of model farmers and peer learning, and also because the extension services got a real boost. At the same time, cooperation between large commercial enterprises and small scale farmers was realised.

Restoration of regional cycles (of nutrients, water and money) and of complex agro-ecological systems. Through integrated projects in the fields of water, soil and energy, problems that still existed in 2015 were efficiently tackled from a landscape point of view.

In developing countries, **NGO's, governments and institutions of knowledge** worked together and started copying and distributing sustainable examples and case studies, instead of exporting western knowledge with its related problems. Examples are the System of Rice Intensification (SRI) from Madagascar; the successful restoration of the Loess plateau in China; the Soil & More project in South Africa; the example of Cuba[153] and the Holistic Management for grazing lands as developed by Allan Savory.

Mutual understanding. The endless, hateful, discussion about the relative efficiency of large scale mechanised agriculture compared to small scale *low input* agriculture died somewhere in 2015. It is now accepted that both types of agriculture are necessary. Wheat and other grain production in the USA are still managed by large-scale enterprises, but in a more ecological manner. Fruits and vegetables are produced on small farms, thus creating a lot of employment. Countries in development now benefit from the development of small-scale mechanisation practices. Everywhere in the world, organic practices for soil improvement are in use.

---

[153] "After the break-up of the Soviet Union, Cuba lost 70% of agrochemical and fuel imports and 50% of livestock feed imports," explains Julia Wright, deputy director of the Centre for Agroecology and Food Security at Coventry University. "It couldn't produce those inputs itself, and since then Cuba has developed some fine examples of ecological agriculture."

Governments created an *enabling environment* for the further development of sustainable agriculture. For industrial agriculture, the impact on the environment and public health will be incorporated into the price of the product under the slogan 'the polluter pays'. Organic, ecological and cyclical agricultural products will thus become cheaper.

Governments in developing countries obliged the donor countries to make agro-ecology and soil health management part and parcel of their development programmes.

Governements and donors invested in farmer oriented and/or participatory driven agricultural research. Local interests, citizens and groups in society had a major say in the research and agricultural projects conducted. Where organic and chemical innovations were involved, their impact on soil, water and health of man and animals were thoroughly investigated. The social and economic implications of these innovations were discussed with all stakeholders.

Donors and funding agencies invested in scaling up of good local practices and innovations on the condition that attention was paid to land rehabilitation and soil health management.

Sustainable agribusiness. The large dominant food companies made a change; their new directions became 1) biodiversity, 2) agro-ecological regional development or development of multifunctional agricultural landscapes (no more asparagus from exploited Peruvian farmers for the European market), 3) restoration of water and nutrient cycles, 4) inclusive and socially responsible business.

Sustainable chains. Consumers and many other 'links' in the value chain realised a substantial reduction of food losses. Every link ensured that, at the source of the food chain, production took place in an ecological and socially responsible way. In the future labels will present the ecological footprint of a product, including its water consumption.

From transfer of knowledge to co-creation. Science, institutes of knowledge and the business community changed from *transfer of knowledge* to *co-creation* of experiential knowledge. They supported the transformation to sustainable agro-ecosystems by practice driven research, with integrated system approaches, facilitation of transitions and the application of ecological principles in agriculture. The exchange of practical experience amongst farmers' networks was supported and strengthened. Cooperation between farmers and businesses got a more long-term character.

Courageous policy and courageous leadership were required to protect and re-introduce agro-ecological principles. Policy and leadership broke with short-termism and created the right conditions for agro-ecological practices, especially so in Western agriculture. Driven by necessity this was first realised in Cuba. In principle it concerns a transition from a fossil fuel driven economy to a green economy.

All of us took the 1990 Asilomar declaration[154] to heart. The recommendations are still valid in 2016 and have opened our eyes to do what we needed to do going forward.

---

[154]   For the declaration and its topics see chapter 6.6

17. Realising the future

"Now is the time! The time to tell your truth. And do not look for the leader beyond yourself" [155]

"We are the ones whom we have been waiting for"

---

[155] This is a message of the Hopi elders, Red Indians who are aware of our role in a larger context and the interconnectedness in time. *A message of the Hopi Elders, 2002.* Various sources with additions of J.Crow

17.1 Rethinking by all

Rethinking is necessary. In 2012 the report *Sustainable Development in the 21st Century* (SD21) was published by the Department of Economic and Social Affairs of the United Nations.[29] In the section *Food and Agriculture* it is stated that the status of our food security and the reduction of our natural resources is mainly caused by industrial agriculture. It also says that the importance of public health in the coming 20 years is a serious matter.

> "Re-thinking is necessary because we are aiming for the wrong goals. Our eating habits result in poor health and the destruction of eco-systems. This is stupid; the importance of healthy food for the worldwide population is the responsibility of the wrong parties and not related to correct agricultural and water management practices. We have to restore the nutritive value and the vitality of food through better soil management. No more empty calories! In the developed countries import of food is more important than its production; while there are 50.000 edible crops in the world, fifty percent of our food consists of three crops, grain, rice and maize; farmers and emerging organisations which contribute to the resilience and reinforcement of natural resources through the use of ecological agriculture and soil management are hardly supported. Industrial agriculture is the largest water user; on top of that it is the cause that annually some 20.00 to 50.000 km2 of productive land is lost as a result of erosion and land degradation."

Many of the interviewed experts plead for a complete change in thinking, *rethinking*: it concerns a transformation of our current habits and ways of thinking and a transformation of our current (Western based) food production and agricultural systems. [30]

Rethinking can be supported by many participative tools.

17.2 Actions by consumers

"Every consumer can promote food security" says Editor in Chief of the British Centre for Ecology and Water Management. Scientists are calling upon the consumers to reduce their meat intake. "Everybody can contribute to a more sustainable production and consumption of nutrients and everybody will benefit from this," says Achim Steiner, director of the UN Environmental Programme. "Whether we live in a region with a shortage or a surplus of nutrients, our daily decisions can make the difference. If we do not act together immediately, the next generation will inherit a world where millions of people will suffer from food insecurity as a result of a shortage of nutrients, while pollution with the same nutrients elsewhere will increase and promote climate change."

The following actions can be carried out by consumers to realise the required future, starting as of this moment.

Think globally, Act locally! Or, be aware of what is happening around the world and adjust your actions at local level accordingly. You can change the world by changing one purchase or one meal from your ordinary pattern. Eat less meat for instance. Each little bit helps. Buy organic products, regional products, products originating from a healthy soil. Ask for the origin or the sustainability label, so you create awareness with the vendors. You can start eating healthier, by paying attention to how your food has been produced. Each purchase is in fact a vote for a healthier future.

Dutch consumers have spent 25 per cent more on sustainable food in 2012. Total turnover was 2,2 billion Euro. Under the heading 'sustainable', food products are included which distinguish themselves by their way of production: animal friendly, organic, environmental friendly and/or ethical. In less than three years consumers have doubled their procurement of sustainable food. "Society shows that sustainable food is getting more and more important" says the Minister. "This confirms that we are on the right way."

Create a beautiful sustainable landscape somewhere in the world, through your own behaviour. Your purchase has an impact on the continuation of its production method and the landscape that is the result of this production method. A multi-functional or a monotonous landscape, an eroded or a lasting fertile landscape. With your purchase you choose for investments in or exploitation of a landscape, be it a Dutch landscape (greenhouse tomatoes), a landscape in South America (maize, soy for export; or maize and beans for local consumption), in Peru (green asparagus for export, or food for home consumption), in Ethiopia (flowers for export, or food for home consumption).

"If you buy organic or related products, you vote in favour of healthy agricultural practices, you eat your soil healthy. If you buy industrial food you vote for unhealthy production methods. The world cannot permit this unsustainable approach any longer. The price that we make our planet and ourselves pay is big. These are choices we make ourselves."[156]

Change your procurement behaviour. The consumer is the critical factor in effecting this change. A structural change is required which acknowledges that agricultural production has to be adapted to the ecological capacities of the region and that this should not be the other way around. This was posed in an article of July 2012 in the Flemish paper by *Wervel*[157].

---

[156] Jane Goodall in "Harvest for Hope, A Guide to Mindful Eating" 2006.

[157] http://www.wervel.be/

Consumers are essential in realising change. They decide to choose for the products of integrated and regional agriculture. Do it! Put questions to your grocer, town council and at provincial level.

As a consumer, you have a voice — and you should use it. You can check where your products come from and how they are produced. If you do not agree you can ask your supermarket to provide another brand.

For example, If your favourite product contains palm oil, contact the manufacturer and ask them to use certified sustainable palm oil from suppliers that have made a clear commitment to halt deforestation. If the manufacturer already uses sustainable palm oil, ask them to indicate this on product packaging to help consumers make the best choice to protect the environment. The RSPO (Round Table for Sustainable Palm Oil) Shopping Guide lists products that carry the RSPO logo. You can find out if a company is a member of the RSPO and see what actions they are taking to improve the sustainability of their supply chains.

Stop using herbicides like glyphosate (*Roundup*)[31] and *neonics* which harm the soil as well as man and animals and cause bees to become extinct. Join an NGO to strengthen the movement and thus contribute to reaching the Tipping Point.

You are what you eat, so stop being cheap, artificial, fast, non-authentic, unfair.

17.3 Actions by farmers, farmers' organisations and NGOs

Restore cycles at farm level (closed-loop farming) and start cooperating in your own region, with consumers and other farmers. Some suggestions:

Switch to integrated systems. This requires planting permanent crops with long roots in your fields as they will retain water, increase groundwater levels, reduce surface run-off, preserve nitrogen and fix carbon. Additional ecosystem measures are: less or no tillage and no additional extra nitrogen, reintroduction of mixed farming, restoration of the food web, restoration of large scale grasslands and rotation grazing.

Return to biodiversity management. Birds in farmland can be promoted by specific measures. For example no ploughing before winter, planting a winter crop, flower rich borders along the fields and protection of nests.

Support (small holder) farmers in countries in development. For medium and large scale farms, promotion of commercial aspects may be considered, especially by balancing supply and demand. Encourage the switch to agro-ecological methods, the reduction of the use of pesticides, quality improvement and sharing of knowledge about closed-loop agriculture (One of the outcomes of the Oxfam/NOVIB internet discussion held in December 2012).

Regional cooperation. This can be done in various ways. In Belgium the VLIF[32] supports farmers' cooperatives or fledgling cooperative movements with the major aim to create a communal market for the participating farmers. The partnership takes the shape of a co-partnership, a not-for-profit organisation, an actual society with at least three active member farmers, who are individually responsible. The support[33] consists of a capital premium with a maximum of 22.500 euro.

Sustainability tag. Ensure that your healthy, regional and sustainable products can be recognised. If the consumer wants to shift to these products they should be easy to recognise. Farmers' cooperatives and farmer-consumer organisations play a major role here. In the UK the association LEAF has achieved this with their own brand for integrated agriculture and its products. *Oregional, Boerenhart* and *Willem & Drees*[158] in The Netherlands represent sustainable and regional production, but all have their own label. It would be preferable if a nationwide label for healthy, integrated food production could be organised. This could be done by applying PGS, *Participatory Guarantee System*, a certification system developed in Brazil[159], in a bottom up approach, which involved the participation of all stakeholders in the production chain. This certification depends on mutual trust, social networks, exchange of knowledge and shared responsibility.

Nature&More developed the Sustainability flower for sustainably grown food products (see footnote 166)

Stop using herbicides like glyphosate (*Roundup*) and *neonics* which harm the soil as well as man and animals and cause bees to become extinct. Join an NGO to strengthen the movement and thus contribute to reaching the Tipping Point.

Start working according to the Conservation Agriculture principle.

Copy good examples in the region.

---

[158] These organisations belong to the 26 frontrunners in the transition to agroecology; see chapter 10 of this book.

[159] See the example by Ecovida in chapter 10.5

17.4 An Agenda for Agribusiness

The SAI platform[160] adds another three sustainability indicators to the existing ones. They are: 1 Biodiversity, 2 Agro-ecological regional development and development of multi-functional agricultural landscapes and 3, restoration of cycles.

Ensure the reduction of food losses throughout the production chain. Ensure an agro-ecological approach in those countries where the basic products originate.

Stop destruction and burning of rainforests for the development of oil palm and other plantations. Avoid mono-cultures (wheat in USA, soy in Brazil, palm oil in Africa and Indonesia) as they result in soil losses and deterioration of soil quality and have a negative impact on the livelihoods of small farmers. Stop land grabbing in the developing countries. Cooperate with development organisations, start producing regionally in a co-creative way, organise agricultural production through nucleus farms[34].

Apply sustainability principles. Use production, consumption and reproduction patterns, which protect and promote the regenerative capacity of the Earth, human rights and social well being. Use the sustainability flower and the grass-root certification system PGS, *Participatory Guarantee System* (EcoVida, Brazil).

Strengthen 'low input' farming enterprises of farmers that know about cyclic agriculture (as done in the Netherlands by the Biodiversity fund of HIVOS/Oxfam Novib); use *multistakeholder* approaches for locally applicable technology, to connect to the local and regional market and the improvement of their logistic situation.

Contribute to new alliances between regional governments and business chains, to develop a certification system which includes landscape. The sustainability Round Tables are things of the past, we have moved ahead.[35]

Use new inviting economical procedures at regional level. There are new approaches which contribute to sustainable landscape development and guarantee income and food security for the local (poor) population at the same time. They can be found in a publication of the IUCN[161] together with

---

[160] Platform Sustainable Agriculture Initiative; a food industry organization, aimed to support the development of sustainable agriculture, involving the stakeholders in the food chain. http://www.saiplatform.org/.

[161] International Union for the Conservation of Nature;

the strategy for Landscape Livelihood (LLS) on a new approach of the economy, markets and incentives[162] at regional level.

Create socio-economic opportunities and unlock organisations and regulations to ensure that small scale and new technologies will reach small farmers to have an impact. Do not stick to old fashioned principles, beliefs or self-interest.

17.5 Investors change their investment plans

Change of mind! "The biggest challenge for the adoption of agro-ecological approaches is not a technical one, but is of a social and political nature. We require a change of mind in the political, economic, and ethical thinking about Agribusiness, which keeps promoting industrial large scale agriculture. The crisis which developed as a result of the worldwide unsustainable agricultural practices is covered by the ever increasing flow of subsidies, even in the shape of scientific research to promote this type of agriculture. It is essential that we leave this path to destruction"[36]

The focus of investments should be with small and medium scale farmers, organised in cooperatives, as individual entrepreneurship, strengthened by responsibility, factual knowledge and creativity. This will lead the way to (the development of) sustainable agriculture. Invest nationwide and at regional level, in both North and South, in agro-eco agriculture and regional economies.

Make different technologies accessible for different socio-economic and ecological situations. Pasture management in the Netherlands requires a different small scale approach from management of savannas. The demand side will participate in the formulation of the criteria to be met by projects.

Facilitate socio-economic opportunities; ensure that small scale and new technologies will reach small farmers and have an impact. Do not stick to old fashioned principles, beliefs or self-interest.

Public sector finance (mainly through grants, subsidies and credit)[163] can enable landscape actors to collaborate on projects that integrate multiple landscape objects. But the public sector must do more to help private investors move beyond niche opportunities. Public sector finance institutions must aggregate and coordinate Integrated Landscape

162 Rethinking Economics, Markets and Incentives: Using Economic Tools at the Landscape Level.
163 http://peoplefoodandnature.org/?s=public+sector+finance&post_type=default

Management (ILM) finance, improve the risk profile of ILM, and mainstream the ILM business case.

Private sector investment (loans, equity, credits) and partnership models for ILM range from those that channel finance into whole landscapes to those that support and are designed to coordinate with landscape objectives. Public-private partnerships enable public and philanthropic actors to more effectively leverage private sector investment for scale, while also providing private sector partners an opportunity to reduce environmental and social risks in their supply chain, fulfil corporate social responsibility goals, maintain a 'license to operate,' and sometimes to access new markets by raising their profile in emerging economies.

17.6 Agenda for policy and governments: a new agricultural revolution

A new agricultural revolution. The IAASTD report appeals for a renewed investment, by governments, in agriculture. **A different type of agriculture however:** one less dependent on fossil fuels, one which is supported by family and agro-ecological approaches and makes use of locally available inputs.

Agriculture with a regional economic impact, promoting local employment and food security, reducing transportation costs as well as the impact on the environment, an agriculture which uses less herbicides, insecticides, water and energy. In all regions in North, East, South and West. It is important that governments start seeing the interconnectedness of systems, and start cooperating at national, provincial, and municipal level to support the transition that is going on.

'Quality food' instead of higher production. Agriculture and agribusiness producing nutritious food should be the goal of policy, industry, and politics. This was one of the outcomes of the Oxfam Novib discussion of November 2012. In 2016 it is high on the agendas of EU countries and the International Food Policy Research Institute IFPRI.

Enable! Make it possible, establish the conditions, facilitate. The private sector runs ahead of the government. They will play an important role in providing sustainable, socially acceptable solutions for our food production and the related agricultural systems, as the sector itself depends on the continuation of these systems and flexibility. Governments have to follow the private sector closely and facilitate development through legislation and tax facilities.

We shall stop the polarisation between advocates of small scale, low external input agriculture and those preferring large scale intensive agriculture as per today.

Cattle breeding and pastoralism return to its ecological and social context. Where Ecology is concerned we restore soil based cyclic movements at regional and local level, improve soil quality and organic self-regulation such as natural resistance of cattle and antibiotics only in extreme cases. Create awareness amongst consumers and promote their support of sustainable cattle breeding.

Green energy, windmills, solar panels. Protect and promote biodiversity. From the social aspects: restore and revitalise the relations between North and South.

The public sector (politics and policy) will provide better thought over support and directives towards agro-ecological solutions, for higher wellbeing of society and long term preservation of natural resources. Various stakeholders participate in this process: politicians, agribusiness, trade, farmers, rural development organisations, for viability of nature and environment. By assessing where differences in opinion exist and where consensus, a selection of realistic movements can be made.

Development of organisations. Support new organisations instead of starting a new one yourself. Change existing organisations so they will follow the new, integrated agricultural movement.

Systematize open air scattering of composted manure and long-fibre fodder for cattle in Europe. In January 2013 research by Dr. Lantinga (Wageningen UR, the Netherlands) demonstrated that open air scattering definitely has a positive impact on the soil and soil life. The association VBBM in the Netherlands is the initiator of a return to open air scattering. Their requests for practical tests to prove that their closed-loop management system in animal husbandry is healthier and more sustainable date from 2002. However, the race is not run yet as it is still very difficult to find support from civil servants[164].

Integrated agro-eco systems are used worldwide. Politics, policy and knowledge development agree on this, they initiate and support this approach. Ecosystems and food production are not mutually exclusive. We now have to manage ecosystems in a healthy manner to realise higher yields. *Oxfam internet discussion. December 2012*

---

[164] http://tinyurl.com/mestuitrijden

Encourage and reward investments and enterprises which contribute to the common good. A label for sustainable-integrated-regional is necessary. Organic is not by all means fair and does not necessarily have a small ecological footprint. Do not re-invent the wheel, join existing initiatives. There is the *Sustainability flower* of Nature&More[165]; there is PGS, the *Participatory Guarantee System* (EcoVida, Brazil) and there are farmers' organisations who want to develop such labels.

Biofuel. Avoid the use of food crops and productive land for the production of biofuel. But investigate the de-centralised production of biofuel, if it contributes to strengthening of the local economy, the diversification of the landscape and strengthening of natural resources.

Complementarity first. There are many roads that can be followed to restore sustainable cycles, food security, and coherent systems. Placing your bets on one horse with a *one size fits all* approach is no solution in view of the heterogeneity of agro-ecological systems, land use, policy, social and cultural change and values. Janvry[166] argues that different models can be applied at the same time depending on the specific characteristics of the region (people and their values, social relations, local economy and soils).

Promote the use of Effective Micro-organisms and stone-meal in agriculture.

17.7 Actions for combined agribusiness & development assistance.

Preferably as per this moment we stop distinguishing between 'Western' and 'Development' agriculture. Until now there was a difference between small scale Low External Input (LEI) 'development' agriculture and large scale, intensive, mechanised, large scale 'Western' High External Input (HEI) agriculture.

Low External Input Subsistence Agriculture (LEISA), also known as development agriculture comprises of:

---

[165]   The sustainability flower was developed in 2009 by an international group of prominent pioneers and innovators of the organic movement, operating under the umbrella of the "Belbis Desert Club". Among them are the founders and leaders of Eosta, Sekem, Alnatura, Lebensbaum, Rapunzel, Fibl, IFOAM, Soil & More, the Soil Association and others. They were looking to unite ecological and social values in a single elegant model. For each aspect of the flower, performance indicators were defined on the basis of the GRI Guidelines. The Sustainability Flower serves as the main evaluation and communication tool in the Nature & More system.

[166]   A.de Janvry et E Sadoulet, 2008.

(1) The *subsistence farmers*, who do not consider their activities as agriculture but as part of their existence. These farmers require a support network, policies to eliminate risks, to guide and strengthen their way of food production and management of water and energy, preferably through existing NGOs.

(2) *Small farmers* and small scale enterprises with low external input. They are mainly supported by NGOs, international donors and other aid organisations and will receive micro credits etc.

Large scale, intensive 'Western' agriculture has a high energy consumption, is strongly mechanised and logistically well organised. This agriculture involves worldwide production chains, like the meat and dairy chains, where grains and soy are grown on different continents from where they will be exported as animal feed. 30 % of the world grain production is used as feed. Farmers in Argentina thus do not produce their own food but European cattle feed. If western countries start producing their own cattle feed again, farmers in Argentina can produce their own food again and start the restoration of their agro-eco systems and soils.

A third road exists. What does it look like? Local farmers in developing countries start producing in a more intensive and sustainable way, for local and export markets. This type of agriculture will use 80% of the total agricultural area. If these farmers are assisted with affordable access to resources and technologies to become self-supportive, for the greater part the problem is solved. These farmers use an ecologically healthy system, which is economically feasible and matches their culture. They have a high potential for carbon fixation. It is high time that their role in the greening of the economy is recognised, small scale as it may be.

In order to do so, we will adhere to the following lines of action:

a. Small scale low input farmers and family enterprises will be strengthened with knowledge on cyclic agriculture, as is done by the Biodiversity Fund of the Nederland's/ Hivos/Oxfam Novib. We can apply multi-stakeholder approaches to develop locally applicable technology, adjust to the local and regional markets, and improve the logistic situation, as Soil&More is doing.

b. Large scale intensive Western agriculture will change to a low-input approach, restoration of cycles, improved soil management, and increase of soil organic matter. This happens both in 'the West' (USA, Canada, Europe, China and Australia) and at the sources (mostly in the South) of the elementary inputs for western oriented production chains. This will have an impact on both small and bigger scale farmers in developing countries, on the producers of soy, palm oil, milk, grain, mushrooms, citrus fruit, flowers, cotton etc.

c. Integration of systems and the uniting of interests create the best conditions to render agriculture and cattle growing sustainable

d. By turning NGO's into partners instead of adversaries, integrated approaches for smallholder farmers will get a better standing. The polarisation between extensive/organic and intensive/industrial can be solved by using the advantages of both production systems in an integrated system.[167]

e. The principle of Nucleus Farming is accepted. Combine the advantages of a commercial farm with smallholder production. See also FAO[37]

f. Use of integrated landscape development principles. Use the 10 principles (below) for decision taking processes. These emphasize that integration of agriculture and environment require a human oriented participative approach with all stakeholders involved. This involved. This involves personal leadership because integrated landscape not easy, and they come with ups and downs. And still they are the best approach for complicated land use and rural development projects. So it is imperative that we gain experience in its use[38]

The 10 principles for an integrated[39] landscape approach are:

1: Continual learning and adaptive management; learning from outcomes can improve management.

2: Shared interest in an issue or problem; build solutions – even to wicked problems where parties have divergent views on possible solutions – around perceptions of common interest.

3: Multiple scales; awareness of numerous system influences and feedbacks that affect management is essential.

4: Multifunctionality; landscapes and their components have multiple uses and purposes that require trade-offs be reconciled.

5: Multiple stakeholders; engaging them in an equitable manner is needed to ensure optimal and ethical outcomes.

6: Negotiated and transparent change logic; transparency is the basis of trust needed to avoid or overcome conflict and is helped by good governance.

---

[167] This debate was organised In February 2013 by the Dutch Dairy Association and the research group for development issues (SKOV), supported by WageningenUR Livestock Research.

7: Clarification of rights and responsibilities; rules on resource access and land use need to be clear to ensure good management and good outcomes.

8: Participatory and user-friendly monitoring; it is valuable to derive information from multiple sources.

9: Resilience; increase system-level resilience through recognition of threats and vulnerabilities and actions to reduce them.

10: Strengthened stakeholder capacity; people require the ability to participate effectively and to accept various roles and responsibilities.

17.8 Urban Food Policy

Change the way in which we feed our cities! The Urban Food Revolution (by Peter Ladner, 2011) contains a prescription for food security for societies, villages, cities, and cooperating citizens and is based on a wide range of innovations in the USA. How cities can become self-supporting through a regional food policy:

Enable, encourage, and engage! Promote community development through the introduction and support of neighbourhood vegetable gardens, communal cooking, and composting programmes. Do not start these kind of programmes as a municipality, but encourage existing neighbourhood programmes, and support them with manpower so that they can grow. This helps against estrangement of food and supports social cohesion. But only through a well-considered policy can the trend be realised.

Exemplify, set the right example. The increased demand for local and sustainable food justifies the development of sustainable and feasible business cases for urban agriculture. Support these!

Restore local food processing (butchers, jam and cheese factories) storage and distribution. Make fresh food from the region available in town centres, at markets and in supermarkets, as done by Willem&Drees, Oregional and MARQT (in Amsterdam).

17.9 Science and research support transition

The Social and Agricultural Sciences can support the transition in many ways.

Social and transition science can support as follows:

Provide insight in the processes of system innovation and transition (how do we do it?). This is already taking place at Telos in Tilburg, the Netherlands, Centre for Development Innovation (CDI) Wageningen, Knowledge Centre Transitions TNO, DRIFT Dutch Research Institute for Transition, Erasmus University Rotterdam and by John Grin at the University of Amsterdam.

Process guidance and stimulation of collective learning. As was done in the crowdsourcing project 'Our Common Future 2.0' started by Jan Jonker[168] in 2010. Over a period of 6 months everybody in the Netherlands, including non-scientists, could participate in one of the thirty discussion groups, each covering an aspect of sustainable development. This resulted in a strong flow of sustainability thinking.

Provide a platform for knowledge development and reflection on the relationship between the various aspects of sustainability; integrate and apply knowledge together with the business community, government and social parties. Utrecht Sustainability Institute[169]

Start pilots to test new options; this is mainly done by private and NGO initiatives, which are less likely to be recognised by science and policy; however, *Innovatie netwerk* and Utrecht Sustainability Institute also use pilots.

Reflexive monitoring! Monitor institutional change as well as practical changes as they are taking place at pioneers' and early followers' level. And support this by rendering the relationships and feedback mechanisms visible.

Supportive regulations. Investigate how regulation – at all levels and for different sectors – can support the restoration of complex agro-ecosystems.

---

[168] Jan Jonker is working on a series of new books the first of which is called: *Strategic Sustainable Organisation, Seduce, Connect and Anchor*. Starting from 2012, sustainable and justified ventures and the realisation of the fundamental change that this requires in, with, and by people in organisations will be in the centre of attention.

[169] http://usi-urban.nl/. With over 1500 researchers the Utrecht Sustainability Institute (USI) is one of the leading network organisations on sustainability in The Netherlands.

Agricultural Sciences will support as follows:

Support the development of endogenic knowledge systems, locally specific experiential knowledge about dealing with the complex agricultural system and landscape.

<u>Emphasize that we are dealing with system innovation</u>: unknown types of cooperation, which cannot yet be contained in a model, will become visible; this requires interdisciplinary and organic science. It will only work if the actors concerned do realise that they are mutually dependent. As a researcher you cannot stand on the side, since you are part of the process.

<u>Substantiate that agro-eco agriculture covers wide range of practices,</u> and works well with practice driven and practice supporting research. Louis Bolk and Agro/Eco apply ecological principles in agricultural practices.

<u>Monitor the change to agro-ecosystems</u>; identify the successes and the failures so institutional support can concentrate on how to remedy the failures and strengthen the successes and the supporting measures.

<u>Prioritise research according to the future needs</u>, take collective action to look forward and implement communal and interrelated research programmes at regional and international level. This was one of the outcomes of the second worldwide conference[170] on agricultural research for development.

<u>Develop technologies</u>, through practical research and effective cooperation with farmers; technologies which are useful for them, instead of imposing something on farmers because you find it important. This is one of the main conclusions of the first Conference on the development of Science in Africa, CoS.1.

<u>Measure and monitor results</u> to manage new developments effectively, because without measuring, feedback and thus modification are impossible. (Oxfam Novib internet discussions December 2012)

<u>Increase action research to reduce post-harvest losses.</u> Only five percent of the budget is currently spent on this problem. It should be increased by 100 percent.

Support the teaching of secondary school teachers on the importance of agricultural practices and agriculture and food production for the world.

---

[170] Second Global Conference on Agricultural Research for Development (GCARD), Uruguay, 2012

17.10 Together: Prevent food losses

The prevention of food losses can only be realised if we tackle the issue together in a worldwide setting. The recent working document[40] of the *World Resources Institute* WRI[171] gives us five recommendations.

Develop a protocol (set of principles) on how to measure food loss and wastage under the slogan "What you can measure, you can manage". It would be a practical aid for organisations, institutions (hospitals, retirement homes), restaurants, and municipalities worldwide to register food losses in the same way and get a better grip on them.

Set targets to reduce food losses in the production chain and at consumers' level. Setting targets helps to create awareness, concentrate attention and organise support. Worldwide, national and regional targets for large and small scale enterprises motivate to take action. The European Union has set its targets to reduce food losses in 2050 by fifty percent in comparison to 2013.

Invest in the reduction of post-harvest losses in developing countries. A large percentage of the food loss in developing countries takes place at farm level, mainly because[41] of poor storage facilities (rodents, mould) and poor packing facilities for transportation to the markets. The percentage of agricultural research spent on this aspect amounts only to five percent, but should be ten percent at least.

Support or create organisations aiming at reducing food loss in the developed countries. WRAP (Working together for a world without waste) is a good example of such an organisation. They are independent from government, but work closely together with government and industry to reduce food loss and promote recycling.

Support and strengthen initiatives aiming at the reduction of food loss and wastage. *SAVE FOOD*[172] and *Think.Eat.Save*[42] are examples of such initiatives. To find a solution they bring the different actors together, they encourage and share best practices.

---

[171]   The World Resources Institute. http://www.wri.org/publication/reducing-food-loss-and-waste

[172]   http://www.fao.org/save-food/en/;

ENDNOTES

[1] In 2006 the average ecological footprint for various countries and continents has been calculated based on data of 2003. Source: WWF Belgium.

[2] The growing push toward industrialization and globalization with its emphasis on export crops including transgenic crops such as soybeans for cattle feed for countries such as China, Europe, USA, and the rapidly increasing demand for biofuel crops (sugar cane, maize, soybean, oil palm, eucalyptus, etc.) are increasingly reshaping the agriculture and food supply of many developing nations, with yet unknown economic, social and ecological impacts and risks (Holt-Gimenez and Patel 2009). Despite these unfolding trends, the peasant or small farm sector that comprises myriad of ecologically based agricultural styles, offers promising models for promoting biodiversity, sustaining yield without agrochemicals, and conserving ecological integrity while accounting for no less than 50% of the agricultural output for domestic consumption in most countries (ETC Group 2009).

The realisation of the contribution of peasant agriculture to food security in the midst of scenarios of climate change, economic and energy crisis led to the concepts of food sovereignty and agroecologically based production systems to gain much worldwide attention in the last two decades. Two recent major international reports (IAASTD 2009; de Schutter 2010) state that in order to feed nine billion people in 2050, we urgently need to adopt the most efficient farming systems and recommend for a fundamental shift towards agroecology as a way to boost food production and improve the situation of the poorest. Both reports based on broad consultations with scientists and extensive literature reviews contend that small-scale farmers can double food production within 10 years in critical regions by using agroecological methods already available. The food challenge will be met using environmentally friendly and socially equitable technologies and methods, in a world with a shrinking arable land base (which is also being diverted to produce biofuels), with less and more expensive petroleum, increasingly limited supplies of water and nitrogen, and within a scenario of a rapidly changing climate, social unrest, and economic uncertainty (IAASTD 2009). The only agricultural system that will be able to confront future challenges is one that will exhibit high levels of diversity, productivity, and efficiency. In the top left quadrant in Fig. 1. Features of green agroecosystems of the future: productivity, diversity, integration, and efficiency (Funes-Monzote 2009).

Given the present and predicted near future climate, energy and economic scenarios, agroecology has emerged as one of the most robust pathways towards equitable and sustainable development available today. Agroecology is providing the scientific, methodological, and technological basis for a new "agrarian revolution" worldwide

(Altieri 2009; Ferguson and Morales 2010; Wezel and Soldat 2009; Wezel et al. 2009). Agroecology-based production systems are biodiverse, resilient, energetically efficient, socially just, and comprise the basis of an energy, productive and food sovereignty strategy (Altieri 1995; Gliessman 1998). Agroecological initiatives aim at transforming industrial agriculture partly by transitioning the existing food systems away from fossil fuel-based production largely for agroexport crops and biofuels towards an alternative agricultural paradigm that encourages local/national food production by small and family farmers based on local innovation, resources, and solar energy. This implies access of peasants to land, seeds, water, credit, and local markets, partly through the creation of supportive economic policies, financial incentives, market opportunities, and agroecological technologies (Vía Campesina 2010). Agroecological systems are deeply rooted in the ecological rationale of traditional small-scale agriculture, representing long established examples of successful agricultural systems characterized by a tremendous diversity of domesticated crop and animal species maintained and enhanced by ingenuous soil, water, and biodiversity management regimes, nourished by complex traditional knowledge systems. Such systems have fed much of the region's population for centuries and continue to feed people in many parts of the planet (Koohafkan and Altieri 2010).

In this paper, we analyze the fundamental reasons why the promotion of an agroecological development paradigm based on the revitalization of small farms which emphasizes diversity, synergy, recycling and integration, and social processes that value community involvement and empowerment, is the only viable option to meet the world's food needs in this age of increasing oil prices and climate change. We also analyze the socioecological features and significance of peasant agriculture and the impacts that hundreds of agroecologically based projects in Cuba, Brazil, Philippines, and some African countries have had on the environment and food production.

Agroecologically efficient agricultural systems for smallholder farmers: contributions to food sovereignty, Miguel A. Altieri, December 2011

[3] From I to WE. 10 jun. 2008 - From I to We: Social identity and the collective self. Hogg, M. A. and Williams, K. D. (2000)....

[4] Farming Matters provides an overview of the importance of small-scale farming and of an agro-ecological approach to agriculture, looking in detail at four key areas: food security, poverty alleviation, energy and climate change. www.farming-matters.org

[5] The history of fertilizer has largely shaped political, economic, and social circumstances in their traditional uses. Subsequently, there has been a radical reshaping of environmental conditions following the

development of chemically synthesized fertilizers. In 1810 J. von Liebig invented fertilizer. Fertilizer is considered to comprise material of non-biologic origin which are added to the soil to promote crop growth. A better definition would be "all materials which are produced artificially". In 1910 Fritz Haber succeeded in converting Nitrogen from the air in ammonia, in order to use that in fertilizers. Saltpetre is of organic origin but is modified in a factory and is then called fertilizer. Practically all fertilizers are salts, which are used in common agriculture. In organic agriculture – and by farmers who cannot afford the high price of chemical fertilizer - no use is made of fertilizers. Here manure and compost (fermented dead material from plants) are used, sometimes mixed with stone meal, since that is rich in minerals. This is much better for the soil fertility and soil structure. http://en.wikipedia.org/wiki/History_of_fertilizer.

6   WWF conducted a research on the annual available water in the large catchment areas of this world and prepared a report on how this water could be used for agriculture in a sustainable manner. See: Agwaterusefinalreport.pdf. Subsequently an awareness campaign was conducted and projects were initiated with the aid of international donors. (Water resources planning for the Red Tahi Bin River basin with the assistance of the Asian Development Bank f.i.)

7   Don Huber, Emeritus Professor at Purdue University and senior scientist on USDA's National Plant Disease Recovery System, has been a plant physiologist and pathologist for over 40 years. His academic career began with 8 years as a cereal pathologist at the University of Idaho, and the next 35 years at Purdue University where he specialised in soil-borne disease control, physiology of disease, and microbial ecology. For the past 20 years, he has conducted extensive research into the effects of glyphosate on crops, in response to the increase in crop diseases on glyphosate-applied fields. Since his letter to the US Secretary of State Tom Vilsak was leaked in February 2011, there has been a great deal of controversy over what Huber described as a pathogen "new to science" and abundant in glyphosate-tolerant GM crops As he concluded in the letter: "We are now seeing an unprecedented trend of increasing plant and animal diseases and disorders. This pathogen may be instrumental to understanding and solving this problem".

8   ISIS Report 26/03/14 Glyphosate and Cancer

New research shows that the low levels of glyphosate, found in human urine, can promote the growth of human breast cancer cells, confirming the carcinogenic potential of the herbicide known since the 1980s. Dr Mae Wan Ho.

GM and herbicide cancer warning suppressed in retracted study. Among the unsettling results of the Séralini study [1], which almost certainly lie behind its notorious retraction by the journal editor a year after it was published ([2] Retracting Seralini Study Violates Science & Ethics, SiS 61), are cancers in rats fed GM maize and/or exposed to Roundup. Although the word 'cancer' was never used by the authors, they recorded three 'metastases' (i.e. cancers) - two in females and one in a male - plus two kidney Wilm's tumours in male rats, which had to be euthanized a year early because the cancerous tumours grew to more than 25% of body size. This makes a total of at least 5 cancers in the treatment groups, in addition to the excess of grotesquely large tumours, premature deaths, pituitary, kidney, liver, and other pathologies compared with the controls. The cancer cases certainly should not be ignored, and to make sure this important paper is not erased from public record, it is now freely available and permanently registered on thesparc [3] a floating knowledge archive for the survival of people and planet. The findings are especially important in the light of new research and indeed, previous research on the carcinogenic potential of glyphosate (and GM food).

Glyphosate promotes growth of human breast cancer cells at minute concentrations. A research team in Thailand led by Jutamaad Satayavivad at the Center of Excellence on Environmental Health and Toxicology, Ministry of Education, and The Chulabhorn Graduate Institute in Bangkok, published a paper [4] in the very same Journal from which the Séralini study was retracted. They found that glyphosate at minute concentrations enhanced the proliferation of human hormone-dependent breast cancer T47D cells, but not hormone-independent breast cancer MDA-MB231 cells. Their detailed experiments showed that glyphosate mimics the action of oestrogen, and uses the same molecular pathways as the natural hormone to promote proliferation of the cancer cells. They also found that glyphosate had synergistic effects in enhancing breast cancer cell growth in combination with genistein, a common phytoestrogen in soybean. Glyphosate at concentrations between 10-12 and 10-6 M (0.169 ng/L to 0.169 mg/L) boosted the proliferation of T47D cells by 15 to 30 %, about half as effectively as the most potent oestrogen, 17 b-estradiol (E2).

That is not all. Glyphosate-based herbicides are widely used for soybean cultivation (especially for Roundup Ready GM soybean); and the researchers also found an additive oestrogenic effect between glyphosate and genistein, a soybeanphytoestrogen.

Read the rest of this report here: http://www.i-sis.org.uk/Glyphosate_and_Cancer.php

9   Gro Harlem Brundtland, author of one of the most important UN reports on sustainability, some 30 years ago, where the three P's people, planet, profit were formulated for the first time.

10   500 years of agriculture F.H. King.

11   No-till farming (also called zero tillage or direct drilling) is a way of growing crops or pasture from year to year without disturbing the soil through tillage. No-till is an agricultural technique, which increases the amount of water that infiltrates into the soil and increases organic matter retention and cycling of nutrients in the soil. In many agricultural regions it can eliminate soil erosion. It increases the amount and variety of life in and on the soil, including disease-causing organisms and disease suppression organisms. The most powerful benefit of no-tillage is improvement in soil biological fertility, making soils more resilient. Farm operations are made much more efficient, particularly improved time of sowing and better traffic ability of farm operations.

12   The word 'permaculture' is made up from the concept of 'Permanent Agriculture'. It was designed in the seventies, by two Australian biologists, Bill Mollison and David Holmgren, in reaction to the then prevailing agricultural system, which brought a lot of irreversible problems, like soil degradation, erosion, salinization. By copying the most important ecological principles from Nature itself, they developed this method that can be easily applied and allows farmers to 'build' a functional agro-ecosystem. Permaculture now integrates land, resources, people and the environment through mutually beneficial synergies – imitating the no waste, closed loop systems seen in diverse natural systems.

13   In the Netherlands there are two associations of farmers and advisors that apply closed-loop farming. One is called Network for Vital Agriculture and Food, netwerkvlv.nl, the other is VBBM, short for Association of Farmers for a better Environment. Closed-loop farming was not known in the Netherlands, let alone it being supported. When the NetworkVLV asked the Ministry of Agriculture to support the knowledge development for close loop farming, a feasibility study was carried out by CLM (Centre for Agriculture and Environment) into the positive effects of closed-loop farming. It was hesitatingly stated that closed-loop farming might be beneficial for the environment.

14   Hairs, on the body and legs of insects, and also in their facet eyes, act as antennae. The length of the hairs is related to the frequencies it can register. Since each gas has its own frequency, it is a way of communication, so that insects can 'know' where they need to be. Roelf Havinga, Team Ecosys.

15   The term 'cross-compliance' refers to the requirement for farmers to comply with a set of Statutory Management Requirements (SMRs) and keep their land in Good Agricultural and Environmental Condition (GAEC) in order to qualify for the full single payment and other direct payments. The SMRs relate to the areas of public, animal and plant health, environment and animal welfare. The standards of GAEC relate to the issues of soil erosion, soil organic matter, soil structure, ensuring

a minimum level of maintenance, avoiding the deterioration of habitats and protection and management of water.

16   Can we feed the world without pesticides? The documentary Crops of the Future (1996) shows that yes, we can! Directed by Marie-Monique Robin, and spanning four continents - from Mexico to Japan, via Kenya, Senegal, Malawi, the United States and Germany - the film has been broadcast by ARTE and five international channels. It has been screened in more than 150 theatres in France. It is available on DVD. For more information, contact m2rfilms.com. Alternatively, you can find it here: http://vimeo.com/52532401

17   In the abundance of seafloor massive sulphide deposits, an international team of geologists attempts to quantify the total available copper and zinc contained in deep-sea massive sulphide mounds. Massive seafloor sulphide mounds are a byproduct of the processes that create deep-sea hydrothermal vents. As super-heated sea water emerges from the vent, it deposits heavy metals and other elements and minerals along the walls of the vent. Over thousands of years, an active vent field can build up a huge mound of metal and mineral rich ore – a massive sulphide mound. In addition to copper and zinc, these mounds can contain gold and silver. Generally, the ore is of much higher quality than its terrestrial counterpart. Over the last few decades, many exploration companies were eyeing these deposits, but it's only recently that technological developments and economic incentives have aligned to permit potentially profitable deep-sea mining.

18   Peak Oil, an event based on M. King Hubbert's theory, is the point in time when the maximum rate of petroleum extraction is reached, after which the rate of production is expected to enter terminal decline. Peak Oil theory is based on the observed rise, peak, (sometimes rapid) fall, and depletion of aggregated production rate in oil fields over time. Mostly due to the development of new production techniques and the exploitation of unconventional supplies, Hubbert's original predictions for world production proved too conservative. Peak oil is often confused with oil depletion; peak oil is the point of maximum production, while depletion refers to a period of falling reserves and supply.

Some observers, such as petroleum industry experts Kenneth S. Deffeyes and Matthew Simmons, predict negative global economy implications following a post-peak production decline and oil price increase because of the high dependence of most modern industrial transport, agricultural, and industrial systems on the low cost and high availability of oil. Predictions vary greatly as to what exactly these negative effects would be.

Optimistic estimations of peak production forecast the global decline will begin after 2020, and assume major investments in alternatives will occur before a crisis, without requiring major changes in the lifestyle of heavily oil-consuming nations. These models show the price of oil at first escalating and then retreating as other types of fuel and energy sources are used Pessimistic predictions of future oil production made after 2007 stated either that the peak had already occurred that oil production was on the cusp of the peak, or that it would occur shortly.

[19] See: http://www.defra.gov.uk/farm/policy/sustain/procurement/index.htm)

[20] Tony Rinaudo. Natural Resource Management Specialist, World Vision Australia. G.P.O. Box 399C, Melbourne, Victoria 3001, Australia. E-mail: tonyrinaudo@worldvision.com.au

[21] In nature, every organism is independent and at the same time systemically interconnected to other organisms. Inspired by ecological principles, representing the wisdom of nature and the universe, we continuously strive to gain and sustain a harmonious balance between the following polarities and to integrate them into our development

Self assertion -   integration

Expansion   -   conservation

Competition-   cooperation

Quantity   -   quality

Sovereignty -   partnership

[22] The 2d Annual Conference of the World Cultural Forum (Taihu, China) in Hangzhou

On May 18th to 19th, 2013, the second annual conference of the World Cultural Forum (Taihu, China) was successfully held in Hangzhou with the theme 'Strengthen International Cooperation for Ecological Civilization'. Chairman of the National Committee of the Chinese People's Political Consultative Conference (CPPCC) Yu Zhengsheng attended this Conference and delivered the keynote address at the opening ceremony. More than 500 people from 23 countries and regions around the world, who are dignitaries and celebrities in ecology, culture, economics and media both at home and abroad including President of the Republic of Mozambique Armando Emilio Guebuza, Governor-General of Antigua and Barbuda Dame Louise Lake-tack, Greek Prime Minister Antonis Samaras. When the Conference concluded, the guests jointly signed a Hangzhou Declaration on Promoting Ecological Civilization Construction based on equal exchanges, each expressing their own opinions and seeking common grounds while reserving differences.

[23] IIED needs to be bold and seek out places and sectors in which we and partners can influence decisions at global, national and local levels. This is our strategy for the next five years — pushing the boundaries of research, building partnerships and engaging for change. Please

get in touch with us, because it is only through collaboration that we can identify, apply and scale up solutions for a fairer, more sustainable world.

24 Within the 'New Partnership for Africa's Development' (NEPAD), a programme of the African Union, the "Comprehensive Africa Agriculture Development Programme" (CAADP) was created that is entirely African-led and African-owned and represents African leaders' collective vision for agriculture in Africa. For example, agricultural reform in Africa aims for an annual growth rate of 6% in agriculture by 2015. CAADP has four pillars: 1) Sustainable land and reliable water control systems; 2) Private sector development, rural infrastructure, improved trade & market access; 3) Increasing food supply and reducing hunger; and 4) Agricultural research and dissemination of agricultural technology. Within this last pillar, CoS-SIS focuses on research on the impact of agricultural innovation systems approaches.

25 An example of the change in behaviour that needs institutional change. In 2012 the FAO advised to produce and consume less meat, worldwide. If we want to follow up on that advise and make the transition, a real systems change in both consumers' and producers' behaviour, we encounter the following barriers, which can only be tackled by 4 synchronic (and probably orchestrated) societal changes.

At the meat-**production** side there are two big barriers, both Cultural and Structural and enhanced by (a conservative) Attitude.

1. A powerful, influential agro-industrial production system, which is not liable to change its approaches drastically or on a short term, unless it is economically viable.

2. Global regulations (WTO) which, by their character, do not stimulate the sitting regime to change toward more sustainable approaches.

Using Wilber's model for the meat- **consumption** side we find barriers in Behaviour, Attitude, Culture (worldviews) and Structure:

Barriers in Behaviour
- In our Western menu, meat plays a dominant role. People are used to eating meat every day. Vegetarian is regarded as alternative.
- Habit: to change to another way of cooking and eating is difficult, needs extra effort.
- Food buying habits: people are often used to buy at a certain supermarket, know their route, and buy habitual food.

Barriers in Attitude

- 'Perception gap.' People assume - and will tell you - that nowadays they eat and buy more sustainably. But when monitored it doesn't appear to be so.
- Consumption is narcistic, focussed on satisfying the Self. Sugar, chocolate, alcohol, fast food or just too much food, is taken when one wants to feel better. This attitude is enhanced by advertisements claiming that "you are worth this", and so offering self-esteem through food or drinks.
- People generally do not see the connection between their individual choices and the societal impact, either here (economy, health) or in other countries.
- A feeling of impotence "It wouldn't make a difference if I stopped eating meat while all those other people won't and on top of that, the Chinese eat meat increasingly, would it?"

Barriers in Culture/ Worldview

- The individual is more important than the community or the relationship with nature. This expresses itself in our (Western) eating culture: "I feel better or more important when I can afford to eat a lot and when I BBQ often. If I want strawberries in December they should be available." Most people are not even aware of the ecological and societal footprint of the products they eat, or the circumstances under which their food is being produced.
- People have lost the connection with food as the final result of a human and natural process. Food is regarded as 'goods' that can be bought; cows are no longer seen as animals but as milk machines, pigs and chicken are not visible at all and are not much more than meat on legs.
- Estrangement; the relationship with the animal behind the meat has gone lost. Hardly anyone realises that the nicely packed 4 chicken breasts, that look not much different from soy, have come from two real life chicken.
- There is a commonly accepted idea that one needs to eat meat to remain healthy.

Barriers in Structure/ Institutional level

- Meat is cheap since many external production costs are not (taken into account in the price) if the environmental, and health costs would be incorporated, then meat and other food products would be unaffordable.
- Regional and organic products however would be cheaper.
- At country-policy level, the seriousness of the effects of excessive meat production and consumption has not been recognised yet. Partly because there are too high stakes in maintaining the

production itself (mport/export, GNP, agribusiness and food conglomerates lobby).
- Few politicians dare risk their short term future, by suggesting a thorough change in our production systems for the longer term.
- The European Union considers itself a protagonist of a rigorous global climate change policy; but she cancelled parliamentary demands for measures toward decreasing meat consumption.

[26] The Tipping Point: How Little Things Can Make a Big Difference (ISBN 0-316- 31696-2). A book by Malcolm Gladwell, first published by Little Brown in 2000

[27] http://www.youtube.co m/watch?v=fW8amMCVAJQ

[28] H.E.Wielinga; de initiatievenspiraal. http://www.toolsfornetworkers.nl/wp/wp-content/uploads/Initiatieven-spiraal-beschriving.pdf

[29] Written by Daniele Diavanucci, Gabriel Scherr, Danielle Nierenberg, Charlotte Hebebrand, Julie Shapiro, Jeffrey Milder, Keith Weeler

[30] Sustainable Development in the 21st Century, SD21. "Re-thinking is necessary because we are aiming for the wrong goals. Our eating habits result in poor health and the destruction of eco-systems. This is stupid; the importance of healthy food for the worldwidepopulation is the responsibility of the wrong parties and not related to correct agricultural and water management practices. We have to restore the nutritive value and the vitality of food through better soil management. No more empty calories! In the developed countries import of food is more important than its production; while there are 50.000 edible crops in the world, fifty percent of our food consists of three crops, grain, rice and maize; farmers and emerging organisations which contribute to the resilience and reinforcement of natural resources through the use of ecological agriculture and soil management are hardly supported. Industrial agriculture is the largest water user; on top of that it is the cause that annually some 20.00 to 50.000 km2 of productive land are lost as a result of erosion and land degradation."

[31] Glyphosate is a non-selective herbicide that kills any plant it comes into contact with, regardless of whether it is a weed or a crop. "Roundup ready" crops, including soy, corn and cotton have been genetically modified to tolerate glyphosate, meaning that farmers can apply as much of the herbicide as they want without worrying about hurting their crops. As a result, glyphosate use has increased tenfold since it was last approved by U.S. Environmental Protection Agency in the early 90s. With the use of glyphosate steadily increasing, it is imperative that JMPR acts to protect the public from being exposed to this probable human carcinogen in their food. Unfortunately, glyphosate is linked to cancer (Group 2A 'probable' human carcinogen) by the International Agency for Research on Cancer (IARC), the prestigious cancer assessment arm of the WHO. But, cancer-causing chemicals

have friends in high places. Monsanto is the world's leading producer of glyphosate, with annual sales of Roundup netting about two billion U.S. dollars. Unsurprisingly, the company quickly fired back with a statement on how the company is "outraged" at IARC's "agenda-driven bias" in its "irresponsible" decision-making. [As a side, since IARC announced its decision, a group of U.S. citizens have filed a class action lawsuit against Monsanto for falsifying safety claims and a group of Chinese citizens have filed a lawsuit against the Chinese government for hiding Monsanto's toxicity studies from the public].

32   The Belgian support for cooperations is called VLIF. It supports the start up of licensed farmers' cooperations and has as its main goal that the farmers create a communal market. The cooperation takes the shape of a cooperative company, a non profit organisation, an actual association of at least three farmers, who are individually responsible. The support consists of an amount of maximal 22.500 euro http://tinyurl.com/VLIFboeren; rudy.geerts@lv.vlaanderen.be

33   http://tinyurl.com/VLIFboeren; rudy.geerts@lv.vlaanderen.be

34   Eaton and Shepherd[2] identify five different contract farming models. Under the centralized model a company provides support to smallholder production, purchases the crop, and then processes it, closely controlling its quality. This model is used for crops such as tobacco, cotton, sugar cane, banana, tea, and rubber. Under the Nucleus Estate model, the company also manages a plantation in order to supplement smallholder production and provide minimum throughput for the processing plant. This approach is mainly used for tree crops such as oil palm and rubber. The Multipartite model usually involves a partnership between government bodies, private companies and farmers. At a lower level of sophistication, the Intermediary model can involve subcontracting by companies to intermediaries who have their own (informal) arrangements with farmers. Finally, the Informal model involves small and medium enterprises who make simple contracts with farmers on a seasonal basis. Although these are usually just seasonal arrangements they are often repeated annually and usually rely for their success on the proximity of the buyer to the seller.

35   Friedman, landscapesblog, FAO.

36   IAASTD, 2008

37   For Nucleus Farming, see http://www.fao.org/docrep/004/y0937e/y0937e05.htm

38   This article was published in a special report of the PNAS, with editors Jeffrey Sayer and Kenneth Cassman. It emphasizes innovations in agriculture which can contribute to an increse in food production without an increased negative impact on the environment.

39   Sayer, J., T. Sunderland, J. Ghazoul, J. Pfund, D. Sheil, E. Meijaard, M. Venter, A.K. Boedhihartono, M. Day, C. Garcia, C. van Oosten, and L.E. Buck. 2013. Ten principles for a landscape approach to reconciling agriculture, conservation, and other competing land uses. PNAS 110(21): 8349-8356.

40   http://blog.ecoagriculture.org/2013/06/06/10-ways-to-cut-global-food-loss-and-waste

41   http://www.wrap.org.uk/ The research further revealed that alf of the waste could have been recycled. After recycling this would have had a value of 1.38 million euros. Annually 26.000 tonnes of waste is dumped illegally.

42   http://www.thinkeatsave.org/

Printed in Great Britain
by Amazon

79512922R00150

BOOK FOUR

Psycho

A DARK MAFIA ROMANCE

CHELLE ROSE

NOTE TO READER

This book is a dark romance with dark themes. Please read the trigger warnings prior to diving in. They can be found on the author's website at www.chelleroseauthor.com

Or scan the QR below

This book is a purely fictional creation, from the author's dark mind. Please don't use it as a 'how to' book. The main characters in this book play dangerously. Do not attempt replicating these scenes at home.

DEDICATION

To all of you who have fantasized about being railed by a pierced psycho. It's gonna be dark, dirty, and bloody. Be a good girl, and take what Psycho has to give you.

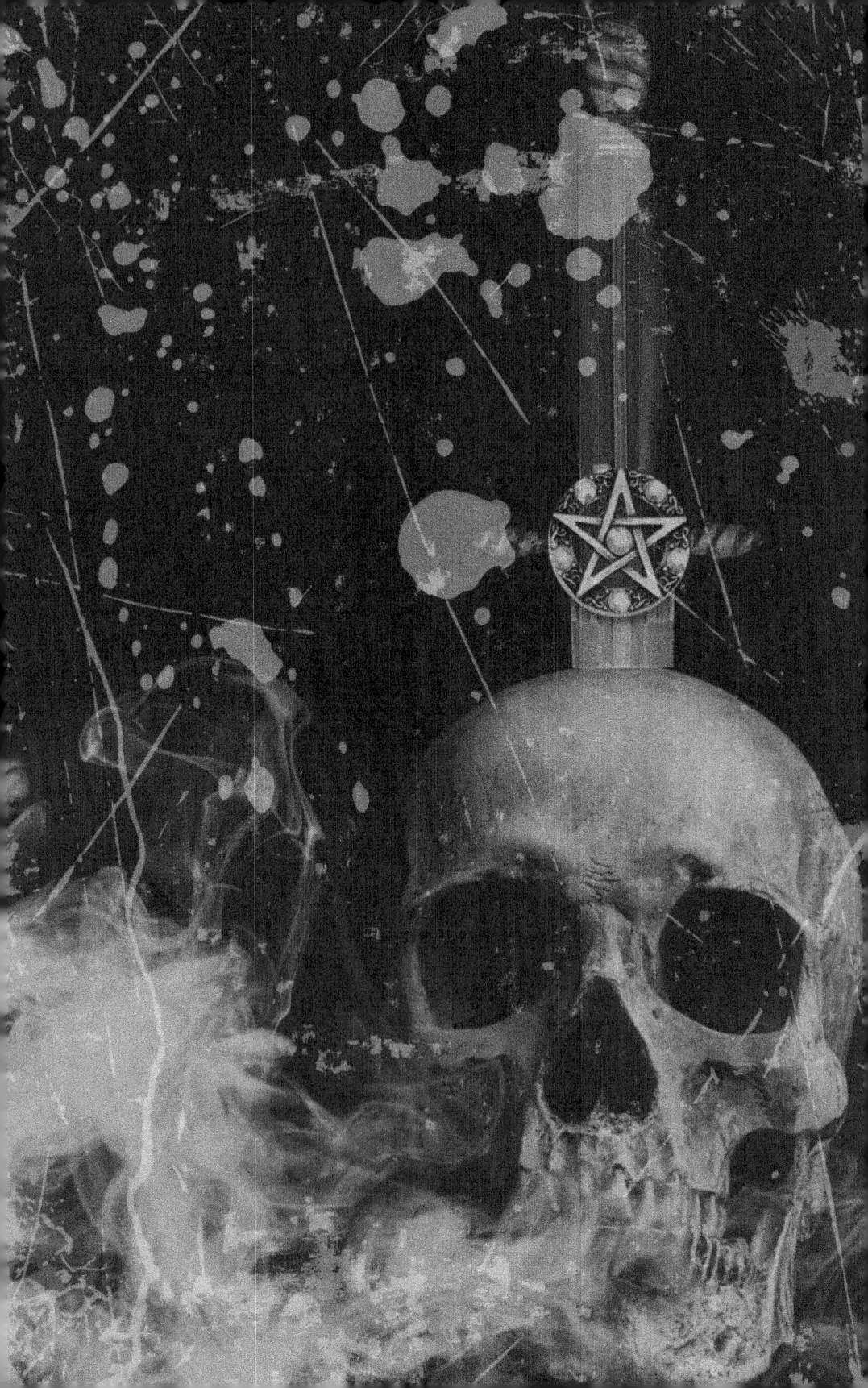

Prologue
ANASTASIA

My life is a sick, twisted joke.

It wasn't always this way.

Once upon a time, I was someone else. Daddy's little girl, blissfully unaware life can change on a dime.

Bonetti.

The name itself is like poison on my tongue.

Everything begins and ends with them, the family that put the collision course of my life into motion. Without them, none of this would have happened.

They took everything from me, and now I'll return the favor.

Revenge is sweet, and mine.

Luca Bonetti.

Lorenzo Bonetti.

Nico Bonetti.

Massimo Bonetti.

I trace over their names on my sheet of paper, and linger on the last one. Shoving away the pang in my chest, I tilt my head back, looking to the sky.

"I'm sorry it has taken so long. Things got complicated. I made you a promise, and I will see it through."

The scent of fresh cut grass surrounds me, as I smile at the red roses in the flower holder attached to the gravestone. I lean forward, and inhale the smell of the bouquet, embracing the instant comfort it provides me. A memory of a better time, before the end of happiness. Pressing a kiss to two of my fingers, I place them against the headstone. My therapist once told me the stages of grief are different, depending on the person. Some people move through them quickly while others do not. I'm beginning to wonder if some people don't move through them at all, because I'm stuck on that day. Whether I'm awake or asleep, it plays on repeat, like a song you can't get out of your head. The visions flash in front of my eyes, and I'm taken back to that time, unwillingly, like I'm being escorted by the ghost of the past, as if I'm a character in some new fucked up version of a *Charles Dickens* novel.

I've contemplated suicide more than once, but that would mean handing them my defeat. I will not give in. I will not let them win.

Gone is the girl they once knew.

From the ashes they left me in, I'll emerge as a new woman. The weak can become strong. The victim becomes the villain. Rising from the wreckage of destruction, caused by evil men in my life, I am reborn.

Chapter One

ANASTASIA

Enemies can become friends, and friends can become enemies. When your so-called friend does something unforgivable, your enemy is born. The guilt is heavy as I collect evidence on the Bonetti brothers because, as a girl, Mama Bonetti was good to me. A second mother, maybe more of a mother than the woman that gave birth to me. I have to ignore the pit in my stomach, that only seems to grow, because I made a promise. One I will not break.

After attempting to get the most recent Bonetti woman, Raina, to turn my witness, and failing miserably, I know I'm going to have to get my hands dirty. I blow out an agitated breath, as I thumb through the contents of the folder with my evidence on the Bonetti brothers, or lack thereof. This is why I needed her. I don't have shit. They've covered their tracks well. Raina Abruzzo was on board until she wasn't.

She fell in love with one of my four targets, refusing to give me anything further. It would've been easy for her to get what I need, with her living inside Kage Bonetti's home. Too easy.

By now, I've made my presence clear. I've tried to get one of their own to my side, and shown my face at Bones Bonetti's house, but I'm confident he didn't recognize me.

They have three warehouses that I've discovered, but I know there are more. I want to know where the weapons are. If we can get an indictment, it will lead the way to searching their various properties. Then a superseding indictment will follow, and we can use everything we find to nail their asses to the wall. Life in prison is not good enough for the Bonetti brothers. I'd prefer death sentences, but I'll settle for seeing them behind bars, for the rest of their natural lives. The man I'd really like to see rot is dead, so his sons will have to do.

Theo comes into my office with an iced coffee in his hand, and a smile on his face.

He hands me the drink, and I smile my thanks, but it's not sincere. Like all men, his kindness has ulterior motives. Call me jaded, but I did not get here on my own, I had a lot of help along the way.

"Dinner tonight?" He asks, his voice dripping with mock sweetness, as he nearly begs me with his gaze.

"You have asked me out every day for the last six months. Why?"

Theo doesn't bother to sit down, because he knows he has five minutes before I tell him to go.

Stuffing his hands into his pockets nervously, he shrugs his shoulders, and speaks far more confidently than he should.

"Eventually, I'll wear you down. You'll give in, and that will be the beginning of our story."

Glancing away from him, I look at the door, hoping he'll catch my drift. I try to be nice, but he makes it difficult. How many times do I have to tell him I'm not interested? He's a nice-looking guy, but I'm not dating anyone. My focus is on work and my mother. There is no room in my life for romance, or whatever else he wants.

'Your pussy. The rest of you is worthless.' I hear Carlo in my head, his voice an always present reminder of my past.

Narrowing his gaze at me, Theo leans over my desk and spots the paperwork, with a photograph of a Bonetti warehouse laying on top. Shaking his head, he says, "I told you to leave them alone. You will not win this, Anastasia. If they catch wind of your investigation, they'll kill you, long before RICO charges are brought against them. There will be no warning, it'll be over and done. These are not men to mess with."

For the second time since he's been in my office, I fight myself to not roll my eyes. He doesn't know my history, but I know this family far better than he does. Yes, if I'm not careful, I'll end up on their long list of victims. Theo is one of the few people that knows my plans. I cannot go to my boss, the DA, without concrete evidence. With an exasperated sigh, he turns on his heel and leaves my office.

My colleagues have reasons for entering the law profession, we all do, but theirs differ from mine. Theo came from a family of lawyers, and it was expected he'd follow in his father's footsteps. Squeaky clean Tabitha wants to change the world for the better. Everybody thinks I'm a good girl that wants to rid the world of scum, and I suppose I do.

Bonetti scum.

My reason is pure vengeance.

They took something from me I can never get back. It's why I'm a lawyer, and worked my ass off to make it to the District Attorney's office.

The end of the Bonetti Brothers is here. Lucky me, I'll have a front-row seat to watch their destruction.

Chapter Two

PSYCHO

One Month Before Reaper's Wedding…

I stitch my victim's arm to slow the bleeding, while whistling. His whimpers are muffled, because of the duct tape over his mouth.

Looking down at him, I flash him an evil grin, and his return gaze is one of terror.

"Shall we start on the other side?"

Theo lies strapped to my metal table, trembling with fear, and unable to speak. I did give him the opportunity to spill everything he knows about the nosy Assistant District Attorney, but he didn't want to talk, so here we are.

I drag the knife down his left arm, and watch the blood spill from the wound. It's a beautiful sight, but not as much as it will be when I get my hands on her. The woman coming after my family. Anastasia Crowne is the true target. Theo is for information purposes, because the goddamn background check on her provided nothing.

"Would you like to talk now, or do I keep going?"

The muffled words against the tape cause me to chuckle. He talks rapidly, but, of course, I can't make out a single unintelligible word.

Grabbing one side of the duct tape, I pull it off, as he gulps for air like he couldn't breathe. He still has a fucking nose. I don't know why he's being dramatic.

"I gave you the opportunity to talk before, and you didn't take it. So now, you talk, and I'll work."

He catches my drift, as I drag my knife down his stomach, cutting into his flesh, but I'm not trying to kill him yet. Just terrorize him a bit. Not only to get him to give over the information I want, but because, fuck, it's fun. Should I feel bad, since he hasn't done a fucking thing to deserve this? Probably, but I don't. He's guilty by association.

"Okay, okay," he sobs loudly.

I chuckle darkly as I pull the knife out, and push it in on the other side of his stomach, deeper, but still not enough to be fatal. This isn't about prolonging torture for my enjoyment, the only thing I seek is information. Although, I'm enjoying it a bit. They don't call me Psycho for no reason. Still, if he gives me what I need, the pain will end. Usually the people on my table have wronged me, or my family. He has done nothing other than take a job at the District Attorney's office. Unfortunate mistake.

"She hates your family."

Holding the knife inside him, I stop moving, as I knit my brows together in confusion. It sounds personal, and doesn't make sense, since we had never met this woman when she started her bullshit.

"You mean she hates mafia families?"

That's something I could at least understand. There are people that hate us simply because of who we are. People fear us, and that causes dislike. I don't blame them really, but if they don't cross us, as the assistant DA did, they have nothing to fear. Aside from my brother, Reaper, we don't hurt innocent people. He kills for the thrill, and I'm confident at least one innocent person has lost their life at his hands.

"No," his nostrils flare, as he exhales a shaky breath, teary blue eyes focused on mine. I know he's hoping for survival, and I'll let him hold onto that hope, for now.

"She hates your family. The Bonettis. I told her to let it go, because I know enough about you to know it's a death sentence."

Why does she have this obsession with us? It could be to further her position in the DA's office. Or maybe she wants to write a book, or some stupid shit like that.

"Why?"

"I don't know. She won't talk about it. Only said it was a personal matter."

How the fuck can it be a personal matter, when we've never met this goddamn woman? While I do believe him, when he says he doesn't know, the lack of information causes the blood in my veins to boil. Fucking dangerous for him.

"Open your mouth."

He does, and I close my forceps around his tongue, gripping it hard enough to make him whine like a little bitch.

"If you're not going to tell me what I want to know, I may as well cut your fucking tongue out."

Theo's face turns beet red as I tighten my forceps on his tongue, holding it firmly in place. His muscles are tense, and his unblinking eyes bulge, as he moans frantically.

"You're fucked, Theo. There is nothing you can do, other than give me what I want."

Sobs wrack his entire body, as his eyes dart back and forth, clearly wondering what's next for him. Shaking his head, he attempts to wriggle free from my grasp, but fails miserably. The only thing he does is cause himself more pain, as the metal digs into his tongue.

"Your death is a guarantee. The only question is, will it be quick, and relatively painless, or slow, and excruciating?"

It's not often they get the choice. I guess I'm feeling generous today.

His red eyes stare at me as he cries. Fuck, he cries a lot for a man. Then again, the Bonetti boys were raised to be stronger than your average man. It was a lesson I learned the hard way, and early in my life. I was twelve, the first time I was tortured, because I was the first-born Bonetti son.

Hanging upside down, from a chain wrapped around my feet, they lower my head into a filthy barrel of water, submerging me for what feels like hours. Each time they pull me up, I cough, and gasp for air.

The Russian man stares at me with boredom.

"Where are the weapons?" he asks in a thick accent.

I say the same thing I've said for the last several days.

"I don't know, I'm just a kid."

My father has been training me, to eventually take over, for the last year. I know where the warehouses are, the man that manufactures them, and everyone involved, yet, I won't tell them a damn thing. A Bonetti will endure whatever torture they hand out, so I'll gladly die, but I will never give any information on my family.

Only weak men succumb to torture. Even as a child, I'm unshakable.

He lowers my head into the water again, and I hold my breath for as long as I can, but eventually end up taking water into my lungs. Kuznetzov pulls me back up, with a grin on his face, as I cough once again and fight for air.

"Ready to talk?" He says, and I nod my head, as much as I can, with all the blood rushing to my brain.

"Sorry, Cuntnetzov, you won't break me. I am a Bonetti. You can kill me, but you'll never force me to tell you a fucking thing about my family."

Theo continues to whimper and cry, snapping me from my memory, and causing me to roll my eyes. I press my blade to his throat, which only makes him squeal louder.

I arch an eyebrow in warning. At this point this asshole is far more annoying than useful.

"Careful, make too much noise and the movement of your throat might be your end."

Pulling the knife back slightly, I tell him how it's going to go.

"You have thirty seconds to tell me everything about Anastasia Crowne. If you're a good boy, then I'll make this quick. If not, I'll be cutting and stitching you up for fucking days. The choice is yours."

More tears roll down his cheeks, as he accepts that this is his end, but he finally gives me what I need.

"She became a lawyer for the sole purpose of destroying your family."

Wow. That's some fucking dedication right there. If I weren't seeing red over the 'destroying my family' part, I'd be impressed. Really fucking impressed.

"Continue," I order, and he does, earning himself a pat on the head.

"What do you want to know?"

I chuckle darkly.

"Everything. There is no detail too tedious. I want to know everything about her."

More tears flow, and I am aware this is painful for him emotionally, as well as physically. Not long after I strapped him to my table, he swore he wouldn't tell me anything, because he's in love with her. When faced with torture, love often vanishes. Few men, not of my world, would stay silent, and accept the brutality of my constant slicing. A man like Theo never stood a chance. Poor sap.

"Her father is dead. Mother lives in a trailer park alone. No siblings. Doesn't date. She's completely focused on work."

By work, I assume he means taking down my family, which would never fucking happen.

"What does she know?"

He tries to shift uncomfortably, but he's stuck. Blowing out a long breath, he tries to calm his nerves, still appearing to be in a fit of terror.

"I don't- don't know everything, but she knows where your warehouse is," he stammers pathetically.

I stare at him, a question on my tongue, but he figures out what it is, before I have a chance to speak again.

"The weapons one. She watches sometimes, and has a notebook for documenting her investigation. She never lets it out of her sight at work, so I don't know everything she has found. Her goal is to get

17

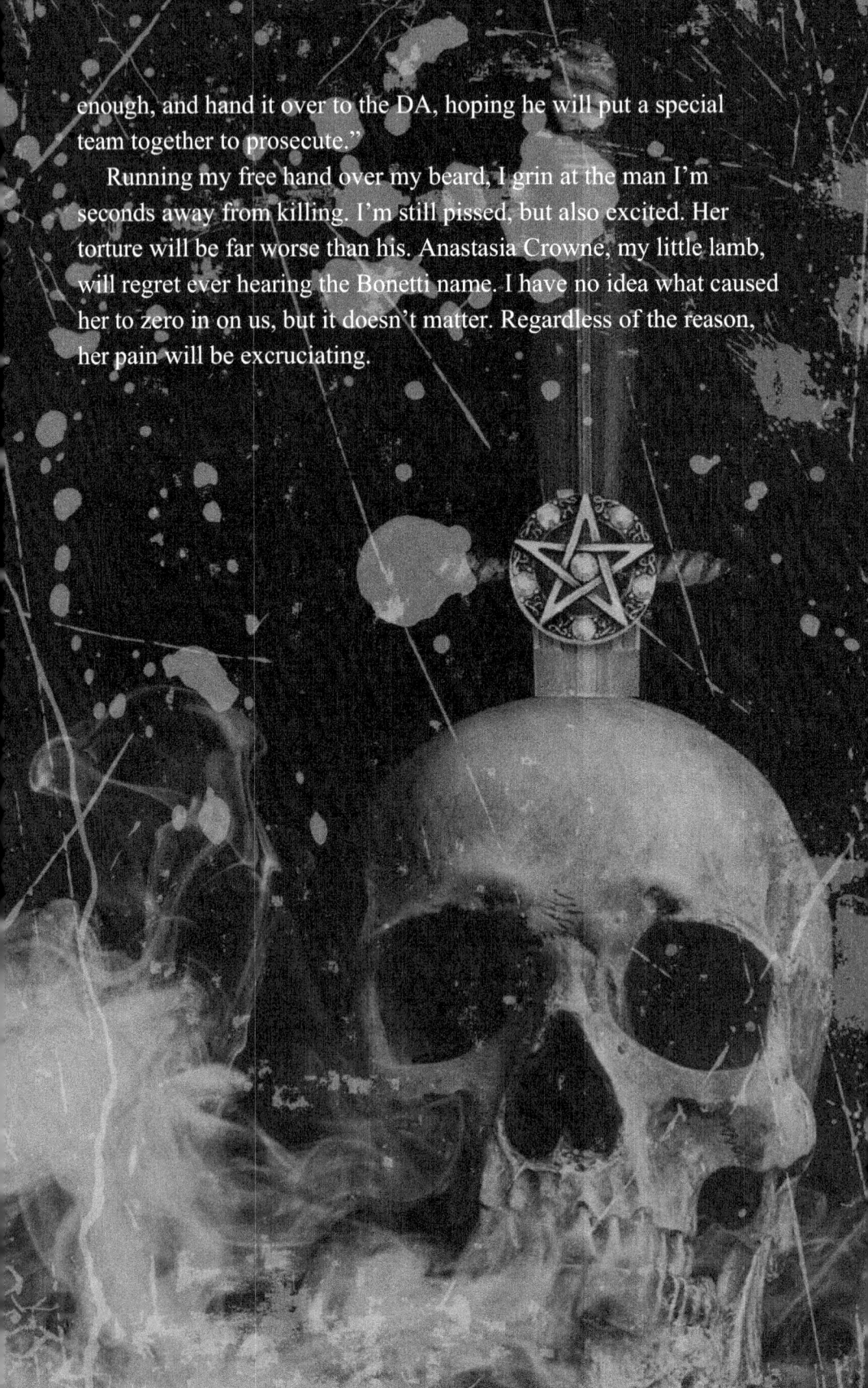

enough, and hand it over to the DA, hoping he will put a special team together to prosecute."

Running my free hand over my beard, I grin at the man I'm seconds away from killing. I'm still pissed, but also excited. Her torture will be far worse than his. Anastasia Crowne, my little lamb, will regret ever hearing the Bonetti name. I have no idea what caused her to zero in on us, but it doesn't matter. Regardless of the reason, her pain will be excruciating.

Chapter Three

PSYCHO

I watch her smile, and collect her coffee from the register of Mounds Coffee Company, which I happen to think is a poorly named business. She smiles, and laughs, with the man at the counter, completely fucking oblivious to the man watching her.

Her killer.

I'm not Reaper. I don't go searching for people to kill, because their eyes look interesting when they die. I'm also not fucking pussy whipped like my three brothers are. Apparently, if they are a good enough fuck, we let traitors live. I cannot touch Kage's firecracker, but the woman that started it all? She's as good as fucking dead.

I lick my lips, as I watch her carry on with her life as if she has nothing but time. Spoiler alert, she does not.

Pretty little lamb, you should not have gone into the wolf's den.

She wanted to know more about the Bonetti Brothers. Her wish is my command. The pretty little counselor will learn firsthand that you do not fuck with us.

One, two, Psycho is coming for you.

Three, four, your blood will coat my floor.

Five, six, you'll beg to live.

Seven, eight, it's too late.

Nine, ten, scream for me again.

I keep my distance for now, so I can learn her routine, as I follow her to the District Attorney's office. She hugs a woman outside, as they laugh about something I don't hear, and walk through the revolving glass door. Pretty little Anastasia Crowne, clueless about what she has started.

I'm her stalker.

Her tormentor.

Her killer.

I stroke my fingers through my short beard, and take a deep sigh in contentment. This will be fun. The girl she is with presses the button for the elevator, as I move closer to her. Am I worried about her recognizing who I am?

Not at all. I'm not stalking her in the shadows, because I want her to know I'm coming for her. When she looks at my face, I want her to know that Massimo Bonetti, also known as Psycho, is coming for her. I step into the elevator, and both women quickly move to the side as they feel my presence, and Anastasia presses number four, never stopping her conversation. We stop on their floor and she glances at me, but there's no recognition on her face. Maybe my aviators disguised me, but I'm disappointed.

She's a few steps ahead of me when I nod to the receptionist. Anastasia stops in her tracks when she hears the words that come out of my mouth.

"Good morning. Mr. Bonetti to see District Attorney Easton."

My eyes dart, from the secretary in front of me, to Anastasia, as the panic visibly sets in. She clenches her free hand into a fist, her muscles tightening as she stops moving, and takes a moment, before she walks down the hall to what I assume is her office. I bet her heart is pounding. Is she struggling to get a full breath? Fuck. I can hardly wait to see the effect my brutality will have on her.

"Is he expecting you?"

I flash her a grin and say, "No," before I walk down the same hallway Anastasia did. As usual, his blinds are down, hiding all his despicable behavior. Without knocking, I open the door, step inside his office, and sit down in the chair across from his desk. He is busy reading something on his computer, and doesn't even notice I'm here. Am I fucking invisible today?

Picking up the picture on his desk, I run my finger along the faces of his wife and daughter.

"I forgot how beautiful they are."

That gets his attention. His gaze snaps to mine, his showing instant uneasiness.

"Mr. Bonetti. Did I miss a meeting? We usually meet outside of the office."

I run my hand over my beard casually, with my eyes glued to the photograph, as I respond to him.

"No. If I want to come into your office, I will. Is there a problem with that?"

He shakes his head emphatically, as I lift my gaze to his.

"No, sir."

Easton does not want me here. There's a risk someone not in our pocket could see me, and cause him some headaches. Other than that, he's fucking petrified of me, as he should be, and doesn't enjoy surprise visits. Every Bonetti brother instills fear, but I like to think I'm more special than they are. I'm known for my psychotic tendencies.

"Tell me everything there is to know about Anastasia Crowne."

He stares at me with a concerned expression, and he should be worried. I don't appreciate questions when I'm asking for answers.

"Is there a problem?"

Sitting back in the black leather chair, I casually cross one leg over the other, and pull my aviators off.

"Nothing I can't handle. I will give you a heads up out of courtesy. You'll need to find a replacement for her. Soon she will disappear and, of course, you won't notice. If her family contacts you, you will have no information for them. The Chief will be concerned enough to handle the investigation himself, but, of course, he won't find anything either. Do we understand each other?"

He swallows hard and nods.

"Yes, sir."

"Now, everything."

I set the picture back on his desk, to let him know his family is safe if he answers my questions. I've never threatened them, because

I haven't had to, but the occasional reminder of what's at stake doesn't hurt.

"She's relatively new to my office. Anastasia has only worked here for a couple of months. She seems eager to serve the community. I think she's the 'change the world' type."

"Her family?" I ask.

Easton shifts in his seat uncomfortably as I glare at him.

"I don't know much, but she was the first in her family to go to college, and most of her pay goes to taking care of her mother."

I scratch the side of my jaw, wondering what the story is, but it doesn't matter.

A sob story will not change the outcome, if there is one.

"Do we understand each other?" I ask with an arched brow.

"Did she do something?"

As I drag my hand down my face, I answer, "She did. It seems your overzealous ADA is doing her own side work. A little investigation into the Bonetti Brothers. I assume you didn't put her up to this? I'm sure you know the consequences of such behavior."

His face goes pale, as he taps his foot under his desk in agitation, likely resisting the urge to run. We both know he wouldn't get far, so it's hardly worth the risk. I've never killed anyone in a government office, but I'm not above it either. I may need to add that to my bucket list.

"No, sir. I know the rules and I play by them. I would never cross your family."

I pull out a bag of cocaine, which is how I bought his silence three years ago. He does whatever the fuck we want, and the drugs keep coming. That's how we control so much of the city. If you find a weak spot, you can easily exploit it.

"Not a word to her, or anyone. If she has a warning to run, you will watch me slice your pretty wife to shreds."

Does he even react to me threatening his wife for the first time? No, of course not, because he's far too focused on his little treat.

Easton stares at the bag on his desk, and I can see him nearly salivate. The second I walk out the door, the white powder will be up his nose. His jaw is clenched, fists tight, like it's taking everything in him to not get high right now. This is why junkies are my fucking favorite. They are the easiest to control.

"I won't betray you. Ever."

I rise from my seat, and pat him on the head.

"Good boy."

Turning away from him, I walk to the door, and hear him rip open the bag before I've even left. Predictable.

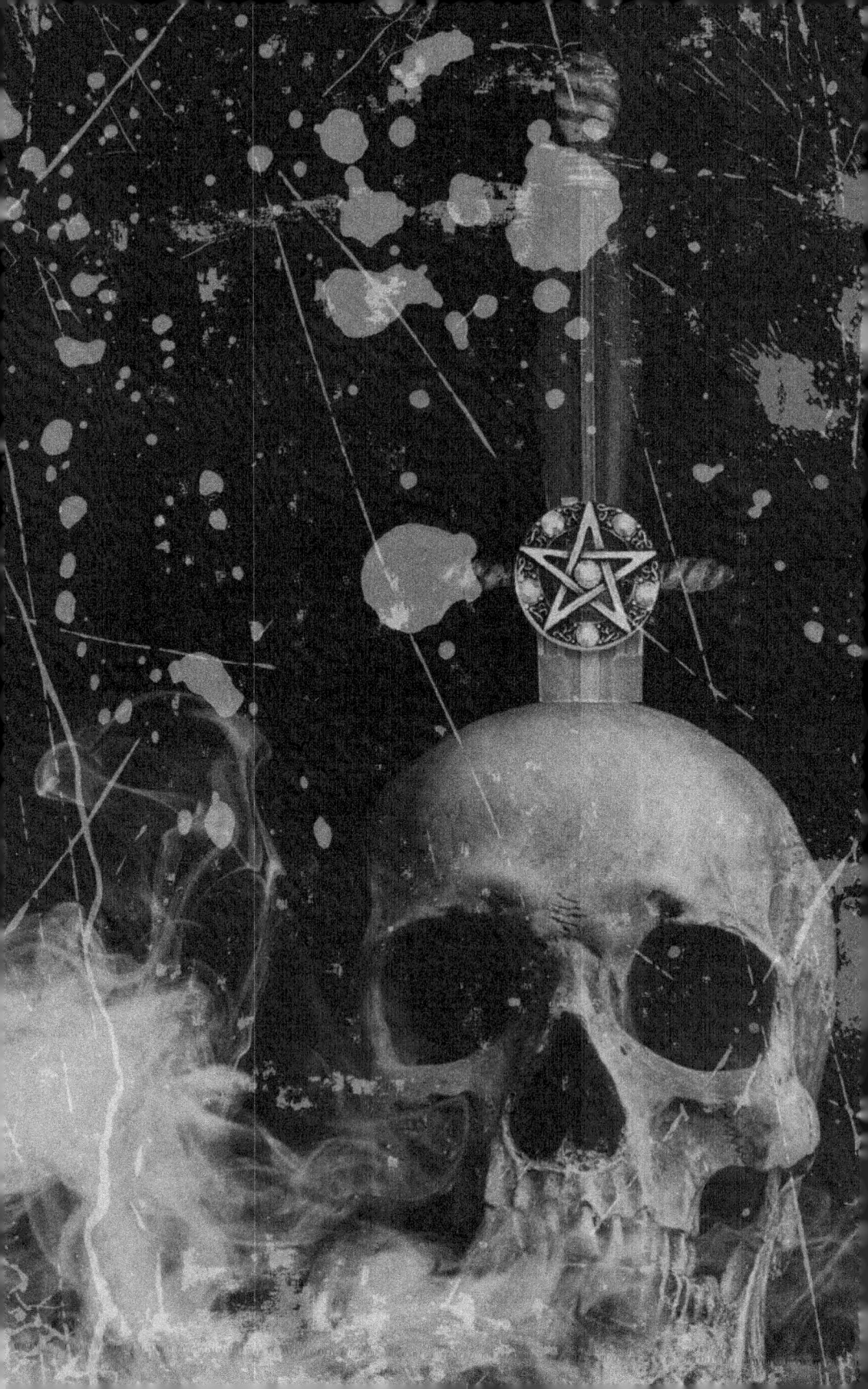

Chapter Four

ANASTASIA

Losing a parent at only twelve years old is tough, but losing two is heartbreaking. My mother isn't dead, but she may as well be. The day my father died, she stopped living. I spend every weekend cleaning her trailer, because it has gotten disgusting. No human should live like this, but she simply doesn't care about anything. Her condition has only gotten worse over time. It started with her eyes glued to the tv, devolving to this nearly catatonic state. I sit beside her bed and stare at her lifeless body, her gaze fixed on something across the room that I'm not sure even exists. Like I'm not here beside her.

"Mom. You can't keep going on like this. I love you and miss you so much. Don't you remember how things used to be? I wish I could even remember the last time I heard you speak to me. Remember how much I hated it when you yelled at me? I'd give anything for you to scream at me right now."

There's no response, like I could've predicted, because there never is. I have not heard my mom's voice in years. Once I moved out, she went further inside herself, and I have no idea how to get her to come back to the land of the living. I have read every medical journal on severe depression, trying to find the answer. I'm no longer certain there is one.

"The doctor says you stopped taking your medication, and that it would probably be best if I put you in a facility."

I draw in a long, steady breath attempting to control the pounding in my head. Her silence causes the frustration to build, and I do my best to not raise my voice. I know it has been hard on her, but I want to scream, 'what about me?' No child should be deserted the way I was, but I also know, she didn't choose this.

"I know you miss him. I understand that, but I can't comprehend why I don't matter to you. When you gave up on living, you abandoned me. I was twelve, and lost everyone and everything that ever mattered to me, in one fell swoop."

Her stillness continues to fill me with a rage that only leads to guilt, so I turn away from her, and stomp to the kitchen like a petulant child. Every cent left, after paying my own bills, goes to caring for my mom. There's a cook that comes in several times a week, to make meals she rarely eats. It's clearly time to hire someone to clean, because I don't think my weekend cleaning sprees are enough anymore. The doctor's bills are more than I can afford, yet I keep paying them in hopes that they can help her. If she's going to refuse the medication she's on for depression and anxiety, they can't do anything. It's a waste of money, but if I take that option from her, she won't ever get better. How can you make someone want to live?

I grab a pot, and warm the soup the cook made for her. It has yesterday's date on it, but doesn't look like it's been touched. I'm not surprised, because over the last several months, she only eats enough to survive. After pouring it into a bowl, I grab a spoon and head back to her bedroom, setting the soup on her worn black end table. There is no point in trying to get her to eat while I'm here, because I already know she won't. I know she does get out of bed occasionally to eat a little, but never when anybody is here. And she is still going to the bathroom on her own, but whenever there are people around, she plays dead.

"I'm going to the graveyard to see Dad. As always, I'll bring him red roses, because I know he'll think of you when he sees them."

She pulls her hand into a fist at the mention of my father. I'm happy to have gotten a reaction from her, even if it's anger. It tells me she's still in there somewhere. My dad loved my mom in a way I think is rare. It was as if he couldn't continue to breathe, if she wasn't near him. It was intense, and beautiful.

26

I pull up to my father's graveyard, and park, before walking over to his grave, with the roses in my hand. When I was a small child, he sent my mother red roses every week. Thursdays were flower delivery days. I once asked him why he had them delivered, instead of bringing them home to her.

"It's more special this way. Any man can buy a cheap bouquet at the grocery store, and bring them home. This is planned, and comes with a card."

"Why every week?" I ask, as I stare at my father with confusion. He chuckles and pats my head.

"It makes her smile, and that means it's worth every cent I spend."

Kneeling in front of his grave, I place the flowers in the metal holder, and sit back on my heels as I talk to him.

"Dad, I miss you. And mom does too. I'm sure she'd be here if she could manage it, but she's trapped in grief. I thought, by now, she would've bounced back, but maybe she never will. It's hard seeing her like this, and I don't know how to help her. She won't take her medication, and only eats barely enough to keep her heart beating."

Talking to a dead man is slightly frustrating, because I need his help desperately, but of course, I won't get it. I've been alone in this world since I was a girl. Had my dad been alive through my Carlo years, he would've saved me from that abusive shit. Yet he wasn't, so I dealt with it alone, and did anything I could to keep my mother safe from him.

Kissing two fingers, and placing them against his headstone, I say my goodbyes.

"I love you. I'm going to see Michael. Please hug him for me, Daddy. I miss you both so much."

Rising, I move to the next gravestone. I brush the dust off the angel carved into the stone, before kneeling beside it.

I don't bother brushing the tears away, I just let them fall, as I speak low.

"I'm sorry, Michael. I tell you that every time I'm here, and I'm going to keep telling you. I miss you, angel. I'd give my life for one more day with you. I still dream about that day, and I have so many regrets. If I had done things differently, you'd still be here. I don't know if I even believe in God anymore, but I hope he's real. I desperately want to believe there's a heaven, and you're up there, enjoying every moment. Is there sunshine there? Remember how you loved sunny days? And soccer," I say, through a teary laugh.

Taking a deep breath, I smile at the memory. Michael running through the grass, kicking the ball all over the place, screaming 'goal' as he kicked it into the play net. There was nobody else there, just the two of us, and it was perfect.

Kissing his grave, the way I did my father's, my breaths come out hard, when talking to him nearly crushes my windpipe. It's always like this, it never gets easier.

"I love you, angel. I'll see you next weekend."

Chapter Five
PSYCHO

The stage has been set at the district attorney's office, but now I want to find out more about her personal life. I have her home address on my cell phone, so I can make a visit. While I can hack, I didn't need to. I rarely do. This is what friendships in government offices buy you. Maybe friendship is not the correct term. Relationships, born from fear. The property tax office in this case.

I smile to myself, as I call the Chief of Police.

"Mr. Bonetti. How can I help you, sir?"

"Bob. How's the family?"

He stammers, "Real good. Real goo-od."

It's a reminder to him why he's in our pocket, and why he wants to stay there.

"Giving you a heads up. There's going to be a break in at 2307 Windover Drive. Be sure to send a detective you can trust, once it's reported."

"Yes, sir. Of course."

I can nearly hear the nerves crackling through the phone line, and can see him wiping his sweaty palms on his slacks, like he always does every time I see him.

"That's all. Give my love to Caroline."

I hang up before he has a chance to respond. People can decide to suddenly grow a conscience, and do the right thing. They need reminders of who will be hurt, if they decide to flip sides. The good guys never win. Not in this world.

She lives in a cozy little neighborhood. There are four houses, including hers, on one side of the street, but only two houses on the other side. They are all cookie cutter, two floor, single-family homes. I park on the street, get out, and go to her back door, with my sledgehammer in my hand. There are a hundred different ways I could get inside without her knowing, but that defeats the purpose. I want little Anastasia to know I'm watching. I want her to jump at every fucking sound, wondering if a Bonetti brother is coming for her. That's the very reason I smash the window on her back door, to let myself in.

My brother, Bones, is the head of our family, and made it clear, in no uncertain terms, that I was not to touch her. I believe his words were to 'not touch a single hair on her head'. He will point to this, and tell me this is the reason our father didn't make me the head of the family. I get really fucking sick of hearing that shit. Am I fucking happy about how things have turned out? Hell no. It should've been me, but I've mostly made peace with it. I am who I am, and I wouldn't change a fucking thing I've done in my life. I've never had any regrets, and this won't be one either.

'You don't think things through, Psycho. You're unhinged and careless.'

I've heard it all, and I don't agree. Okay, yeah, maybe I'm a little unhinged, but I'm not careless. Bones thinks, since she has nothing on us, there's no harm. Nothing can touch us, but that's not the fucking point. If you come after us, you die. I don't mind picking up his slack, because if you want a job done right, you do it yourself. Again, the thought enters my mind that it was always supposed to be me to take over, but I shove the thought away, because now is not the time to be thinking about my goddamn family drama.

People draw comparisons between myself and my brother, Reaper, constantly, because we're both the same brand of evil. There's one big difference though. He'll kill you quickly. I'll do it slow, because the torture is what I'm after. When they finally die, I always have a slight pang of sadness, because I can't hurt them anymore.

After glancing around her spotless kitchen, I make my way to the carpeted stairs, to find her bedroom. That's where secrets are always kept. Is there a boyfriend? This is where I'll find whatever I need to know about her.

I stop mid-step, when I spot photographs on the wall. An image of a small child catches my attention. A little boy that looks to be three or four. Further up, there's another picture, of a man in his thirties, holding an infant. I stare at it for a long moment, feeling that weird deja vu, like I've seen him before, but dismiss it, because no recognition follows. This must be her family, but I don't know who they are. I don't really care.

I walk through the first door, and instantly know it must be the master bedroom. It's large, with an ensuite bathroom. A queen sized bed sits in the middle of the room, with a deep purple satin comforter. An arrangement of flowers is placed on the matching white end table, beside the bed. On the other side of the room sits a matching dresser. Everything has an innocence to it, and it makes me smile. There's something beautiful about evil destroying purity.

Walking over to her dresser, I open the drawer, and pull out a purple vibrator.

Okay, maybe not as pure as I thought.

I hold it up to my nose and inhale. A faint scent remains, along with the soap she must have used to clean it. I'm not planning on fucking her, but I wouldn't rule it out either. I've seen her in person now, along with her pictures, and little Anastasia is fucking gorgeous, and her screams will only make her more appealing. Slipping the toy into my pocket, I go through her assortment of lace panties. So much fucking purple.

Little lamb, I think you have a problem.

There's nothing here that suggests she has a boyfriend. I'm confident she lives alone, since there are only women's clothing in the dresser, and closet.

I have one more thing to do, to let her know I was here, before I can leave. Walking back over to her bed, I unzip my pants and pull my cock out, stroking it, while I imagine what she'll look like with blood dripping down her skin. The way she'll cry for me. The bargaining. She'll tell me she'll do anything, if I make the pain stop. Then she'll realize that only intensifies the pain, and she'll break into a million fucking pieces.

Gripping my length harder, I fuck the palm of my hand, and can almost taste her tears, as I climax with a groan all over her pretty comforter. With a grin, I pull out my knife, and shred her pillows. I toss a card down on her, now destroyed, pillow, with 'Psycho' scrawled just underneath the Bonetti Brothers logo, along with her now empty notebook.

I tuck myself back into my pants, before setting up a camera that's going to catch her reaction, when she walks into her bedroom, and finds my cum on her bed, ruining the angelic look she has created with this room.

Eyeing the white bookshelf in the corner, I decide that's the best spot for the camera. I set it among three porcelain angels, as I snicker to myself. Fitting. Her collection of books is interesting. Trial Law makes sense, given what she does. However, The Complete Mafia History makes me laugh. If this is how she plans to take us down, she never had a chance.

I head down the stairs to leave, and place a camera in her kitchen, among her collection of teas. When she calls the police, and I'm confident she will, this is where they'll start, most likely, and I want to watch her fucking unravel, as they essentially do nothing. Letting the Chief know to watch for this ensures no surprises. He knows damn well to only send dirty cops. Odds are, it would've been fine anyway, since we own close to the entire department at this point, but I don't need the added headache of dealing with some asshole that wants to save the world.

Chapter Six
PSYCHO

I've been watching this camera for the last hour, and my patience is wearing thin. Where the fuck is she? My phone vibrates, as my eyes dart from the two camera feeds on my laptop in my office. 'Reaper' flashes across the screen, and I have no choice but to answer, while I eagerly await her appearance on my monitor.

"Black or blue?" He asks, before I even say hello.

"What?"

"Black or blue? For my vest."

"Right." I groan, "The wedding. Black."

I have no idea why anyone would want to vow to be faithful to someone for the rest of their life. It doesn't make any fucking sense in my brain, but I'm glad my brother chose Bella, if he had to choose someone. She's as crazy as he is. I like her a lot more than my brother Kage's girl, Raina. I'd still kill her if I got the go ahead. If they betray you once, they will betray you twice. It's that simple. I see things in black and white, there's no gray. Either you can be trusted or not. If it's the latter, you will cease to exist.

"Gotta go, Reaper," I say, when I spot her back door opening.

I disconnect the call, before he has a chance to keep me on the phone longer, and zoom in on the camera in her kitchen. She steps over the broken glass, as her eyes dart around the kitchen, surely wondering if her intruder is still in the house. I turn the sound up all the way, and I can just hear her panicked breaths, as she walks through the kitchen. Once she's out of camera view, I wait while she inspects the rest of her house. I'm surprised she hasn't called the police yet, but I wait for her to make it to the bedroom, while I mentally berate myself for not putting cameras everywhere.

Finally, her bedroom door opens, and she walks into view. Anastasia appears to notice the pillows first, as she moves closer to the bed. Unfortunately, her face is hidden, since my current viewing point is her back, which isn't bad to look at, but I'd prefer to see her fear. She shakes her head, turns, and sits on the edge of the bed. I chuckle as she places her hand, palm down, on my cum, and jumps up in a frenzy. I turn the volume up, and listen to her freaking out.

She holds her hand in front of her, spreading her fingers, as the white substance strings from one finger to the other.

"No!" she says in utter disbelief.

Her face turns red, and I can't help but laugh at her misery, as I kick my feet up on my desk and lean back in my chair.

"This is not cum," she nearly chants, as she races toward the bathroom, I assume to wash her hands, as I continue laughing. Pretty little Anastasia will learn there are a lot of things I'll do to her that she never fucking imagined anyone would. Game on, ADA.

My entertainment continues, after the police come and go, and of course, they did nothing. They barely glanced at her bedroom. The blanket was left untouched. No DNA testing. Of course, this is not a surprising outcome. It happened exactly the way I knew it would, after all, I orchestrated it, although there is something unexpected happening right now. Putting my feet back on the floor, I move closer to the screen as she takes a spoon, and scoops a spoonful of my cum into an evidence bag.

I tilt my head to the side, and she shivers, as if she can feel the weight of my stare.

"Bad fucking girl," I say out loud, and even though she can't hear me, she turns to the camera once again, as if she did, and I fucking groan from the look on her face. Furious eyes stare back at me, before she turns back to the bed, to collect her evidence that will fucking go nowhere.

34

I'm lost in a fantasy of cutting deep into her flesh, and watching the blood drip from her skin, when she leaves the room. After waiting, for what feels like a long time, she comes back into view.

I watch Anastasia walk into the bedroom with a gas can. She douses the comforter with gasoline as I watch, enthralled.

She is not going to set her bed on fire.

Few people surprise me, but this astonishes me. I can't tear my eyes from the crazy woman on my screen, as I adjust myself in my pants. I'm hard again, from watching her melt down like this.

"Fucking disgusting Bonetti Brothers," she complains, as she sets the can on the floor beside her dresser. I smile at her angry expression on the monitor. This is precisely why I left the card. I want her to know it's us. Before I kill her, for being the nosy bitch she is, I want her fucking terror. And that, I can promise, I will have.

Grabbing the lighter beside a candle on the nightstand, she lights the fabric and stands back with a fucking smile on her face, as her bed ignites.

I'm fucking mesmerized as I watch her, with a satisfied smile on her face. Her expression turns to one of panic as the flames rise. I think she just realized that her house could burn down. Either that, or she is remembering that arson is indeed a crime.

She goes into the bathroom, comes out with a fire extinguisher, and goes to work on putting out the flames. She's very lucky that it was effective, because the fire could have spread far quicker than it did. If she reacts to my cum on her bed like that, I can hardly wait to see how she responds, when I come all over her face.

35

Reaper's Wedding Day

I shake my head, as I watch my little brother kissing his bride. All three of my brothers are married, or fucking close to it. Kage broke our pact, and I'm the only one with an ounce of sanity left. My phone vibrates in my pocket, as they all play the part of good husbands.

Retrieving it, I answer it quickly, since it's one of our security guys.

"Boss, you warned us about a dark-haired woman lurking. I can't tell if it's the one from the picture, but it might be."

"Keep your distance. Unless she attempts to leave, and in that case, stop her."

For a brief moment, I consider saying something to my brothers, instead of just leaving, but decide against it. It's better to ask for forgiveness, than to ask for permission you know would be denied.

I head out to my dark blue McLaren, and make my exit from my brother's wedding in a hurry. The excitement of what's coming travels through my veins. Call me a bad guy, but I enjoy torture. And when it's a person planning to destroy my entire family, it's a little sweeter. Anastasia Crowne has her reasons, they always do, but I don't give a fuck what they are. It doesn't matter. Every threat will be eliminated. Even a gorgeous one. And she is fucking gorgeous. My cock hardens behind my zipper, as I imagine her beautiful screams. Will they be loud and screeching? Or more of a breathy whimper? I am about to find out.

As I approach the warehouse, I pull over and go on foot, so I can surprise her. Our guys were told to stand down, and I know, without hearing from them, that they obeyed my orders. I nod to my security guy, Mark, who moves his head in the direction she's in. I don't see her at first, because it's dark, and she's far away. I make it through the gate, and travel to the spot he motioned to. As I get closer, I spot her behind a tree, long dark hair falling in waves to her full ass. A small hand rests on the bark of the tree, as she looks around, searching for something she'll never find. I walk closer to her, quietly, so I don't alert her to my presence.

I stop when I'm standing behind her, close enough to touch, but I keep my hands to myself, for now.

"Find anything useful?"

She spins around with a squeak, and raises her fists, like she has any chance of fighting me off. I narrow my gaze at her.

"Lay one finger on me, and I'll have you arrested."

I smirk before chuckling.

"You're on my property, little lamb. Maybe I should have you arrested."

Chapter Seven

ANASTASIA

Twenty-six years ago, he was my protector, whether I wanted him to be or not.

I stand holding my two cut braids in my hands, with tears running down my face. All four Bonetti brothers are mean, so this shouldn't surprise me, but it does.

Massimo comes into the kitchen, after returning from his run, and stops in his tracks when he spots me, knitting his brows, his expression showing concern for me.

"What happened?"

His gaze travels, from the tears on my cheeks, down to the hair in my hands. I am like any other 12-year-old girl. My hair is important to me, and this is devastating.

"Luca cut my hair!" I say, as I continue to look at the damage he has done. I don't know how I am supposed to go to school on Monday, looking like this. He darts out of the room, yelling, "Luca! Get in here!"

The Bonetti brothers aren't the kind of boys that talk things over. It's no surprise, when I go after them, and find Massimo on top of Luca, punching his face repeatedly.

The weird thing about Massimo Bonetti is that he is mean to me, but apparently he's the only one who is allowed to be.

I tilt my head back, and look into his eyes, and am grateful at the lack of recognition in his gaze.

"I'm sorry for coming onto your property. I was curious what this place was. I'll be going now."

He rubs his hand over his beard, without taking his eyes from mine.

"That's the game we're playing?"

I shake my head, trying to convince him to let me go.

"It was an accident. I'm sorry. You don't know me, and I don't know you. I'll be sure to never come on your property again."

I've been to his brother's house recently, but he wasn't there, so I'm hoping he doesn't know what I look like.

He is not the boy I knew. Massimo has some of the same features, but he has filled out since he was sixteen, the last time I saw him. His shirt is tight around his muscles, as they flex with his movements. His gaze, more threatening. And his voice? I don't remember it being the deep tone it is now.

His lips turn up into a smirk, as his eyes darken with obvious malicious intent.

"That's the problem, Anastasia. We both know that's not the truth. Don't we, counselor?"

"That's not my name. I'm Jenny."

He strokes his fingers down my cheek, giving the illusion of a gentle touch, before he places his hand around my throat and squeezes.

"Liars don't live long in my presence. You'd serve yourself well to remember that."

I cough, as I gasp for air, when he releases his hold on me.

"Leave me alone, or I'll call the police."

He steps back, with a sadistic grin on his face, and a challenge in his eyes, as if this is some sort of entertaining game.

"Call them. I'll wait."

I tilt my head at him, not believing for a second that he's going to allow me to call for help.

Massimo nods. "Go right ahead, little lamb. I will not touch you before they get here. Scout's honor."

I roll my eyes at him, because I'm quite sure this man was never a boy scout. In a split second decision, I call the Chief of Police, instead of dialing 9-1-1, simply because I don't want to bother them.

He answers with surprise.

"Anastasia?" He questions quietly, like maybe his wife is sleeping.

"I'm at the Bonetti warehouse on third street, and I need assistance. It's urgent."

If he is wondering why I didn't call 9-1-1, he doesn't say anything.

"I'll send for a couple cars, and be there myself in a few minutes."

Massimo stands staring at me, while his gaze travels the length of my body several times, as he runs his tongue over his bottom lip, giving me the impression the look on his face right now is why they started calling him Psycho.

"Stop looking at me like that."

He chuckles, with an evil expression, leaning his head down and staring into my eyes, as his own darken, with a predatory glare.

"Like what? Like I'm the wolf, about to teach the pretty little lamb the consequences of walking into the wolf's den?"

My eyes widen at his words, but I don't speak. I'm not sure I could if I tried.

"That's right, counselor. I'm going to rip you to shreds, before I devour you. The louder you fucking scream, the harder I'll dig my blade into your sweet flesh. I'm a well-controlled man, so I'll wait patiently for that part, but mark my words, I'll watch you bleed. It'll be a pure fucking pleasure."

He rubs his hands together with excitement, when he notices the flashing lights. I don't know what he's excited about, but I'm happy that this is about over. I want to get the hell out of here, and never see this evil man again. Well, until he's behind bars.

The chief of police, Bob Roberts, approaches us, with six police officers flanking him.

"Mr. Bonetti, good to see you, sir. Is there anything you need assistance with?"

I look at him, waiting for his response, but he shrugs his shoulders.

41

"I'm not the one that called you, Bob."

The chief asks him, "Did you want us to remove her? If she's causing problems for you, we're happy to take care of it."

What? I called him for help, and he is asking if Massimo wants me removed from the premises? He has not even addressed me, and I know my face is turning red from the anger surging through me.

Massimo chuckles, as he stares at me with an unreadable expression.

"I'm perfectly capable of removing anyone I want removed. I'm sorry she wasted your time."

Glancing at Roberts, he nods at Massimo. "No bother at all. Have a pleasant evening, Mr. Bonetti."

And they turn to leave.

What the fuck just happened?

All the air escapes from my lungs. This is insane. What the hell happened to 'serve and protect'?

I turn back to him, my panic visible on my face, and, judging by his evil expression, he is enjoying this far too much.

"Do you see now, counselor? We're untouchable, because we own everyone."

I straighten my back and glare at him.

"Not everyone. You don't own me."

He steps forward. "Oh, but I will. Once I catch you, I own you."

"Once you catch me?" I question, honestly because there's no catching what's already in front of you.

Massimo runs his tongue over his bottom lip again, and growls in a deep voice.

"Run, little lamb. Run like your life depends on it. If I catch you, I will devour you."

I stand, frozen, from his words, as he growls louder, his voice deeper, and as threatening as his large stature.

"Run."

He pulls out his knife, and I do what he said, I run for my life.

Chapter Eight
PSYCHO

She takes off running, and I give her a head start, not because I planned to, but I can't stop watching her ass as she sprints, trying to find a way off the property. There isn't one. The front gate is the only exit. I know she thinks she found our weapons warehouse. And it is, in a way, but not really. It's where we keep ammo, which is why it's guarded around the clock. Bullets in the wrong hands can be dangerous, kids. She was never going to find shipments of weapons being delivered. Those are underground. Silly little lamb.

I walk casually, whistling, as I look for her. Walking through the trees, following the route she took, I taunt her.

"One, two, Psycho's coming for you."

She makes the sweetest little yip I've ever heard. Anastasia keeps running, trying to find her way out of my trap.

"Three, four, your blood will coat my floor."

I watch as she squats down behind a large crate of our supplies.

"Five, six, you'll beg to live."

Her breathing is heavy. I know she's probably trying like hell to control it, and not give away her location, but she can't. The panic is too severe.

"Seven, eight, it's too late."

I chuckle darkly as I reach her, lowering my head as she raises hers, and meets my gaze, fucking trembling like such a good girl.

"Nine, ten, scream for me again."

Her eyes are wide with terror, but she doesn't cry.

Fucking unfortunate, because I want her tears. I stare at her stunning face, taking in her gorgeous features. From her dark hair, hazel eyes, hips that beg to be held onto with a bruising grip, back to her trembling bottom lip. Gorgeous.

"Stand."

She does, and I grin at her.

"This is your final chance. Fucking run. I promise you, you don't want me to catch you, little lamb."

Anastasia takes off again, this time right smack into my security detail. Reggie goes to grab her, but I give him a look, and he raises his hands in the air.

"Vanish. All of you, inside the warehouse."

He moves quickly, and does as he's told. It wasn't much of a choice, because they know the consequences of not following orders.

She runs past where Reggie was, and again I watch her sweet little ass run, with nowhere to fucking go. Anastasia may as well be on a goddamn treadmill. Still, she's fun to watch. The kill will be beautiful, but it's the hunt that's truly exquisite. The way my little lamb tries so hard to save her life. I run to her and push her, so that she falls onto the earth with a thud, facedown, followed by a scream. Climbing over her, I pin her in place, as she tries to fight me off. It's futile. She never had a chance of winning this fight. Placing my nose against her neck, I inhale the sweetest scent of pomegranate and, is that mango?

"Fuck," I growl, because she smells fucking delicious. Goddamn edible.

When I decided to take her and kill her, I never planned to fuck her, but now it doesn't seem like such a bad idea.

Anastasia bucks her hips, trying to fight me off, and I chuckle against the sweet skin just below her ear.

"I know you're trying to get me off, little lamb, and I promise, you will… *get me off.*"

"Don't you fucking dare," she says. I don't know if she's trying to sound strong, but she doesn't. Instead, her shaky breath only makes me want to be inside her, with a desire I haven't felt in a long time, if ever.

Reaching under her, I force my arm around her belly, and unbutton her pants, while she continues to struggle beneath me.

"Do you feel how hard you're making me, little lamb?"

She whimpers underneath the weight of my body, still trying unsuccessfully to wiggle free, but I give her an 'A' for effort.

"Please don't."

The sound of her cries, her helpless wriggling, and the panic in her shaky voice, makes me feral. I growl, "Fuck. Already the begging begins."

Without moving off her, I pull the gun from her hip, and press the barrel against her temple, before sliding it down the side of her face.

"Oh, little lamb, don't you know how dangerous firearms are? How ironic that you brought it for protection, and yet I could kill you with it right now. Shhh, don't worry, counselor. I promise you a better ending than that."

Grinding my hard length against her ass, I chuckle in her ear.

"Fucking with the Bonetti Brothers is a dangerous game to play. You're about to find out the consequences of your stupid fucking choices."

Yanking her pants down, I grow harder by the second, with every one of her breathy pleas. Once I have her bare ass in front of me, I unzip my pants, and pull my cock out.

"No. I said no!"

With a growl, I say, "And I said yes. As your owner, that's all that matters. Now be a good girl, and come all over my cock."

"I don't come for rapists," she bites, causing me to laugh again.

I bury myself inside her with one single thrust, and groan louder than I mean to.

"Fuck, little lamb. Such a tight pussy."

Anastasia has nowhere to go. I fuck her like she's my enemy, with punishing thrusts, so hard it likely knocks the wind out of her. Gripping the back of her neck, I squeeze hard, as I bottom out inside her pussy repeatedly. Every time I pull my hips back and slide back inside her, she whimpers for me, and then, as if talking to herself, says, "What the fuck?"

It's cute she thought she could prevent herself from coming.

She digs her fingers into the earth, as she moans against the ground. Moving back onto my knees, I grab her hips firmly, and she tries to move away from me, but I don't allow it.

"Your mouth says stop, but your drenched cunt says fuck me. Which is it, little lamb?"

Anastasia screams out an annoyed huff, that turns to a moan, and I can't help but laugh softly, because she's so fucking angry, but she likes my cock far more than she'll admit.

"I hate you."

While she barely knows me, I don't doubt her words. In fact, I know her hatred will grow, in leaps and bounds, by the time I'm done with her. Her execution will not be swift, and when that day comes, she'll know pure fear and hatred.

She screams as I drive into her, over and over again, and her pussy clenches around my length. Wetness gushes out of her, and drips onto my balls, and I know I'm going to have a lot of fun before I end her life. Every time she comes for me, she'll hate herself more, until she isn't sure which one of us she despises most.

I pull my hips back and snap forward, slamming completely inside her again, as I fill her with my cum. Will I enjoy knowing that she'll be dripping of me, all night long? Definitely, because she'll feel it, remembering the way I made her climax, and her own self-hatred will grow. No matter how hard you try, you cannot get away from yourself. She'll want to crawl out of her skin to escape the way she feels about herself, but she'll be stuck with the growing resentment for the person she has become. And me? I'll enjoy watching her fall apart.

Getting off her, I stand, and tuck my cock back inside my pants.

"Up you get."

She rises to her feet, pulls her pants up, and turns to me with a glare that might be bristling, if I were anybody else.

"You will never do that to me again."

I rub my temples, trying to ease the ache she's responsible for. "Let's go."

She holds her fists up, like she's going to attack me, and I don't move. I stand still with an arched brow, waiting to see what she does.

"I'm not going anywhere with you," she says, far more confidently than she should. She can fight me if she wants, I'll only enjoy it more, but she will be going wherever the fuck I tell her to.

Chapter Nine

ANASTASIA

My brain says to not look at him, and my eyes blatantly disobey. Instead of looking anywhere else, my gaze travels the length of his body, from his feet to his muscular chest, deliciously stretching the fabric of his shirt. Tattoos peek out from the top, as well as under his sleeves. The ink on his hands is interesting; skulls, which definitely match the man. He has a dark beard, matching his short dark hair, and a scowl I remember from a long time ago, but it's his eyes that steal the breath from my lungs. They're different now. Somehow darker, and full of such malicious intent.

The massive white warehouse, bigger than three homes, is to my right. I still don't know what's inside there, and now I'm thinking I never will. Along the side of the building are shipping containers, that probably hold weapons, but I don't know that for sure either. The more I thought I was finding out, I think the less I actually knew. I'm not an idiot, if I knew he was going to show up here, I wouldn't have come. I glance to my left, seeing trees, and then more trees. I have a feeling there's no way out of here, and he knows that. All he's doing is playing with his food before he eats it.

Reaching into his pocket, he pulls out a knife, and gazes at me with an evil grin on his face.

"I'd prefer for you to not lose blood yet, but if you insist, I'm happy to slice through your pretty skin right here."

He places the blade against my neck, and I whimper as he drags the tip down my throat, not cutting me, but making his threat clear.

"Pretty little lambs do not belong in the wolf's den. They never escape with their lives. Whatever you think I'm capable of, I promise you, I can do things you never imagined. I'll cause you pain you never thought possible. Once you break, I'll find new ways to break you all over again."

His voice is deep, threatening, and filled with the promise that the end is near. Massimo Bonetti is going to kill me, and there is nothing I can do to prevent it.

"Let's go," he growls, as he removes the blade from my skin, and I follow beside him, because what else can I do? If I refuse to go wherever he plans to take me, he'll kill me right here. He started going by Psycho when I was still a kid. I'm not sure why, but I never questioned it. Probably because I still called him Massimo, so it didn't affect me. Now I know why. It's not just a name for him, it's part of his identity.

We approach a two door sports car, a dark blue McLaren, which only screams how much money he has. Psycho wraps my hair around his fist and pushes my front up against the car, slamming my face against the roof, as he drags his free hand down my body, like he's searching me for other weapons. Trust me, if I had one, I would've already shot him. He opens the car door and I get in.

Psycho walks around to the driver's side, gets in, and immediately locks my door, as if he could read my mind. Taking my chances with moving vehicles is no longer an option.

He runs his tongue over his bottom lip before speaking. His voice comes out deep, and filled with the danger this man promises at every turn.

"There's no way out, little lamb. Every time you think there is one, I'll take it away."

I turn away from him, and stare out the window, as I attempt to figure a way out of the predicament I've put myself in.

"Look. I didn't see anything, and I don't want to die."

He chuckles, as he pulls onto a property with a massive black metal gate. I don't know where we are, but the building looks like it could be a luxury hotel. There's a spiral stone staircase on either side of the large white house. The grass is landscaped to perfection, with

50

dozens of red roses all around the front, which, of course, makes me think of my mom, and the fact that there is no one to take care of her, if I'm gone. Everyone involved with her care is paid by automatic payment, but eventually the money will run out, without anything more going in.

I spot three balconies in total. One on either side of the house above the first floor, and another at the top, in the center. It's clear they make a lot of money, more than I imagined. One look at this place tells me they may be far more powerful than I realized. When I was a kid, I knew they had money, but never questioned how much, or what they did for it. Information has been difficult to find, so I was only beginning to get anything. Which is, once again, why I needed Raina Abruzzo on my side.

"Where are we?"

"My home," he answers, as he pulls to the front of the house.

"Are you married?"

Please let there be a wife and kids, that will make him let me go. He chuckles softly as he opens his door, and walks around to my side of the car.

"I'm not married. I live here alone, and now you're here, but, of course, that's temporary."

He pulls me out of the car, and I say, "Right, because my body will be thrown into the ocean."

Psycho laughs, like I truly amuse him.

"We don't do that. Maybe at one point that's what mafia families did, but not anymore. I have never in my life seen any Bonetti toss a body into an ocean, lake, river, or whatever other fucking body of water there is."

The burning question in my mind is, why am I at his house? Surely he isn't going to kill me here. Or is he?

Grabbing my arm, he pulls me into the massive house, and down a hallway, before pulling so hard he nearly causes me to fall down the stairs, to what I quickly figure out is a basement.

Chapter Ten
PSYCHO

I could've brought her to the back of the house, and directly to the basement, but it's better this way. Going from the surroundings of a beautiful house, to what my brother calls my torture chamber, is jarring. It will heighten her fear and, at this moment, I want that more than anything. We walk through my collection of cars, and turn a corner. Her expression shows her curiosity, as I enter the code to get into my favorite place. The doors slide open, and I yank her through the doorway, before it closes behind us automatically. She glances behind her, and realizes there's no escape. Turning back to the room, she looks around, taking it all in. The metal tables with restraints, the drains on the floor, a cage I don't use very often, and a St Andrew's Cross, bought just for my little lamb. The moment I saw her picture, I wanted to tie her up, and now I'm moments away from realizing that fantasy.

"Get undressed."

Tilting her head to the side, she flashes me a 'fuck you' look, and I don't hate it. Fuck, I think I like it.

"No."

This is not about sex, it's about pain that she fucking owes me, but my dick is hard as a rock for her again. Her defiance means a fight, and that's my favorite thing. I step closer to her, and she raises her tiny fists.

"No."

I can't help the grin that overtakes my face.

"Yes," I say, with a narrowed gaze. This is not optional.

Pulling her fist back, she hits me in the chest, hard. I chuckle when she starts jumping up and down, while holding her right fist in her left hand.

"Motherfucker. You asshole."

I arch an eyebrow at her, but I'm not pissed. I'm fucking entertained.

"You hit me and I'm the asshole?"

"I was protecting myself."

As I move closer to her, she steps back frantically, until she hits the wall. I can hardly wait for her to find out that, behind her head, sits my collection of blades. Once she can't go any further, I wrap my hand around her throat, while I retrieve my favorite knife from my pocket. My brothers make fun of me, but I have an emotional attachment to this knife. It was custom made for me, and cuts through almost fucking anything.

"Is that what you're doing, little lamb? Protecting yourself?"

Her heart rate, and breathing, both pick up at the same time, as she glares at me. This woman is fucking fascinating. Anybody else would have tears streaming down their face, but not her. She stands strong, even though I know she's terrified. Her heartbeat betrays her, as does the trembling of her bottom lip. The same goddamn lip I want to suck into my mouth, and bite, until it bleeds.

Standing over her, I jerk my chin down, my gaze connecting with hers, as I take in the fire in her eyes. The same one I'll destroy. Tracing my thumb over her bottom lip, I speak low, and stifle a groan as her breath brushes over my skin.

"Last chance, little lamb. Would you like to take your clothes off on your own? Or do you prefer I cut them from your body? I will warn you, when I get angry, I get careless with my knife."

"I'll do it," she whispers, and I step away from her, to give her room to get undressed.

She pulls her black t-shirt over her head, and angrily throws it on the ground.

"You're insane. You know that, right?"

I shake my head no, because she's wrong; I am many things, but my sanity is intact.

"I'm not insane. I'm a psycho. Maybe look up the difference."

She unbuttons her pants and pulls them off, as she continues her pointless argument.

"Insane means a state of mind that prevents normal perception, behavior, or social interaction. Or," she waves her hand in the air, while standing in a pink bra and matching panties, "severely mentally ill. I believe this situation describes it well."

"Psycho, not insane."

She rolls her eyes at me like I'm an idiot, and I stop myself from cutting her throat right now. The temptation is intense, but I have bigger plans for her.

Patience, Psycho. You'll get there.

"An unstable and aggressive person. Again, either fits."

I'm not the idiot this woman probably thinks I am. I do know it's not normal to be the way I am. I shouldn't be excited to see blood dripping down her skin. I shouldn't be wondering what it tastes like. We kill our enemies. The fact that I will take pleasure in torturing her, before ending her life, is probably not a good thing, but I don't fucking care. Call me insane, but I've been the person I am since I was twelve. I don't know another way, and I don't even want to.

"Bra and panties too."

She shakes her head like she cannot believe she's here, but does as she's told. I watch her as she slides the bra straps down her arms until it hits the floor. It's not lost on me that this woman is beautiful. Long dark hair, hazel eyes made to seduce and torture a man, perfect 'C' tits, and a small waist, with wide hips. She's tantalizing from head to toe. Even so, it won't save her life. I'm not my brothers, and her beauty does not change the fact that she wronged us. Maybe Kage can look past it, but I can't. I won't. She's stunning, but it's business as usual for me. After she removes her lacy panties, I direct her to the cross.

Anastasia walks to the cross, with her head hanging down in defeat, as I remove my suit jacket, and dress shirt, before folding them, and placing them on the metal table.

I walk over to her, grab her arm, and tie her to the post, using a square knot, then do the same with her other arm, and legs.

"Is this what you do to all the people you murder?"

Standing back, I admire my exquisite canvas.

"No. Most of the people I kill aren't as beautiful as you. I've never wanted to watch someone bleed the way I do you. I could kill you quickly to be done with it, but I want to savor it. Now, tell me, pretty girl. Are you ready to tell me why you came after us?"

I pull my knife out of my pocket, and she whimpers softly.

"Please don't."

I slash the inside of one thigh, and then the other, and watch, captivated, as her blood trickles down her skin. Pressing my fingers into the scars on her stomach, I'm lost in her beauty. Even the deep scars begging to tell a story are stunning.

"So beautiful."

She hisses from the pain, but does not shed a tear, and it fascinates me.

"Why aren't you crying?"

Shrugging her shoulders as much as she can, she glances away from me.

"When you've been through the pain I have, you find a way to manage it. Tears show weakness. Do your best, Bonetti, but you'll never see me cry. If that's what you're after, you'll be left with nothing other than disappointment."

I pull out my cell phone and take a picture of her, earning me an instant glare.

"What the hell are you doing?"

Instead of responding, I dial Raina's phone number. They are all together at the reception still, so I'm not surprised when the voice of my brother, Bones, is the first one I hear.

56

"Where are you?" Bones asks.

"Doesn't matter," I respond, and then add, "Raina, I'm sending you a picture, and need you to tell me if you recognize the person in the photo."

"That's the ADA. That's Anastasia Crowne," Raina gasps.

I drag the blade over her tit, and circle the tip around her nipple. "Oh, little lamb. You lied about who you are."

Bones says, "Psycho, you cannot fucking kidnap the Assistant District Attorney."

"You're wrong, Bones. I already did."

I disconnect the call and get back to work. As I stare at her horrified expression, and then the blood trickling down her thighs, I smile to myself.

Fuck, I love my job. They say to do what you love for work, and I do love this. It's not very often we have to deal with a woman coming after us. It's usually a man, either from a rival family, or someone we do business with, trying to steal from us. Theft is one of the biggest reasons, because money makes people stupid. Lack of it causes them to do dangerous things. This is a unique opportunity, and I plan to fucking enjoy every moment of it.

Chapter Eleven

ANASTASIA

I don't know if there's a word for it, but this man is an insane psycho. He cuts into the skin on the side of my breast, not deep enough to cause me to die, but fuck, it stings like a bitch.

"You will cry, little lamb. I'm going to fucking break you, until you have nothing left."

Leaning down, he licks at the blood on my skin like a wild animal, and the soft lashes of his tongue ease the pain from the cut, but instead of relief, it causes the anger to surge through me.

He drags the knife slowly up my slit and, for a moment, I can't breathe. The fear is immobilizing. Not that I can move anyway, but I don't want to be butchered, and I'm pretty sure that's where we are heading.

Running his tongue over his bottom lip, he arches an eyebrow, and his expression is taunting, as I wonder what the fuck happened to him. What made him turn into this?

"Was it worth it, little lamb? You got nothing, and will give me everything. Even your last breath is mine."

"No," I whimper, because, right now, it was not worth it. If he were behind bars, it would have been, but tied to this damn cross, in some dark *Christian Grey* fantasy? Definitely not.

"Tell me why," he says, as he lowers his head and stares at me, with a gaze that promises violence. For a moment, I consider telling him everything, including who I am. Massimo is anything but stupid, and will figure it out at some point. Unless he already has, and is playing games with me. I do look different than the last time he saw me. There's a big difference between thirty-eight and twelve. Would it save me, or infuriate him more?

"I wanted you gone. All of you. The Bonetti Brothers are criminals, that hurt innocent people. I stand before you as evidence."

He pulls the blade over my nipple, and my breath hitches, as my entire body goes rigid. There is fear, and there is terror, the same thing, only one is more heightened. This is the latter, and he knows it, one look at him, and it's clear he gets off on it.

"Let's talk about innocence, *Anastasia*." The way he growls my name sends shivers up my spine, and makes me think he does know. Stepping back from me only slightly, he crosses his arms over his chest, and his knife hangs down, still firmly in his grip, as he stares at me with those eyes. The ones I remember from so long ago. He wasn't friendly all those years ago, but now, his gaze is sadistic, and rattles me to the core, as I'm sure is his intention.

"I don't cut innocent people. And I don't kill them either. Nosy bitches, trying to hurt my family, are far from innocent."

Without warning, he steps closer again, and slashes my nipple, causing me to scream. I've never been great at holding my tongue, and I'm not now either, as I speak my mind honestly while he licks at the blood once again, before pulling my nipple between his lips.

"You are a sick and twisted bastard, like your father was."

Psycho wasn't exactly a nice man to begin with, but he switches in an instant, to one that turns my blood cold. Pure evil stares back at me. His already dark eyes turn the shade of coal, as his gaze intensifies. The anger is palpable, as he tightens his hold on his knife with a death grip, turning his knuckles white. He presses the blade to my throat, and speaks to me in a dark, threatening tone.

"It would be so easy, little lamb. I could slaughter you right now. All it would take is for me to cut into your flesh right here, and I'd have what I want, to watch you fucking bleed to death. Is that what you want, Anastasia?"

"No," I whimper quietly, afraid to move a muscle, with his blade pressed to my throat.

"Let's play a little game."

He pulls the knife away from my skin, and I take my first full breath in several minutes.

I roll my eyes at him, risking pissing him off, and knowing I shouldn't. I can't stop myself.

"I don't think I want to play any game you'd want to play."

With a chuckle, he runs his tongue up the side of his blade, licking up the small amount of my blood on it.

"I'll ask you a question. You'll answer truthfully, and I'll answer a question for you in return. As a reward. But," he points his knife at my face, as an obvious threat, "if you lie to me, I'll cut you." Stroking his finger down my cheek, he adds, "Right here. A nice slash, right across this beautiful face."

I don't move, but it's ironic. There was a time I would've done anything to hear Massimo call me beautiful. Although, not quite like that.

"How will you know if I'm lying?"

If he already knows the answer to a question, why would he bother asking it?

"I'll know."

I swallow hard and ask, "How will I know if you're telling me the truth?"

He arches an eyebrow, and his lips pull up into a smirk that shouldn't be attractive. I hate him, and his perfect body. His handsome face can't have an effect on me. Not his perfectly sculpted arms, or the gorgeous ink covering his upper body, and definitely not his full lips. Most of all, not that deep voice, that makes my insides ache with need. I will not allow it.

"I don't lie, little lamb. Ever. If I can't tell the truth, I'll refuse to answer the question, but you are never leaving, so there's no reason I can't answer any question you ask."

"Okay," I say softly, because I don't have a choice anyway, but there are things I want to know, even if I can't ever do anything

61

about it. More than anything, I want to hear him say it, admit what his family did to mine.

"You'll go first, since you were a bad girl and started this."

He moves closer to me, and his brows knit together, his anger crackling like a tangible force. If I weren't tied up, I think I could reach out and touch it.

"Why my family? There is no open investigation, we both know that. So why?"

I tilt my head, and look at him with curiosity. There isn't one, but why is he so sure about that?

"How would you know that?"

I know they obviously have some officers in their pocket, but not the DA's office. There's no way. I would know. Every day I go to work, and go through new case files, hoping to find one name that will give me the closure I need.

Bonetti.

When there's hope, it's only followed by disappointment, yet it's all I have. I've lost everyone. Taking them down has become my reason for existing.

He drags the spine of the knife down his beard, as he stares at me with a curious gaze. I wonder if he does it to remind me about the blade. If so, rest assured I have not forgotten. My skin still stings, serving as a constant reminder.

"My question first, and if you're a good girl, and tell the truth, then I'll tell you how I know."

I squeeze my eyes shut, hating that I have to talk about this. The familiar lump in my throat grows, as flashes of his face form behind my eyes. The way I found him is seared into my brain. Time keeps going after we lose people, but the pain remains. Sometimes it dulls, but it never truly goes away. My voice comes out as broken as my heart still feels, as I speak.

"My father worked for your father. One day when I was a little girl, I came home, and found his head on our doorstep. Your father decapitated mine, and left such a vile image that it was burned into my brain. It destroyed my mother. His hands showed up a few days later. And his heart, days after that. Such brutality. I vowed, the day we put his severed parts in the ground, to get revenge for him, by putting every Bonetti in prison."

Chapter Twelve
Psycho

I'm not surprised by much, but this absolutely floors me. I didn't know her father had worked for our family, so that's interesting, but it's the manner of death that has me raising a brow. That's not something we would do. Kage was the first in our family to decapitate anyone, I'm fairly certain. Sending a message like that to a family isn't our way. If he worked for our family, they aren't a rival family, so it doesn't make sense for my father to do this. In a mafia war, anything goes, but this? No, she's wrong.

I run my knife through my beard as I think. The Bonetti brothers all kill in their own ways, but my father was not into torture, he was quick, and to the point. The only time he tormented someone was for information. He was not one to send messages like she's suggesting. It was not his style to leave a child to find her father that way.

"What makes you think that was our family?"

She shakes her head, like I'm an idiot, when, if one of us is an idiot, it sure as fuck is not me.

"He worked for you. It had to be you, well, not you personally, but your father."

I gaze down at my lost little lamb, as I realize making her hate herself has just gotten a lot easier. When she realizes what she has done, for fucking nothing, the devastation will be visible to the naked eye. I almost feel bad for her. *Almost.*

"You came after my family, and brought this on yourself, when it wasn't us that did this to your father. It's not something my father would've done. If he thought your father had done something, yes, he would've been killed. I guarantee you, torturing an innocent family isn't how he would've handled it. Perhaps another family may have done this, because he worked for us, but this wouldn't have been our doing. Lorenzo Bonetti would never have done this. Instead, he likely paid for your father's funeral."

That's our way. We take care of our men, and unfortunately shit like this happens, but not at our hands. If, for some reason, my father had wanted to decapitate him, he would have. Leaving the evidence for his child to find? Not a fucking chance. Contrary to what my little lamb thinks, we are not vile monsters. Don't get me wrong, we are bad men, and we do bad things, but we leave children the fuck out of it. And the women too, unless, of course, they're like Anastasia, and have come for us. There are families that would do this shit, but we've never seen the point of it. A mafia man should be powerful on his own, without the need to wave his dick around.

A tear rolls down her cheek, and it's simply beautiful, but confusing.

"You don't cry when I cut you, but now you do."

It's not really a question, but more of a statement. An observation.

"Do you think you're the first man to torture me, Massimo?"

I arch an eyebrow in surprise, at her using my given name. It's different, and confuses me. My mother is the only one that calls me that, ever. Bones has never even done that when he's pissed at me. He has with my brothers, but not me. Although it might be coming, since I've been ignoring his repeated phone calls.

"Who else has tortured you, little lamb?"

She shakes her head, refusing to answer my question. I allow it for now, mostly because I don't actually give a fuck. Judging her decision-making skills, she likely deserved it.

"It's my turn."

I smirk at her and nod.

"Very well. Ask your burning question, ADA."

"Were you in my house?"

I'm more than a little surprised at her question. I thought the first thing she wanted to know would be about my family.

"I was."

Her eyes widen in response, like she's shocked I would do such a thing.

"So it was you that, umm, finished on my bed."

"Cum, little lamb. You can say the word. Yes, it was my cum on your bed. Until you set it on fire like a goddamn pyro. I should also let you know your little evidence bag won't accomplish anything."

She shakes her head in disgust, like she has never seen semen before, which can't possibly be the case. This woman is fucking gorgeous, and I'm sure, without even asking, she's had many men chasing after her. Why that thought pisses me off, I have no goddamn idea.

"Why would you do that?"

I chuckle, as I drag my hand down my face, remembering watching her anger flare, as she doused her own fucking bed in gasoline.

"I wanted to rattle you. I wanted you to know I was watching you. While I didn't know you'd go crazy, and set your bed on fire, I'm not sorry. It was hot."

Arching an eyebrow, I grin at her, which seems to only unsettle her further, as her eyes grow ferocious and narrow at me.

"I'm not talking about the fire. Lunatic looks good on you, little lamb."

She scoffs, as she looks at me like she's better than me, and it pisses me off. It's at that moment that I decide I'm going to torment this girl. I knew that already, but now it's going to be far more prolonged. The desire to mark every inch of her, knowing how angry it will make her, is intense.

"My turn. Who tortured you before me?"

I allow my eyes to scan her delicious naked body, only looking into her eyes when she speaks her answer.

"Carlo, my ex-husband."

My irritation grows that I didn't know this piece of information, that's not hard to find. How the fuck does she have a husband I didn't know about?

"I did a background check on you. Marriage records are public records, so explain how I did not find this information?"

Grinding my teeth, I can feel my pulse quicken, as my nostrils flare. How the fuck did I find so little on her?

She scowls at me, dismissing my goddamn question, and bites, "That's two questions. I answered yours. It's my turn."

It's easy for a woman to be a brat under normal circumstances. This woman is tied to a cross, naked, with dried blood on her body, and still giving an attitude, and it excites me far more than I care to admit. Much like the goddamn picture in her house, there's a familiarity with her, but it's something I can't place. Maybe I saw her in one of our clubs at some point, because the name does not ring a bell. It's that odd feeling that you've seen someone before, maybe in another lifetime, because I know if I saw her, I would have fucked her. Anastasia is not the kind of woman you fuck and forget. You remember it.

I nod in agreement, and wait for her to ask her next question.

"How have you never been convicted of any crimes?"

I flash her a grin, because it amuses me that she really doesn't know. On one hand, I think maybe she's terrible at her job, but on the other, I know people in the DA's office would be tight-lipped about my family, certainly to a new person. After all, it's literally their skin on the line, if people start talking, and causing headaches for us.

"I assume you aren't asking about me specifically, but my family. Nearly every person in law enforcement is in our pocket. We own them all. The Chief, your boss, all of them. Those we can't control usually die. If they're a liability, they can't exist."

"Easton," she gasps in surprise.

68

I nod and continue, "He has a drug problem, and has gotten himself into trouble with the Juarez Cartel. We've bailed him out more than once, in exchange for his cooperation. I supply him with cocaine, and he does whatever the fuck I need him to."

"I was getting the information I needed, and planned to hand it over to him. What would've happened?"

It's not her turn anymore, but I decide to answer her question anyway.

"He would have brought you to me, and I would've killed you. There was no chance you wouldn't have ended up in my basement. The second you decided to go after my family, your fate was sealed."

Swallowing hard, she says, "I don't want to die," in a small, broken voice. I might feel bad for her, if she hadn't done this to herself. The information she thought she had on my family was all wrong. She wanted to destroy us for killing her father, and I'm certain we didn't even have a hand in it. So she has sacrificed her life for nothing.

Stepping closer to her, I place my hand on her chin, and hold her face in a tight grip, while once again dragging my knife down her stomach.

"You did this, little lamb. Surely you knew the danger of coming after a mafia family. We kill people, you knew that, but you came for us anyway. One woman will never take the Bonetti Brothers down, yet you tried. We have killed for far less, and I will end your life. The only question is, what will you do to prolong it?"

Her hazel eyes stare into mine, and I can't help but notice the golden circle around them, reminding me of a fucking halo, but this woman is no angel. She's the fucking devil, yet I can't help myself with this delicious body made for sin. I'm going to have it again.

"Anything," she whispers.

"Anything," I repeat with a grin on my face, as ideas pop into my mind. If she sees the wheels turning in my brain, I can promise, it's

not what she thinks. Anastasia thinks she's going to get fucked again, and I suppose she will be. Literally and figuratively.

Chapter Thirteen
ANASTASIA

"Anything leaves an awful lot on the table, counselor."

He releases my face, and rubs his thumb over my cut nipple, before pinching it hard, causing me to whimper from the pain.

Leaning his head down, he inhales the scent of my skin before biting me, making me cry out again, and he chuckles darkly.

"Are you prepared to be my filthy whore, Anastasia?"

The last thing I want to do is let this monster touch me again sexually, but I don't have a choice. I can either die now, or hope if I live long enough, I might convince him to let me live. Although, it's becoming more and more clear, with each passing minute, that is unlikely.

"Yes. I said anything, and I meant it."

He moans this sexy sound I'd like to ignore, but can't, as he moves his hand between my spread legs, and shoves two fingers inside me, forcefully stretching me, but it's his words that cause the harshest sting, and bile to rise in my throat.

"Imagine if your husband could see you now. Tied up, and consenting to be my personal slut."

"Ex-husband," I bite, as he moves his fingers inside me.

Psycho drops his knife to the floor, and reaches up and pinches my nipple, while he continues fucking me with his other hand.

"Look at how wet you are. You hate me so much, and yet, you're going to come all over my hand, aren't you, little lamb?"

"Nothing has changed. I still hate you."

He runs his tongue over his bottom lip, while he stares at my face like he doesn't want to miss anything. I close my eyes, the intensity in his gaze too much, and he growls in response.

"Open your fucking eyes."

My lashes flutter, as I force myself to do as he says, and am once again met by his hungry gaze.

"You're still going to die. Nothing has changed."

I open my mouth to speak, but he shoves his fingers into my mouth aggressively.

"Fucking suck. Before you ask why, I'll tell you. It pleases me, and that's your job now. The second you refuse an order, you die."

When he pulls his fingers from my mouth, I tilt my head and glare at him.

"Order?"

His lips pull up into an evil grin, that chills me to the bone. I can see the devious thoughts running through his mind. I don't know what they are, but I can tell they aren't good.

"Before I end your life, you won't even recognize yourself, little lamb. You won't have a choice. You will do everything I say."

I plead for my life like a pathetic person, because this isn't only about me. If I am not there to pay expenses, my mother will get worse, and die.

"Please let me go. I will do anything you want. Just let me go. Cut me, but let me live."

He folds his arms over his chest, while he stares at me like he's making a decision. The knife is still in his hand, and I watch it closely, willing it to kill him, but it doesn't even cut his arm.

"You're offering to make a deal with the devil, little lamb. Are you prepared for what that could mean for you?"

I nod my head, because it doesn't matter. As long as I survive, I will have to deal with whatever he throws at me. For my mother, I have to survive this.

Psycho steps closer to me, and takes my face in his hands, forcing me to look him in the eyes.

"This is a one-time offer and, if I'm honest, I'm only making it, because I know you won't hold up your end. I'll keep you for thirty days, and you'll do everything I say. If you refuse any order, the deal is over, and you'll die immediately. If you somehow manage to do everything I want you to, I'll let you go."

He's wrong. I will hold up my end of the deal, because I don't have a choice. I don't want to die, so I'll sacrifice the next month of my life for my freedom. I know something he doesn't though. I'll be the one to rid the world of the Bonetti Brothers. I'll just need to be more careful once he lets me go. I try to stay strong but, against my will, my body trembles, as it has the entire time I've been in this basement, giving him what he clearly thrives on, my fear. I want to hide it away, but as mean as Massimo the boy was, the man is far worse than I imagined. He's beautiful and cruel. Brutal, and if my hopes for living are contingent on him having an ounce of kindness, I'm in big trouble. I don't think he has any left.

"Consider this your first test. I'm going to untie you. You will immediately get on your knees, and put your hands behind your back. I won't give you reminders of what's at stake. I trust the consequences are severe enough for you to remember on your own."

Psycho unties my wrists, and I rub them, while he does the same with my legs.

Silently, he arches an eyebrow expectantly. I step away from the cross, and drop to my knees.

After kicking his shoes off, he unbuttons his pants, and I stare at him in confusion, while he pulls his lips up into a wicked grin.

He removes his black pants and matching boxers, and I sit on my knees, staring. No, what I'm doing would probably be considered gawking.

"What the actual fuck?"

Chapter Fourteen

PSYCHO

This is not a normal response to my dick. First time for everything, I guess. I've already been inside her. She didn't realize it was my piercings making her scream with pleasure.

"Please tell me you weren't a fucking virgin."

She rolls her eyes at me, which makes me want to say our deal is off, but of course, that wasn't part of it, so I dismiss it.

"I've been pregnant. Of course I'm not a virgin."

I drag my hand down my face. Fuck. She's got a goddamn kid. Call me a softie, but I don't love the thought of leaving a kid without his mother. It won't change much, but I don't like it. We'll have to give money to whoever ends up with the kid. It's the right thing to do, and I already know Bones will insist on it. See, we're not as bad as people say we are.

"You have kids? How many?"

Her gaze drops to the floor, and the sadness in her expression is visceral. It's like looking at a damn puppy that has been kicked one too many times. The sorrow etched on her face, when I ask about her children, says there's a story, but it's one she isn't interested in reliving.

"He's dead. End of story."

Stepping closer to her, I grab her chin with my thumb and forefinger, and lift, forcing her head back.

"Let me make one thing clear, Anastasia. If I want to know the story, you will tell me. In this case, I don't give a fuck, but if I want to know something, you won't refuse me. We've already discussed what happens if you don't do as you're told."

Her glare is fucking fierce, and her anger is palpable. I definitely struck a nerve. *Good.*

"Understand?"

"Yes," she whispers.

I tilt my head and narrow my gaze, feeling the need to push her further, wanting her to break. When she finally does, it's going to be a beautiful show, and patience isn't my strong suit. I fucking want it, now.

"Yes, what?"

She trembles before me, and it only makes her more stunning.

"Yes, sir," she says with a shaky voice. All her confidence seems to have gone for the moment. The defiant, smart mouth is silent until I let go of her. Her eyes lift to my dick, as she stares at my piercings. Has she never seen a pierced dick? Even on fucking google? Not every man has one, but I didn't think anybody didn't know about them. I have a Prince Albert in the head, but I also have a Jacob's ladder. Most women are excited when they see the six bars in my cock. However, my little lamb, not so much. Her eyes are wide, as she stares at me in what appears to be shock.

"It's a piercing. It's not going to hurt you."

She shakes her head and gazes up at me. Fuck, she looks good like this.

"I'm afraid I'll hurt you. I'm pretty sure I know why I'm on my knees."

Her concern causes me to chuckle softly. Pain is never a deterrent for me, it's a goddamn aphrodisiac. I could tell her that, but I won't, because while pain gets me off, so does fear. And the way she trembles before me, has me hard as a goddamn rock.

"Open wide."

She parts her lips obediently, and, if I'm honest with myself, I'm not sure if I prefer the brat or the good girl more.

"Run your tongue over the bars."

She opens her mouth wider, and flattens her tongue against the underside of my cock, eliciting an instant groan from me. The feel of her moving along the rungs has me ready to slam into her throat, but

I pace myself, while I stare down at the woman that wants to destroy me, as I defile her. If she thinks this is as bad as it gets, she's wrong. Thirty days is a long time, and she'll regret her choices. The things I plan to do to her, and force her to do, will change her. In a month, she'll hate herself so much, she'll be begging me to take her life. Even better, she'll take her own life, if I don't do it for her. Watching her fall apart will be a pleasure greater than her tongue gliding against my shaft, and I must admit, that's pretty fucking great.

"Fuck," I groan out, as she circles her soft tongue over the head of my cock, paying special attention to the slit, as she laps up my pre-cum.

"Open wide, and when I tell you to hold still, do not fucking move."

I slide my cock into her open mouth with a chuckle.

"You wanted to destroy me, little lamb, but the tables have turned. I can't wait to break you, until there's nothing left. Should you live through what I will do to you, you'll be left a fucking shattered mess. It's going to be beautiful, and completely deserved."

Wrapping her hair around my fist, so I can control her, I watch my cock slide in and out of her mouth. This isn't about feeling good, this is about wrecking her, but fuck, she does feel good. Better than I want her to.

"Spread your thighs."

Again, she does as she's told immediately, and fuck me, I enjoy it. Pulling my hips back, I push my cock back inside her mouth, not stopping until I hit the back of her throat. She gags, as tears leak from her eyes, but doesn't fight me.

"Suck harder."

She tightens her lips around my cock, and sucks me hard. The suction is so strong it nearly causes pain, and I love it. I tighten my fist around her hair, and pull her off me.

"Don't move."

Her eyes are wide, as she continues to tremble for me. I like her like this, naked, afraid, and waiting for me to come. The greatest part of any sexual act is not the release, but the anticipation. For her, right now, the anticipation and fear are one.

I grip my cock in my hand, mere inches from her face, as I give myself quick strokes. Once she figures out my plan, her eyes widen in stunning horror.

"No," she whispers, but I don't slow down. With my free hand, I grab the back of her head, wind her hair tightly around my fist, and yank her head back.

She watches my cock slide in and out of my hand, and quickly closes her eyes, as I paint her face with my cum.

"Fuck," I growl, as I look down at her beautiful defiled face.

Anastasia is a stunning woman on her own, but with my cum on her face, she looks even better. It's on her cheekbone, all over her lips, and a small amount dribbles from her chin. I think I like her best like this. I know how angry she was, when she found my cum on her bed. I'm sure this is worse. I'm hoping it is.

"Stand up."

I place my thumb and forefinger on her chin, and tilt her head back. Leaning down, I scoop up some of the cum with my tongue, before forcefully pushing it inside her mouth.

The raw need to mark her, in every fucking way, is overwhelming. Anastasia surprises me when she kisses me back. Her taste is sweet, with a slight bitterness from my tongue. She places her hands on my chest and digs her nails into my skin, when I pull her hair and tilt her head to the side, so I can change my angle. I shouldn't want her at all, but I can't stop myself from licking all over the inside of her mouth.

Pulling back, I take a moment to gaze at her, thoroughly enjoying my work.

"Kneel in front of the cross, and wait for your master to return. Do not wipe that off. If you do, well, you know what happens."

Her glare is stunning, that halo in her eyes more prominent as her jaw clenches.

Oh, poor little lamb. Are you angry?

"Do you degrade all women, or just me?"

I chuckle darkly before responding. Degradation isn't really a kink of mine, but I think it might be with her. That fire in her eyes, her tiny fists at her sides, and a clenched jaw. She may not want me to know, but I can see the beginning of the break. It's only a tiny crack right now, but eventually it'll be a complete fracture.

"Oh, poor little counselor. Let's remember, you started this, not me. I guess you could say, you fucked around and found out. Trust me, you're going to like your next task far less than taking my cock in your throat, which, if you were an honest woman, you'd admit you liked."

Tilting her head to the side, she stares at me with a curious gaze, but she doesn't ask. I wouldn't have told her, and ruined the element of surprise, even if she had. This little game may end quickly, along with her life, when it's time for her next job anyway. I'd bet everything I own that she will not complete it. She says she'll do anything, but everyone has limits, and this is beyond hers.

"You may get dressed, but you will not clean your face. And I will come back to find you on your knees."

"Yes, master," she says with a bite, laced with sweet venom, and again, making my cock hard. I know she hates me, but shortly, my little lamb will experience self-hatred like she has never known. I can't fucking wait.

Chapter Fifteen
ANASTASIA

The second he leaves, I put my clothes on, to cover not only my body, but the shame I feel for what happened. It shouldn't even be possible to be turned on by Psycho. He's a madman. Massimo Bonetti is sexy as hell on the outside, but cold and dead on the inside. There are no redeeming qualities. If there's a worse man on earth, I've never met him, or at least that's what I'm currently telling myself. None of that matters because, for a long month, I have to do everything he tells me to. I'll obey his every command for my survival, but also because letting him kill me feels like handing him a win. It would prove him right, like I'm as weak as he thinks I am. He doesn't know the shit I've endured in my life. Men that have taken from me, until I had nothing left to give. He's only one of many on a long list. He isn't the first monster I've encountered. I can handle anything he dishes out. After what Carlo did to me, it will pale in comparison.

Kneeling in front of the cross, I wait. I shift uncomfortably, as I wonder how long he'll be gone, or what awaits me when he returns. The urge to clean my face is intense, my skin is tight, and feels disgusting, but I fight it. I glance around the room while I wait, and take in the various spots that I assume are for torture. The St Andrew's Cross behind me is the only item in the room that people would normally think is BDSM equipment, but I think it's simply another device for him to hurt people on. There are two metal tables on the other side of the room, with straps hanging down on both ends. The white floor with the drain on it is telling. It's probably for easy cleanup of blood. This entire basement is a serial killer's dream, and a victim's worst nightmare. I can't help but wonder how many people have died here. Is it hundreds or thousands? I swallow hard at the thought. The Assistant District Attorney in me wants to know, but the terrified woman kneeling in wait doesn't want to even think about it.

I get up to see if there's a bathroom, and walk past the metal tables to find a door. Upon opening it, I find another room. The walls are red, the floor black, and there's a king sized bed on one side, and a chair on the other. The kind you'd find in a dentist's office, that can lie back, or be left upright. A small metal table sits beside it, with what looks like a tattoo machine. Shaking my head in confusion, I walk back out and close the door, before finding the place I'm looking for. The bathroom is small and plain. White walls, a white toilet, and a single shower stall, with a glass sliding door. I am quick to relieve myself, and wash my hands, when I find one thing that makes me smile. *Mouthwash.* I can finally get the taste of him out of my mouth, because I am not willing to admit that I liked his taste on my tongue. My first fantasy as a teenager was Massimo, but not like this. Glancing in the mirror, I spot my face, and repulsion fills me, as Carlo's voice pops into my mind.

'Disgusting fucking whore.'

Massimo is not the first man to degrade me, or make me feel two inches tall. I swallow the emotion, causing a lump in my throat.

That's how you know you'll get through this.

I quickly make my way back to the cross, and kneel, while breathing out a relieved sigh that I'm back in position, right when I hear noise on the other side of the door, and my heart pounds like a jackhammer inside my chest.

"Stop fucking whining, and get inside," Psycho says, as my boss walks in, with his hand gripping the back of his neck.

My eyes widen, as I blink fast, trying to make sense of what's in front of me, and my mouth opens in a near gape, as Psycho directs him to the metal table. This is not happening, I try to tell myself. He is not going to make you watch him kill Easton.

"Clothes off," he orders, and much to my surprise, my boss complies. I tend to think this is likely not unusual for Psycho. Even when people know the outcome won't be good, they probably still do as they're told, as I have, because pissing him off will only cause things to escalate.

I turn away, because I don't really want to see him naked. And I don't want to watch whatever Psycho plans to do to him.

"Please. I have never crossed you."

His tormentor chuckles darkly, and if there ever was a doubt, there is none now. Psycho is a psycho, and he enjoys this.

"I know. Shame, isn't it? Unfortunately, my little lamb has a test. We're going to see if she will pass or fail. My money is on failure, but people do surprising things, when their lives are on the line."

I glance up at him when he says that, wondering how this is my test. Does he think I'll try to save him? Easton is alright, I suppose, but I won't trade my life for his. He lies naked on the metal table, shivering, with a strap holding his biceps down, and another over his thighs. This really is great firsthand knowledge to get, so I can get out of here, and have them prosecuted, assuming I ever find someone high up that they haven't paid off. I'm a witness now. I won't be involved in the case, but that doesn't matter to me. The Bonetti brothers, going to prison where they belong, is enough for me. If I can take down Psycho, and not the others, that's at least something. One is better than none of them. Besides, this may lead to uncovering other things about this violent family.

Psycho walks over to me, and I swear evil practically glows around him like some kind of neon warning sign. Before he says a word, I know his plans are diabolical. His lips pull up into a slight smile, but it's his words that cause my head to spin.

"Little lamb, it's time for 'anything'."

"What?"

If he's planning on making me fuck my boss, I'm not doing it. Not a chance.

He chuckles, and shakes his head like I'm a disappointment.

"I asked you what you would do to prolong your life. You said anything. Now we will find out if that's true. If it's not, then I'll kill you both, and be done with this. Stand up."

Wrapping his hand around my bicep, he grips me hard, pulling me to the table where Easton lies petrified. His trembles are so intense, he looks like he's having a seizure.

"If you look at his dick, you'll be punished."

Rolling my eyes, I say, "I don't want anything to do with his dick."

I'm still worried he plans to make me fuck my boss, but his last statement gives me a little hope.

Psycho reaches into his pocket and pulls out his knife, and now Easton isn't the only one in this room shaking. I glance at his smug face, as he grins at me like he knows what a psychotic asshole he is.

"Do not, for a second, think you can overpower me. Play stupid games, win stupid prizes, lamb. Open your hand."

I do, while staring at him with confusion. He places the knife in my hand, and the lack of understanding grows. What the hell does he have planned?

"Cut him. Anywhere you want."

All the air escapes my lungs, as I shake my head no. I am not stabbing a man. That is something Psycho does, not me. I have never hurt anyone in my life, if they hadn't first hurt me. Not even when I had good reason to do so.

He tilts his head, while clicking his tongue in disapproval.

"What happens if you refuse an order, Anastasia?"

"You kill me," I whisper.

He drags his fingers through his dark beard and nods.

"That's right. Make your choice wisely, because you will not get another chance. Refuse me again, and you'll die where you stand."

I can do this, right? I cleaned deer with my dad when I was a kid, although the deer was already dead. Jesus, I can't do this. Except I have to.

I take a deep breath, attempting to calm my nerves, which are beyond frayed at this point.

It's just a different animal. Okay, he's a human, not an animal, but that's what I'll have to tell myself to get through this. That's the only way.

"You have five seconds to make a cut, little lamb. If you can't do it though, it's okay. I'll be more than happy to slice your beautiful flesh again. Only this time it won't be knife play, it'll be your death."

I look down at the knife in my hand, and take another deep breath as I grip the handle. His name is engraved on the blade, and I arch an eyebrow.

"Afraid someone will mistake your knife for theirs?"

I roll my eyes, because it reminds me of the way your mom puts your name on everything when you're little.

"Instead of being a bitch, try to be grateful. I let very few people use my knife."

Am I tempted to tell him it's a little strange, the way he is with a weapon used to torture people? Yes, but I know better, so I don't.

I step closer to the table, and look down at Easton's wide eyes.

"Please don't do it."

I take a deep breath and hold the blade up.

"I'm sorry, so sorry. I don't have a choice. If I don't do this, he'll kill me, and I can't die. It's not just my life on the line. My mother will die too. I promised my dad I'd take care of her."

Chapter Sixteen

PSYCHO

Listening to her talk about her mother, as a tear rolls down her cheek, makes me curious about things I shouldn't be. I wonder what the deal is with her mother, that she cannot care for herself. I can't stop myself from asking, even though it's going to confuse her, and make her think I care. Which I don't.

"Is she sick?"

She nods and admits.

"Very. When my father was killed, she lost her way. Her depression is killing her, slowly."

Interesting. I assumed it would be cancer, or something like that.

"Make your cut. I'm growing impatient."

"I hate you, Massimo Bonetti. I fucking hate you," she says as she pierces his flesh, and drags the knife over his stomach, like she watched me do to her.

"Deeper."

When I cut her, I wasn't trying to fatally wound her. It was lighter treatment than she deserved. She will do far worse to her boss than I have done to her so far. Easton's screams become annoying, so I grab duct tape from under the table, tear a piece off, and cover his mouth. His face is red, and covered with tears and snot. Way to die like a man, buddy. I've always known he was a coward, but now he's proving I was right all along.

Bones is going to be pissed, because eventually a new District Attorney will be elected, and we'll have to go through everything to get that person in our pocket. This is all his fault, though. He is the one that didn't want to fuck with the pretty ADA, and waited until shit got out of hand. So now I'm doing his fucking job.

Her hands tremble as she pulls the knife out, and plunges it deep inside his abdomen.

"Fuck. Good girl."

This is a first for me, forcing someone to kill another is different, but I think I like it. Maybe I'm more depraved than I thought, because my dick is hard as fucking steel.

Easton bucks his hips up, but he isn't going anywhere. His screams are muffled now, but I can still hear them. Sometimes I like to hear them cry out in pain, but not now, because I'm solely focused on Anastasia. I don't think she realizes it yet, but she's going to kill him. Today is a big day for her. Your first kill is something you never forget.

I remember mine well, after my father found me with the Russians.

"How much did you tell them, Massimo?"

I shake my head and answer, "Nothing. Bonetti men are never rats."

He grins at me while he pats his chest.

"You make me proud, figlio."

My heart swells with pride, because my father is everything I strive to become. The thought of disappointing him is not something I can bear.

"It's time for your next lesson, Massimo."

I nod, ready for anything he wants me to do, as I look at the six Russian men of the Kuznetsov family, hanging upside down from chains, much like I was.

My father hands me a knife, and I take it, staring at it with a feeling I can't quite describe. I think maybe this is what it's like, when you become a man. Gone is the awkward little boy, unsure of his place in the world, replaced with the carbon copy of my father. Everything I want to be. All boys look up to their father, but for me, it's different. For the last four years, I have asked to take part in the business. He has always said I was too young, and was not ready. After what I've endured, he knows I can handle it.

"This is a custom made blade for you, figlio. It can cut through flesh and bone with ease. That means you are careful with it. This is yours now. Use it now to exact your revenge. How much, or how little, is up to you, Massimo. If you cannot finish it, I will."

I start with the man that beat me to a pulp. Maybe I should savor it, and drag out his pain, but at this moment, I want instant gratification.

I plunge the knife into his stomach, and smile at the blood pouring from his wound. It's better than I ever imagined, his screams fill the large warehouse, his red face nearly matching the blood seeping onto the floor.

My father says, "Twist it, if you want him to die quickly. If you want to prolong it, go for a straight angle."

Turning to my father with curious eyes, I beam at him.

"Could he be stitched up, so I could do it again?"

He chuckles, with what looks like beaming pride, and pats me on the head.

"If you don't hit a vital organ, that will work."

Shaking his head, my father laughs under his breath.

"It does make sense that my son would be a complete psycho."

From that day forward, I became known as Psycho. It's not just a name, I fucking earned it.

She turns her head to me, and asks, "Is that good?"

I lean forward, and run my tongue up the side of her cheek, tasting her tears. So fucking beautiful.

"It's a good start, little lamb, but you aren't done until he's no longer breathing."

She squeezes her eyes tight, and clenches her fist around the handle of my knife.

"You're going to make me kill him," she whispers, as the truth finally sinks in.

Placing my finger on her chin, I tilt her head back, and her eyes open, as she stares at me with a pain filled expression.

"For thirty days, you do as I say. Then, and only then, will you no longer be my property. You agreed to this deal."

She blows out a long breath, as if trying to release stress.

"Can I do it, and get it over with? Or does it have to be slow?"

I run my fingers through my beard, while I contemplate how I should answer. Normally, I drag out torture, but I'm also aware Easton is mostly innocent. However, this is her test, and the reason she's here is because she did cross us.

"I'll allow a quick kill, because there will be time for me to make you torment someone, if I decide that's what I want. If you want him to die quickly, plunge the knife into his chest, and twist it."

She moves beside his head, and holds the bloody knife in her hand. Anastasia lowers the blade to his throat, and I could stop her from making the mistake she's about to make, but where's the fun in that? I'm surprised she decided on his throat, instead of doing as I said, but I like it.

"I'm sorry," she says as she cuts into his flesh, and blood squirts all over her for a solid thirty seconds, while she stands screaming in horror. I fight the chuckle threatening to erupt, as I stare at what looks like a hot version of *Carrie*.

"You should have stood on the other side of him."

Her neck is coated in blood, and her eyes radiate fury. It's fucking exquisite. She drops the knife.

"You fucking asshole. Instead of telling me, you said nothing. I don't know how to murder people. You're a fucking monster!" She screams, and now, believe it or not, my cock hardens even further.

I fist my hand in her hair, pull her to me, and lean down, slamming my lips to hers aggressively. She holds her lips closed tightly, and I growl, "Fucking open. Do not fucking test me, little lamb. You won't enjoy the outcome."

I slide my tongue into her mouth when she parts her lips, and she kisses me back with equal aggression. The little mewl that erupts from her sweet mouth is intoxicating. Placing her bloody hands on my chest, she grips onto my shirt, pulling me closer to her. Her anger is palpable, and I don't fucking hate it. Anastasia would kill me if she could, yet she wants me. Without a doubt, her pussy is drenched for me.

Moving to pull back, I stop momentarily, when she sucks on my goddamn tongue like she did my dick, and I snap. I grab her hair tighter, and yank her head back.

"Are you playing games with me, little lamb?"

"No," she whimpers.

She tries to push my chest to get me to release her, but I don't move an inch. I told her she would never overpower me, and I meant it.

"Do you think if you make me think you want me, that I'll fall to my knees for you, and let you live?"

"I don't think you fall to your knees. You feel nothing for anyone. Whatever is beating in your chest is not a heart. You're far more monster than man. So no, I don't think there's anything I could do, that would make you choose to let me live."

I slide my hand down the front of her pants, and she freezes, like she's unsure of what I'm going to do when, in reality, she should know.

Circling my thumb on her clit, I lower my head, and speak into her ear.

"You think you have a magical pussy, little lamb? One that will change me into a man I wouldn't recognize? Trust me, sweetheart. There's nothing special about your cunt."

I'm lying through my teeth, her pussy is goddamn wet perfection, and if I weren't the man I am, it might actually save her life. Her eyes darken with a glare. If looks could kill, I'd be dead.

"Yeah? And there's nothing special about your dick. You think it's special, because you went and put a bunch of metal in it, like the psychopath you are."

I mock a pout.

"You don't think it's special, little lamb? I'll show you how wrong you are, but first, I'm going to mark you, because for the next thirty days, or until you die, you're mine."

Chapter Seventeen

PSYCHO

Why is the thought of her blood mingling with his bothering me? I don't fucking know. It shouldn't matter. Anastasia is going to die anyway. Yet, the second it enters my brain, I know I have to rectify it. I need his blood gone from her, in a nearly obsessive way.

I pull her by her arm to the bathroom.

"Clothes off."

After turning on the water, I spot her questioning expression, as she slowly removes her shirt.

"You have his blood all over you. Do you want to risk a fatal blood infection? He was a goddamn addict. Who knows what he could have? I know he injected heroin more than once."

Her giggle catches me off guard, the sound more fucking pleasurable to my ears than it should be. It's not just the sound though, her eyes light up with something I can't decide if I like.

"You're planning to kill me, Psycho. Now you're suddenly worried about my well-being?"

Shaking my head, I dismiss the thought that I'm at all concerned about her health, because she's right. I'll end up killing her, so it shouldn't matter.

"We will likely be in a situation where our blood mixes. It's not about you, little lamb. It's me I'm worried about. It's not about your safety, but mine."

"Asshole," she mutters under her breath, as she drops her pants to the floor. While I know I should be annoyed by her attitude, I'm not. I like this feisty behavior, although it surprises me. It makes me think a struggle is coming, and call me fucked up, but I love the idea of that.

The fight. Whimpers of both pleasure and pain. Fingernails scratching at my skin. That's right, little lamb, give me everything I want.

I get undressed as she gets into the shower. Once I'm naked, I get in behind her, and chuckle at the scowl she gives me, over her shoulder.

"I don't want you in here with me."

Too fucking bad. My clothes were bloody from her touching them, although I'm not, but I want to touch her naked body again.

Trailing my palm over her ass, my eyes take in the way her back arches, telling me how conflicted she is. She doesn't want to like my touch, but she does. I move my hand behind her, pushing two fingers inside her, and the breathy moan that escapes her lips is telling.

"You don't want me in here, little lamb? Or-"

Curving my fingers inside her, I groan when her pussy squeezes my digits.

"Do you just want me in here?"

"No," she whimpers, as the water falls down her back. Her dark hair is wet, so is her pussy she wants to insist doesn't like my fingers fucking her. Dirty fucking liar.

I reach my free hand around her waist, and pull her up against me, my cock pressed against her ass, while I move my fingers in and out of her wet heat.

"Lean forward, hands on the wall."

Pulling my fingers from her pussy, I spread her ass cheeks, and watch the water fall along her crack, enticing me.

"Fucking beautiful temptation. Do you know what I think, little lamb?"

Leaning my face into her neck, I bite into her flesh, as I push my fingers back inside her.

"I think you like being my pretty little whore. Don't you?"

Her answering whine, as her pussy clenches down on my fingers, says a lot more than she likely wants to.

94

When I know she's close to an orgasm, I pull my fingers from her, and ignore her annoyed glare as she spins toward me.

"You come when I decide, and not before. Get the soap and wash the blood off."

Her soapy hands rub down her neck to her perky tits, and my eyes follow every movement, as blood falls, along with water, from her body, and down the drain. I grip my cock in my hand and squeeze, trying to relieve the pressure, as she flashes me her pissed off scowl again.

"If you're going to get your rocks off by watching me, can I at least wash my face?"

With a nod, I allow it, because I can always come all over her face again, and probably will.

Chapter Eighteen

ANASTASIA

He yanks me by my hair, and practically drags me back to the room I found earlier.

Psycho is never gentle or kind that I've seen. Right now he seems angry, and that worries me, because I can only imagine what he's capable of when he's mad. He watches me like a wolf watches its prey, and the irony isn't lost on me. I expect him to direct me to the bed, but he doesn't.

"Get in the chair, and put your hands on the armrests."

Psycho stares at me with a heated gaze, as I do as he said. I have no idea what's happening, and I'm still confused when he grabs a strap from underneath the armrest, and secures my arm in place, before doing the same with my other one.

"What are you doing?"

He doesn't answer. Instead he grabs my leg and pushes it back beside my head, strapping it there, before also restraining my other leg beside my head.

"What the fuck?"

With a smirk, he drops his gaze between my legs. I'm spread wide open, and I don't like it. I've never had a man look at me like this.

"Pretty boring pussy, but we'll fix that."

He opens a drawer on the table beside the chair, and pulls out a needle and a tube.

"What is that?"

I hate the stupid grin on his face, like my misery brings him joy.

"It's for your piercing."

He holds up a little piece of jewelry. A fucking knife, because, of course, he would have piercings that are tiny little knives, just like the one he has.

"I'm piercing your hood, little lamb."

My mouth opens and forms an 'O', before I react angrily.

"You are not fucking piercing me!"

He sets the items on the table and, for a moment, I think maybe he's realized how insane this is, and might stop this madness. I force myself to ignore his body. I will not look at the beautiful ink, that is an artistic masterpiece. The large skull in the middle of his chest, or the ones on his arms. Vibrant colors, that make this dark man appear lighter than he is. I'll pretend all of it doesn't exist.

What is it about bad guys that attract me? Why can I even notice how hot this man is? He has me strapped to a chair, like a goddamn x-rated pretzel, and plans to pierce a part of me he doesn't even have a right to touch. I've always thought Carlo was the monster of all monsters, but now I'm not so sure.

"Why are you doing this to me?"

He stares at me in quiet contemplation, and I wonder if he even knows the answer.

He sits in front of me on the chair, with the stupid needle, and tiny knife, in his hands.

"It pleases me. Also, because you mocked my piercings, and I feel the need to show you how pleasurable it is."

I glare at him as he lowers the tool just over my clit, and my breathing gets heavy, as I pant out, "How is piercing me going to show me that? It's going to fucking hurt."

His lips pull into that smirk that irritates me to no end. I fucking hate him.

Except when he made you come harder than you have in your entire life.

"Again, it pleases me, little lamb. Greatly. Few things turn me on more than your pain."

I take a deep breath, trying to calm myself, because showing him fear only means more torture, since he gets off on it.

Psycho chuckles softly, as if he can read my mind.

"It'll be a slight pinch," he says, as he shoves the needle into my sensitive skin, and he's a goddamn liar. It's not a pinch. And it's not anything slight. I scream out in pain, and Psycho stares at me with an intense gaze, that should not take my breath away.

Without looking away from the jewelry, he tosses his supplies on the table.

"Fuck, little lamb. Look how pretty your pussy is with my knife in it."

I still cannot believe he just put a piece of jewelry on my body that's a tiny gold knife. My blood pounds in my ears, as I see red. Massimo, the boy, was never sweet and gentle, still I never imagined he'd turn into this. I knew he did terrible things, but this crosses a line I didn't expect.

He strokes his cock a few times, lining it up with my entrance, and I want to push him away, but he has me restrained, so I can't do anything.

"Don't."

The corners of his lips pull up into a smirk, equally sexy and dangerous.

"For thirty days, you're mine to do with as I please, unless you're telling me I can't fuck you. I won't take you without consent, counselor."

'You already have' is on the tip of my tongue, but I swallow my words. I'm not a violent person, but right now I wish I had the use of my hands, and could punch him in his smug face, because we both know I have no choice but to consent. It's either let him do whatever he wants to me, or he kills me, for not obeying his every word. That's not fucking consent. It's coercion. I'm tempted to inform him under the law that's still rape. If a person is unable to say no, it's sexual assault by coercion. Then again, nearly everything he has done is against the law, and I know he doesn't care. He's untouchable. Or so he thinks.

"I don't want this," I say, in a voice barely above a whisper.

Psycho arches a brow as he stares at me.

"Are you saying no, little lamb? Is this you giving up on day one?"

"I'm not saying no, I'm making it clear I don't want this. We both know you're going to do what you want to, anyway. Can you at least put a condom on, so I don't get pregnant?"

He pushes the tip of his cock inside me.

"Not a chance. We both know you won't be alive in thirty days, so we don't need to worry about any babies."

With a single thrust, he's buried to the hilt. Leaning over me, he places a hand on either side of my shoulders, and his voice comes out deep, and filled with need I wish I didn't recognize.

"I'm going to go slow, because I want you to feel every piece of metal in my cock. Every movement will bring you closer to an orgasm. I promise you, it'll be better than the toy you had in your dresser."

Every time he thrusts into me, he grinds his pelvis against the damn piercing, causing pain and then pleasure, forcing moans out of me, that I wish I could keep stuffed down. My body is a traitor. I should be able to control whether or not I want to orgasm, but I can't. He has control over me in every single way, and I hate it.

I already knew he was in my house, and did disgusting things while he was there. Somehow, him seeing my toy has me turning red with humiliation, and equal rage. Everything about Psycho is a violation.

"Wait. Had? You said had, as in past tense. Like it was there, but it isn't now."

Psycho swipes his tongue over my lips, and groans.

"I like it when you're angry, lamb. It's sexy as fuck, but you have reason to be suspicious. I have your toy, and I'd be happy to fuck you in the ass with it, while you come all over my cock, if you like."

"I would not."

Chapter Nineteen
PSYCHO

I pull my hips back and push inside her slowly, so she can feel every groove. Every time I move inside her, her pussy squeezes my cock, even though I'm supposed to believe she doesn't want this. Reaching up, I untie her legs, and she puts them on either side of me with a whimper. I push her legs back, and reach up to remove the restraints on her wrists.

"Trust me when I say you want to behave yourself. I'm going to bring you upstairs shortly. If you can't obey me, you'll be left down here, tied to the cross."

Anastasia rotates her wrists. I'm sure she wasn't in pain, but it likely wasn't comfortable either.

"Understood?"

"Yes, sir," she says with a bite, causing me to pinch her nipple.

"Maybe we should pierce these too."

"No. Please. I'm sorry. I understand, and I will behave."

She doesn't know it, but her nipples will be pierced, just not tonight. I only had one piece of jewelry custom made. I'll need to call my guy, and have him make two more.

I place my hand around her throat and squeeze lightly.

"Are you ready to see Jesus, little lamb?"

The panic in her gaze somehow makes her tight pussy feel even better.

"When I kill you, it won't be by choking the life out of you, counselor. There will be blood. So much fucking blood. It'll be beautiful. That will be the last time I taste you, because I won't be able to help myself. A man like me can't refuse the taste of heaven. When I die, I'll never get near the pearly gates. I know I'm evil, little lamb. A man with no redeeming qualities. There's no good in me.

While you're alive, I suggest you take the pleasure I offer you, because it's the only thing I will give you."

She trails her fingers up my arms to my shoulders, and I actually hate her more than I ever have, because her touching my skin feels better than it should. Her touch should not feel like this. I snap my hips back, and begin fucking her with punishing thrusts. I push inside her and intentionally hit her clit with my pelvis, to cause her pain from her new piercing. I want to hurt her. I want to make her scream. Yet it has the opposite effect, and she fucking moans with pleasure.

"Massimo," she gasps breathlessly. I need to nip that shit in the bud immediately. My given name falling from her lips is wrong. It sounds fucking intimate, as if we mean something to each other and we don't.

Pinching her nipple, I growl, "It's Psycho."

She laughs, but there's no humor behind it.

"Do your worst, Massimo. It's nothing I haven't heard before. The most devastating thing has already been done to me. It doesn't matter what you do, you'll never top the last man. I am unbreakable. You cannot ruin what has already been destroyed."

Am I curious what the fuck some man did, that's worse than what I'm capable of? Obviously I am, but it can wait.

Pulling out of her, I flip her over and smack her ass.

"On your knees."

She whimpers as I push her head down, and hold onto the back of her neck, while I fuck her like I want to. Like she's the bitch that wants to lock me up. Anastasia can cry all she wants, because she deserves every single punishment. When I end her life, she'll deserve that too. I pull my hips back, and slam into her over and over again.

In. Out. In. Out.

Her helpless cries sound out when I slam into her pussy violently. If I weren't holding her down, her head would likely hit the wall behind the chair.

My punishment fails. Her pussy clenches my cock like it never wants to let me go, and she cries out my name again.

"Yes, Massimo. Oh my God."

Anastasia should be punished for disobeying my order. I clearly told her to call me Psycho, and yet hearing her breathy words, as she comes all over my cock, just makes me want to make her do it all over again.

Leaning over her, I growl into her ear.

"You're going to do that again, and then you'll clean up the mess you've made of my cock. Understood?"

I grab a fistful of her hair and yank her up, so she's riding me with her back to me, and with my free hand, I pinch her nipple. The sound that comes from her, combined with the way she's once again clenching my cock, pulls my climax from me. I groan out my release, while I sink my teeth into her neck, tasting her delicious flesh until I draw blood. Darting my tongue over her skin, I lap up the coppery sweetness, as she whimpers, before it turns to a moan, and makes my cock hard inside her all over again. As good as her pussy feels, that's not what the next thirty days is about. It's punishment. And exactly what she deserves.

"Get on the floor and kneel."

Reluctantly, I pull out of her, and she climbs off the chair to stand, staring at me with an arched brow.

"Counselor, don't make me tell you twice."

I follow her as she gets up and walks a few feet over, and turns to me with a glare.

"I can't figure out how the man that made me feel so good, can also make me feel so bad about myself."

She kneels on the floor and lowers her gaze, as if she can't look at me. *Good.* Women tend to confuse sex with romantic shit. This is not a romance, and she should be clear that this is about hurting her. Maybe I'll make her come in the process, but it changes nothing. She's mine to use, and dispose of, when I see fit.

Leaning down, I grab her chin and lift her head, forcing her gaze to mine.

"I own you, little lamb. You will obey every single order. I don't give a shit if it makes you feel bad about yourself. In fact, it's the goal. If you miraculously survive thirty days, you'll never be the same. If I don't kill you, you'll kill yourself."

She blinks back tears as she sighs sadly.

"Clean up your mess."

"Fuck," I groan, as she slides her tongue up the underside of my cock. Knowing she's tasting not only me, but her pussy, makes me want to fuck her again. She swirls her tongue around the tip and I grab her hair, and slam into her mouth. Anastasia gags slightly, when I push aggressively to the back of her throat. She looks stunning like this. On her knees, taking the cock of the man she hates, her eyes watering, as she does the only thing she can. She takes me, like she will take everything I have to give her. I guess we're about to find out if that's true.

"When I come, you'll take every fucking drop."

She moans around my length, so I reach down and plug her nose, and she panics. Unable to breathe, she pulls off of me as I release, coming once again on her face, a little on her hand, and some on the floor.

"Oh, little lamb, you should not have done that. I said, every drop. Now, lick it up."

Chapter Twenty

ANASTASIA

He has to be kidding. I am not licking his cum off the floor. Somewhere there has to be a line, and this is it. After a few years of therapy, I have learned that people treat you the way you allow them to. This is not a normal situation, because my life is hanging in the balance, but I can't do this. I won't.

"No."

In a flash, Psycho's eyes darken to the shade of coal, and he grabs me by my hair, pulling me down to the floor. Putting his weight on my back, he growls angrily.

"Drink up, little lamb. This is not a fucking request. It's an order."

With a whimper, I continue to refuse to be treated like this, when he pushes my face down into his cum.

"This is what cum sluts do. Now lick it up."

Leaning over me, he speaks low into my ear, his voice coming out deep and lethal sounding. I know I don't have a choice, so I scoop it up with my tongue, while any respect I had for myself disappears without a trace. The bile rises in my throat as I swallow, and I nearly vomit. Not because of how he tastes, but the fact that I just licked the floor like a dog. This is what he meant, when he said I'd hate myself so much, that I'd kill myself if he didn't. He's wrong though. This man does not know me, and he doesn't know I can, and will, survive him.

Psycho gets off me, and pulls me to my feet.

"Where is this ex of yours? Is he over you, or should I expect him to come looking for you?"

I shake my head in irritation, because Carlo is not a subject I talk about. The mere mention of him is all it takes for the stabbing pain in my chest to return. Long after the person that hurts us is removed from our life, the pain remains. It's the one constant that follows me everywhere I go. Some days it lessens slightly, as a smile crosses my face for one reason or another, surprising me. Without warning, it comes back with the strength of a hurricane, threatening to rip apart all the pieces I glued back together.

"No. He's in prison. Maybe one day you'll meet."

He grabs my arm and pulls me to the stairs, before entering the code on the keypad to the left of the door. It's not lost on me that no one gets in or out without those numbers, and I try to see them, but other than a six, I fail miserably. I don't know where we're going, but it's also not lost on me that we're both naked. As if reading my mind, Psycho chuckles softly.

"I'm taking you to your bedroom. You can take a shower and get ready for bed. You'll be locked inside, but if you can behave, it'll be a better environment than the basement."

I don't bother to ask what happens if I can't behave, because I already know the answer. He takes me across a vast living room that screams money. The floor is a stunning white marble, and the vaulted ceiling is painted a deep red, with two crystal chandeliers hanging overhead. All the furniture is black, a sectional, and two oversized chairs. The painting on the far wall catches my attention. It matches the tattoo on his stomach. It has fire, a knife plunged through a skull and says 'Your death is a gift'. It makes me curious, and he questions my gaze, as it's drawn to the large canvas.

"What?"

"Your death is a gift. Does that mean something to you?"

He nods with a smirk.

"It means a great deal to me. Death is freedom from pain. Most of the time when I end a life, they've earned the relief. The torture they have endured has gone on for weeks at a time. By the time I kill them, they don't want to live anymore. The will to live is gone, replaced with the readiness to die."

I shake my head, and make a disgusted face.

"You're a serial killer."

He chuckles as he takes my hand in his, and pulls me to the red, double-sided spiral staircase.

"That would be my brother, counselor. Not me. I kill out of necessity, not for sport."

As we walk up the stairs, I say, "A serial killer is defined as a person who murders three or more people, in a period of over a month, with a cooling down period between the murders. Is that not you? Have you not killed that many?"

While it's not surprising, Psycho doesn't answer my questions.

We make it up to a bedroom, and he nods for me to enter. The room is large, but doesn't have a lot to it. There's a large bed with a deep red comforter, and a small dresser.

"You must really like red."

He chuckles darkly.

"Red is the color of blood, little lamb."

I fight myself to not roll my eyes. It's weird and a little gross.

Psycho points and says, "There's clothing in there for you."

I tilt my head and look at him, as puzzle pieces slam together in my mind.

"Was this planned? Even if I hadn't gone to your warehouse, this was going to happen, wasn't it?"

His movements are quick, as he wraps his hand around my throat, and slams me against the wall, shaking the dresser where it stands.

"Was this premeditated, counselor? Yes. Let's not get shit twisted. You are not a goddamn victim. I never would have laid a finger on you, had you not gotten into my business. This is a dangerous game, little lamb, but I'm more than happy to play with you. While you're crying about all the things I will do to you, remember, you started this."

His breathing is heavy, as he stares into my eyes with that dark gaze, that promises what he has done to me is simply the tip of the iceberg. He has far more sinister plans for me.

Psycho squeezes his hand around my throat, not cutting off my air supply completely, but enough that I begin to panic. My heart pounds in my chest, and his lips pull up into a smirk.

"I suggest you take a shower, and get some rest. You're Psycho's plaything now, and you never know when I'll get an itch that I just can't scratch."

He removes his hand from my throat, and steps away with a chuckle, as I gasp and cough, nearly falling to the floor. I take my first full breath when he leaves the room, and shuts the door. A shiver runs down my spine, as I hear the click of a lock. I'm never getting away from him. There's no chance.

I run to the window and look outside at the world around me. The bedroom faces a massive pool, and gardens, as far as the eye can see. I was not looking for an escape, but it becomes clear it wouldn't have been an option, when bars slide down outside the window. I look around the room, trying to find cameras, because I know Psycho made those bars come down. Is he watching me? Probably. I don't see any signs of surveillance, but I don't doubt that, somewhere in here, there are cameras.

"I hate you," I say out loud, hoping he hears me, before turning and walking to the bathroom, to take a hot shower.

I stand under the rainfall showerhead, soaking up the warmth, as I think about the man I wish I had never seen again. What made him this way? There has to be some traumatic event that led him down this path of madness. Children are not born evil, they are made. Was he abused? Mafia men are terrible people, so maybe his father beat him, and made him like this. I certainly don't remember his dad being abusive, but maybe I wasn't around for it. I'm fascinated by human behavior, and believe there's normally a rational reason people snap, and do heinous things. It doesn't make it okay, but it does explain how it happened.

After finishing in the shower, and drying off, I open the drawer to the dresser to find my clothes. Not clothes he bought for me.

My clothes.

He took them when he was in my house, which shouldn't be surprising at this point, but it is. I groan in frustration, and get dressed in my favorite pink pajama pants, and a matching tank top. Crawling into bed, I squeeze my eyes shut tight, as the grief seizes me. I don't cry, I never do. That part of me is dead. After Michael died, love was replaced with hate. Losing a child is the most painful trauma any mother can experience. It's how I know I can survive this madman, no matter what he dishes out. Nothing could be worse than the day he was taken from me.

I let out a shaky breath, and force myself to sleep, knowing tomorrow I'll go through the same things I did today, or maybe worse. My only solace is the hope that, if I die, I'll get to hold my baby again.

Chapter Twenty-One
PSYCHO

After taking a shower myself, I turn on my monitor to observe my little lamb. I watch as she gets dressed in fluffy pink pants, and my fingers itch to touch them, and drag them down her legs. I grip my cock hard as she slips into bed. Her expression is pained as she closes her eyes, but it's her voice that makes me take notice.

"Goodnight, Michael," she says, in a voice drenched with anguish.

Humans are curious by nature, which is the only reason I wonder who Michael is, and why she sounded so damn sad. I don't really give a fuck about her feelings. As I reminded her a little while ago, she did this. Had she stayed out of our family business, she wouldn't be here. I don't kidnap random fucking women. Had she not started asking questions about the Bonetti Brothers, she'd still be safe in her own bed. We own the majority of the city. There is nowhere she could've safely asked questions about us, and it not gotten back to me. Showing up at my brother's house? Dangerous game. Not just dangerous, but fucking stupid.

Deep down, I'm a nice guy, so I let her sleep for an hour, before I get up and grab my knife. I chuckle to myself, okay, maybe not really nice, but I have my moments of decency. I walk to her bedroom and open the door quietly. Stepping over to the bed, I grip my knife, while the desire to cut her surges through me, like a wildfire out of control.

I give myself a minute, and allow my eyes to take her in as I drag the comforter off her, tossing it to the floor. So beautiful. Her long dark hair is splayed across the pillow. Her chest moves with heavy breaths, as her eyelashes flutter subtly. I pull her shirt up over her tits, and smile at the mark I've already left. I've never seen a pair I didn't like, but hers are perfect, a 'C' cup, so big and perky. They pebble under my gaze, like they know I'm here. I need to call my jeweler again and get her nipple jewelry rushed, so I can get that done. I run the blade of my knife over her nipple and stifle a groan. She'll look exquisite with two knives in her rosy nipples, matching the one in her hood.

Climbing on the bed, I straddle her thighs without putting my weight on her. The thought of tying her up did occur to me, but I'm hoping for a fight, which restraining her would prevent. Leaning over Anastasia, I cut the side of her breast, just enough to make her bleed. I train my eyes on her face as I swipe my tongue up her skin, tasting her sweet blood, as her eyes pop open and a loud gasp leaves her lips.

Exquisite.

Her eyes widen with delicious fear, as they dart back and forth, as if she's trying to make sense of her current predicament. Her tits rise and fall with her panicked breaths, and her bottom lip quivers, as she speaks quietly, almost like she's at her breaking point.

Fuck, I hope so.

"I've done everything you've wanted me to. I don't deserve to die, Massimo."

She digs her nails into the sheets, her body trembling like a leaf, and I can see the fight to remain brave, and not crumble in front of me. Cutting her stunning skin does not mean I came in here to kill her.

"I'm not here to kill you, little lamb. Not yet anyway. I want to play with my pretty little fuck doll."

She whimpers sweetly, as I move down her body and slice her stomach, just above her belly button.

"Why are you doing this to me?"

Her voice sounds devastated, but when I look up at her face, there are no tears. Just a look of fury, mixed with alarm, and a side of lust, which makes my cock weep for her.

"Your skin is beautiful, little lamb. The perfect fair shade, that only looks more appealing when it drips for me. The contrast of the dark red color against your light skin does things to me. You taste like heaven. I can't wait to find out if your pussy tastes as good as your blood."

Moving further down the bed, I forcefully spread her legs, press my face to her pussy, and inhale her scent. Jesus, she smells good.

"Since you like playing games, we're going to have a little fun, counselor. If you're a good girl, I will reward you. If you're a bad girl, I'll fuck you with the blade of my knife."

She releases another gasp, and I swear I can almost hear her heart pounding in her chest.

"You wouldn't," she says, in a voice barely above a whisper.

I chuckle softly against her skin. "You still doubt me, little lamb? I promise you, I will. You would look so stunning, lying here stiff as a board. Afraid to move, because you might get shredded by my knife. You'd still get wet for me, you'd still come, even if you don't want to. The struggle to stay still would be difficult, and you'd lose your battle. I already know you'd fuck my knife back, unable to stop yourself, all the while knowing the consequences."

I run the blade cautiously over her clit, eliciting a whimper from her as the blade hits the piercing, and she instinctively attempts to shut her thighs.

"Oh, bad idea, little lamb. That's going to get you cut, unless that's what you're after. Do you like bleeding for me, Anastasia?"

"No," is the word that comes from her lips, but her drenched pussy tells an entirely different story.

I swipe my tongue up her slit, tasting her, while I press my knife to the inside of her thigh. She raises her hips, wanting more of my tongue, and cuts herself on the blade. I quickly slide my tongue along her skin, collecting her blood, before going back to her sweet cunt. The flavor is almost too much to take. I push the handle of my knife inside her, and she moans loudly. I move it inside her, and the sound she makes nearly causes me to release all over the damn bed.

"Look at you, little lamb. This pussy is ravenous, swallowing the handle of my knife, so desperate to be filled."

"More," she whimpers pathetically, and it pisses me off. She is not supposed to want this. This is no longer a goddamn punishment. I'm going to need to escalate things.

I pull the knife from her pussy and stare at her eyes, blown wide with pure lust, as I lick the handle of my knife clean. Climbing over her, I say, "Your secret is out, little lamb. This isn't working anymore. I'm going to have to reassess things. Find a way to break you. Torture you. Punish you."

I slam inside her, and she gasps my name.

"Massimo."

It makes me irrationally angry. Is she delusional? Thinking this is something other than what it is? Nothing has changed for me. I press my knife to her neck, not cutting her, but making sure she feels the metal threatening to slice her flesh.

"My name is Psycho. To you, it will always be Psycho. Do not get confused, and think this is something other than you trying to live through thirty days. I feel nothing for you. I will feel nothing for you. I'm fucking you out of convenience. Tomorrow, I have shit to deal with, and I'll be inside another pussy, before I even get home."

She turns her head away from me, causing me to nick her skin, and bites, "Just shut up and fuck me."

Chapter Twenty-Two
ANASTASIA

Does he think I feel anything for him? I don't. That hasn't always been the case, but it is now. When I was a stupid little kid, I had a crush on him. Even though he was mean to me, the way he protected me made me think I loved him. Now I feel nothing for him, other than pure hatred, but I can't deny the piercings on his dick feel really fucking good. He told me to take the pleasure, because there's nothing more he'd give me. That's what I'm doing, because it's not like I have a choice. If he wants to have sex with me, he will, and it doesn't matter how loud I scream. The fact is, Massimo Bonetti may have no other redeeming qualities, but he's good in bed.

I will never admit it to him, but yes, I like the pain. There are a few depraved things I'm learning about myself that I don't like. The pain, and the degradation, are not what he thinks they are. I like it, fucking love it. The only thing he has done, that I didn't get off on, was licking the damn floor. That was disgusting, but the rest, I don't hate like I should.

Leaning his head down, he licks at the blood on my neck with a groan. Drawing his hips back as he bites down on the wound, he pushes back inside me. I moan instantly from the feeling of the metal massaging my insides. It's not just the piercings, but the way he knows how to move, to hit that delicious spot exactly right.

"Mmm," he groans against my skin, "I think you like being my fuck doll, little lamb."

I don't respond. Instead, I dig my nails into his shoulders, while he moves inside me like a man possessed. Psycho pulls out slowly, making sure I feel every rung of his piercings, before he slams back inside my pussy.

He hovers over me, a hand on either side of my shoulders, and stares at me, with a light coating of my blood on his lips. Leaning down further, he captures my lips with his. He growls into my mouth, as he pushes his tongue against mine, forcing me to taste my own blood. Fucking me with long strokes, he hits that sweet spot inside me repeatedly. The one that makes my body climb higher and higher. For a moment, I think I see him. The person I once knew, and I'm sure I spot something familiar, and then I come, and everything changes in an instant.

"Psycho," I cry out in an orgasm, and his gaze turns cold as ice, as he presses the knife into my skin again, harder than before.

"I want to watch you bleed to death. Never do I go back on my agreements, but I want to. I've never wanted to kill someone more than I want to kill you," he growls angrily, which is confusing, because I don't know what I did.

Picking up his pace, he fucks me like an angry animal, with hard, punishing thrusts. After he finishes inside me, he gets up.

"You'll be locked inside this room. My staff will feed you three meals, nothing more, nothing less."

I stare at him with confusion, because I know he doesn't like me. He hates me, but the sudden spike in anger has me feeling more off balance than I already was.

"Are you leaving?"

"Yes," he answers with a glare.

"When are you coming back?"

Psycho turns his head to the door, and speaks low, but matter-of-factly.

"When I can stomach looking at you."

The flashback is instant, and attacks me head on, as he slams the door shut.

"I can't even stand to look at you," Carlo says, as he stands with his belt in his hand. I know what happens next. He's going to beat me with it, it's become his go to, whenever we argue, which lately is

constantly. His green eyes are wide with anger, as he steps closer to me. I won't fight him. We both know I won't, because I won't risk waking Michael. The last thing I need is for our three-year-old to walk in on his daddy beating mommy. Children learn what they see, so I'm careful to never cause him to lose his temper when Michael is awake. It's my fault, I know it is. I shouldn't have questioned where he had been. I knew how this would play out, but I was pissed when I saw a smear of lipstick on his shirt. Now it's not worth it.

He wraps the belt around my throat, and tightens it, until he cuts off my air supply.

"I told you I'd make you learn your place, one way or another. Of course, I'm fucking other women. You disgust me."

I'd like to ask him why he makes me have sex with him every day, if I'm so repulsive, but I can't, with a belt strangling me.

"Mommy. Mommy," my little boy cries, as he races toward Carlo.

The evil glint in my husband's eyes causes me to shake my head, as his grip loosens. I take in a gulp of air, and plead with him to not hurt my son. When Carlo becomes angry, there's no stopping it, so I know this is going to get worse before it gets better.

"Don't hurt him. It was me, all me. I'm sorry."

He removes the belt from my neck, and turns to the son we created together. Carlo has never been a great father, but he's never hit Michael either. With the belt in his hand, he raises it, and I grab a knife. I've never fought him off, but for my son, I will kill him with my bare hands, if I have to.

Racing over to him, he places the leather around Michael's neck and, as he tightens it, I stab him in the back with a butcher knife, but it doesn't stop him. It doesn't slow him down. I wrap my arm around his throat, trying to pull him back, and away from our boy. My everything. It doesn't work. Instead, he pulls tighter, until I watch my sweet dark-haired boy slump to the floor.

I pull the knife out, and plunge it into his back over and over again, until he falls to the floor, beside the little boy that not only made me a mother. He gave me life. In only minutes, Carlo took everything from me.

That day is never far from my mind, and neither is my part in it. The guilt weighs heavily on me, and I spend most days feeling like I'm carrying a boulder on my back. After it happened, I had no one to turn to. Mrs. Bonetti was no longer in my life, and my own mother was already in her depressed state. The loneliness was crippling, and the flashbacks are still intense.

I let out a shaky sigh, as I try to remind myself that I hate Massimo Bonetti. His words don't matter. Yet, somehow they do.

There are some things in life you never get over. Losing your child, to an act of violence at the hands of his father, is one of those. The darkness fills your heart and never leaves. You somehow manage to keep breathing, even when you don't want to. The pain never leaves. It's always there, and all-consuming. The only thing possibly worse than the pain itself is the guilt. I am the reason my son is dead. I knew better than to fight with Carlo. His blood is on my hands, and I will never forgive myself.

Chapter Twenty-Three

ANASTASIA

I've been staring out the window, through the bars, for hours. His property is beautiful, and I'd love nothing more than to explore it. I won't ask for that. Making Massimo angry seems easy, and dangerous.

I spot movement near one of the two large gardens, and it catches my eye.

He catches my eye.

Massimo is running back toward the house, in black sweatpants and no shirt. My breath hitches, because he's evil, but beautiful. A large frame, with chiseled muscles, and so much ink. When I last saw him, he had one tattoo on his arm, but now, he's covered with them. As he gets closer, I notice his chest rising and falling with heavy breaths, and ignore my drenched panties.

You will not be attracted to him.

First crushes die hard, but this one has to. After Carlo, I vowed to stay away from bad boys. I didn't know, when I met my ex, that he was affiliated with a mafia family. I didn't find that out until after I got pregnant, three months to the day after we started dating. Then it was too late.

His gaze lifts to the window, and I know I'm caught. I dart away so he can't see me, and run back to the bed with my hand on my chest, as my heart thumps wildly.

When we were kids, he was both kind and cruel, although mostly the latter. There were times he showed me that he cared. I wonder if that part of him is gone, or if there's any of the boy I knew left at all.

I lay on the ground, blood covering my knees, and Massimo and Lorenzo run through the empty field to me, like they somehow knew I was here.

"Lorenzo," he barks, "Grab that fucker."

Kneeling beside me, Massimo stares at me with concern, as he pulls my dress down, now covering my thighs appropriately.

"You are not supposed to be over here by yourself. What the fuck did he do to you?"

I shake my head no, not wanting to talk about it, but he insists.

"Tell me."

Glancing down at my skinned knees, unable to meet his gaze, I admit, "He pulled my dress up and, when I told him no, he pushed me to the ground, and got on top of me. Then he ran off, because he heard you coming."

He sighs audibly, like he's relieved I'm okay, and the butterflies swirl in my belly. When he leans down, and softly kisses each of my knees, my heart soars like it's trying to take flight. I love Massimo Bonetti. I will always love him.

Several minutes later, I hear the locks clicking on the door, which does not calm my racing heart. If anything, it makes it speed up so fast, I feel it in my throat.

The door opens and Massimo stands in the doorway, his gaze leisurely traveling my body, making me feel like I forgot to put clothing on. His lips pull up into a smirk, as if he knows that I was eye fucking him. What the hell is wrong with me?

"Come on, little lamb."

I don't know where he's taking me, but I follow him anyway. The entire way downstairs, I'm hoping it's not to the basement. That place is the worst. Every time he's done something horrible to me, it's been there.

"I thought you might like to take a walk."

I glance at him, as we walk toward the French doors.

"Thank you."

Placing his hand on the small of my back, he reminds me once again, that he's in charge. As if I could forget.

"If you don't behave, you'll never go outside again."

122

I jerk my chin up, and flash my annoyance to him.

"You don't have to keep threatening me. I get it, already."

Grabbing my arm, he pulls me to a sudden stop, and runs his fingers down my cheek.

"I don't think you do get it, little lamb. Every time I remind you of what's at stake for you, I see fear. Beautiful fucking fear. Your eyes widen, lips part, breaths get heavy, and fuck, I like it. So I'll keep reminding you, continue causing you terror, because it pleases me."

I shove down the urge to tell him he's a complete psychopath, because he already knows that.

"I'm being nice right now, so maybe be thankful, and keep your bitchy attitude to yourself."

Cocking my head to the side, I lift an eyebrow, challenging him, because maybe he likes my fear, but I like pushing him just a little.

"This is nice, Massimo? We'll have to agree to disagree. Nice would be letting me go. Do that, and I'll think you're nice."

He chuckles soft and low, as he yanks my hand and starts walking again.

"I like it when you're delusional, little lamb. It's cute."

We step outside into the warm sunshine, and I let out a gasp, at the sight of what I guess is the backyard. It's so massive that the word feels inadequate. He wraps his hand around mine tightly, like I might make a run for it. I learned my lesson, trying to run from him the first night at his warehouse, although he told me to. I'm sure if there's a place to run to, he would know, and follow. He's in great shape, so I have no doubt that he could outrun me anyway.

We walk past an Olympic sized pool, with water that might be bluer than the ocean, and over to a massive garden, that is mixed with greenery, and red roses, designed in a spiral pattern. There's a walkway between the two gardens, with some kind of grey concrete, and I spot the logo stamped into the cement. Three skulls, one with a crown and wings. It says Bonetti Brothers, but I remember from my childhood his father had one just like this, on the gate to their home. It didn't say brothers though, it only had their last name.

I walk away from him to get a better look at the flowers, and he allows it, no doubt still watching me. There's no need to look behind me, because I can feel his eyes on me. Heat licks up my skin, and I try to block it out. Leaning down, I inhale the scent of the most perfect roses I've ever seen in my life. There's not a hint of dying leaves, it's all landscaped meticulously.

"This is gorgeous," I breathe, as the sun warms my skin. Not knowing when you'll ever see outside again, or if, makes you appreciate it differently. His breath brushes over my bare shoulder, before he sinks his teeth into my flesh with a growl.

"You're gorgeous."

A moan slips between my lips, when he licks the spot he bit.

"Are your panties wet, little lamb?"

"No," I answer, the high tone in my voice betraying me.

Wrapping his arm around me, he splays his hand over my stomach, and makes a deep humming noise in my ear.

"I might believe you, except for one thing. I can fucking smell your arousal."

Shaking my head, I continue to deny it.

"You're wrong. I'm not."

"Wet," he says, finishing my sentence, sounding out each letter, causing my panties to become more damp. Why does his damn voice do this to me?

"Let's see, little lamb. Do you think I didn't see the way you were watching me from the window? Were you clenching your thighs, trying to get some relief? Would you have played with my pretty pussy, if I hadn't come to you right away? Or would you have waited, and only given in when the throbbing became unbearable?"

He slides his hand up my thigh, underneath my favorite light blue dress, and drags his fingers over my skin slowly, causing goosebumps to appear. Placing his hand over my panties, a groan vibrates through his chest, into my back.

"Fucking. Beautiful. Liar."

Slipping his hand inside my lace panties, he slides two fingers up my soaked slit.

"Drenched. You can't hide the way I make your body feel. Has any man ever made you come the way I do?"

Like the way he pulls my orgasms from me, the words come the same, with honesty I'll probably regret.

"No."

He circles his fingers over my swollen clit, commanding me with his touch to come. Nobody has ever touched me the way he does, with such precision, as if he knows exactly what I want. How hard or soft his strokes should be. Massimo may be an asshole, but he can play my body like a musician plays their instrument.

I lean my head back against his chest, and grab onto his arm, as the pleasure climbs through my body.

"I still don't like you," I bite, and I'm not lying entirely. I at least don't *want* to like him.

He chuckles against my neck, as he circles his finger over my clit and retorts.

"I know. Yet your ravenous pussy can't get enough of me."

"Massimo," I cry out, as he pushes two fingers inside me, fucking me aggressively, giving me the delicious stretch I crave.

"Fuck," he says in a low, dark growl, that nearly brings me to my knees.

Suddenly, he withdraws his fingers, and I turn to find him sucking them clean, as he stares at me with a heated gaze. Taking my hand, he pulls me out of the garden, and I stare at him in question, as he pulls me up against the wall outside the house.

"Panties off. Now."

I reach under my dress, pulling my panties down and stepping out of them, as he angrily lowers his pants, and pulls his cock out.

"I didn't do that. You did. So stop acting pissed at me."

He grabs my hips on either side, lifts me and impales me on his hard cock, causing me to whimper.

"I didn't plan on fucking you, and I hate myself for it. You are my fucking enemy, and I don't fuck my enemies, little lamb. You're so goddamn beautiful, and I can't help myself. So yeah, Anastasia, I'm fucking angry."

Chapter Twenty-Four
PSYCHO

I dig my fingers into her ass cheeks, sure to leave marks, pull her up, and slam her back down, burying my cock to the hilt. Every whimper escaping from her lips only spurs me on. I fuck her like I hate her, but she doesn't get the message. Digging her hands into my hair, she pulls my head down, pressing her lips to mine with a sweet little moan. Her velvet tongue slides against mine, her fingers dig into my scalp, and I swallow down her cries, as her pussy clenches down on my cock.

She feels amazing, but it's not enough. Moving my hands behind her back, I lower her to the ground, kneel between her thighs, and continue fucking her. Anastasia lies on the ground, looking fucking breathtaking, taking my cock like a goddamn queen. Every time I'm inside her, I know I'll want her again, and it's fucking with my head. It wasn't supposed to be like this, and I know damn well, I'm the only one that can put a stop to this. I've told myself multiple times to just fucking end it.

"Massimo," she says in a breathy moan, as she digs her nails into the skull tattoo on my chest.

So fucking beautiful. She lies on the grass underneath me, with her dark hair splayed around her, eyes wide with lust, and lips parted with heavy breaths. How can my enemy look so fucking perfect like this?

Her eyes roll back into her head, and her back arches off the ground, as a strangled scream comes from her throat. Jesus Christ, this woman does things no woman should be capable of. My head screams at me, 'she should be dead'.

Leaning over her, a hand on either side of her, I continue fucking her, dragging my pelvis over her clit with every thrust, and I'm rewarded with a sweet mewling sound from her slender throat.

"Massimo," she cries out, and the familiarity sends shivers down my spine. I stare into her eyes, and her pussy squeezes my length again, taking my orgasm, and my thoughts, from me.

I grunt out my pleasure as I fill her with my cum, and she hums her appreciation, knocking me off kilter once again. Do I want to kill her? I don't. Not really, but she can't know that. There's some confused part of me that wants to protect her, and I don't know why. That's not an option. Black and white, I remind myself. She came after us, and has to be punished. Knowing damn well it won't only be her that suffers doesn't change a goddamn thing.

My head tells me to take her back inside, and lock her in the room again. Space. We need a lot of it, because she's fucking with me. Confusing me. Making me see her as more than my goddamn enemy. She can't ever be anything other than that.

Black and white, I remind myself, for the umpteenth time in the last hour.

Opening my mouth to speak, my mouth defies my brain.

"Let's get some lunch. We'll eat on the patio."

I help her up, and stare at the blush forming on her cheeks, with the slight lift of her lips, as I tuck myself back inside my pants.

"Thank you," she says, with a soft sweetness that makes me rub at the ache in my chest.

She walks over, grabs her panties off the ground, and pulls them on under her dress. I don't take my eyes off her. I can't. Anastasia is too fucking beautiful. Gorgeous in an almost painful way. It's not a good thing. Instead, it causes the fury to travel through my veins, and makes me want to hurt her. Really fucking hurt her.

I grab her arm, pull her through the garden, and around to the other side of the house, where the patio is.

"You're hurting me," she complains, while trying to get out of my grip.

Nodding to the chair, I order her, "Sit."

She places her hands on her hips, and tilts her head at me in annoyance. Her gaze is full of anger, pulling me in, trapping me in place. Anastasia is not the one with no escape. I am. If I don't do something drastic to alter this course, I'm going to live to see my own goddamn ending.

Pretty little ruiner, I think to myself.

My gaze travels the length of her body, taking in every soft curve, as my cock swells in my pants, wanting her again already. Snapping my eyes back to her face, I swallow hard, as I meet her eyes again.

"Sit. The. Fuck. Down."

Anastasia takes a seat at the black, wrought- iron table with a heavy sigh. I know she's wondering why I have to be such an asshole, but I have my reasons. It's the only way.

My chef comes to the table and takes our order. She orders parmesan chicken, and I choose seared scallops with a pomegranate glaze. Oscar brings us both a glass of white wine, and I watch her as she sips it.

"Mmm."

I palm my face as I try to control the twitching in my pants.

The sweet smile on her full lips does nothing to talk my cock down.

"Thank you for this, Massimo."

I shrug my shoulders. "It's just lunch."

She shakes her head in disagreement, as she reaches across the table and rakes her nails along the inside of my forearm.

Fuck.

"It's not just anything. Thank you."

Oscar brings our food, and she looks up at him sweetly, speaking her thanks.

We start eating, and she speaks with a far-away gaze to her eyes. She's looking directly at me, but she's lost in the past.

"My mom used to make this every Sunday. Before I lost her. We were happy, and she was always smiling. I would watch her cook, while she sang her favorite song at the top of her lungs."

I can't help but be drawn into her musings.

"What song?"

She smiles softly.

"Bella Ciao. Do you know it?"

I do know it, but I shake my head.

She sings quietly, as her embarrassment shows on her skin, turning her cheeks a beautiful shade of pink.

"O Bella ciao, bella ciao, bella ciao, ciao, ciao."

Anastasia giggles, as her cheeks turn from pink to crimson.

"Your name is Russian, but you're Italian?"

She tilts her head to the side, and gazes at me for a moment, before she responds.

"It actually comes from the Greek word anastasis, which means resurrection."

Shrugging her shoulders before continuing, she looks at me pointedly, and it feels like her statement means more than the words she says.

"It's just a name. Like Massimo."

Rolling her eyes, she says, "Or Psycho. You could live without it. If you decided your name was William, it wouldn't change the person you are. People become far too attached to names, and it's insignificant. It's the least important thing about any person."

The sadness in her eyes makes me think of my father, even though it's a completely different situation. He's dead, and her mother is lost.

"Is she under medical care?"

She wipes a tear from her cheek, and nods slowly.

"Yes, but she won't take her medication. My mother eats only enough to survive. There's little they can do for her. If she stops eating altogether, they can put a tube in her stomach, but all they can do is keep her breathing. Sometimes I wonder if I'm helping by keeping her alive? What's the point, if you're going to live like that? She isn't even living. Only existing."

I swallow down a bite of my scallops, as I watch her eat her food.

"She wasn't always like this, though? It sounds like you have good memories of her from your childhood."

A sad expression crosses her face, as she sighs heavily, like the weight of the world is resting on her beautiful shoulders.

"When my father was alive, it wasn't like this. The day he died, I think she did too. At least the part that matters. The heart. The soul. After we buried him, she never recovered."

I think of my mother, and the constant traveling she has done. We all think it's her way of coping with the loss of my father, but I prefer that over a lifeless existence.

"If you give me her address, I'll send a specialist to see her."

I already have her mother's information, but I don't feel the need to tell her that.

She tilts her head back, and stares at me with an emotion filled gaze.

"Seriously? Why? Why would you do that?"

I don't have a fucking answer to that question, because I don't know. Her eyes become teary, and it's too much to think about, so I revert back to the asshole I am.

"Say fucking thank you, Anastasia. It doesn't matter why, if I can get someone to help her. Stop being an ungrateful bitch."

She bristles at my words, and bites her thank you, before focusing on her meal.

Chapter Twenty-Five

ANASTASIA

I glance up from the book I found in the nightstand drawer, and find Massimo staring at me in the doorway, holding a shopping bag, and wearing a smirk. My gaze travels down his chest to the black swimming trunks he's wearing, and eventually to his feet, before moving back up and meeting his eyes.

He may have been forged from the flames of hell, but he isn't hard to look at. I just wish he didn't know how gorgeous he is.

"Want to go swimming?"

I jump up off the bed, and can't help the huge smile on my face.

"Please don't be kidding."

He holds his hand out, passing me the bag with an impassive expression.

"Let's not make a big deal out of this, Anastasia. This doesn't change things for you."

I snatch the bag from his hands, and flash him a grin, as I bounce like a little girl on my toes.

"Thank you anyway, you big grump."

Massimo shakes his head, and I spot him trying to hide a smile, as I run into the bathroom to change. I'm a little surprised he didn't make me change in front of him, but I'm happy for the odd moment of decent behavior. I'm sure it won't last, but I'll take what I can get.

Opening the bag, I roll my eyes when I spot a skimpy bikini. Of course, Psycho would pick out one that's blood red. After getting changed, I stare in the mirror, and decide I don't look bad. It's a simple two piece, no design, just the dark red color. The bottoms are a thong and I don't love that, but I'll deal with it for a few minutes of normalcy.

I throw my clothes into the hamper beside the shower, and open the door. Massimo's gaze travels down my body slowly, before making its way back to my face. He drags his hand down his cheek, a heated expression on his face before he groans.

"Fuck."

"Interesting choice of color," I say dryly, as we walk down the spiral staircase to go to the pool.

"I told you. Red is my favorite color, and when I saw this, it reminded me of how pretty you are when you bleed for me."

As we turn the corner and go to the French doors, he opens it for me.

"Does that mean you left your knife inside?"

He chuckles loudly, and I swear it's the first genuine laugh I have heard come out of his mouth since we were kids. It's deep, beautiful, and makes my heart skip a beat. It's hard to reconcile the boy I knew with the man he has become, but it's moments like this that I can see it. The Massimo that stole my heart is in there, somewhere.

"I don't go anywhere without my knife, little lamb."

He slides his thumb down my bare back, and I shiver from the contact. I bite back a moan when he sinks his teeth into my shoulder, but it escapes from my throat, when he licks away the pain. Dropping his hand to my ass cheek, he squeezes my bare flesh, hard.

Wrapping his arm around me, he pulls my back against his chest and slides his hand up the center of my body, until he reaches my throat. With a squeeze, he groans into my ear, his hot breath fanning over my skin, and causing more tingles, that I feel all the way to my feet.

"I want to punish you, little lamb."

"For what?" I gasp out, both of us knowing I haven't done a damn thing, other than what he has told me to.

"Mmm," he murmurs, "For coming after my family, putting you in my house in the first place. For being so goddamn beautiful I can't keep my fucking hands off you. Maybe for having such a tight pussy, that it feels like it was fucking made for my cock. So many reasons, pretty little lamb. I want to cut you, and watch you bleed, so bad it hurts. You should go get into the pool, before I do just that."

As he releases his light grip on my throat, I turn to him, and spot the devilish smirk on his lips, ignoring the shiver running down my spine. I don't move. I can't. I'm trapped in his gaze, and the only thought in my head is that maybe I want to be punished.

I run my fingers up his bare muscular chest, and admit my truth.

"My mother is the only reason I'm not begging you to take my life, Massimo. While I don't think I deserve to be punished for anything I've done to you, I do deserve to be hurt. It's not for the reasons you think. The guilt, for things I've allowed to happen, is all consuming, and some days, I think it might swallow me whole. If I died, that pain would end. Yet, I beg you to let me live for her. For the promise I made to my father. I said I'd take care of her, and I cannot do that, if I'm six feet under. You understand that, right? Family means everything to you, and the little family I have left means everything to me too."

His eyes flash a look of pain, before he returns to his impassive expression, the one he almost always wears on his impossibly handsome face. His Adam's apple bobs as he swallows hard, and I have no idea why that's so hot.

Running his thumb over my bottom lip, he speaks low.

"Get in the pool, little lamb. My control is hanging by a thread. Go enjoy the water before I lose my goddamn mind, and take the option away from you."

He slaps my pussy, and I yelp from the sting, before darting off in the direction of the pool while feeling his heated gaze follow me, like the wolf tracking the lamb, but I'm not afraid. I like it. And that's how I know I'm in serious trouble.

For years I have thought I hated Massimo, not because of anything he had done, but because he was a Bonetti. He's convinced his father didn't kill mine, and if that's true, it makes this vendetta worse. As it was, holding an entire family responsible for one man's actions may not have been right, but now, I don't know anything anymore. I convinced myself I hated him, all of them, but now I'm more conflicted than ever. The truth is, I had a silly little crush on Massimo when I was a kid, but now I am not so sure it was so silly. My heart is like a magnet, pulling me to him, feeling less like the captive I am, and more like a willing participant.

I move down the steps into the water, and sigh at the warmth on my skin. The pool must be heated because it's in the low seventies today, but the water feels more like eighty. It's Olympic sized, with a rock garden on the far end, complete with a waterfall, and I swim to it, wanting to get a closer look. Grabbing onto the side of the pool, I let the water flow over me. It feels far cooler than the temperature of the pool, but still I welcome it. The sun is shining on this cloudless day, and for a moment, everything feels perfect. I'm calm, and at peace, but I know that could end in a nanosecond.

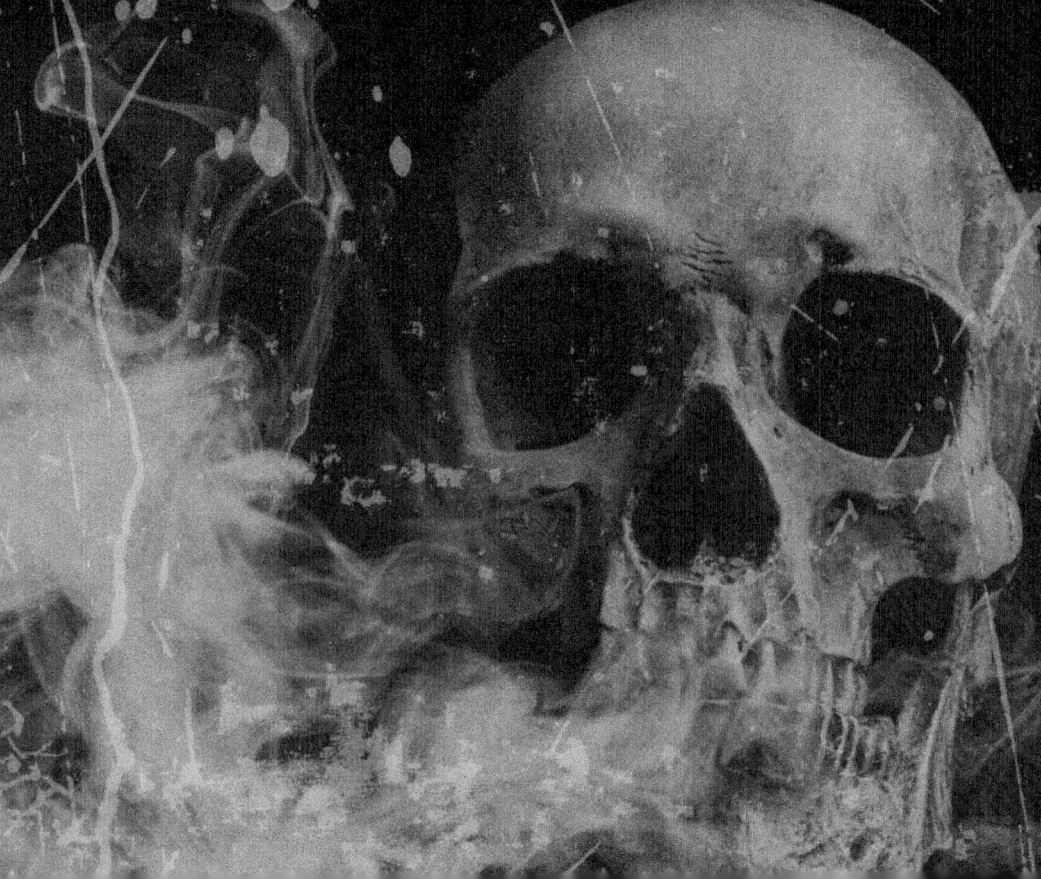

Chapter Twenty-Six

PSYCHO

Black and white, black and white, I chant in my head like a goddamn crazy person. It's time for drastic measures, because my head is becoming entirely too fucked up. I need her gone. I need her to disappear, not only from my home, but my life. This entire thing has gotten way off track.

I'm sitting in a lounge chair instead of getting into the water, because every time she's within touching distance, I cannot stop myself. It's not just fucking her, if it were, this would be much easier. It's fucking everything. The softness of her skin, the way her fingers feel as they drag down my chest, the goddamn way she places her hand on my face, and stares at me like I'm not the bad guy I know I am. Her eyes tell me she sees a man that does not exist.

"Massimo," she coos, in a sweet voice dripping with honey.

I lift my chin in a 'what' action, and her smile fucking steals my breath.

It's time to set things in motion, because I don't know if she's doing this intentionally, but I need to get back to life as I know it.

"I'm lonely. Will you please come in the pool?"

She stands in the shallow end, with the water just under her belly button. Her hair is wet, and hanging below the bathing suit top, and that fucking red bikini, her pebbled nipples pressing against the fabric, calling to me like a goddamn siren. Begging for me. I should tell her no, and stay the fuck away from her gorgeous body, but I'm an idiot, so that's not what I'm going to do.

Rising from my chair, I make my way to the pool and step into the water. Anastasia's eyes follow my every movement, only making my cock harder. Then I walk over to her, and my equilibrium is knocked out of the fucking atmosphere. She all but jumps into my arms, wrapping her legs around my waist, and arms around my neck, while she smiles at me and whispers a sweet 'thank you'.

My brother, Reaper, would tell me to kill her, get it done with, but things aren't that simple, because I don't think I can. The thought of being the one to end her life, causes physical pain in my chest. I know she has to die, and I knew it when I made the 'thirty day' deal. There was never a moment when I believed the words I spoke to her. Letting her go was never an option.

Black and white, I think to myself, as she presses her lips to my neck. Soft kisses graze my skin, causing a groan to erupt from me.

This needs to end. I have let this go on far too long already. She can't keep fucking with my head if she's not here. This is the first time in my life I've felt so out of control. I've never struggled to end a life. It's as easy as breathing for me. Except now.

Then it occurs to me that she can die the way she was supposed to, and I don't have to lift a finger. I don't know what the fuck is wrong with me, but this is the solution. Let somebody else handle her, since I can't bring myself to do it.

Anastasia gently brushes her lips over my beard, her soft breath on my skin feeling like a heaven I don't deserve, before she kisses me on the lips softly. Digging her fingers into my back, she pulls my bottom lip into her mouth, and sucks gently.

"Massimo," she breathes, as she releases my lip.

Fuck.

Her eyes bore into mine, and I swallow hard. I have no right to have her, with what my plans are. Not having a right doesn't change the fact that I will take what I want, and right now, I want her. My need for her is out of fucking control, and so I do what I shouldn't even want.

I take her lips.

I slide my hand inside her bathing suit.

I stroke her soaked slit.

Then I take her confession I don't deserve, as I yank my shorts down, pull her bottoms to the side, and sink into her.

"Massimo," she says, sounding breathy, and desperate for more.

"I'm falling in love with you," she cries out as I slam into her, burying my cock to the hilt. Her words nearly cause my brain to explode.

This was not part of the plan.

I go back to chanting in my head. It's entirely possible that she was right before; I might be insane.

Black and white. Black and white. This changes nothing.

Winding my fist in her hair, I pull her head back, and run my tongue from the base of her neck to her chin, eliciting a sweet little moan from her.

Laying her down on the pool deck, I hook my thumbs into the sides of her bottoms, and drag them down her legs, revealing her pretty pussy, pink and perfect, with my jewelry at the top. I move closer to her, push her thighs back, and lean down to inhale my favorite scent, knowing soon, I'll never have this again. I know there's no chance of survival, and yet, I'll do it anyway. While I won't be the one to end her life, I will be responsible.

No. That's wrong. *Black and white.* She came after my family, not the other way around. Anastasia is responsible for her own demise.

"Please," she moans desperately, snapping me out of my own thoughts.

"What do you want? Tell me what you need, little lamb," I ask gruffly.

"Your tongue," she nearly begs, her eyes blown wide with lust, and her legs trembling slightly with anticipation.

Making a V with my fingers, I spread her pussy wide open, and admire how wet she's getting, from only my gaze, and spit on her clit.

"Ask me to make you come."

She reaches behind me, grabs my hair with a tight grip, and attempts to move my face to her pussy, but I don't move. I growl.

"Fucking ask me like a good girl, or you're not getting it."

She groans in frustration, but when she does as she's told, it's fucking beautiful.

"Please, Massimo, please make me come."

"Fuck, little lamb, you make me want things I cannot have," I admit. She opens her mouth to question the words I shouldn't have said out loud, but I silence her, with a swipe of my tongue across her clit.

Circling my tongue around her swollen nub has her legs shaking. Fuck, she's perfect, except for that one, not so minor, detail, but I put that out of my mind.

I push two fingers inside her, as I pull her clit between my lips, sucking hard, while she mewls on the patio with desperate need. Anastasia is close, I feel it in her pussy, and see it on her gorgeous face, but it's not until I bite down on her clit that she erupts, screaming my name.

Pretty little pain slut.

I had my suspicions that she got off on me hurting her. It wasn't how I planned things, but I can't honestly say I don't like it. I'm slightly disappointed that it's going to take another man to break her, because it wasn't supposed to be this way, but there's nothing I can do about it.

Wrapping my arms around her, I carry her up to her room. I can't take any more at this moment. As much as I'd like to fuck her, I can't.

Laying her down in her bed, she yawns, and, with heavy eyes, darts her gaze away from me.

"I have to tell you who I really am, Massimo."

I stare at her, with confusion wracking my brain, but I don't get more than that, because she crashes, like she hasn't slept in days.

Chapter Twenty-Seven
PSYCHO

The ache in my chest continues to grow, as I watch her on the screen, before my brother steals my attention away.

Bones: *We need to discuss this, Psycho.*

Me: *Nothing to discuss.*

Bones: *Is she alive?*

Me: *Yes.*

Bones: *The DA is missing. Am I silly to assume you know something about this?*

Me: *I wasn't responsible for that exactly.*

Bones: *Goddamn it, Psycho. What do you think will happen with a new DA? There will be an interim DA, and then a new DA. One we don't have control over. This is why you weren't made the head of the family. You don't fucking think.*

Me: *Well, you got what you wanted, little brother. See you Sunday.*

I turn my phone off, and go back to watching Anastasia. She sits on her bed, her fingers twisting like she's agitated.
Poor lost little lamb.

I chuckle to myself as I watch her talk to herself, but I can't hear her because she's speaking so low. Tomorrow, I'll escalate things, and it will break her. By the time tomorrow is over, she'll be begging for death. Anything to never go through it again.

I enjoy torturing people. Cutting them, making them scream. Sometimes suffocating them slowly over days, with a bag over their head. The pain she'll go through isn't only physical. Emotional torment can be far worse than the physical kind.

With a smile on my face, I stare at the screen, as she lies down in the bed.

"Tomorrow, little lamb. You're going to regret ever hearing the name Bonetti."

She has twisted me all up, but I've gained clarity. It's funny how dreams can fuck with you, but this one fixed my thinking. My father stood in front of me, and gave me the lecture I've heard so many times.

If they are a risk to our family, we wipe them from existence. This is how we survive all things. Are they for or against us? If they are against us, the answer is always the same, figlio. No exceptions.

I arch an eyebrow with pure annoyance, when two of my brothers come into my house. They've always come and gone without an invitation, but now I'm annoyed. I shut the monitor off, as Kage looks at me with a shake of his head. He takes a seat on the sofa across from me, and Reaper joins him.

Kage leans back and makes himself comfortable, staring at me with a smug grin.

"Bones is pissed."

I roll my eyes. "What's new? Ever since he became the head of our family, he's been a whiny little bitch."

Reaper chuckles, but other than that, there's no response.

I'm not an idiot, I know Bones has a lot on his plate now, especially with two brothers that tend to do whatever the fuck they want. I also understand his concerns about a new DA being elected. There are few rewards without risk. This is one we needed to take, because pretty little Anastasia was only going to cause problems.

"What's the plan?" Reaper asks.

Kage nods in agreement, and says, "I know there is one."

I'm not much of a planner by nature, which is why Bones is always pissed at me, I suppose, but also my brothers know by now there'd be a plan, or she'd already be dead.

"Jimmy," I state plainly, and both my brothers look at me like I've lost my fucking mind, and they may not be wrong.

"What are you planning, Psycho?"

Jimmy isn't a good guy, but not like the Bonetti brothers. He hurts women specifically, for no reason other than receiving pleasure from it. We've suspected for a long time the strippers that work in his club are trafficking victims. Normally, none of us would ever have business dealings with him. In fact, it's strictly forbidden. I know that, but I frequently don't follow rules to a 'T'.

"He's going to take her off my hands."

Kage arches a brow at me, as he shakes his head with clear disapproval.

"Are you talking about trafficking her? We do not fucking do that. Jesus, Psycho."

My younger brother tilts his head, and stares at me in that crazy way he does, as if he's trying to figure me out.

"Do you have feelings for her?"

"Of course not."

That's ridiculous. He knows I don't feel for fucking anything. It's not my way. If I were ever to fall for a woman the way my brothers have, it would not be the goddamn enemy. The woman that wants to destroy us all.

"Why don't you kill her?" Reaper asks, as he continues to examine me like I'm something complicated, when really I'm not.

I shake my head, without giving him more, because it's not a conversation I'm interested in having, with him or anyone else.

"You're going to regret this, man. I don't know what the fuck is going on, but we don't do this. You don't do this. Also, chances are pretty good Bones will push you out of the family. He's never going to accept this."

I glance at my brothers, and feel the weight of their judgement in their eyes. Nobody would blame me for killing her, but selling her to a man like Jimmy is beneath us, and I know that.

"I told her I'd give her thirty days, and if she obeyed every order, I'd let her go."

Reaper covers up a grin with his hand, and I have to fight myself to not get up and punch him in the face.

Kage says, "This is not some 'my word is my bond' bullshit, something bigger is going on with you."

I groan loudly, as I drag a hand down my face. "Go home to your women. I'm sure they're missing you."

As if I summoned them, they both walk in, causing me to groan fucking louder. I know exactly why they're here, and I don't fucking like it.

"We were looking at the garden," Bella says with a beaming smile.

"You know that's a must for Raina."

Kage's girl glares at me, as she crosses her arms over her chest. She's getting far too brave for my liking.

"I'm here to do a welfare check. After all, it's my fault she's here."

I turn on the monitor, and she moves closer, as if she's inspecting every inch of Anastasia. Does she really think she's the reason my little lamb is here? She's not. As much as I don't like Raina, and definitely don't fucking trust her, I don't blame her for this. There's little doubt though, that my brother has already had this conversation with her.

144

"What are you going to do with her?" Raina asks, as she continues to watch Anastasia closely.

Bella shakes her head and answers for me.

"You don't want to know."

Reaper echoes her sentiments with a nod.

"You really don't. She's alive, as you can both see, and I think that's enough for today."

My youngest brother walks to the door, with a shake of his head, and Bella grabs Raina and walks with her close, while Kage stares at me.

"I'm quoting my girl here, but it bears repeating. *Regret is a poison like cancer. It kills slowly, painfully. It eats away at you, until there's nothing left.*"

I smirk at him.

"Your girl into poetry, man?"

He shakes his head, and punches me in the shoulder.

"I'm going to fucking stab you, when you realize you have feelings for her. The problem is, I think the damage is going to be so catastrophic, you'll welcome it, and beg for me to kill you."

I ignore his words, because I feel nothing for her. I'm not like my brothers. A man in love does not sell his woman. I'll do it without batting an eye, because I always do what needs to be done. And because I don't feel a goddamn thing for her.

Chapter Twenty-Eight

ANASTASIA

"You're being relocated," Psycho says, with about as much emotion as if he were saying we're having eggs for breakfast. His words don't make sense to me. Am I moving rooms?

"Relocated?" I ask, as I stare at him with confusion.

Staring down at the floor, like he can't even look at me, he nods slowly.

"You're being sold."

I try to make sense of his words. Massimo Bonetti is capable of many things, things that would terrify anyone, but selling a person? No. He wouldn't.

"This is our last night together, Anastasia. Tomorrow, Jimmy will pick you up."

"No!" I scream. My heart is thundering in my ears, and tears I've fought so hard to prevent, spring to my eyes. I tell him I'm falling for him, and he sells me? Fucking sells me?

"We made an agreement. You have to let me go after thirty days, because I've done everything you wanted me to. Everything, Massimo."

A sorrowful expression crosses his face, but it's gone so fast, I think I may have imagined it.

"I know. I am truly sorry for not honoring my agreement, but this is happening."

The urge to shake him, and demand to know why he would do this to me, is strong, but I also know Massimo will not tell me more than he wants to. "He's going to kill me."

I already know that has to be the plan.

Psycho steps closer to me, placing his hand on my face, as I lift my gaze to his.

"Maybe. He's far more violent than I am, so be a good girl. Don't give him reasons to hurt you."

Mimicking his actions, I place my hand on his face, feeling his beard under my fingertips.

"Don't do this."

He closes his eyes before he re-opens them, the quick flash of regret showing through, before he hides it away. This man is a master at hiding his emotions, but I know he has them. Meanwhile, mine crash into my chest, feeling like a freight train slamming into me.

"I can't let you live after coming for my family. This is the only way. I am a fucking coward, and I can't be there to watch you die."

"If you love me, you can't do this. You feel something for me, Massimo, I know you do. I have to believe you won't do this to me."

He shakes his head in refusal.

"I don't love you, little lamb. Did I get addicted to your pussy? Maybe, but I don't love you. I feel nothing for you."

I sigh a shaky breath, and drop my hand from his face. I try to stay strong, but it's difficult, with a million conflicting emotions running through me. Processing one thing is hard enough, but the anger, heartbreak, sadness, and pure devastation, all at once, is so overwhelming I can barely see straight.

"You're lying, Massimo. To me, and to yourself."

He chuckles, but there's no humor behind it.

"Little lamb, I don't lie, and I don't love."

Do I love him? I do, but there's no coming back from this. I was so close to the month being over, and now he's selling me? Like I'm nothing. Not a human being with any worth whatsoever.

I still don't understand. He said he'd let me go, if I did everything he told me to, and like the stupid girl I am, I believed him. I killed a man, and for what? I'm going to go from a bad situation to something of my worst nightmares. I did my thesis, when I got my master's degree, on human trafficking. It's the most brutal, inhumane treatment a person can go through. And the man I think I'm falling in love with is the person doing this to me?

"Why are you doing this to me?"

He darts his eyes away from me, like it's painful to meet my gaze, and now I know he is aware how disgusting his actions are.

"I'm an evil man, little lamb. I do bad things, and no one gets freedom after coming for my family."

Charging for him, I push him in his chest, and he stands solid like a damn boulder, only infuriating me more.

"You're weak, Massimo Bonetti. You can't handle whatever the fuck this is between us, so you want me gone. Because it makes you fucking uncomfortable. I'll be tortured, and probably killed, because poor little Massimo can't handle his big feelings."

I hit a button, clearly, and he growls as he closes the distance between us, slides his hands in my hair, and kisses me. It's not aggressive, it's desperate and needy. He swirls his tongue against mine, as he walks me backward to the bed.

Pulling back from our kiss, he pulls my t-shirt off and drops it to the floor, while staring at me with a heated expression. Unsnapping my bra, he pulls the straps down my arms, until it falls to the floor. He kneels in front of me, as he silently pulls my skirt down, along with my panties. Pressing his nose to my pussy, he inhales, before letting out a soft groan.

Psycho swipes his tongue up my slit, and I grab onto his head for balance, whimpering as he hits my piercing repeatedly. The urge to push him away is there, but even now, my physical need for him overpowers anything else. It makes me hate myself, just like he wanted. The sight of him should make me sick, but this monster is the only thing that brings me comfort. I must have some kind of mental disorder, because this is insane, yet I can't fight it. I wish I could. Massimo confuses me. In one breath, he makes me feel beautiful, and cherished. In the next, completely worthless. This man who is doing the worst things to me, things I never thought even a

Bonetti would ever do, lights me on fire. I don't want to want him, but I do. Desperately.

"Massimo," I cry out, the pleasure all-consuming, just like he is. I look down at him, this powerful mafia man on his knees for me. At the moment, I feel safe. Safety is an illusion, since tomorrow he'll throw me away like I'm trash. Like I don't matter. If he goes through with it, I'll know he's right, and doesn't feel a thing for me.

Rising to his feet, he lifts me and lies me down on the bed. I've never seen him like this. So quiet. He kicks his pants off, and climbs over me.

"I wish you had not come after my family."

"Me too," I whisper, and I mean it with my whole heart.

He pushes inside me, with a deep growl that I feel vibrate through my body, with his chest against mine.

"Massimo, please don't do this to me."

"Shhh," he says, with his lips brushing against mine.

"What's done is done. Let me have you one last time. Let me make you feel good, little lamb. Let me have what's mine, until it's not mine anymore."

I wrap my arms around his neck, and cry into his shoulder, as he moves inside me. Had he killed me the night he took me, it'd be easier than this. The moment you realize you mean so little, to the man that you're falling for, that he'd sell you, is not an easy one. The ache in my chest is so heavy, as he finishes inside me. He rolls over and pulls me into his arms, like I mean something, continuing to fuck with my head.

"Tell me about him."

He sighs audibly.

"I told you, he's violent. So you will need to behave. You don't need details. The fear will be worse than what he actually does to you. It's not helpful."

Somehow, I don't think that's going to be the case. Why does he even care if I'm afraid? After all, he's in control here, if he really gave a shit, he wouldn't do this. Even Carlo never trafficked me.

"Have you ever bought a person?"

"No," he answers, in a flat, emotionless tone.

"Would you?"

"No," he responds the same way.

I bury my face in his chest, so angry at myself for wanting his scent, his touch, everything Massimo. Now I know, the boy I loved is gone, because he never would've done this to me.

"I'll never forgive you for this. Ever. I'll breathe my last breath while hating you."

"I know," he says, as he holds me tighter.

I've never been more confused in my life. He touches me like I matter, holds me like he never wants to let me go, but he's selling me to a man that will be my killer. It doesn't make sense to me.

How can one human do this to another?

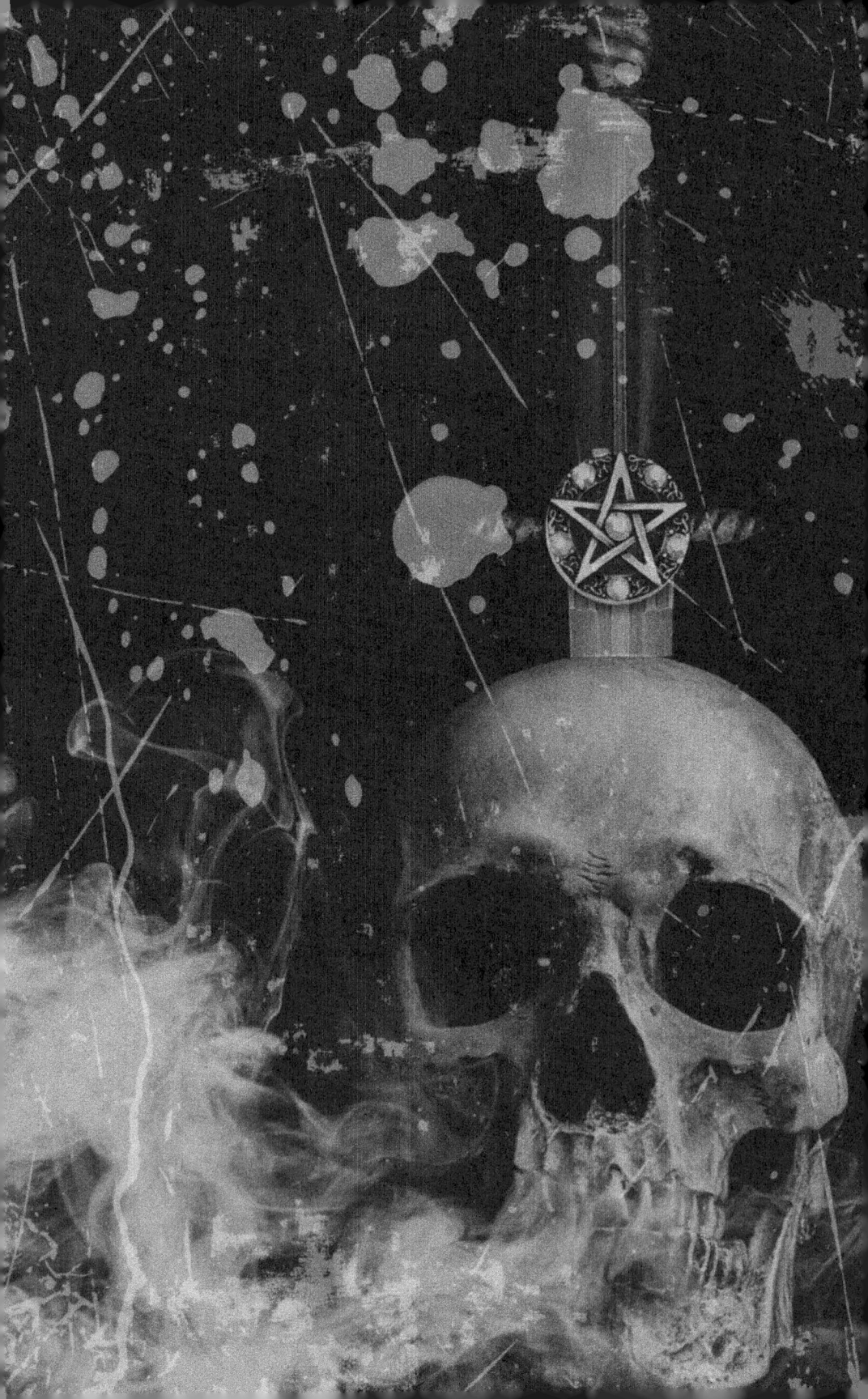

Chapter Twenty-Nine

PSYCHO

I fucked her three times, attempting to get my fill, and held her while she cried. Then, I watched her sleep restlessly. I've never seen a more beautiful woman. Everything about her is simply stunning. Still, I can't forget her plans, and I can't trust her in the future. Yet, I can't kill her because, as she said, I'm fucking weak, so I'll let another man do it for me. One I won't be forced to look at again. Hell, I'll probably kill him for it.

Things have always been black and white for me. I don't forgive and I don't forget. If you come for what's mine, you don't exist. Anastasia can't be different. Yet, every time I think of killing her, I physically feel ill.

Anastasia lies on my chest sleeping, but begins to stir. She claws her fingernails into my chest, while whimpering my name repeatedly.

"Massimo," she cries, obviously having a nightmare.

"It's okay," I coo, knowing full well I'm a goddamn liar. In mere hours, her world is going to go from dark to pitch black. Jimmy will beat her and rape her brutally. His favorite is chasing a woman straight into a bear trap. He'll sit laughing, as the steel claws sink into her skin and bones. Am I any better than he is? I get off on cutting her skin. It's simply a different type of torture.

She pops her head up, her wide eyes on my face, as a gasp escapes from her lips. Tears fall down her face, twisting something inside me, and I don't like it. I've wanted her tears in such a feral way, but not now, not because of what another man will do to her.

"Now you cry, little lamb?"

"I've never been more heartbroken. Not since my son died."

Rolling her over to her back, I gaze into her eyes with curiosity.

"Heartbroken? Not scared?"

She blinks fast, trying to stop the tears, but they keep falling.

"I'm scared. Terrified, but knowing I love you, and you feel so little for me that you're doing this…"

Anastasia closes her eyes, and takes a shaky breath before continuing.

"That's worse than anything he'll do to me."

I don't understand how a woman could think she loves a man that kidnapped her, and tortured her, but I don't say anything, as much as it confuses me. She's clearly mistaken. I'm not the man a woman falls for. I can't love, and I can't be loved. Fucking her good, and often, has made her think she feels something she doesn't. She can't.

"Is your mother alive?" She asks, and I swallow hard as I nod, because I know where she's going with this.

"Does she know what you're doing? Would she be okay with this?"

She wouldn't, although there's no doubt my mother would agree to put family first, always. My brothers won't forgive this, even though they wouldn't have said much if I had killed her. We eliminate threats. It's what we do, but this is something we don't do. I keep hearing my brother's voice in my head.

'We don't traffic people.'

I don't respond to her about my mother, and I'm sure I don't need to. She continues trying to change my mind.

"Let me go, Massimo. You can even tell him I ran. I'll go, and you'll never see me again."

Narrowing my gaze at her, I look at her like what she said is fucking stupid, and it is.

"Let you go? I was never going to let you go, little lamb. That's not an option. You cannot walk out of here and live your happy life. You cannot be fucking trusted. I should be the one to take your life. This is the punishment you deserve. But I can't."

Anastasia collapses in my arms, like she's lost all her fight. The same one she's going to need, to have any chance of surviving Jimmy.

For the entire time I've had her, she has never cried for herself, but she does now. Burying her face in my chest, she drenches my skin with her tears.

"I know what I did. What I planned to do, but it's different now. I would never hurt you or your family," she cries through hiccups. I wish I could believe her, but I lost all ability to trust anyone outside of my family years ago.

"What have you done?" My mother cries, while rubbing her hands over her face.

I stare at her with confusion, and try to take her hand, but she pulls it away.

"Only you could have given Julia the information she needed. Only you."

Continuing to stare at her in bewilderment, I stand waiting for clarity. I have no idea what has my mother so upset, and how it involves my girlfriend of a year.

She shakes her head in disgust.

"I told you she was using you. Your father told you, but you would not listen. Her name is not even Julia!" She all but screams.

I wait for her to tell me more, and when she does, my world implodes.

"Danielle Mindar is her name. Her father works for the FBI, in the Organized Crime division. And now, your father is in jail. Charged with serious crimes, figlio. Do you see what you've done?"

I rub at the spot on my chest; the burning is intense and immediate. My father is in jail, and it's because of me. Maybe not directly my doing, but my fault, just the same.

Hanging my head down, I place my face in my hands, as the devastation devours me.

155

"Oh, figlio. We have attorneys. He'll likely be home for dinner. This is why we do not trust outside of our famiglia. Not until it has been proven that someone is worthy."

My mother's words hit me hard that day, and they've stayed with me for every day since. I cannot risk my family for her. And I cannot bring myself to kill her. Why don't I have my brother kill her? Reaper would do it without batting an eye. I've considered it, but then I'd never see him the same way again. I don't love her, but this girl has gotten under my skin.

Again, I want to tell her everything will be okay, and that I'll protect her. I clench my jaw at my own thoughts. I fucking want to, but I can't.

"You should take a shower before he gets here, Anastasia," I say softly.

She climbs off me and stands naked beside the bed, as stunning as ever, fists clenched, eyes radiating fire, as she screams.

"You're really going to do this to me?"

I nod wordlessly.

"When you hear that I'm dead, I want you to remember, you killed me. It was your choice. You did not have to do this. You chose it. Loving you is a cruel fucking joke, Massimo. I thought Carlo was the worst man I had ever met, and he was..."

She hangs her head down, and her voice comes out broken.

"Until you."

I clear my throat and get dressed, feeling her hot gaze scorching my back.

"I'll give you a few minutes to yourself, and meet you downstairs."

Chapter Thirty

PSYCHO

Jimmy enters my home, flanked by four of my guards. He is the kind of man you watch from all angles, because even if you think he's a friend, I promise you, he's not.

"Bonetti," he says with a slimy grin.

I shake off the war currently going on in my head. Like there's an angel on my right shoulder, saying to not do this, and the devil on my left, is screaming that she can't be trusted, and this is my only option.

"She ready? After seeing that picture, I can't wait to fuck her. Is she a screamer?"

Clenching my jaw, I tighten my hands into fists at my sides. I want to kill him. How dare he talk about my little lamb like that? I want to reach into his chest, grab his beating heart, and stuff it down his throat. Instead, I take a deep breath, because this is my doing. My guards stand staring at him, not really listening to his vile words, but ready for any threat.

"Anastasia is in the shower. She'll be down in a few minutes. Do you want me to grab her suitcase while you wait?"

He laughs, like someone told a hilarious joke, before shaking his head.

"No. She won't need any of it."

Images of him, torturing her, flash through my mind. Jimmy, fucking what belongs to me, and my chest aches with regret, before it has even happened.

What the fuck am I doing? I cannot fucking hand her over to him for two reasons. One, I can't let him destroy her, and two, she fucking belongs to me.

"Deal's off, Jimmy. Get off my property."

He stares at me with shock, and throws his hands in the air in a 'what the fuck' motion.

"We had a deal, Bonetti. I brought the money, and you need to give me the girl. I'm not leaving without her."

I nod to my guards, and instruct them to get him out of my house.

"Help him off the property. Be sure he actually leaves. If he doesn't, feel free to put a bullet in his brain."

As they drag him away, he shouts at me, but his words don't worry me.

"You're going to regret this, Bonetti. I don't give a fuck who your family is. You will be sorry."

Ignoring him, I go back upstairs to tell my little lamb that it's off. She's safe. I don't know what the hell the future holds for her, but Jimmy is not part of it.

I make it up to the bedroom, and wait outside the bathroom.

"Anastasia?" I say, after it feels like at least ten minutes. She doesn't respond, so I walk over and attempt to open the door, but it's locked. After calling her name repeatedly, she doesn't answer, the only sound is her sobs.

I smash down the door, and find the woman I broke, on the floor sobbing, while she attempts to open a vein with the end of a pair of tweezers. I'm sure it would've been a knife, if she could've found one.

"I'm not going," she cries.

She looks so fucking delicate, and broken, on the floor. It's not lost on me that this was my plan. Tears streaming down her cheeks, eyes lost, and far away, the way she shakes with her sobs, this should please me, and it doesn't.

I knew I was doing a terrible thing, I'm not an idiot, but seeing her like this now makes it very fucking real.

Kneeling beside her, I take the tweezers and throw them in the corner, before grabbing her wrists, and pressing soft kisses to the one she was successful in cutting.

158

Her lashes flutter as she lifts her gaze to mine, and she stares at me for a long minute, before she speaks in a low voice.

"I'm not going. You can't do this to a person. Massimo, even you must know this isn't okay."

She sits on the floor in front of the shower, with pure devastation in her gaze. The pain in her eyes cracks my chest wide open.

"I know," I admit.

Reaching out, I place my hand on her cheek, and she pulls away with obvious fury.

"No! You don't get to touch me. How dare you? Massimo, you have no right."

I retract my hand with a nod. Am I going to let her suddenly control things? No, but I can give her a fucking minute.

"I told him the deal is off."

She trembles as she stares at me incredulously. Shaking her head, like she can't begin to understand my words, she speaks in a broken voice.

"Do you think that makes it right? You didn't go through with it, so it's okay? You're absolved of wrongdoing?"

Her gaze locks on mine, her hands shaking, and eyes darting back and forth. The bathroom is filled with her labored breaths, as the anger vibrates from her body. She looks at me with so much disdain, I'm certain I am going to force her to stay.

"Let's get you into bed, you need rest."

Taking her hand into mine, I help her to her feet, and she quickly pulls back from me.

"Are you going to kill me?"

"No," I answer in a clipped tone.

She places a hand on her hip as she demands, "Then let me go. I want to leave."

That's not happening. There's no fucking chance of her walking away from me, but I don't say that because, for once, I don't want her fight.

159

"After you rest," I say, and am pleased my lie was convincing enough. She storms into the bedroom, and gets under the sheets with an exasperated sigh.

Reaching under the cabinet, I grab what I need, and shove it into my pocket.

I come out of the bathroom and stand in the doorway, unable to take my eyes off her. I drink her in, every delicious inch, even as she scowls at me.

"Do you really have to watch me sleep?"

"Yes," is my only answer, because I like watching her. It doesn't matter if she's awake, mouthing off to me, coming all over my cock, or sleeping. Anastasia captivates me in all things, but right now I'm waiting for her to fall asleep, to make my next move.

I pull my cell phone out, and check my messages, so she thinks I'm not watching her. Rolling my eyes, I respond to my brother's text.

Reaper: Bella could do it.

Me: No. Nobody is killing her.

He sends me an immediate bulging eye emoji, which I know is all the effect of his wife, because he didn't do this annoying cutesy shit before he met her.

Reaper: Nobody is killing her?

Then he sends a thinking emoji, and I'm officially done with this conversation. I glance back over to Anastasia, and grin when I notice her parted lips, as she sleeps. Walking over to her, I take a second to get a good look at her features. Her lashes flutter as she sleeps, her cheeks have a light blush to them, and those full lips are the perfect shade of pink. She is stunning, but when she wakes up tomorrow, she will not be this calm. Once again she'll call me a monster, but I was nice. I could've done this while she was awake. She should be grateful. Yet, I know she won't be.

After grabbing the alcohol, I clean her skin before placing the needle to her neck, and slowly push it through her flesh. I know she's out for the night, but I keep my voice low anyway.

"My sweet little lamb, tomorrow is the day. You'll realize when you wake up, I'll never let you go. I don't love you, I never will. It's not something I am capable of, but what is greater than love? Obsession. You have that."

Lifting her into my arms, I hold her close to my chest, and carry her back down to the basement where my fixation started. Taking her into my tattoo room, I lay her on the chair, and stroke my finger over her lower back as I hum.

"You're going to look so stunning with my knife on your back."

Chapter Thirty-One

PSYCHO

I watch her sleeping peacefully, or at least that's how it appears, until she starts crying. Eyes still closed, tears run down her cheeks, as she calls the name I've heard before.

"Michael!" she sobs.

"No! Michael, please."

She opens her eyes and stares in confusion, likely wondering how she ended up down here. Rolling from her side to her back, she winces from the pain with a hiss.

I walk over to her, and gaze at her perplexed expression.

"Easy, little lamb."

"Did you beat me?"

I reach down to brush the hair from her face, and she flinches.

"Oh my God. You did."

Pointing to the Advil, and a glass of water, on the bedside table, I answer her question.

"I did not fucking beat you."

I'm annoyed that she would think I would beat a woman, but then, I realize, in her mind, it's probably not a far stretch from the things I've done. The things I will likely continue to do.

I help her sit up, and she glances down at her bare breasts and squeals.

"You pierced my nipples."

She glares at them, like she can somehow make them disappear.

"You pierced my fucking nipples," she repeats, with something that sounds like disbelief.

Crossing my arms over my chest, I shrug my shoulders, and admit it.

"It seemed best for you to get it all done at the same time. Less pain."

She grabs the pain medication, takes it, and is quiet for a few minutes, while she sits with the glass on her lap. It's almost as if she doesn't want to ask.

"If you didn't beat me, why does my back hurt, Massimo?"

I bite down on my lip, stifling the laugh, and then give her the answer.

"That's from the tattoo, little lamb."

"Tat-?"

She doesn't finish her word. Instead, Anastasia lifts her gaze to mine, and her eyes widen, as her cheeks flush bright red. I could dodge the glass that comes hurtling toward me, but I don't. I'll give her this. It hits me in the stomach with a hard thud, causing me to grunt, before crashing to the floor, and shattering.

"You cannot tattoo someone against their will."

Rising off the chair, she stomps over to me, with fists balled tight.

"You cannot pierce someone against their will. Do you fucking understand me?"

Fuck, she's adorable like this. I enjoy her angry side. The victim behavior does not do it for me, but this. Fuck, it's beautiful.

I drag my fingers through my beard, as I tilt my head at her, with a smirk on my lips.

"I think I do. You're saying that I cannot pierce, and tattoo, someone against their will, correct?"

"Yes!" she screams, the anger radiating from her.

"I understand your words, but you're wrong, little lamb, because I just did."

She steps on the broken glass to get to me, and punches me, as she screams in pain. I growl, "Goddamn it."

Quickly, I sweep her into my arms and rush her to the bathroom. Setting her on the counter, I grab tweezers from the cabinet, and pull out the pieces of glass, while my blood boils.

"So careless. You threw the damn glass, and shattered it."

I inspect her foot, making sure it's not deep enough to require stitches.

"Who's Michael?"

She darts her eyes to the wall, as she hangs her head down, with a sadness I don't think I've ever seen on her face.

"He was my son."

"What happened?" I ask, as I clean her skin, to make sure she doesn't end up with an infection.

Her bottom lip quivers as more tears fall from her eyes. I know what it was like for my brother and Bella to lose a child, so this time her tears don't do anything for me. I don't like it, and wish for a moment to be the kind of man that could make things better for her, but I'm not.

"My ex-husband, Carlo, killed him in front of me, to teach me a lesson in obedience."

I place a bandage on her foot, covering the three cuts, and lift her off the counter.

"Was the child not his?"

To me, the question makes perfect sense: what kind of a man would kill his flesh and blood? For her, it doesn't, and she gets angry all over again.

"Of course Michael was his, you asshole."

Normally, I'd scold her for calling me names, but not right now, because I want to keep her talking. Suddenly, I want to know everything there is to know about her life.

"How old was he?"

"Three," she answers, as my head spins. He murdered a goddamn toddler? Because she was disobedient? I make a mental note to find this guy, and kill him. What kind of a piece of shit does this, to not only a child, but his own child?

"He hit you, didn't he?"

She nods, with a laugh that doesn't reach her eyes. Then she shakes her head no, as if taking it back.

"No, he didn't hit me, Massimo. He attacked me, brutally, as often as he could."

I stroke my fingers down her arm, and she lets me.

"I'm sorry. He won't be serving out his prison time. I'll take care of him."

She shakes her head, and rolls her eyes at me.

"Always with the violence."

I smirk at her. "Always."

Anastasia may think, since he's in prison, that I can't get to him, but she'd be wrong. I'll have to call in favors, but it's not a problem. Not by a long shot.

I grab the robe hanging in the bathroom, and help her into it.

"What's on my back?"

I pull out my phone, and show her the picture I took, after I finished last night, and show it to her. She stares at the knife covering her lower back with my name on it.

"I have a knife on my back permanently. And knives in my nipples. This is unbelievable, Massimo."

Flashing her a grin, I say, "Don't forget the knife in your sweet pussy."

I bend down and scoop her into my arms, and she puts her arms around my neck.

"What are you doing?"

Arching a brow at her, I sigh heavily.

"You have cuts on your foot. I don't want you to hurt yourself."

She buries her face into my chest, and laughs maniacally.

"Nobody causes more pain than you, and you're worried about a little cut on my foot?"

"Even Carlo?" I ask, as we head upstairs.

Pulling her head back, she gasps.

"No. He cost me my identity, and my son. He took everything from me."

Her words rattle around in my head, as I carry her to my kitchen, and set her on the counter beside my stainless steel refrigerator.

Chapter Thirty-Two
PSYCHO

I open the refrigerator and start grabbing food. After hearing her stomach rumbling while she was still sleeping, I know I need to feed her.

She watches me as I press ground beef into hamburger patties.

"What did you mean, you lost your identity?"

Anastasia doesn't immediately respond. Her gaze is on me, but the look in her eyes is far away, as if she's somewhere else.

"Anastasia?"

With a roll of her eyes, she says, "I can't tell you. I'm afraid you'll kill me for real. Or change your mind, and sell me to that asshole. Unless you're playing games, and already know everything about me."

I walk over to wash my hands, after putting the patties in the pan, and my head swirls with confusion. What the fuck is she talking about?

Going back over to the counter, I stand in front of her, and place my hands on the granite, caging her in. Lowering my head, she tilts her head back, and stares up at me.

"This is what I know, little lamb. Anastasia Crowne, assistant district attorney. Your father is deceased, mother unwell, and you have a vendetta against my family, because you think we're responsible. And after tonight, now I know that your ex husband Carlo is in prison, for killing your child, and hurting you."

She speaks in a whisper.

"He was never charged for hurting me, Massimo."

"Why couldn't I find anything on you? It is as if you appeared out of thin air, when you started college, but you didn't exist before then."

A soft gasp leaves her lips as she questions me, although it sounds like more of a statement.

"You don't know. He really didn't tell you. You acted like you didn't know, but I thought you must have."

I move to flip over the hamburgers, and immediately return to her.

"He who? Little lamb, I'm running out of what little patience I had."

After the hamburgers are ready, I quickly plate them before moving them to the table. She needs to eat, but I need fucking answers.

She takes a seat across from me, and I tell her, "Eat and talk. I want answers."

"After Carlo was arrested, your father contacted me."

The mention of my father feels like a gut punch, and I'm not inclined to believe her.

"Do not fucking lie to me."

She tilts her head at me, with a glare in her hazel eyes, puts her hamburger down, and places her clenched fists on the table, on either side of her plate.

"I'm not fucking lying to you, Massimo. Carlo worked for a rival family, and when your father heard what happened, he knew, even with him behind bars, I'd never be safe. And with our families once connected, he wanted to help."

I assume she's referring to her father allegedly working for our family. The fact is I've never heard the name Crowne until her, so I have no fucking idea who her father was.

"I didn't want to accept any assistance from him, because I didn't trust him."

Arching an eyebrow, I speak in an annoyed tone.

"Because you thought he killed your father?"

She nods and takes a sip of her drink, eyeing me warily.

"I didn't have a choice. I knew I was a sitting duck staying put, and it was only a matter of time, before someone would come for both me and my mother."

Rubbing at the ache in my chest, I wait for her to tell me what my father did. I'm annoyed that he didn't tell me, as I wonder if Bones has this information, since he was made the head of the family. Surely he would have told me, after finding out that I took her.

"My family name is Amici. Your father got me a new identity. My name is not Anastasia Crowne. It's Hadley Amici."

All the air vanishes from my lungs, as I stare at her in shock, and I'm pulled into the memory of the first time I heard that name.

My mother scowls at me.

"Massimo, you will be nice to Hadley."

She's annoying, following me everywhere, looking up at me with those eyes that say I'm a hero. I know she's just a little girl, but for a reason I cannot explain, I want to hurt her. I like making her cry.

"Why is she here?"

My mother glances at me with a soft smile, and she shakes her head, as if to say I'm being impossible.

"Her mother had somewhere to be, so she's hanging out here because, as you know, the men are working."

The men.

I clench my fists at my sides with her words, because, while I've proven I can handle enemies, I'm still not working with my father, because I'm only sixteen. My mother has urged me repeatedly to go to college, but it's not what I want. I've known, since I was a young boy, that I want to work with the family. With my father.

"Behave," she scolds me, and I nod with a groan.

"Massimoooo," I hear from down the hall, and I bristle at the sound of her high-pitched voice. I bet I'd like it better if she were screaming.

My mother reminds me.

"She's a little girl, figlio."

"Massimo?" She speaks low, but loud enough to snap me out of my memory.

I gaze at her silently, as I attempt to make a connection between the gorgeous woman in front of me, and the annoying little girl, that liked to follow me around like a lost puppy. The same fair skin, slender neck, the lone freckle on her right cheekbone, and the fucking halo around her irises, that seems different now. More intense.

"I didn't recognize you," I say, as I scratch my head in confusion.

Giggling, she says, "I was a little girl. I would like to think I've changed."

A million questions pop into my mind. Why didn't my father tell me? Does my mother know? And who the fuck killed her father?

"Where did you get the information that my father was responsible for your father's death?"

"Carlo," she admits, after a hard swallow.

I stare at her incredulously.

"You're fucking kidding me, right? That's your source?"

"Yup," she answers in a squeaky voice, telling me that she knows where she made a critical error.

She lets out a soft gasp when she catches my glare.

"Are you thinking of killing me again?"

I nod in response, refusing to tell her what I'm really thinking about. She spots my heated gaze, and gasps my name, telling me she's thinking about the same thing.

Chapter Thirty-Three

HADLEY

He stares at me, and I feel as transparent as glass. It's like he can see right through me.

"Hadley," he says in a gravelly voice, sounding more like a plea than anything. It raises goosebumps on my flesh, and steals the breath from my lungs.

"Come here, little lamb."

I rise from my chair, heart pounding in my chest, as I walk around the four empty chairs to him. Never taking his eyes from mine, he moves his chair back, and pulls me onto his lap.

"You were an annoying little shit," he growls, as he wraps his arms around my back, holding me close to him.

"I still am," I breathe.

It feels like a million years ago, when I had a wild crush on him. Never did I imagine, back then, as mean as he was to me, that, in the future, he'd do the things to me he has.

"I'm still mad at you. And I don't understand why you did it. I ask for you to let me go, and you respond by tattooing me against my will?"

He runs his tongue over his lower lip, as he stares at mine like he's imagining the taste.

"I'm a bad guy, little lamb. A really bad fucking guy. The reason why I didn't sell you isn't so you could go free. It was because I wanted to keep you all to myself. You belong to me."

The deep rumble of his voice sends shivers down my spine, his tone laced with possession, his gaze heated and intense.

"Massimo," I whimper, as he kisses the skin below my ear.

"Fuck," he says with a groan, as he sinks his teeth into my flesh.

"I wanted to break you, ruin you, make you want to die, and then watch the blood drain from your body. Now, I just want to be inside you. If you're the poisonous apple, I want to devour you. If you're my undoing, I welcome it. You can be angry with me, little lamb. As long as you scream my name."

He rips the robe open, and drops his gaze to my breasts. Leaning forward, he strokes his thumb over my nipple, causing me to yelp in pain. They are tender to his touch, but when he swipes his tongue over my nipple, somehow it eases the discomfort, and turns to pain mixed with pleasure. The moan that slips out of me is louder than it should've been, and slightly embarrassing.

Pushing the robe over my shoulders, he runs his hands up my thighs until they sit under my ass, and he rises from the chair, carrying me back upstairs to his bedroom. Lying me down on the bed, his gaze swallows me, as he removes his shirt.

"What? I told you, you had no right."

Tilting his head with a smirk, he chuckles soft and low.

"I tattooed you. Pierced you. I'll mark you in any way I deem necessary, because you belong to me. And…"

He drops his shirt to the floor, and I swallow hard, as I take in every ink-covered muscle. If I were standing, I know my legs would be shaky.

"I want to feel you come for me. I want to watch you bleed. I want to hear you scream."

Massimo removes his pants, along with his boxers, and my gaze instantly drops between his legs. His cock is heavy, thick, and causes a gasp to slip out of me.

Forcing my eyes back to his face, I say, "No cutting, unless I can cut you."

I know he's the one in control, and if he wants to slice my flesh, he will.

Tilting his head to the side, he appears to be deciding how he wants to play this.

Bending down, he grabs his pants, pulls the knife from his sheath, and grins at me. It's not a smile exactly, it's dark and devious.

He climbs onto the bed, and I spread my legs. Placing the knife beside my arm, he hovers over me, a hand on either side of me, as he stares into my eyes with so much heat my clit pulses. The way he looks at me might be enough to make me come.

"I have rules with blood play, little lamb. If you make me bleed, you'll caress the ache with your tongue. You'll consume my blood. Are you prepared to do that?"

"Yes," I breathe.

"So fucking perfect."

Lifting onto his knees, he picks up the knife and hands it to me.

"Do not try to kill me. It will not end well."

I swallow hard at his threat, and shake my head.

"I wouldn't."

He rolls over onto his back, and motions for me to come closer. I straddle his hips, his hard cock underneath me, causing me to moan lightly.

"A muscular area is best. Avoid the forearm and neck."

My hand shakes slightly as I grip the knife.

"Are you sure about this? Have you done this before?"

He places his hand over mine, steadying the tremble.

"I've been stabbed, but not like this. Don't cut too deep, and I'll be fine. Make me bleed for you, little lamb."

Chapter Thirty-Four
PSYCHO

Her fear does nothing to relax my erection. I'm not sure I've ever wanted inside a woman like I do her at this exact moment. The anticipation nearly kills me, as I wrap my hand around her wrist, lift it gently, and pull her hand down to cut into my chest. Her eyes widen, as she spots the slow flow of blood oozing from the wound. She leans down and I grab her hair, moving it out of the way, as she slides her tongue over the cut, taking my blood into her mouth.

"Fuck," I growl.

The soft flicks of her tongue, knowing she's drinking from me, have my cock so hard, it's difficult to control myself. She lifts her head slightly, staring directly into my soul, as she licks her lips seductively. Reaching under her arms, I grab her, and throw her onto her back, ripping my knife from her hand.

"My turn."

Pushing her legs back beside her ears, I kiss her ass cheeks while she whimpers. I cut into her flesh, and she hisses slightly from the pain. Her hiss turns to a moan, when I slide my tongue over her cut skin.

"Hadley," I groan, all of my senses firing off like an explosion. The way she looks, tastes, feels, and fucking sounds, drives me insane.

"Look how drenched you are," I say, as I push two fingers inside her, and am immediately rewarded with the buck of her hips, coupled with a soft breathy moan.

I press my nose to the inside of her thigh, and inhale her scent, before moving to her pussy, taking that in too. Gazing up at her body, I'm marveled by the pure beauty. Her dark hair splayed over my pillows, eyes blown wide with lust, that halo around her irises more prominent than normal, and the piercings I gave her. She's so goddamn beautiful it almost hurts. The little girl that followed me around like a lost puppy is long gone. Replaced with a fucking siren. The most tempting of temptresses. This stunning woman wanted to take my family down, for crimes we didn't commit. I should be punishing her, she deserves it. As I lower my head and slide my tongue up her slit, I know I'm coming undone. I've always seen things in black and white. She's my grey. For the first time in my life, I want to get lost in something other than vengeance.

"Fuck."

It takes me less than twenty seconds to realize I made a vital fucking mistake. Climbing over her, I quickly push my cock inside her, and close my eyes with a groan. I have no fucking idea how the hell the knife got close enough for her to grab it, but when the blade is pressed to my throat, I know I'm in a bit of trouble. My eyes pop open, and I stare at the stunning woman under me.

"Hadley," I whisper softly, being careful not to move my throat too much. Her eyes glow with fury, and this time, her hand doesn't shake. She's steady as a rock.

"Let me make something perfectly clear, Massimo."

I don't move. I wait. The beauty of the moment isn't lost on me.

"You said before you'd be inside another woman before the end of the day. Were you?"

"No," I answer in a clipped tone, but it's the fucking truth. I never left the house.

"Good," she breathes, "If you're fucking me, it means you aren't fucking anyone else. Do you understand me?"

She catches me off guard. I've never been a monogamous man, and I certainly have never promised to not fuck another woman, but as hard as this should be, it's pretty fucking easy.

"I don't want to fuck anyone else. Only you."

It's not a life-long commitment, but for now, it's the truth.

Pulling the knife away from my flesh, I grab it and toss it behind me, unwilling to take the risk of her having a change of heart.

"Very brave, little lamb. The next time you press a knife to my throat, I'd advise you to slash it, because the price will be more than you can afford to pay."

I crush my lips to hers, swallowing her soft moan, as I slide my tongue into her mouth, licking every fucking corner, unable to get enough while I move inside her. Every time I reach her 'G' spot, I rock back and forth, while she digs her nails into my shoulders. Pulling my hips back, I slam forward with punishing thrusts, desperate to hear more of those whimpers.

She places one hand in my hair, the other on the side of my face, and her back arches as the pleasure consumes her. My name falls from her lips in a garbled scream, and it makes me feral for her. Driving into her soaked pussy, as it squeezes my cock, I feel something I've never felt for a woman. Pure obsession. I'm possessed with the need to own her.

Placing both of her hands in my hair, she pulls my head down and whispers, her breath fanning my lips, "Come for me, Massimo."

And I do, because this woman is my fucking downfall.

I hold her in my arms and rub her back, careful to avoid the tattoo. Her head is on my shoulder, her tits against my chest, and one leg draped over me. I like the way she feels, but I have to ruin this serene moment, because I need information.

"You said Carlo was from a rival family?"

Hadley lets out a long sigh, as she balls up her fist on my chest. "Yes."

A few years ago, I heard rumblings of Carlo Bianchi being in prison. I never found out why, because I didn't care. The De Lucas wiped out the majority of the Bianchi line, but clearly didn't want to go to the trouble to take care of the man in prison.

"Bianchi?" I ask, needing confirmation.

Popping her head up, I'm met with pleading eyes.

"Yes. Please don't go asking questions, Massimo. You will get me killed."

She's more afraid of him than she is of me, and that I find interesting.

Rolling her over to her back, I grip her chin in my hand, forcing her to see me. Hear me.

"I will not let him hurt you. If I had known of the situation, he wouldn't have gone to prison."

Her eyes widen, and it causes a dark chuckle to escape from me.

"He'd be dead, Hadley."

I fucking hate how sad her expression is, when she talks about him.

"What did he do to you?"

She closes her eyes tight as I witness the pain visibly consuming her, like a wave pulling her under.

"I told you, he was brutal. He beat me far more often than he didn't. Choked me with a belt, until I passed out. The only thing that kept me going was Michael. Then he took him from me too."

It's not lost on me that she once told me I was a worse man than Carlo. I don't say that though, because this isn't about me.

"I swear to you, I'll protect you. That asshole, and any of his associates, will never get close enough to touch you. Whenever you leave my home, you'll be protected. You belong to me, little lamb, and I protect what's mine."

Chapter Thirty-Five

PSYCHO

If Kage could see me now, I'd have a knife in my flesh, but I don't fucking care. When I asked her if she wanted to watch a movie, her answering smile was all that mattered. The light in her eyes had me once again rubbing that spot in my chest.

She cuddles up against me on the couch, while she watches the chick flick on the screen. She covers her mouth with a gasp, and tears roll down her cheeks, as the hero of the movie drops to his knees, declaring his love for the blonde on screen, that he's been away from. The moral to this story is that love wins in the end, even when tragedy after tragedy threatens everything. As the credits roll, she turns to me and catches me watching her, instead of the lame movie.

Folding her arms over her chest, she scolds me.

"Were you even watching the movie?"

I move a hair out of her face, and lean in, brushing my lips over hers.

"You watched what you enjoy watching, and so did I."

"Massimo," she sighs my name, her breath dancing over my lips.

Placing her hand on the back of my head, she pulls me closer, closing the distance between our lips, and presses hers to mine. She pushes her tongue into my mouth, and it's a slow sweet kiss until she whimpers, and I lose my mind. I move my hands to her hair, and take control as I always do. She doesn't complain, instead responding by matching my hungry pace, and giving me the moans that I fucking love. When I pull back, she's completely dazed, when a slow smile appears on her face.

"You're so fucking beautiful, Hadley."

She blushes and shakes her head, like she's trying to right her mind.

"It's been a long time since I've heard that name."

Grabbing her waist, I pull her onto my lap, kiss the side of her neck, and fight my groan.

Fucking pomegranates and mango.

I'll never get used to her scent, so I let it fill me as I close my eyes, and kiss her gently, again and again.

Looking up at me with a hopeful gaze, she asks the question I wish I had an answer for.

"Do you know who killed my father?"

"I don't, but I promise you, I will find out."

She lays her head against my chest, and I wrap my arms around her back, holding her tight.

"Where did you go after you left?"

With a soft sigh, she says, "We moved to the trailer park. Your father wanted to help, but my mother was convinced it was his doing, so she flat out refused any help."

I kiss her on the top of the head, not ignorant to the tears on my chest.

"Did she immediately decline?"

She nods against my chest, as she exhales a shaky breath.

"After the burial, she was never the same. I was a child, but I had to do everything she couldn't bring herself to. Your mom left food on our porch every week for years, but eventually she stopped. It always put a smile on my face. It was like a link to my old life."

"I didn't know. If I did, I would've done something. I don't know what, because I was also a kid at the time, but fuck, I would've done something."

She gazes up at me with emotion in her eyes, and my breath catches in my throat. Don't say it, Hadley. *Don't fucking say it.*

"I love you, Massimo."

My heart pounds, and my head spins.

"That's not what this is, little lamb. I don't love. I'll take care of you, but love, marriage, and babies? I can't give you that. I won't."

Turning in my lap, she straddles me and places her hands on my face, as she stares at me with a sad expression.

"You deserve to be loved too, Massimo."

She lays her head on my shoulder, and speaks in a voice barely above a whisper.

"I think I loved you when I was twelve. The anger of what I thought your father did, took me down a different road, one of vengeance, but if I'm honest, I think I always loved you. It doesn't matter what you say, Massimo. Love is not a decision, it chooses you. You have given me every reason to not love you, and yet, I still do. If I had the choice, though, Massimo, I'd choose you. I see the real you. Not the Psycho, because that's a small part of the man you are. You're so much more, and I love all of you. Even the broken, jagged edges."

I hold her closer, unable to reciprocate her feelings, but knowing damn well, I don't want to spend a day without her.

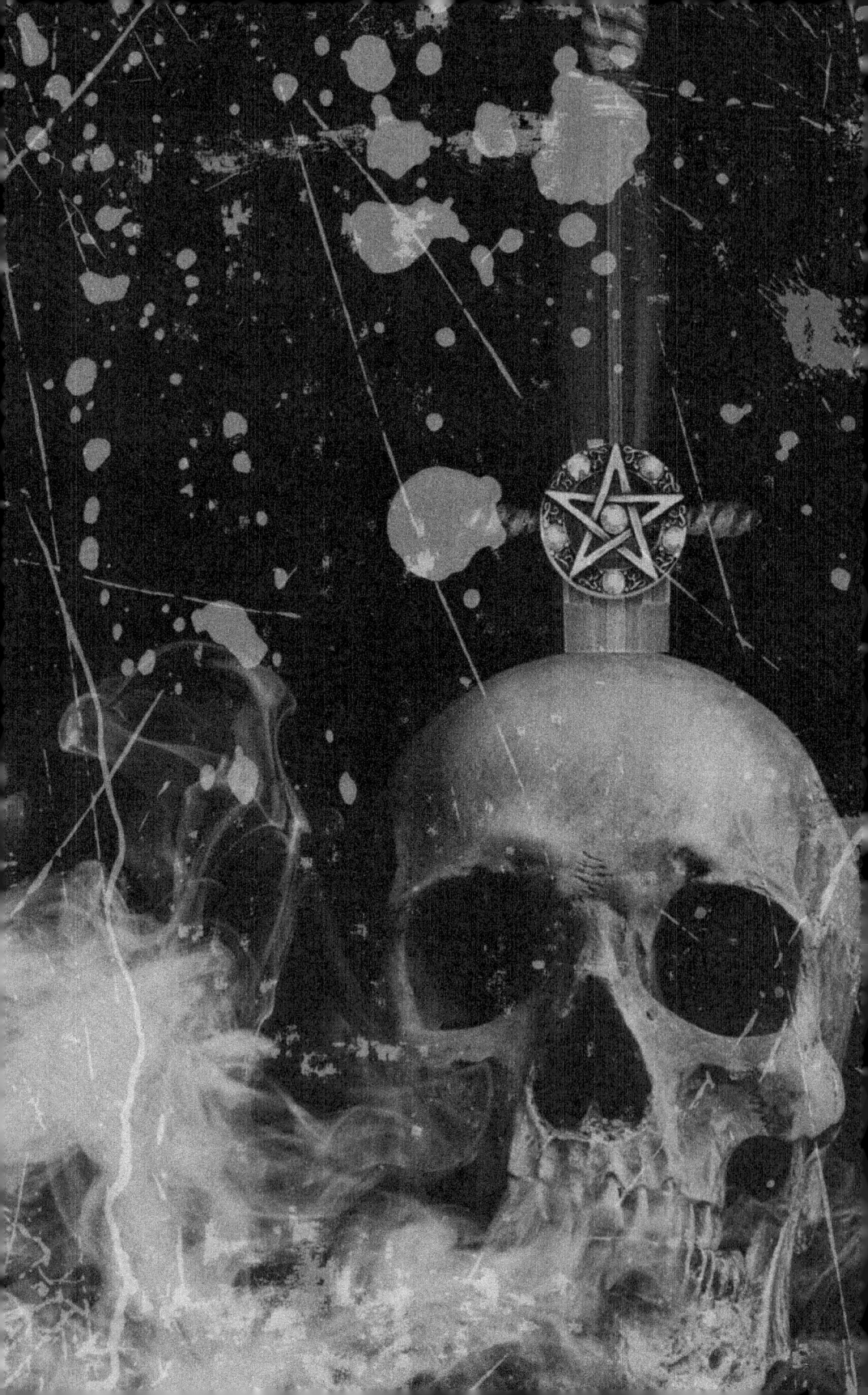

Chapter Thirty-Six

PSYCHO

I don't want to leave her, I'd prefer to stay buried in her sweet pussy all day long, but I need information from my family. Somebody has to know something about all this shit. I plan to extract Carlo from prison and deal with him, but there's still the matter of her father. I want to know who the fuck killed him. It's important, for some reason I cannot identify, that she knows it was not a Bonetti. I know that already, but I need her to as well.

"I don't want you to go," she pouts, as she pulls up her t-shirt, tempting me with her pierced nipples.

Reaching out, I pinch her rose bud as she squeals.

"Behave. I need to do this."

Leaning my head down, I capture her lips, and kiss her softly.

I turn to leave, but stop halfway to the door.

"Oh, and Hadley?"

Looking over my shoulder, I catch her gaze on my ass, and chuckle softly.

"Keep your goddamn hands off my pussy."

The sound of her giggle follows me in the entryway of my home, and I rub at that familiar spot in my chest, because fuck me, I don't hate it.

The first words Bones speaks to me have me annoyed.

"Is she dead yet?"

I don't respond audibly, just answering with a shake of my head.

While I knew my mother would be here, since it was my request, I'm pleased to see her. Since my father died, she has spent a lot of time traveling the world, and we don't see her nearly enough.

I waste no time scooping her into my arms, squeezing her tight, and placing a kiss on her cheek.

Taking a seat on the sofa, I nod a greeting to my brothers; Bones, Reaper, and Kage.

"Mama, do you remember Hadley?"

A soft smile crosses her lips as she nods.

"Of course. She's unforgettable."

I glance at Bones, who is eyeing me curiously, wondering why I am asking about a girl we have not seen in years.

"Hadley is the ADA. Anastasia and Hadley are the same person."

My mother is the only person in the room that is not wearing a shocked expression.

She holds her hands up, as we all point our gazes at her.

"Her father died tragically, and she got herself caught up with that Bianchi brother. If your father hadn't helped her, she'd be dead. Where did you see her?"

Bones groans, knowing full well I'm not going to lie to my mother. I'm not ashamed of the things I do. And she knows the man that I am.

"I kidnapped her."

Her eyes widen, as she slaps her hand over her mouth with a gasp.

"Oh no, figlio. Please tell me you did not hurt her. She has been through so much pain."

Reaper speaks, before I have a chance to respond.

"She was trying to take us down. Whatever he did to her is within his right."

I rub at my temples, hearing those words from a goddamn serial killer. Reaper has little concern over the line between right and wrong. His date nights with his wife involve murder. I'm not opposed to it, but I know his words are of little comfort to my mother.

My mother shakes her head, and wipes away a tear.

"Not if she's Hadley."

I turn to Bones, ignoring the glare from my mother focused on the side of my head.

"Did you know?"

He laughs, but it's not sincere.

"I did not. I also don't understand what her issue is with our family. She was practically one of us."

Rubbing my temples again, I tell him the absurd truth.

"She thinks Padre killed her dad."

After I fill Bones in on everything I know, which doesn't feel like enough, my mother grabs my arm.

"Figlio, I won't ask again. Did you hurt my Hadley?"

I had honestly forgotten the relationship my mother had with her. The distant memory of her playing barbies with my mother. The last time I saw Hadley was three days before her father was murdered.

Tears spring to her eyes, her hands balled into fists, as she screams at me.

"Why did you do that? Why, Massimo, why?"

I shrug my shoulders, not giving an answer, because I don't really have much of one.

"You're too young to have a boyfriend," I come up with, but she's not buying it.

Placing her hands on my chest, she shoves me backward with a grunt.

"Why, Massimo, why?"

If my brothers called me by my first name, I'd punch them in the face. Everybody knows me as Psycho, and I fucking earned that name. Yet, when she does it, I have to fight back the smile that wants to come to my face.

Leaning down, I narrow my gaze at her, meeting her glare with one of my own.

"I didn't like it. Okay? That's fucking why. You are under my protection, and that's what I was doing."

She doesn't back down. Her back straightens, and her head raises, as she roars at me.

"I don't want your protection."

After her father died, she didn't come around anymore. Her mother never brought her to see us, even when my mother all but begged to see her.

I look at my mother and raise my hands in defense.

"I didn't kill her, which was my plan. I did not know she was Hadley, but it doesn't change what she did."

My abnormally quiet brother speaks up, and we all turn to him.

"I wasn't happy that Psycho took it upon himself to capture the fucking assistant district attorney, but now that he has, I don't see any solution, other than ending her life. She is a threat, and if Psycho lets her go, all kinds of trouble will end up at our door. Sure, we'll probably get out of it, but I'm not interested in dealing with unnecessary situations."

"No," I answer in a clipped tone.

Bones arches an eyebrow and repeats my word.

"No?"

I don't respond, because I said no the first fucking time, and it does not need to be repeated. My answer is final.

"Fine. One of us will take care of it."

He glances at my mother's horrified expression.

"Mama, I'm sorry, but Bonettis come first. All threats must be eliminated."

When I speak again, they all stare at me, with almost identical faces of shock.

"That would be a bad idea. She's under my protection."

The large room is so silent, you could hear a pin drop, until Kage roars with laughter. I flash him a pointed glare, and his laughter instantly subsides.

My mother takes my hand in hers.

"I want to see her, figlio. Right now."

I stare at each of my brothers, and issue a warning.

"If you're coming, that's fine, but you'll be in my house. Hadley is under my protection."

I am the only man that gets to hurt her. She belongs to me, and I don't want to fight with my brothers, but I will.

Chapter Thirty-Seven

PSYCHO

My mother gets into my SUV, and my brothers drive separately. I don't know how long they'll be, but Bones didn't seem to be in much of a hurry. When my mom urged that we had to go, and go now, his dry reply was, 'Where's the fire?'

She sits in the passenger seat, tapping her foot anxiously.

I reach over, and grab her hand while I drive, to attempt to calm her. She looks over at me with a teary gaze.

"When your father told me how her life had been, the sadness consumed me. I begged to see her then, but she declined."

With her free hand, she wipes a tear that falls down her cheek.

"How does she look? Is she healthy?"

I nod slowly as I turn onto the highway.

"She's fucking beautiful, Mama. I don't think her life has been easy, and she probably refused to see you, because she thought Padre murdered her father."

Squeezing my hand, she laughs under her breath.

"All she had to do was ask, and I could've told her he didn't. Alejandro was his friend. Her mother must think the same. After he died, your father offered to pay for the funeral, and provide for them. He wanted to pay for her college, everything. You know how he was. It was all refused."

I nod.

"I know, Mama. Instead, she chose to raise her daughter in poverty."

I can't contain the bite in my tone, because it's fucking ridiculous. And somehow Carlo, who will fucking die, convinced her that her mother was right. We do a lot of bad shit, but we don't go after our own men unless there's no choice. If we're faced with that, we don't make a goddamn show of it.

Pulling up to my house, I throw my SUV into park, and climb out, as my heart drops to my fucking feet. My guards are dead, laying just past the gates, and my house is on fucking fire. My brothers pull up, and I yell to Bones to watch my mother, who stands horrified, looking at the flames. As I run toward my house, I hear my brother bark orders at me.

"Psycho, no! Massimo, I said no!"

Kage comes up behind me, and grabs my shoulder.

"What the fuck are you doing? Wait for the fire department."

I turn to him with a glare and shove him off me.

"If she's in there, I'm getting her out. Would you wait for the fucking fire department, if it was Raina locked inside a burning house?"

I don't wait for an answer, because we both know what he would do. Exactly what I'm going to do. I rush up the steps to my open door, and prepare myself to find Hadley unconscious at best. I rub at my chest as I walk inside with Kage behind me.

"What the fuck are you doing?"

He shrugs as I step over debris.

"We're brothers. We do stupid shit together."

Walking through my house, we enter the kitchen first, finding flames near the gas stove, which I don't imagine is a good thing. I go through each room quickly, only looking for one thing.

Hadley.

Three firefighters appear behind us, as we begin to take the stairs.

"Mr. Bonetti, would it be okay if one of us goes in front of you?"

I move to the side and wave him through.

If I were anybody else they'd be dragging me out, kicking and screaming, but they know better. I'd hate to kill a man trying to do his job, but nothing, and fucking no one, is going to keep me from her.

Every room we go into, and don't find her, the harder my heart pounds, as I begin to wonder if she's here.

Kage echoes my sentiments as we stare into my bedroom, and again come up empty.

"Someone started that fire, Psycho. They probably took her, and the arson is to slow you down. Get your attention elsewhere."

Bones appears when we get back downstairs, and he shakes his head.

"Nobody is in the basement."

One of the firefighters comes up to us as smoke filters in.

"Sir. The fire is mostly contained on the other side of the house, but I have to suggest you get out. Fire is dangerous, but so is smoke inhalation."

I nod and make my way to the door, the smoke stinging my eyes, and causing all of us to cough, as we walk through the threshold.

Standing outside, as the firefighters work to get the fire out, Bones gets right to work.

"Any idea what this bullshit is about?"

I swallow hard, a thick feeling in my throat before I speak, when Kage's words about regret come back to me, and hit me far differently than when they were spoken.

"Regret is a poison like cancer. It kills slowly, painfully. It eats away at you, until there's nothing left."

Telling Bones the story of how I pulled Jimmy into our world, sounds worse to me than it did in my mind, when I made the call. And there it is.

Regret.

My brother rubs his temples, staring at me incredulously, and his voice reflects how I currently feel about myself.

"Jesus Christ, Psycho. You sold her?"

I shake my head.

"I told him the deal was off."

Bones narrows his gaze at me, disdain written all over his face, and sounding in his voice.

"I'm going to guess Jimmy didn't fucking agree, Massimo. You don't dangle bloody meat in front of a rabid fucking dog, and think when you tell him no, he'll tuck his tail between his legs, and go home. That is not how men like Jimmy Valentine work."

My other brothers watch our standoff with worried glances, because they know I may not be welcome in the family business anymore, but I say the only thing that keeps circling my brain.

"I have to find her."

Reaper holds my sobbing mother, and that's another person I'll have to deal with after this. The heartbreak in her gaze is heavy. I didn't know she was Hadley at the time, but I think that will be little comfort to anyone.

Bones drags his hand down his face, the agitation with me nearly palpable. I did this. This was all me.

"I need to call Max Esposito. What you have dragged us all into, is something we don't have experience in, but he does."

I've heard of Max, and his team of vigilante assassins, but never met him. Rumor is, he started as a man that took jobs like any assassin, and when he found his long lost sister, everything changed. Finding her altered his business, and now they have a team that only goes after traffickers, and their buyers. I thought at some point, Bones said he was retired, but I don't say anything, because I don't have a fucking clue where Hadley is, and I'll take anybody's help.

The guilt gnaws at me as I rub my chest in circles, as if there's any way to make the pain subside. I did this.

If he beats her.
I did it.
If he rapes her.
I did it.
If he tortures her.
I did it.

If he kills her.
I fucking did it.

Chapter Thirty-Eight

HADLEY

He stands over me, belt in his hand, greasy blonde hair and an equally slimy grin, but it's his words that drench me in fear.

"Carlo says hi. He wishes he could be here for this, but you made that impossible."

Lying on the cold, hard ground, I glare at him with more confidence than I probably should have.

"Psycho is going to kill you."

He shrugs like he's not worried, before shattering my world.

"He's dead."

Tapping on his head, like he thought everything through, he grins at me, showing his disgusting teeth.

"I knew he'd come for you. That's why I set the fire. I knew he'd go into a burning house to save you, but unfortunately for you, he didn't make it out alive."

Swinging the belt down, he hits me on the side of my face, and the pain is immediate, so I do what Carlo taught me to do, go somewhere else.

The lashes continue, but I force myself to disassociate in memories of Massimo. When he was a boy, we fought because he was possessive, even back then.

"You don't own me, Massimo."

He steps forward, closing the gap between us, and places his hands against the refrigerator behind me, caging me in. His proximity, too close, his stare too intense, and his scent, too intoxicating. Running his tongue over his bottom lip, he looks at me like he wants to eat me, devour me, and it's unsettling.

"I don't own you, Hadley, but I will. Until then, I'll still protect you from everyone, including yourself."

My mind snaps to more recent times.

Us sitting under the blanket watching a movie, me in his arms, his warmth spreading through me, and fingers on my skin. The way he kissed me, and I knew he was lying, when he said he didn't feel anything for me.

I try to stay in the memory, but the lashes become too intense.

Blinding pain.

My heart cracks wide open at the loss of him, and the end of my life, because I know it's coming. That's the entire point of this. The pain is a prelude to what's coming. My mother flashes in front of my eyes, as I succumb to the physical and emotional anguish, causing everything to go black.

I wake to more lashes of the belt. He's relentless, as I cry out in pain.

"Why are you doing this?"

He chuckles sadistically.

"Carlo hired me, but I couldn't find you. Psycho called me, and said he had a woman he wanted to sell and, when I saw the picture, I knew who you were. I finally found you, with his help. This isn't just a job, though. Psycho changing his mind, and refusing me what had been promised, only made me obsess over you. And now, you'll pay for being so hard to find."

Chapter Thirty-Nine
PSYCHO

Bones is supposed to be working on finding her, even though he thought she needed to be killed. Even if I would allow that shit, my mother wouldn't. Killing Hadley would break Mama beyond repair. Losing my dad was hard enough for her, but Hadley, at the hands of her son? She'd never get over that. It wasn't happening anyway. When we say someone is under our protection, we fucking mean it. Bones knew my meaning. If it came down to it, I'd fight my brothers. Every fucking one of them.

I walk into Lollipop, Jimmy's strip club, determined to find him, so I can find her. They will give me answers, or everybody dies.

Malcolm eyes me skeptically when I walk in, and I instantly decide he knows something. I lock the door behind me; nobody is getting in or out, until I have Hadley.

"Walk slowly to the main room. Don't try me, Malcolm. I'm pissed. Very. Fucking. Pissed."

When we make it into the room with stripper poles, and a bar, I nod for him to sit at the table. I pull my gun out and aim at the bar, shooting their top shelf selection. I don't use my gun often, but it gets attention better than a knife. People don't pay any mind to a blade until it's cutting into them. It's an underrated weapon.

All it takes is one gunshot and people start screaming, and running back and forth, like a chicken with its head cut off.

I growl, "Everybody shut the fuck up, or I'll start spilling blood, real quick."

I point to the far side of the room. "Ladies, over there, grab a table, and don't fucking think about doing anything stupid. No purses. No cell phones. The men are on this side, same rules."

Motioning to the two dancers on stages, I tell them, "You too. Everybody."

While I'm not feeling particularly patient, I give them a few minutes to do as they were told.

"Now, this is how it's going to go. I'm going to count to ten, and if someone does not tell me where to find Jimmy Valentine, someone dies. I'm going to start with the men, before moving to the women. Mark my words, ladies, I will fucking kill a woman, so you are not safe."

I ignore the worried glances, and begin counting.

"One."

The whimpers sound out across the room, men and women alike, but no one speaks up.

"Two."

Gripping the back of Malcolm's hair, I yank his head back.

"Where the fuck is he?"

He mouths off, "I don't fucking know. I'm not his goddamn keeper."

"Oh, Malcolm," I coo sarcastically, "Bad fucking day to piss me off, you see, I'm a man on edge, and you know how I am. I'm a goddamn psycho."

He holds his hands up in defense, as if he has one.

"Look, man, I'm sorry, alright. I don't know where he is. He said he'd be gone for a week, to take care of a wayward whore."

Malcolm realizes the error of his words far too late. I put my gun back in my holster, pull my knife out, move behind him, and pull his head back again, while pressing the knife to his throat.

"Last chance, Malcolm. Jimmy took what belongs to me. I want her back. Where the fuck is he?"

"I don't-" he gets out, a second before I cut his throat, to the sounds of so many screams it makes me smile.

I wipe his blood from my knife on his shirt, and take a cleansing breath, as his body slumps back onto the table behind him. His dead eyes stare up at me and a smile crosses my lips.

"Alright, let's try this again."

Moving to one of the other men in the club; another bouncer, Patrick, I tilt my head as I grin at him sadistically. He trembles, so I know it has the desired effect. The club is quiet, with only hushed whispers, that I'm choosing to ignore.

"One."

"Fuck," he says under his breath, knowing what's about to happen.

"Two."

He shakes his head. "I don't know where he is. Psycho, come on, don't punish innocent people."

These fuckers are far from innocent. They are involved in a lot of illegal activity. Drugs, illegal gambling, trafficking, and anything else they can make money from. Mostly things that my family does as well, only better. Except for trafficking. I swallow hard at that thought, and get back to work, because I have to find her before... I can't even finish the thought without bile rising in my throat.

I cut his throat, the same way I did Malcolm's, as a round of 'oh my god' breaks out.

Now they know I'm fucking serious.

Sixteen dead bodies later, I'm covered in blood, and I still don't have any answers. I'm losing my grip. Hell, maybe I already lost it. Where the fuck is she? I will wipe out the entire fucking state if I have to. No one is safe, until Hadley is in my arms where she belongs.

I walk over to the tables where the women sit, trembling, and wide eyed. When I speak, my voice sounds as crazy as I fucking feel.

"I didn't want to hurt anybody here tonight. He took her, and I can't stop until I have her again. You understand, right?"

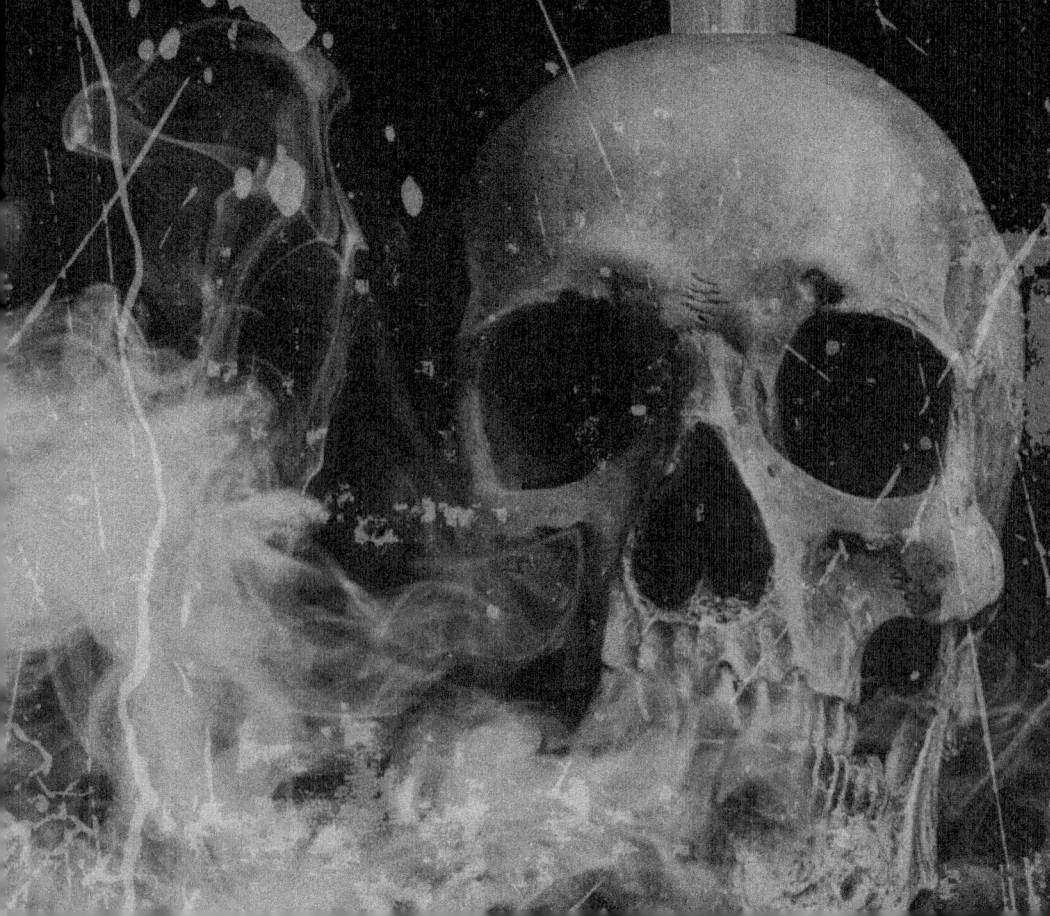

The woman beside me is a young blonde, with pretty blue eyes, although a little hazy right now, with the sobbing.

"What's your name?"

I have no idea why I ask, but when she answers me, my chest cracks wide open with so much pain, I think someone is ripping my heart from my chest.

"Hadley," she answers softly between hiccups, and I just shake my head.

Such a fucking unusual name, and here it is.

Pulling out my phone, I dial Chief Roberts' number.

"There's a bloodbath at Lollipop. Sixteen dead bodies, and a bunch of women that I suspect may be trafficking victims. As always, send your trusted."

I disconnect the call, and put my phone in my pocket.

"Stay here. The police will be here soon."

Chapter Forty

PSYCHO

Two Days Later…

Bones talked this guy up, and made me believe, with my whole fucking black heart, that he'd find her, so his words stun me.

He scratches his head and stares at me regretfully.

"We don't know where she is, man. Not a fucking clue."

I grip the glass in my hand, and my nostrils flare, as my brother watches me cautiously. He knows I'm on the edge of an explosion.

Throwing the glass at the wall behind Max's head, it shatters, and he jumps out of his seat angrily, as my brother jumps up with the same speed.

"I've got this."

He stands over me, as I continue to sit on the sofa, with my other brothers on either side of me. Bones glares at me, but it doesn't faze me, but his words cut like a goddamn knife.

"We will fucking find her. Nobody is giving up, but let's not forget that you set this into motion, brother. You decided to sell your favorite toy, like trash you had no further use for. We will find Hadley, and then you're going to let her go, because you don't fucking deserve her."

"Never," I growl in response.

My brother arches an eyebrow at me, and stares at me like he wants to kill me right here, right now, and I'm not sure I'd even fight him if he tried.

"I fucking know I don't deserve her. That does not change anything. She belongs to me now, and she will be mine, forever. Do what you need to, *brother,* but this won't change."

Max clears his throat, clearly done with our family bullshit, and says, "As I was saying, we don't know where she is, and I think we need to bring in the De Luca family. Their IT guy is the best there is. Besides, once we locate her, it won't hurt to have extra men."

"Benji," Bones and I say in unison.

My brother is close with Domenic De Luca, although I'm better friends with Drake. He's a little more my speed, a little closer to my side of crazy. They are a good family, and have always had our back, and we have theirs.

I nod, because I know Max is right. There's nobody better at finding shit that someone doesn't want found, than Benji.

"When can we get him here? It has been two days, and we all know what he's doing to her."

I fist my hands at my sides, my blood boiling, as I try to push those thoughts from my mind. Max jerks his chin to the door as Benji walks in.

"Everybody knows you as Psycho, because that's how you conduct yourself. That's fine in your family business. In my house, you'll conduct yourself with the respect I deserve. I have a family, and will not have some asshole in my home, throwing shit like an angry two-year-old. If you weren't a Bonetti, you'd be eliminated for arranging the sale of a goddamn woman. A woman I'd bet my bank account you love. Figure your shit out on your own time."

"Noted," I say, while my three brothers watch me, expecting me to tell him to go fuck himself. Another day, perhaps, but not today. Until I find Hadley, I'll act like a goddamn choir boy if I have to.

Benji stands with all four De Luca brothers with him, and then other people I don't know. Max quickly introduces them.

He points out a tiny blonde.

"My sister, Mia. Technically, she's in charge. Remember what I said, respect."

He continues on, "Hunter, Jade, Nash, and Trevor. This is my team, and they will accompany us."

204

Benji clears his throat, and I watch the tiny man as he begins to talk.

"Hadley, before she disappeared and became Anastasia, was married to Carlo Bianchi, brother of Enzo Bianchi."

Domenic groans, while he runs a hand through his hair.

"Fuck."

I don't doubt that information hits him hard, considering what Enzo did to his wife for a year. He nearly lost her permanently. The Bianchis are all disgusting men. They went after Damian De Luca, and his ex-girlfriend at the time. I was convinced, at one point, that they'd take out the entire De Luca family.

"Carlo has been putting hits on her for years, but nobody could find her, because your father facilitated a name change for her. Tell me about Jimmy."

I rub at my chest, because the ache is fucking unbearable.

"Jimmy Valentine. Bloody Valentine is his gang. Most of them were eliminated a while back, but he's still around."

The expression on Bones' face shows a lightbulb going off. I don't think he realized the connection until just now, which is odd.

"My buddy Sin had some issues in Vegas with them. I personally eliminated many of them."

Benji nods, as he stuffs his hands into his pockets.

"It appears, without the rest of his gang, Jimmy may be trying to create something new with Bianchi. Jimmy has been visiting him in the prison, and according to a few people on the inside, he's bringing in drugs. Also, as Domenic probably remembers well, his house was set on fire. The Bianchis were all arsonists, so it makes sense to me."

"Any idea where she is?"

Benji shakes his head, as he eyes me warily.

"I really don't have anything solid on that front, but I think he may be using Bianchi properties. I have a list for you, and I don't have any order for them."

Rising off the couch, I walk over to him. "Can I see?"

He hands me the list, and I go through it. Nine fucking properties scattered. It could take us a goddamn month to rule these out, and still not have a clue where Hadley is.

"Any of these have a substantial outside area? Forest like areas? That's his thing."

Bones arches an eyebrow at me once again, probably wondering how I know so much about Jimmy.

I hold up my hands in defense, knowing what he's thinking.

"We are not fucking friends. I knew a girl years ago, that had a long relationship with him."

I'm using the term relationship a little loosely. He fucked her, that part was consensual, but the repeated beatings were not. I wanted to kill him, but my father ordered me to stand down because it wasn't Bonetti related, and we don't rescue women.

Unless they are ours. Hadley is mine, and I know my father would approve. Although, it wouldn't matter if he didn't.

"You want to start with the property that backs into the woods then, Psycho?" Max asks, and I nod appreciatively, ready to get this shit started, and find Hadley before it's too fucking late.

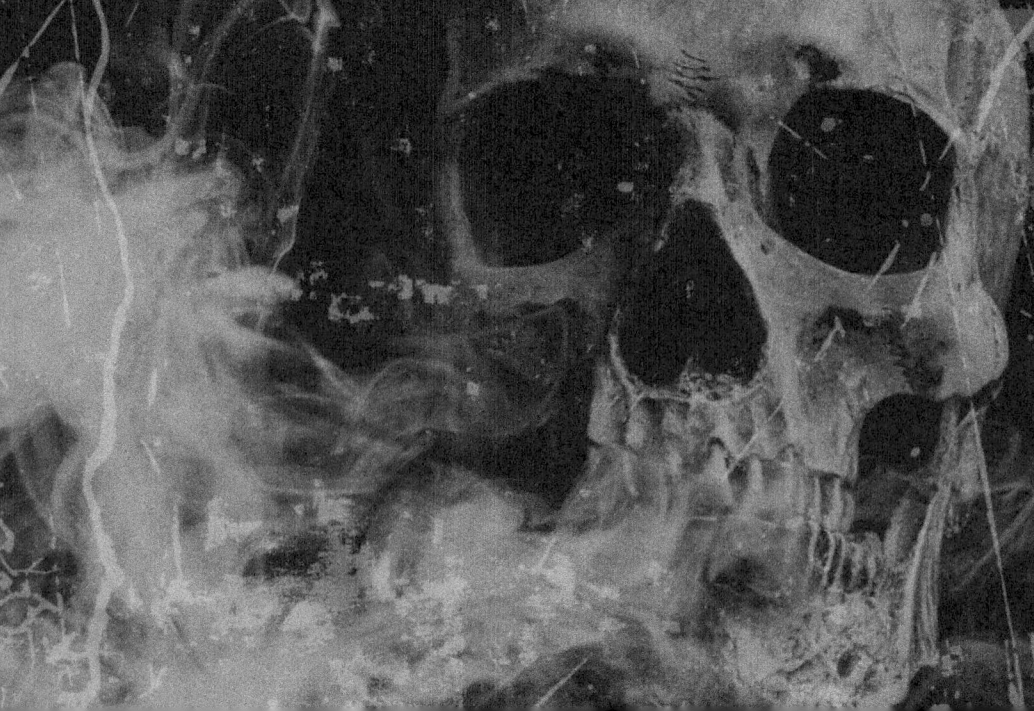

Chapter Forty-One

HADLEY

My bloody hair sticks to the side of my face, as the man I now know is Jimmy, the same one Massimo was going to sell me to, pulls his leg back to kick me again. This time, his boot lands right at my chin, knocking me to my back.

A harsh cry escapes from my throat. I can't run from him, because I'm too weak. I have not eaten, or had even a sip of water, since I got here, and I don't even know how long I've been here. My will to live is nearly non-existent, because I just want this to be over. Massimo is dead, and I will be too, soon, but not soon enough. My heart aches, thinking of him dying in that house, burning to death. The pain in my chest is almost worse than the rest of my body.

Finally, he stops the attack, and I look at him through my swollen eyes to spot him on the phone.

"It's for you." He looks down at me with humor dancing in his eyes.

"The man of your dreams, I think."

He chuckles as he presses a button, and the voice I thought I'd never hear again sends a bolt of terror down my spine.

"Hello, whore," Carlo says, with venom dripping through his words.

My limbs shake uncontrollably, even though I know he can't touch me. Instead, Jimmy's hands will be Carlo's. All of his bidding will be done. There have been many times I wished he would've killed me instead of Michael. How I ever thought I got away from Carlo is beyond me. Stupid girl. I should have known one day he'd get me exactly where he wants me.

Massimo's face enters my mind again. The possessive boy that stole my heart all those years ago, and the man he was only days ago.

My real name falling from his lips, as recognition set in. I'd give my life to hear that again, just one more time.

"Your whore looks white as a ghost, man," Jimmy says over the speaker-phone.

"Good," Carlos quips.

My eyes dart between Jimmy and the phone, wishing I had a way out of here, but I don't. After being beaten the way I have been, I don't have it in me to run. I'm exhausted. There's simply nothing left. As if reading my mind, Carlo laughs maniacally.

"Today you die, *Hadley*," he says my name with pure disdain. I know he hates me, because he's in prison, but it wasn't me that murdered our son. Still, he blames me.

"Jimmy is going to take you outside. If you run and get away, then you're free, but I doubt that's what will happen. It's the end of day three with no food or water. I don't imagine you have much time left, so make a run for it. Oh, and be careful, whore. There are traps, and it's going to be hard to see in the dark. I hope you think of Michael dying while you die. Wouldn't that be beautiful?"

"You're a sick bastard," I scream with a shaky voice.

He laughs again, thoroughly enjoying my pain. This isn't new for him. He has always gotten off on hurting me, whether the torment has been physical or emotional.

They disconnect the call, and Jimmy leans down, grabs me by my hair, and drags me to the back door facing a wooded area, while I kick and scream, trying to get free from him. When he lets go of my hair, I make it to my feet, breathing hard, my heart racing in my chest, and he shoves me forward.

"Run, bitch. Straight into a bear trap, hopefully."

My eyes dart around, trying to figure out where to go, there's nothing but trees, and I have no idea what's on the other side, if anything. I already know there's no way out of here. This was their perfectly executed plan.

The sky is dark; the only light is from the moon, a sliver shining through, as I try to make it through the trees, crawling, not running, because I'm so fucking tired. I want to curl up in a ball right here, and sleep forever.

"Move. Or I'll come kick your ass into gear."

His voice is loud, and echoes in the night like he's using some kind of loudspeaker. I move slowly, my eyes scanning each area before I progress, watching to see if there are actually traps, or if he was attempting to scare me. If it was a scare tactic, it fucking worked.

If I'm honest with myself, everything Massimo did to me was better than this. I swallow past the lump in my throat, trying to stop myself from thinking about never seeing him again.

"Massimo!" I scream for him, even though I know he's not here. Tears blind my vision, as I move forward, and a loud snap of metal echoes in the quiet night.

The noise causes me to scream, as I look down and realize it narrowly missed my leg, as I am met with laughter from the loudspeaker.

"Oops. Looks like you found a bear trap."

The ground is covered with leaves, making it more difficult to see. On either side of me, another trap snaps. The loud metallic clunk causes my heart rate to spike, as it thunders in my eardrums, and my panic rises. I stop for a moment, attempting to breathe.

Calm down. Showing fear makes you weak. You are going to get through this. Breathe.

I nearly laugh at my attempt to think positive, in this very fucked up situation. Every time I move, I might be going right into a trap. What kind of person does something like this? I already know he is following Carlo's instructions.

Taking another cleansing breath, I move forward again, and breathe a sigh of relief when I don't find another trap. I keep going for what feels like a long time, when multiple traps snap all around me, causing the terror to rise, my heart pounding in my chest as I scramble out of the way. I reach a pile of leaves and, against my better judgement, crawl through it and scream, when I realize it's a fucking hole in the ground, figuring it out too late, as I'm falling until I hit the bottom, with a thud that causes instant pain in my legs and back.

It's at this moment that I give up. There's nothing to hold onto. I'm never getting away from this asshole. Carlo wins. He always wins.

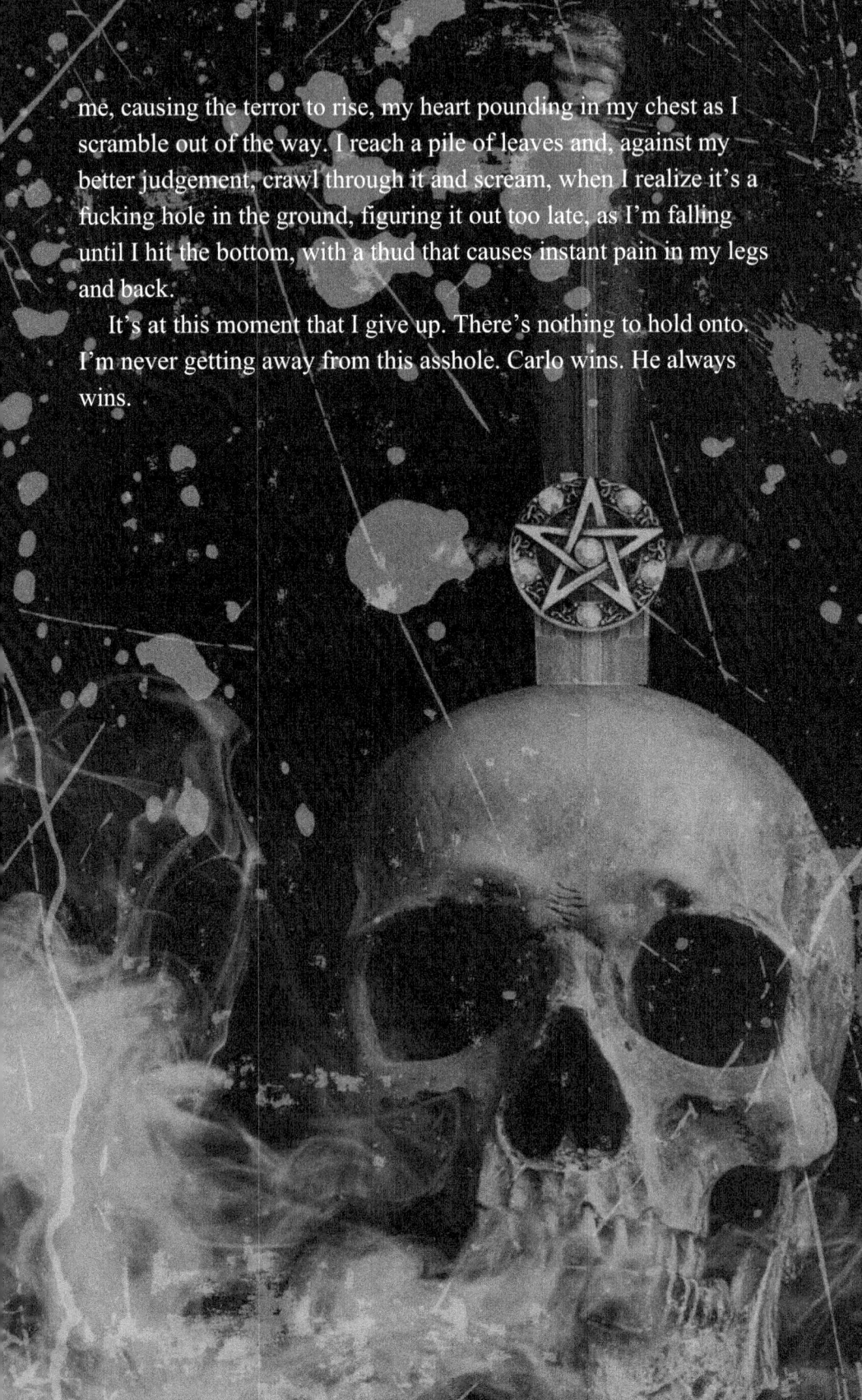

Chapter Forty-Two
PSYCHO

"Any chance you'll stand back, and let people less emotionally involved take the lead?" Max asks, with a smirk on his face.

"Nope," I say bluntly, because that's not fucking happening. If this asshole is hurting my girl, *mine*, nobody is going to handle this but me.

He jerks his chin toward the door.

"After you then."

I walk through the overgrown lawn, spot the boarded windows, and shake my head. My fingers are itching to cut this motherfucker. We climb up the three rickety wooden steps, and I try to turn the doorknob, but it's locked, so I glance back at Max. He steps forward and rams into the door, splintering the doorframe, and kicks it to the ground.

Jimmy comes running, with a "What the fuck!" as his wide eyes dart between all of us, probably realizing he's seriously outnumbered.

"What the fuck?" he repeats.

I step forward, glaring directly into his eyes as he shakes.

"I'm here to collect what belongs to me."

He moves back a few paces and lies to my fucking face.

"I'm afraid I don't know what you're talking about, Psycho."

He's going to be more than fucking afraid.

Pulling my fist back, I punch him in the face, and my lips pull into a slight smile as blood gushes from his nose. That felt good. Too fucking good. I don't bother telling him if he tells me where she is, I'll take it easy on him, because I won't. Sometimes, I'll give someone an easy out. This is not one of those times.

"You took something that belongs to me, and we're going to rectify that, right now. Where the fuck is she?"

Jimmy babies his nose, cradling it in his hand. "Oh, you mean Anastasia? Or is it Hadley? Or do you even fucking know?"

I pull my fist back again, but Bones stops me.

"Do you want to beat him to death, or do you want to find her, and then beat him to death?"

Nodding my agreement, I say, while retrieving my knife, "You have five seconds to tell me where she is, or I'll start by cutting your dick off."

I look to my left, at Bones chuckling, while shaking his head.

"Your wife is a fucking inspiration."

Jimmy glances around, likely looking for a way out, but he's fucked. There's fourteen people, all ready, and able, to take his life. Four of us ready, and willing, to torture him, until he thinks death is a gift.

"Look, man. I was only doing what I was hired to do. She's somewhere in the woods, but she's probably not alive by now."

Damian De Luca growls loudly.

"Go find her. This fucker isn't going anywhere."

I nod, and head towards the back door of this run down hellhole. I'm sure Damian and the others won't let him go. There are few men that hate a woman being hurt more than him. They call him *the saint* for a reason.

My brothers follow behind me as I stare at the trees, so many goddamn trees. They go so far there's no end in sight, possibly for miles. Finding Hadley out here is going to be difficult. Nearly impossible.

"Fuck."

It's a lot of ground to cover with little light, and waiting until daybreak is not an option. I'll stab anyone who even suggests it.

Reaper turns his flashlight on.

"I'll stay with you. Watch the ground, if this asshole likes traps."

We move into the woods, slowly, everybody with flashlights except for me, as I call for her.

"Hadley!"

My heart sinks as I call for her again, and get no response.

Reaper says, "Don't do that. There could be many reasons why she isn't answering. Until you can see with your own eyes that your worst fear is true, she's alive."

Bones yells out to us confirming our suspicions.

"There's traps."

Kage warns immediately after, "We found two. Be careful."

Just after that, we spot three, one after the other. Jesus Christ.

"She's in a trap," I speak low, more to myself than anybody else, but Reaper agrees.

"Probably, but people live through that."

Do they? I don't know shit about fucking bear traps. I've never used one. I don't see the point. It seems a little more humane to shoot a goddamn bear, instead of setting traps.

The emotion fills me, as I realize this woman wanted to take my brothers down, along with me, yet here they are. Is it because they know I care, on some level? Or is it because we all remember little Hadley? All of us except for Reaper, because he was little when she left us. Still, they're here with me, even though I know they're pissed at me. As if he can hear the words rambling through my brain, Reaper glances at me.

"It doesn't matter. You're our brother. A bad decision doesn't change that."

"I think it was more than a bad decision."

He chuckles low and says, "I think you made me look good for a change. Thanks for that, by the way. Psycho, man, you don't get it. The three of us, Bones, Kage, and myself, are assholes. We do terrible things to people, regularly. Me, probably, more than them, but it doesn't mean you don't have a fucking heart. I already know that's why you did it. She scares you, and you couldn't deal with it."

213

We move forward a little more, catching sight of more traps, and it pisses me off, but I keep my conversation going with my little brother.

"Dad always taught us that if someone was against us, they were to be eliminated. It's how I've always operated. I don't know another way."

He shakes his head like I'm an idiot.

"You have to find another way. Don't admit it, I don't give a fuck, but you love this woman. We wouldn't be out here if you didn't."

I palm my face with irritation.

"Jesus. I should've gone with one of them."

Again, he stares at me like I'm an idiot.

"You think they don't love their wives? They do. Fine. Answer this, asshole. Can you let her go, like Bones wants you to? Can you let her walk out the door, and let her live her life without you?"

I rub at that spot on my chest that keeps fucking burning, as I walk, and look all around me.

Where the fuck is she?

"No. I can't. It won't fucking happen."

I don't know what the fuck I feel for her, but as Reaper shines his flashlight, I spot what appears to be a giant hole in the ground, and approach it cautiously.

"Hadley!" I yell for the hundredth time, and again there's no response.

"Shine the flashlight in the hole."

Reaper moves beside me, lights up the dark space, and I spot her. She appears to be passed out, and my chest burns like it's on fucking fire. Now I have to figure out how the fuck I'm getting her out of there.

"What the fuck are you doing?" Reaper asks, as I jump into the fucking hole. How we're getting out, well, I don't know, but I'm not leaving her alone, so it wasn't much of a choice.

I land on my feet with a thud. The hole is about six feet deep, and six feet wide. Wasting no time, I sit down on the ground, and take her into my arms.

"I've got you, baby. You're going to be okay."

Her eyes pop open, wide with fear one second, and the next, she sobs.

"Massimo, are you here to take me to heaven?"

I chuckle against her neck.

"Wrong guy for that, little lamb."

She reaches up and touches my face, like she's trying to make sure she isn't dreaming.

"He said you were dead. I don't understand."

My heart feels heavy, as I take in her swollen face. Thanks to my brother's flashlight, I spot the bruises, as well as the puffiness.

"Are you hurt?"

Hadley grips onto my shirt like it's a lifeline, and presses her face to my chest.

"I'm okay. My legs and back hurt, but I don't think anything is broken."

Gently, I brush the hair out of her face, lean my head down, and kiss her cheek softly.

"How did you find me?"

"You're mine, Hadley. Finding you was never a question. I would've killed every motherfucker on this planet until I located you."

I brush my lips over hers, when my brother interrupts me.

"Hey, Romeo, think you can climb out?"

Chuckling as I pull back from her, I say, "Probably, but I don't want to risk hurting her worse. See if someone has some rope."

Bones and Kage eventually come over with a ladder. Okay, that's better than rope, I suppose.

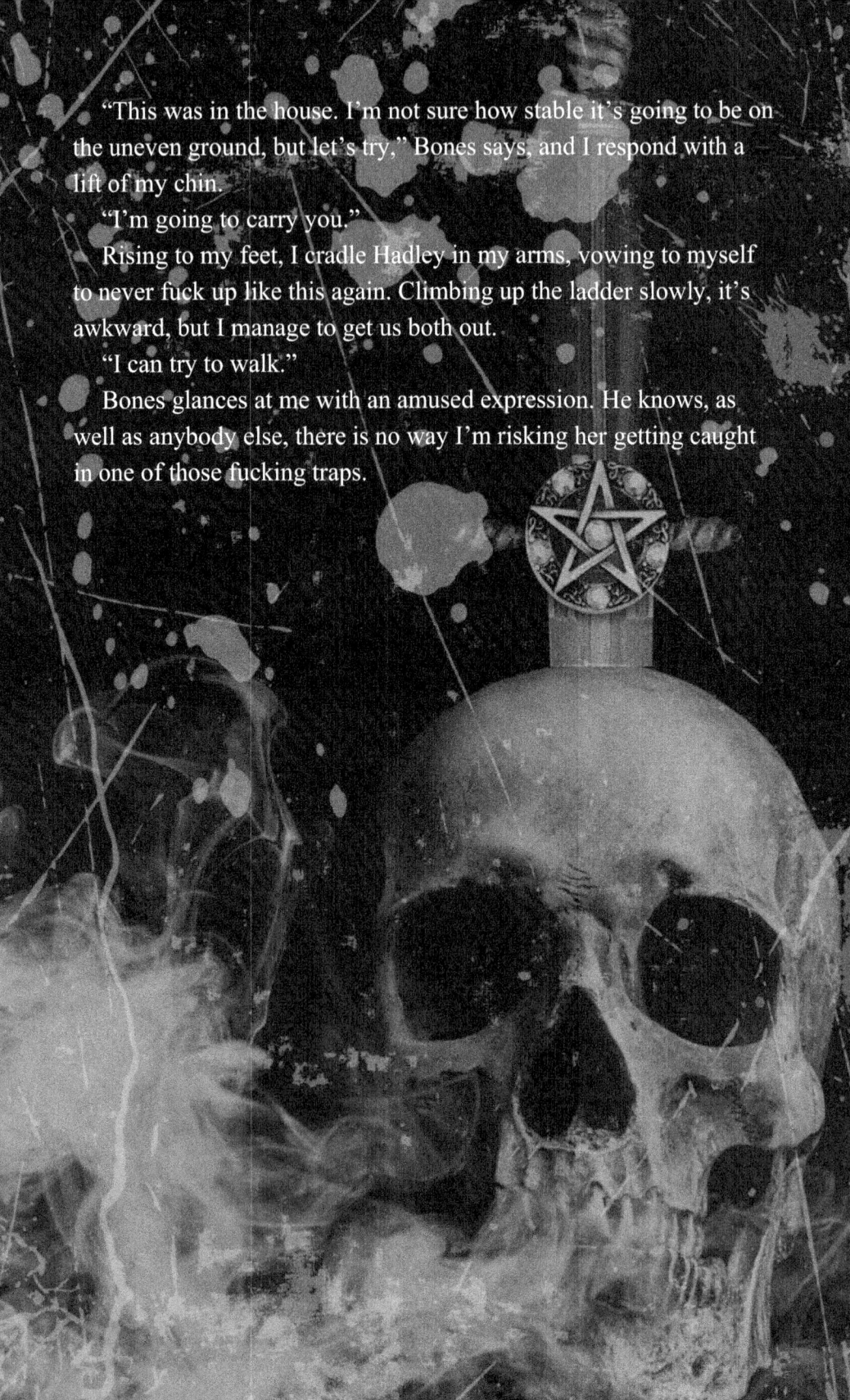

"This was in the house. I'm not sure how stable it's going to be on the uneven ground, but let's try," Bones says, and I respond with a lift of my chin.

"I'm going to carry you."

Rising to my feet, I cradle Hadley in my arms, vowing to myself to never fuck up like this again. Climbing up the ladder slowly, it's awkward, but I manage to get us both out.

"I can try to walk."

Bones glances at me with an amused expression. He knows, as well as anybody else, there is no way I'm risking her getting caught in one of those fucking traps.

Chapter Forty-Three

HADLEY

"We have a doctor on his way to make sure you're okay."

I whisper my okay, as he carries me to the house, and press my face into his chest, allowing his scent to envelop me. Even as a teenager, he smelled like citrus and wood. Nothing has changed, but it's more intense now, with a hint of bourbon thrown in.

"I must look like hell."

He glances down at me with a smirk on his lips, as he holds me in his arms.

"No, baby. You look fucking beautiful."

A man I'm guessing is one of his brothers runs up ahead, and opens the door for us, and he carries us through. I haven't seen them in so long, that they aren't the boys I remember, but full-grown men. None of them are hard on the eyes, there must be some kind of hot DNA in the Bonetti bloodline.

We move into the living room and there's a bunch of men, a few women, and Jimmy, on the couch, with three guns on him, but the weapons bring me no solace. I shake in Massimo's hold, and he pulls me tighter against his chest.

"He can't hurt you, baby."

A man approaches us, and his gaze scans over me, before moving back to Massimo.

"The doctor is set up in a bedroom."

He jerks his chin to the hallway behind us.

"What do you want us to do with him?"

Massimo looks over at Jimmy, then back to the man in front of us.

"Max, you know my plan. I want him stripped and secured in a room. I don't give a fuck which one."

The man I now know is Max nods, and Massimo walks us down the hallway. We enter the first bedroom, and a man with gray hair, and a matching beard, greets us.

"Dr. Palmer. If you place her on the bed, I'll take a look."

He lays me down, and I hiss from the pain in my lower back.

Taking my arm, he presses his fingers to my skin, while wearing a frustrated expression.

"She's dehydrated," he says, addressing Massimo.

I offer the information he's likely wondering about.

"I haven't eaten or drank anything since I've been there."

"Motherfucker," Massimo growls, as the doctor pushes a needle into my skin for an IV, before hanging it from a portable pole that sits beside the bed. I'm guessing he brought it with him, but I don't ask.

"Do you want pain medication?"

"Yes," Massimo answers, before I have a chance to speak.

He reaches over to the end table beside the bed, covered with a towel, and various medical supplies, and grabs a syringe.

"This will help with the pain, but it's not going to knock you out. If you try to sleep, however, it'll make it easier."

The doctor injects it into the IV line, causing near immediate relief, and I sigh a long breath.

Pulling my hand to his lips, Massimo kisses my skin softly, before setting it beside me on the bed. I stare into his face, taking in his handsome features. His dark eyes, dark beard, tattoos peeking out at the neck of his shirt, and more appearing at his wrists, down to his knuckles. He's beautiful. And cruel. I have not forgotten what Jimmy said. Massimo is the only reason he found me. When he contacted him to sell me, he knew, when he saw my picture, who I really was.

Sell me.

As if he can read my mind, he reaches for my hand again, pain reflecting in his eyes as I pull back.

"Don't."

The doctor nods at Massimo.

"I think she'll be fine. She'll likely be sore for a few days, but I don't see anything permanent, or life threatening. Rest and rehydration will help."

"Thank you," I say, and he leaves the room.

"You're angry with me."

Am I? I don't know what I am. He tried to sell me, and yes, changed his mind, but does that make it okay? No, it doesn't. How was that even a thought? Sure, he didn't know who I was, or his connection to me at the time, but I'm a person. And his choices led me right into Jimmy's hands.

"We're going to talk about this, but I have to go deal with him. You can come with me, or stay here in this room. If you choose to come with me, you need to prepare yourself. You're going to see things that might be hard to watch. If you don't hate me already, you might, after seeing what I'm going to do to that asshole. I'm not a good man, Hadley. This is how I handle scum that hurts what's mine. And you can be angry, baby, but you are still mine. Are you coming or staying?"

"Coming. I want to watch him suffer."

"Good girl." He winks at me, and I ignore the butterflies in my stomach, as he lifts me into his arms, holding me with one arm, as he pulls the IV on the pole behind us. Massimo carries me into the room, where there are far too many people.

One of the men exits the room, and comes back with a chair. Massimo says, "Thanks, Drake."

He sets me in the chair, and my eyes go to a naked, trembling Jimmy, on what looks like a small kitchen table, his arms chained to the wall, and his legs connected to the opposite wall, with longer chains.

Four men approach him, and the one says, "We're going to head out. You could've handled this alone, but you know if you need us, call."

Massimo shakes his hand.

"Thank you, Domenic. And we couldn't have done it alone. If it weren't for you, I might never have found her in time. Thank you."

A pretty blonde bounces over to me excitedly.

"Hi. I'm Mia."

She points out the other people in the room.

"That's Trevor, Hunter, Jade, Nash, and my big bro, Max."

Mia watches me with obvious interest.

"You're with Psycho?"

I shake my head no.

"Not exactly."

A growl sounds out across the room, from Massimo, where he stands beside Jimmy.

"Yes. She belongs to me."

"Possessive asshole," I say under my breath, but apparently loud enough for her to hear, because she giggles.

"Possessive men are where it's at. Does he even love you, if he won't kill a man for looking at you?"

I shift in my seat uncomfortably, because the pain is a lot better, but my leg still doesn't feel good.

"You're bubbly," I say, more to myself than her.

With a wink, she responds, "I'm a pitch black, ray of sunshine. Generally friendly and warm. Not unlike you, men tried to destroy the good in me, and I developed another side. Now, I fear no one, instead, I instill it."

Chapter Forty-Four
PSYCHO

Jerking my jaw down, I stare at him with pure hatred I feel to my core, as blood boils in my veins.

"This is where you talk. You'll tell me how, and why."

His wide eyes stare at the knife in my hand, waiting for me to strike him, but I won't. Not yet. The anticipation is the best part, and I want his words first.

"I'm going to vomit."

I chuckle softly as I warn him, "I wouldn't do that. You will lick it up."

Kage laughs somewhere behind me, knowing full well I mean it.

"He's not kidding, man. I would swallow that shit down."

Touching the tip of my knife over his heart, I repeat my order, which I fucking hate.

"How and why. If you don't answer me, I'll cut your heart out and feed it to you."

This man is barely a man, pathetic and weak. Beating a defenseless woman proves that.

Tears run down his face, and he tells me what I want to know.

"She stabbed Carlo multiple times, and called the police. Hadley is the reason he's in prison."

I turn momentarily to look at my girl, and wink at her, showing her how much I fucking approve of what she did. Her cheeks flush pink, as she fidgets in her seat. Fuck, I can't wait for this to be done, so I can hold her, and never let her out of my sight. She's mad at me, rightfully so, and might fight me, but I don't care. I'll let her fight, scream, whatever she needs, but she will be in my arms.

"Where do you come in?"

"I'll tell you anything, just get the knife away from me."

I pull the knife away from his flesh. It's only a brief reprieve. Once he tells me what I need to know, he's going to suffer.

His bottom lip trembles as he begins talking again. Pathetic.

"I got into business with Carlo. He was the only one left in his family. All my brothers are dead, so I was alone too. It made sense to build something together. I supply him with drugs he sells in prison, and when he needs it, I get him weapons. Early on, in our arrangement, he told me about Hadley. And our agreement was, I'd get a higher cut for ten years if I killed her, but he didn't just want her dead. He wanted it to be brutal. He wanted her to suffer."

Turning to my brother, Bones, I speak, and my voice comes out thick with the emotion swelling in my chest.

"I want someone to get that fucker out, so I can kill him. Otherwise, I'll go for a visit and do it right there, in front of anybody. You're right, I'm unhinged. For her. And that piece of garbage will not continue breathing after what he has done to her."

I swallow hard as he nods. It all makes me see red. My next question, I feel like I have the answer to, but I ask for her.

"Do you know anything about her father's death?"

"The Bianchis," he says in a flat tone.

"Why?"

The De Lucas have had a beef with them, but we never did. Not to my knowledge anyway, unless it goes back to my father's days, and was yet another thing he decided not to tell us.

"You'll have to ask him that, I don't know. Please, don't," he says, eyeing the knife warily.

Leaning my head over him, I stare into his teary brown eyes.

"One more question, and I promise if you lie to me, I'll make you regret it."

I speak low, so only he hears me, because I'm not looking to humiliate Hadley.

"Did you stick your dick in my girl?"

His eyes dart back and forth, and the anxiety he exhibits is enough to answer the question for me, but I wait for the word.

"Yes," he says, low, and white hot burning fury travels through me, but I hold it together, for her. Stepping back from him, I rub my chest, feeling like my world just imploded.

"Can everybody leave for a minute, please. Except Reaper. I need a second with my girl."

Silently, everybody steps out, other than my youngest brother.

"Do your thing, but do not let him die. Strangle him repeatedly, but he lives."

Reaper rolls his sleeves up, with a glint to his eye, and says, "Gladly, brother."

Walking over to Hadley, I kneel in front of her, and speak words I've never said to anybody.

"I'm sorry, baby. I'm so fucking sorry. Everything he did is my fault."

Her eyes well up with tears, as she reaches down and gently strokes my cheek. A tenderness I don't fucking deserve. It changes nothing. I have had few regrets in life. I live on my own terms, and apologize for nothing, but this, it fucking guts me, because I did this. I put her in his path.

"This isn't your fault, Massimo. The other things you did are, but not this. Are you sorry for those things too?"

I know she wants me to say yes, but I can't.

"No, baby, I'm not sorry for anything else. This piece of shit, putting him in your path and allowing him to hurt you, fuck, baby, for that I'm sorry. My guilt is my penance. I'll live with that for the rest of my days, while it consumes me. I know it's not enough, but it's all I have."

She darts her eyes away, as Jimmy's coughing, and sputtering for breath, interrupts us. I take her hand and kiss her palm, before I get back up and relieve my brother of his duties.

"Did you have fun?" I ask, as I glower at him. He shakes his head profusely.

"I agree, Jimmy. Strangling people is not fun, but cutting them is."

I push my knife into his flesh, and pull it down, as he screams.

"Fuck! Fuck! Fuck!"

Chuckling darkly, I say, "You took what's mine. You touched what's mine. I'm not even pissed about the fire. If I had any use for touching your dick, I'd do what my sister-in-law did once. A man hurt her, I'll spare you the details, but she cut his junk off."

A smile crosses my face at the memory.

"And then she choked him with it. Imagine dying, by choking to death on your own fucking dick."

"I'll do it," Hadley says, causing me to grin with pride. *That's my girl.*

I cock my head at Jimmy, who now screams louder than anyone I've ever heard.

"I know. She's fucking amazing, isn't she?"

Bones walks back in and arches an eyebrow at me, having heard my conversation with Jimmy.

"I told you, your wife is a goddamn inspiration."

Turning my gaze to Hadley, I tell her, "This will be the one, and only, time, I let you touch any dick, but mine."

A slow smile forms on her battered face, and it starts the rage all over again. I'm an asshole, but I would've never done this shit to her. Again, she surprises me.

"He made me watch him eat, while I starved. He likes his steak well done. Maybe he'd prefer his dick that way too."

My brothers share a shocked glance, before Bones chuckles loudly.

"Psycho's girl is a, well, *psycho*. How fitting."

Walking away from Jimmy, I look down at Hadley, and tilt her head back with my free hand.

"If that's what you want, you'll need to give me a few minutes first. I'll make sure he's still alive for you to do it."

She motions for me to come closer, so I do. Leaning my head down, she whispers in my ear,

"He made me cry, Massimo. Make him cry louder."

I swallow hard as her words hit me. She knows. I don't know how, but Hadley knows her tears are only for me. It's one of many things he took from her that he had no right to.

It's hard to turn away from her, when all I want to do is take her in, but I do what needs to be done. Call me a sick bastard, because I've always enjoyed torturing my enemies, but this isn't for me. It's for her.

Chapter Forty-Five

HADLEY

I'm not sure which of us is more insane, as Massimo cuts Jimmy's skin for the umpteenth time. He's the one with the knife in his hand, but I watch like it's a riveting movie, unable to look away, afraid I'll miss some important part of the plot.

Massimo slices.

Jimmy screams.

I used to be a good person, and something like this would've made me sick to my stomach. Something broke inside me out there in the woods. It wasn't the bear traps, it was something deeper. I've had so much taken from me. My father, mother, my son, then Massimo. The loss gets to a point where it's too much to handle. The way Jimmy and Carlo thought they could do what they wanted to me, with no consequence. Maybe Massimo too, although I'll admit it's different with him. He has hurt me, but I know deep in my soul, he'd never beat me. Even the first night, when he caught me at the warehouse, and said he'd kill me, I know, he never would've done to me what they did. Is he a good guy? Hell no. He did things to me he had no right to do, and he may not know it right now, but he'll pay for those choices. In the last few hours, he has taught me that I like dishing out what I have been given.

A smile crosses my lips, as a decision is made. Massimo catches the look on my face, and drags his non bloody hand down his face.

"You look like you're planning to take over the world, little lamb."

"Something like that," I respond, refusing to give him more.

Setting his knife on a small table in the corner of the room, he comes back to me and squats down.

"Tell me your thoughts."

I shake my head and say, "It's something I know, and something you'll find out."

Arching an eyebrow, he grins at me, something equally curious, and slightly afraid, in his eyes.

"If you're planning to stab me, I welcome it, and it's deserved. I won't try to stop you."

He clears his throat, like he's pushing away emotions. Massimo likes to make people believe he doesn't feel a damn thing, but I know otherwise. He can keep that secret from the rest of the world, but not from me.

"Ready to roast his dick?"

I go to stand, and he barks, "Sit the fuck down."

He isn't the guy that will ever buy me flowers, and tell me how much I mean to him, but it's there in moments like this. Massimo doesn't want me to get hurt, and that's how he shows that I mean at least something to him.

"Let me stand, I need to do this. You can stay close by, but I need to be on my feet."

The reluctance in his expression is clear as day, as he drags a hand down his face, before finally relenting. He nods and helps me out of the chair.

"Hey, Bones. I need one of those bbq lighters, and gasoline, or something flammable."

He grumbles something about taking orders instead of giving orders, which leads to his brothers rolling their eyes, as he leaves the room. Jimmy lays there sobbing. I don't know why he's so worried about it, obviously at this point he knows he's gonna die. You don't take your cock with you, so I am not sure why it matters. Then again, men are so attached to them, it's the worst-case scenario, I think, for any man.

Bones returns a few minutes later with Max, a BBQ lighter, and a can of gas in his hands, and a fire extinguisher. For the first time, he addresses me instead of his brother.

"Be careful, Hadley."

Again, emotion swirls in my chest at the use of my actual name, as I stare at the man that I haven't seen in so long. Memories assault me as he hands me the lighter.

Luca looks ridiculous, staring down at me with toilet paper hanging from his bloody nose, compliments of his brother, Massimo. I don't feel bad, because he cut my hair off. He deserved worse than he got.

"I'm sorry for cutting your hair."

I place my hands on my hips and glare at him.

"You should be, you big jerk! You're a bully, Luca, and nobody likes a bully."

It's not lost on me that his older brother bullies me all the time, and I have no idea why that's different. I scold myself inwardly. I know exactly why. Any attention I get from Massimo, I'll take, even if it's negative, but Luca is not him.

"Hadley?" he asks, snapping me out of my memory.

I glance up at him, and wonder if reading people's minds is a Bonetti family trait, when he smiles at me and says, "Your hair grew back nicely."

Massimo chuckles as he pours gas all over Jimmy's dick, and I'm afraid we may be running for our lives. I learned, when I set my bed on fire, it tends to spread quickly.

After setting the gas can down, he comes back to me with a delicious smirk on his lips. "Careful, little pyro."

As I get the lighter ready, Massimo barks out, "Jimmy, wake up, man. You don't want to miss this."

His chuckle is sadistic, but it doesn't bother me, because I instantly decide it's well deserved.

Massimo wraps his arm around my waist, reaching behind him with his free hand to grab the IV pole, moving it closer, so it doesn't pull on my arm.

Jimmy glances at me, sees the lighter, and freaks the fuck out, screaming and trying like hell to move his legs.

"Not gonna work, man," Massimo says with a dark chuckle, as I light the flame and start at Jimmy's hairy balls. I know he likes the knife, but this is worse for this scumbag. He didn't react like this with the cutting. It makes me happy that I get to be the one causing this level of terror and pain.

"I'm sorry," he sobs, loud enough that Max and his team come in.

Mia comes for a closer look and giggles.

"Don't worry, Jimmy. A dick that small can't take long to burn."

Once flames surround his pathetic member, and the smell of burned flesh fills my nose, I decide I've had enough. Burning humans do not smell good. Taking the lighter away from him, I turn to Massimo, and shake my head.

"Can we cut it now? That smells really gross."

Bones comes up, puts the fire out with an extinguisher, and flashes me a look of disgust.

"Fucking psycho, indeed."

Massimo hands me his knife and chuckles loudly. "This might cut easier than you think, I don't know. I've never used it to cut cooked meat."

I gape at him in utter shock.

"You've never done this?"

He stares at me like he's lost for a moment, before clearing his throat, something like pride shining in his eyes.

"Never, baby. This is the first for me."

Mia says, "There's no bone in the penis, so it'll probably cut like butter."

I place the knife at the base of his dick, which looks kind of like a burnt vienna sausage, and he screams.

"Please, I'm sorry. Please. I told you everything. Don't do this to me."

Massimo whispers in my ear, as he notices what likely looks like hesitation, but it isn't. I was remembering saying those exact words to him, yet he didn't stop.

Chapter Forty-Six

PSYCHO

I'm not especially happy when my girl is holding his severed dick in her hand, but neither is he, judging by the violent screams.

I watch Hadley with curiosity as she walks over to Jimmy's head. There's an unsettled feeling in my chest as she stands close to him. I'm not sure why, because he's restrained and can't touch her but still, I don't like it.

"Open wide," she says, as she cuts the end of it, like you might a hot dog for a little kid.

"Jesus Christ," Bones says, echoing my very thought. She is not going to make this man actually eat his dick. When Athena did it, he choked on it, but he didn't have to actually chew it.

"Be a good boy and chew well, I wouldn't want you to get it stuck in your throat," she says, as she pops the first piece into his mouth.

Kage steps closer to me and speaks low, while Jimmy chews his fucking junk, and after a lot of gagging, swallows.

Hadley immediately goes to cut the next bite for him, and Kage says, "So…"

Without taking my gaze from her, I ask, "So what?"

He chuckles low.

"I've been thinking when the right time is to stab you, but I'm also thinking your girl may have it covered. What the fuck did you do to her? That is not the Hadley I remember."

Watching Jimmy gag more with his second bite, I watch my girl in fucking awe.

"She's been through some shit that had nothing to do with me. I think it wasn't one thing, but many, and fuck, she's more perfect now than ever."

Jimmy gags more, and shakes his head back and forth, as he begins to vomit. Grabbing his chin, she covers his mouth, and holds it closed.

"Swallow it all."

Kage leans in and speaks low, probably trying to make sure she doesn't hear him.

"I'm just saying, brother, maybe watch your back. This is the type of girl that will fucking stab you while you sleep."

I can't help the grin that overtakes my face, as I spare him a quick glance.

"Fuck. I hope so."

Reaper rubs his hands together excitedly when Jimmy swallows the last piece of his own goddamn dick, and says, "Bella is going to love her."

Bones says, "Little Psycho, when you're done there, the doctor is in the other room, waiting to remove your IV."

She turns to me, knife still in her hand, and wraps her arms around my neck, and Kage is quick to take it from her, so no accidents happen. I'm completely thrown off when she sobs into my chest.

"Thank you," she cries.

I didn't set out for her to enact revenge. The plan was to come get my girl, and kill the fucker that took her from me, but now I see it clearly. She needed this. This was Hadley taking back her power, and fuck, I know more than anybody the power she holds. There was something about her, even from the moment I found her at my warehouse, that captivated me. Normally, I would've killed her, sure there would've been torture, but not fucking. I don't fuck my victims. She was so goddamn beautiful, I couldn't help it. I still can't.

Walking her into the other room, Kage follows with the IV pole, and I sit her on the bed, as Dr. Palmer glances at me with a disapproving look. He knows what we do, but he won't say a damn word. He wouldn't dare, and he's paid well for looking the other way. Chances are quite good that he heard Jimmy's screams. Quickly, he pulls the IV from her arm, and places a bandage on it.

"Keep your fluid intake up. You're out of the danger zone, but that could quickly change."

He hands her a bag of medication.

"Antibiotics for seven days, and pain meds, in the event that you need them. Antibiotics are important. If you have further swelling or a fever, you need to call me immediately."

I sit on the bed with her as Kage walks the doctor out.

"Look, Hadley, I don't know what I'm doing here, so I'm going to have to ask you to tell me what you need. I'm not good at this."

She smiles softly.

"You're better than you think you are, but I'll tell you what I need. Right now, I need to wash my hands, because I have bits of burnt weiner stuck to them."

Rising off the bed, as I shake my head at her, I lift her in my arms and carry her to the bathroom. Setting her on the counter, I turn the water on for her, and get the soap ready.

"The doctor didn't say I couldn't walk."

Giving her a glare, I let her know it's not up for negotiation.

"Until I'm convinced you won't hurt yourself, I will fucking carry you everywhere. Don't argue with me, because you won't win. Not when it comes to your wellbeing."

"Fine. Carry my fat ass everywhere, but your arms are going to get tired."

I narrow my gaze at her. "I don't want to hear that shit again. I don't know what kind of things you're used to hearing about yourself, but that's not something I'll tolerate."

The look on her face tells me everything I need to know. I shut the water off and lean down, kissing her neck, before I speak low.

"You're perfect, Hadley. You always have been. Fucking beautiful. I promise you, anything that asshole said to you was a lie. Now, let's get you home, so you can take a shower."

"Home? Your house was set on fire."

Right. Fuck. How had I forgotten that? It feels like a lifetime ago at this point.

Scooping her into my arms, I say, "Hotel then. The where doesn't matter."

I hold back my tongue, and don't tell her that she's my home. Wherever the fuck she is, is where I choose to be.

Bones stands outside the bedroom door when we exit.

"Your house is probably going to need some work. Come stay with us," he glances at Hadley, before adding, "Both of you."

"Thanks, brother, I appreciate it, but we'll get a hotel."

He arches an eyebrow and shakes his head.

"Mama wants to see her. She's at my house waiting."

I sigh heavily. I hate making her wait, but she needs to.

"Hadley has to be exhausted. We'll come by for breakfast tomorrow. Tonight, she needs quiet and rest."

He pats my shoulder as he turns away from us.

"Go get your girl settled. We will take care of shit here."

I walk her out of the house, and she sighs a shaky breath. We get to my SUV, and I set her in the front seat, noticing tears streaming down her face.

"I did not think I'd leave there alive," she says when she spots my concerned expression.

Kissing her on the cheek, I admit, "I wasn't sure myself. This was the first time in my adult life where I experienced true terror."

I close her door, walk around to the driver's side, and get inside, releasing a heavy sigh as guilt gnaws at me once again. My brother was right, maybe it's not love, but I feel something for this girl, and I always have. Even before I knew who she was, I felt something, and it scared the fuck out of me. If I'm honest with myself, it still does.

Chapter Forty-Seven

HADLEY

I thought, by the time we got to the hotel, he would've dropped this carrying me everywhere nonsense, but he didn't. The embarrassment of that, added to the way I look, is too much. The glances, as people wonder what the hell happened to me.

My clothes are filthy, and my face looks like it lost a fight with a truck. I can't say anything, because I've already been scolded about talking bad about myself.

"Ignore them," he growls, as we step into the elevator.

"Does anything bother you, Massimo?"

He jerks his head down, and stares at me like I'm confusing him.

"Losing you bothers me. Men hurting you. Fucking touching you, yeah, that really fucking bothers me. What random strangers think about me? No, little lamb, that does not bother me, because it doesn't matter. Why should I pay any attention to the thoughts of someone I will likely never see again?"

He has a valid point. Everybody does that though, other than Massimo. We all worry what strangers think when they look at us. Why do we do that? I don't have a clue, but I'd love to be more like him. I never thought I'd say that about anything, but it's true. Also, it doesn't hurt that he looks like he just stepped off some dangerous men edition of a fashion magazine, and doesn't have marks all over his face.

He walks out of the elevator, takes a right, walking down the long hallway, and swipes the keycard for the room. Moving to the bathroom, I don't get to see much of the room, other than spotting the massive size. He sets me on the bathroom counter and starts the shower.

"Normally, I won't give you a choice, but after what you've been through, I will. Do you want to shower alone, or have company?"

I twitch my fingers in front of me as he stares at me, waiting for a response, and I have none, because I'm afraid of how he'll react if I tell him the truth.

"Baby, remember our deal? You tell me what you need, and I give it to you."

I sigh audibly.

"I want you with me, but I'm not ready for sex."

"Jesus Christ. You were tortured for three days. And raped, I don't even want to fucking know how many times. I did not bring you to a hotel to fuck you. I'm a bad man, not a vile one. I have every intention of letting you fucking heal before I get my dick wet."

"Thank you," I whisper.

He takes the few steps to me and grabs the hem of my shirt.

"Hands up."

Pulling up my shirt, he's careful around my face when he pulls it off, and drops it to the floor. He's gentle, which is new from him. Every piece of clothing he removes from me, he does it as if he's terrified of hurting me. His eyes drop to the marks on my naked body, and pure anguish reflects in his.

"How did these happen?"

"Belt," I answer quietly.

He balls up his fists like he's ready to attack, but I know it's not me. Squeezing his eyes closed for a moment, before re-opening them, he quickly averts his gaze.

"I'm going to go out there. I'll give you time alone."

I grab his hand, and nearly beg him, as my voice breaks.

"Please don't leave me. I told you what I needed. This is what I need."

"Alright." He nods and gets undressed, before helping me off the counter, and walking me into the shower.

With a gentleness I didn't know he was capable of, he washes my hair and rinses it, before moving to my body. Every time he touches me, I can see the pain.

"I'm okay, Massimo."

He shakes his head and looks into my eyes.

"Have you ever felt so guilty about something, you thought it would swallow you whole?"

I nod slowly.

"Yes, after Michael died, I thought the never-ending guilt would take me too."

Sliding his fingers down my arm, he stops, and stares at me with a somber expression.

"That was not your fault."

I argue, "And this was not something you did. Yes, you were going to sell me to him, and we'll talk about that another time, Massimo, but you did not tell him to beat me, or anything else. He found me because of you, but he probably would have, at some point, anyway. It does not make you responsible for what he did to me."

I trace the line of his jaw with my fingers. "You have many things to regret, but that isn't one."

The look in his eyes is far away, like he's lost in a memory.

"Regret is a poison like cancer. It kills slowly. Painfully."

Standing on my toes, I press a kiss to his jaw.

"Yes, it is. Let it go."

He wraps his arms around me, and holds me tight against his chest. His heart pounds against me, as he takes my chin in his hand, and tilts my head back. Leaning his head down, he kisses me softly. Once, twice, three times, and pulls away.

"You need sleep. Two minutes, and if you're not out on your own, I'll come back and carry you to bed."

Chapter Forty-Eight

PSYCHO

"I'm so glad the bathroom is fully stocked. Brushing my teeth has never felt so good."

Pulling the blankets back, I pat the mattress.

"Drop the towel. I will not touch that beautiful pussy, but I want to feel you in my arms."

Her cheeks turn red, and when she drops the towel, fuck, she's gorgeous. My cock automatically springs to life, like it always does around her, even when I know I can't do what I want. Hadley climbs into bed beside me, and I don't waste any time pulling her into my arms. She lies with her head on my shoulder, as she peers up at me. I pull the covers over her, and kiss the tip of her nose.

"What is going through your mind?"

"Does she hate me?"

I brush the fallen hair out of her face.

"Who? Nobody could hate you, Hadley."

"Your mother," she whispers.

I can't help the chuckle that comes out of me, although she makes it clear it wasn't appreciated, with a cute little scowl on her face.

"No. She does not hate you. My mother has missed you more than you can imagine. I couldn't get her to wait to see you, so she came home with me, when I found my house on fire. To say she was devastated, would be a gross understatement. Mama Bonetti is far more insightful than the rest of us, and I think she understands how everything happened. Her only concern was if I hurt you."

Placing her hand on my chest, she strokes her fingers down the center, and I have to clench my jaw for a moment, to stop myself from doing the same to her.

"Does she know everything?"

I bark out a laugh as I stare at her incredulously.

"Jesus Christ, Hadley. I already lost one parent. I'm not looking to give the other one a heart attack."

She giggles softly, her breath fanning over my skin.

"What did you tell her? I'm trying to prepare myself mentally."

"Just be yourself. You don't need to rehearse your conversation with a woman that loves you."

I spot the sadness in her eyes, before she tries to shutter it from me. It was the word 'love', and I know my inability to love her is going to be a problem. Is it not enough that I care about her? That I would fucking kill anybody that hurts her? Apparently not, but I don't have it in me to argue with her tonight. So I change the subject.

"She knows I kidnapped you."

Making the perfect 'O' with her lips, she stares at me in shock, and covers her mouth.

"Massimo!"

Hadley starts laughing like a maniac, the vibrating of her chest into mine, as I stare at her, does something to me I can't quite figure out. I stare at her like an idiot, as if I've never seen someone laugh before.

"Do you remember when Kage locked me in a cage?"

I arch an eyebrow.

"You were such a brat, you know. You told him you wanted to go in the cage, and when you went in and he locked it, you fucking cried straight to Mama. And Kage got his ass beat with a wooden spoon."

Hadley pops her head up and scowls at me once again.

"If you're going to take a walk down memory lane, at least be honest about it, Massimo. Now tell me what urged me to want to get him in trouble."

I shake my head, annoyed at the memory.

"Fucking Uno."

"Right. You guys didn't tell me you took all the plus fours, and plus twos from four other decks, and pummeled me with them. That was not fair."

I chuckle at how serious she is, all these years later, about that stupid game.

"Uno is war, baby. There are no rules in a battle, you do what you have to, in order to win."

She tilts her head to the side, and taps her finger on her head.

"And who won that battle, Massimo? I did. It wasn't my ass getting a wooden spoon to it."

'Brat,' I mouth, and I am rewarded with a beaming smile.

"You may want to lie down. You're showing off your tits, and it's making it difficult for me to control myself."

She lies back down, and my eyes drop to her lips. I've wanted to fucking kiss her properly since I found her, but haven't, because I am really trying to not be an asshole.

"Massimo," she says in a breathy voice, as she places her hand to my face, dragging her fingers over my beard. No woman has ever touched my face; it's a simple gesture, with something deeper behind it.

Tentatively, I press my lips to hers to see how she reacts, and when I slide my tongue into her mouth, she kisses me back with eagerness, as a whimper escapes from her mouth to mine. I hold the side of her face, careful not to touch any of the swollen areas. There's a few, and I won't be surprised if she has a black eye tomorrow.

I pull back and she flutters her eyelashes as she opens her eyes, and fixes her gaze on mine. So much affection is staring at me, and it physically makes my chest hurt.

"Go to sleep, beautiful little lamb."

Settling into my arms, she closes her eyes, and she sleeps, while I lie awake watching her. I can't take my eyes off her because, while I can't predict the future, I have a feeling a dark cloud is following

me, and something is going to happen, out of my control, and she'll be gone.

Chapter Forty-Nine

HADLEY

I wake up alone, and frown, until I see the note on the bed beside me.

Good morning,

There's coffee in the kitchen. Help yourself. I'll be back in a few minutes with clothing for you.

Massimo

There were no sweet words, but still, I smile to myself, because he signed Massimo, instead of Psycho. Walking out of the bedroom, and into the living room of the hotel room, I gasp as my eyes widen. *Tell me you're loaded, without telling me you're loaded, Massimo.*

Directly in front of me is a large living space, with a black 'L' shaped sofa, a matching chaise lounge off to the side, a fireplace built into the wall on the other side, and massive floor-to-ceiling windows. To the left is the door to the hotel room, and further to the left is a kitchen, complete with black appliances, and a gold sink. Stepping over to the window, I look out at the amazing skyline, taking it in, while making a mental note to see this tonight, because I know it'll be amazing at night with all the lights.

A hand grips the back of my neck, as I'm shoved against the glass, and his body pushes against my back, as a low growl escapes from his throat, making me gasp.

"You belong to me, little lamb. Mine. I will not tolerate you showing it off to all of New York City."

Grabbing my shoulders, he spins me around, and his eyes immediately drop to my breasts before continuing downward, sweeping my body, making my skin heat, like he's touching me.

"My eyes are up here, Massimo."

His gaze snaps to mine, the intensity making my skin heat up further, as if I'm standing in front of an inferno.

"I will not tell you again. This is mine, and I will kill any man that sees you like this. Any fucking questions?"

Forcing my back to straighten, I place my hands on my hips, and reflect the same glare he's giving me.

"Is it just the two personalities you have? Or are there others that will show themselves?"

His eyes flash with amusement, as the corner of his lips lift into the smallest of smirks.

"I suggest you put clothes on this delicious body. My control is limited, and you're fucking testing it."

Rolling my eyes at him, I move around him, my body brushing up against his, as I go to grab the bag of clothing at his feet. Shivers run down my back like a bolt of electricity.

"Stupid hot jackass," I blurt out, as I take the bag and all but run back to the bedroom.

I throw the bag onto the bed with a huff. Reaching in, I pull out a pair of jeans, and a black t-shirt that has my eyebrows raising.

It has a logo on it, with a large 'B' appearing like there are wings carrying it away, and the other letters 'o-n-e-t-t-i' making me gasp.

Bonetti Luxury Hotel.

How did I not know they own hotels? They probably have hotels as a legitimate business to launder funds. I let out a long breath, and tell my brain to let it go, but my lawyer mind won't stop turning, even though I'd never do anything with it. Not now. If I had known his father didn't kill mine, I never would have.

Grabbing a pair of black lacy panties, and a matching bra from the bag, I spot a box of medication. I grab it with curiosity, and my stomach drops when I see what it is.

The morning-after pill.

After I am dressed, I take the box, storm out to Massimo, and throw it at him.

"I'm not taking this."

He jerks his chin to the glass of water on the counter.

"Yes, you are."

I pick up the glass of water, as a glint of satisfaction shows in his eyes, and down the entire glass, before slamming it on the counter.

"No, I am not."

He steps forward, and I step back repeatedly, until my back hits the wall.

"Defiant fucking brat," he says as he raises a hand, and wraps it around my throat.

"What are we fighting about, little lamb? You want to have that asshole's baby?"

I don't know why I'm refusing to take it. Obviously, I don't want to have Jimmy's child, although he used a condom anyway, so pregnancy is unlikely.

Pressing his lips to mine, he kisses me, slowly, passionately, as his tongue sweeps into my mouth, eliciting a moan from me. He licks into my mouth, as if he wants every bit of me, and groans, before pulling away.

Both of us are breathing heavily as we stare each other down.

"Let me take care of you, Hadley. I'm trying, so stop fighting me."

He releases his hand from my throat, but doesn't break his stare.

"Do we understand each other?"

I roll my eyes at him, as his flare with irritation.

"Your mood swings are giving me whiplash."

He chuckles softly as his lips lift into a smile, my heart beating faster at the sight of it, and he shakes his head at me.

"Impossible, beautiful woman, take your medicine, so we can go see my mother."

Chapter Fifty

HADLEY

"Where are we going? This isn't even the right area."

I know this isn't where his brother lives, because we are about a mile from where my mother lives, and there's no way a wealthy as fuck Bonetti lives here.

The corners of his mouth lift up into a knowing smirk.

"I have a surprise for you."

"A surprise?" I question, as he chuckles softly.

"I thought you might like to have a coffee."

Opening my mouth to speak again, I quickly snap it shut, as we pull up in front of my mother's trailer. I must be seeing things. This can't be real. My mother sits at a patio table in the front of her home. She is not in bed. Her eyes meet mine, as I jump out of the car.

"Mom?"

"Hadley," she says with an emotion filled gaze, as she opens her arms, encouraging a hug from me. I run to her, as a sob erupts from my chest. I don't understand what's happening but my mother spoke, said my name, and now I'm in her arms. It feels like she died, and years later, has been brought back to life. The loss of my mother felt as real as the loss of my father.

"Sit," she says, as I spot three cups of coffee on the patio table, and sit between my mother and Massimo. He winks at me when I glance at him.

"See. Coffee."

"Why? When?"

He takes my hand and lifts it to his lips, kissing the back gently.

"I told you I'd get specialists to see your mother, and that's what I did. Why? For you, Hadley. I can't give your father back to you, but this I could do."

I swallow past the lump in my throat, and turn to my mom.

"Are you okay?"

Reaching up, my mom gently touches the bruises on my face, as she exhales a sad sigh.

"I hate that he did this to you, and I know, without asking, it wasn't the first time. I'm sorry."

A tear rolls down my cheek, as she brushes it away with all the tenderness you'd expect a mother to have.

"I'm okay. Now, are you okay?"

She nods and admits, "I have a lot to make up for, and I will, but it'll take time. I'm a work in progress. Some days are better than others, but I have the right doctors and therapist now. Thanks to Massimo."

I look her over, like I'm checking for injuries, but it's because I'm still having trouble believing that what's in front of me is real.

"Mr. Bonetti didn't-"

She holds her hand up, telling me to stop talking, and I do.

"We had bad information, and I think we both know that now. I've made so many mistakes, Hadley. You're a stranger to me now, and that's my doing. I hope you'll let me at least try to fix things between us."

We drink our coffee, and talk about everything past and present. It feels good to have my mother back. I don't want to leave her here, but I know we can't stay here all day.

I glance at Massimo with a questioning look, and as if he understands my thoughts, he nods slowly.

"Mom, we have to go see Mama Bonetti. Would you like to come? I'm sure she'd want to see you."

I'm really not all that sure if that's the truth, but I go with it anyway, hoping it's the case.

She shakes her head no, and speaks after a sad smile crosses her face.

"No, honey. Not today. Baby steps, and today should be about you. I would like it if you'd go with me soon to your father's grave."

I nod. "And Michael's."

My mother sighs, with her hand over her heart.

"I will never forgive myself for not being his grandmother. I should have been there, but I was barely aware of anything outside of my grief."

She's not wrong, and I am not sure I'll ever understand how it happened. How do you lose yourself like that, and all but forget you have a daughter who needs you?

Rising from my chair, I hug my mom.

"I love you. I'm glad you're back where you belong."

Massimo growls.

"This is not where she fucking belongs, and she's moving, as soon as I find an appropriate house for her."

Both my mother and I exchange a glance, but neither of us says a word. Leaving is hard, because I worry that, when I come back, things will be back the way they were. For now, I try to enjoy the gift he has given me.

"Thank you," I whisper when we get back into the car.

Chapter Fifty-One
PSYCHO

She has fidgeted for the entire drive, appearing nervous about seeing my mother. Hadley doesn't realize she has nothing to worry about, unless hugs are a problem. My mother is likely to sweep her into her arms, and never let go. Mama felt the loss, when her mother took her away, more than any of us. She considered Hadley a daughter, and it took years for her to come to terms with it. As I pull in front of Bones and Athena's house, she chews on her lip, riddled with anxiety, as I grab her hand, pull it to my lips, and kiss the back softly.

"Do your brothers want me dead?"

It's the first time she has asked about them, so I'm taken aback, but it does make perfect sense that she'd be concerned about her safety.

"Baby, I would never let them fucking touch you, but I'm pretty sure at least one of them is afraid of you."

She glances at me incredulously.

"I'm sure the big, bad Bonetti brothers are afraid of me."

I arch an eyebrow at her and chuckle.

"Little lamb, you are the first woman we have ever seen roast a dick, cut it into pieces, and feed it to the owner. Any man would be at least a little afraid after seeing that."

I put my SUV into park as she giggles softly. I kiss her on the lips before I get out and walk around to her side, opening the door for her. We turn to walk toward the door, and there stands my mother, already sobbing, with her hands covering her face.

The emotion is thick as my mother races toward her, takes her into her arms, and, as I suspected, holds her like she may never let her go.

"Mama, can we go inside now?"

She removes her hold on my girl, taking her hands and appraising her. Spotting the yellow bruises on her face, she shakes her head with disapproval.

"My sweet Hadley."

Mama brushes the side of her cheek softly, and says, "You're home now, where you belong, with my Massimo. He will love you the way you deserve."

I nearly choke on my goddamn tongue. Does she even know me? I don't fucking love. If I tried, I'd need some fucking idiot's guide, because I don't have a clue how it feels, or how it happens. The cold hard truth is, I don't want it. I don't want what my brothers have, being all consumed by a woman. Losing control, because they are always the target with our enemies. It's not lost on me, that is what I just went through with her, but that wasn't related to my family. That was all because of her piece of shit ex.

I rub the spot on my chest as I order them both inside. We walk in, and are immediately greeted by the entire family. Reaper, Kage, and Bones stand to the side, as our women meet for the first time, except, of course, she has already met Raina, who stares at her with tear-filled eyes, before she darts her gaze to me, and a glare washes away her emotion.

I should've fucking killed her.

Raina is a pain in the ass, but she doesn't own responsibility for Hadley coming after us, or anything that happened before, leading to it. Even if I don't like a person, I will never shift responsibility for my purpose.

Bella, my serial killer sister-in-law, takes Hadley's hand and beams, as her gaze darts between mine and my girl's.

"You're my actual hero," she croons, before adding, "I want all the details."

"Bella," I snap, and nod to my mother.

Mama stares at me and shakes her head.

"I already know, figlio. I don't like it, but he deserved it."

She knows the type of men we are, but we don't give her details. Normally. I don't know who told her, or why, but she didn't need that information. We try to protect her as much as we can.

Bones jerks his jaw toward the kitchen, summoning us, and I lean down, kissing Hadley on the forehead, before I follow after my brothers.

My brother passes us all a glass of whiskey, before darting his gaze, to make sure the women aren't within earshot, before he speaks.

"I've been doing some digging, with a little help from Benji."

I nod my understanding, urging him to continue.

"You aren't going to like this, brother. Other than Jimmy, Carlo has had one visitor coming to see him weekly."

Glaring at him, ready to bark at him to spit it out, he says, "Danielle."

"Who the fuck is Danielle?"

Bones arches an eyebrow at me, as if I should know the answer to my question.

"Mindar."

"Oh, fuck," Kage says beside me, but I don't say a word, because my goddamn mind is reeling.

"Is he turning?" I finally ask.

Bones shrugs his shoulders, before taking a gulp of his drink.

"I don't fucking know, but it can't be good, either way."

"It's awfully early for whiskey, boys," Athena sing-songs as she walks into the kitchen, and goes straight for my brother.

"Butterfly." Bones gazes down at her, with so much love, it nearly makes me physically ill. He places his hand on her swollen belly, and kisses her.

"Go meet Hadley. We'll be with you in a few minutes."

Danielle, the only girlfriend I ever had. She was using me for her father, high up in the FBI, and her only goal was to get information on my family.

"I want him out, Bones."

He nods in understanding.

"I know, brother, and if it were Athena, I'd want the same thing, but there are logistics involved."

I arch an eyebrow, and glare at him, intending to make myself abundantly clear.

"If it's not possible, I'll walk into that prison, and kill anybody that stands between me and Carlo. It's not an if, it's when. He will not continue breathing after what he has done to her."

And then it happens. I should have seen it coming, but I didn't. The knife stabs into my goddamn ass, as I grab Kage by the throat and groan.

"Asshole."

He grins at me, like the cat that ate the canary.

Fucker stabbed me in the ass.

Chapter Fifty-Two

HADLEY

Mama Bonetti takes my hand and tilts her head in question.

"Let's go sit outside for a few minutes, so we can talk alone."

While it has been a while, I know that look well, and it wasn't a question but more of a statement, an order, no room for negotiation.

I rise from the sofa, all three of the brothers' wives eyeing me warily, as I follow her to the French doors that lead to the patio, and an expansive yard, with an in-ground pool. I wonder if all their houses look like a luxury hotel, as I glance around. More expertly manicured gardens, although this one less impressive than Massimo's was, before the fire. We take a seat at a black wrought-iron table, with a large blue umbrella overhead. Within minutes, a man brings us both orange juice.

She winks at me with a grin. "Mimosas, because this is a celebration."

I nod my thanks and take a sip of the drink, and it's delicious. It's not only orange juice and champagne. There's something sweeter in it, that I can't place.

Mrs. Bonetti smiles. "Mango."

Reaching across the table, she takes my hand in hers, with a sad expression, as she gazes over at me.

"Lorenzo did not kill your father, sweetheart. He wouldn't have."

I swallow hard, my eyes stinging from tears threatening to fall.

"I know," I whisper.

"What made you come to that conclusion, Hadley? Make me understand why you came after my sons."

The guilt is heavy as she stares at me, searching my face for answers, and I hate myself more than I ever thought possible. This woman was good to me, and I was wrong about everything.

"After my father was killed, things became difficult. As you know, my mother moved us out of our house, and into a trailer park. She refused to use any of my father's money, because it was 'blood money' from Mr. Bonetti."

I take a sip of my drink and she does the same, giving me a minute before I continue my regretful story.

"I was only twelve, but I was suspicious because of that. In my mind, he must have had a part in it, if my mother would prefer us to live in poverty, than to use the money he had worked so hard for."

I sigh audibly.

"I was fourteen when I met Carlo. After two years of living off food you left on our porch every Sunday, he was a welcome reprieve. He provided for me; I had food, and clothing. Whatever I needed, he provided for me. When he told me he was from a mafia family, I didn't bat an eye, because I grew up around yours. When you're young, you don't know what you don't know."

She laughs lightly.

"That is not something we grow out of, *figlia*."

My throat burns at the endearing term she once used for me. *Daughter.*

"I believed everything he told me. He told me he had gotten information from his father, that Mr. Bonetti had killed my father, and wanted everyone to know, as a message to all families. Carlo said, if he'd do that to his own men, imagine what he'd do to enemies."

A tear I have been fighting falls down my cheek, as I do the only thing I can do at this point; apologize.

"I'm sorry. I believed the words of a monster. Our entire relationship was built on manipulation, and I should have known. If you never trust me again, I understand."

She gets up, scoots her chair beside me, and places her arm around my shoulders, pulling me into her while I sob.

"My sweet Hadley, the past is over now. No harm was done. It's water under the bridge. Now, we rebuild, and remain grateful for another chance. I was afraid I would die without ever seeing you again."

I hear the door open, but it's behind me, so I don't see whoever is standing there.

"What did you do?" Massimo growls.

"Massimo, get!" she barks in response.

Turning in my chair, my eyes snap to his dark gaze, filled with concern. The way he stares at me, with an intensity that could start a forest fire, makes it difficult to break away.

"Are you okay?" He asks, causing me to break into a fit of giggles.

"Other than the severe case of whiplash, I'm fine. We'll be in shortly."

When Massimo heads back inside, I face his mother again, and she smiles.

"He loves you."

I shake my head no, because he doesn't. He has made that clear, and while she has only seen a few moments of concern, she has not seen everything. The things he has done to me shout hate, not love.

"It's not like that between us."

She tilts her head, and gazes at me incredulously.

"Am I to believe you're only friends?"

I bark out an insincere laugh, and shake my head.

"No, not friends either. Frenemies."

She laughs along with me, but says, "We'll see. I've seen how my son looks at you. Massimo, my guarded boy, will realize what he has. I just hope it's not too late by then."

259

Chapter Fifty-Three

PSYCHO

It only took two weeks for the workers to fix my house, although the gardens Hadley loves so much were destroyed. I promised her the gardener would make it right, but it'll take time. I haven't touched her much at all, because I'm trying to not be an asshole with her, and let her decide when it's right. For her. It's completely at odds with the man I am. I'm used to taking what I want, when I want it, but I'm truly afraid of pushing her too far. Hadley acts like she's fine, but I know she's not. I see it in her far away glances, the way she sits in a spot, still as stone, before her hands tremble, yet she won't talk to me about it. When I move the hair that's fallen on her face, the way she flinches from my touch, it all tells me what those assholes did to her is still with her.

I sit in my office working, when something on my camera feed catches my eye. What the fuck is she doing? Pulling up camera three to get a closer look, I expand it so it covers my entire screen, as I watch Hadley crawl across my living room floor. Turning the sound up all the way, I hear her heavy breathing, along with a strangled sob, and get off my chair and race to her.

When I reach her, I stand staring at her like an idiot, unsure what to do. It's clear she's not here, but remembering what she went through. She has had a few nightmares since I found her in that goddamn hole, but this is new. Every few minutes, she screams out like someone is striking her, and I'm not sure I've ever been so fucking lost in my life.

Dropping to my knees, I say her name softly, afraid of making things worse.

"Hadley. Baby, it's me."

Her face is drenched with tears, and her eyes are wide, with what can only be described as sheer terror. For the first time, I can see what I did to her, what she must have gone through, and it does not fucking feel good. When I was a boy, my mother frequently said to be careful what you wish for, because you might actually get it. She's broken, exactly like I wanted her to be, as the truth crashes into my chest.

Her pain is my pain.

Hurting her means hurting myself.

I pull her into my arms, and hold her tight against me.

"Hadley, come back to me, little lamb."

She blinks fast at the sound of my voice, as if she's trying to adjust to new surroundings, before gasping my name.

"Massimo."

I haven't held her in my arms since that first night, because she hasn't wanted me to. Maybe I'm an asshole, but I like it when she wraps her arms around me, and clings to me like I'm the only thing holding her together. I've had several conversations with my brother, Bones, about her state of mind, and the nightmares haunting her. She has refused to talk to a therapist, but right now I'm thinking Bones is right. I need to force the issue.

"Hadley."

She tilts her head back, and gazes at me the way she used to when we were kids. Like I'm a fucking hero, and I almost wish I was worthy of her devotion.

"I'm going to make an appointment for you to talk through this shit, with someone that can help you. You went through a lot, not just with Jimmy, but the loss of your little boy."

I can see it in her eyes, she is considering fighting me on this once again, but this time I won't give in. Personally, I'd never talk to someone about the shit in my head. Hell, they'd probably fucking lock me away, but she needs this, and I know Athena saw someone for a while and it helped.

She nods slowly.

"Alright, but can you just hold me a little longer?"

I rise to my feet, holding her in my arms, walk to the couch and sit down. Hadley lays her head on my shoulder, and breathes out a sweet sigh.

"I love you," she whispers softly, and I want to give her the words back. It's what she's desperate to hear, but I can't, so I just hold her.

Chapter Fifty-Four
PSYCHO

Three Months Later...

I sit behind my desk as the frustration builds, not only behind my eyes, but in my pants. Hadley has tortured me for days, by brushing up against me with her ass, as she pretends like there isn't enough room to get by me. When I kiss her, she sucks on my tongue like she did my cock, and every fucking day it's all I can do to control myself. Now, I turn on my camera system to check on her, she knows damn well they're there, and she lies on my bed in a black lacy negligee, with her hand between her legs. She tosses her head back, stares right at the goddamn camera, and moans loudly.

"Massimo."

Rising from my chair, I storm to the bedroom, open the door and slam it behind me. She freezes, with her hand covering her pretty pussy, eyes wide with what I'm guessing is mock surprise.

"Are you trying to kill me, little lamb?"

"No," she says in a breathy voice.

I move over to her, rip her hand from her pussy, and press her fingers to my nose, inhaling deeply.

"Fuck."

My eyes trail the length of her barely covered body, as I fist the back of my shirt, pulling it over my head. Her tits rise and fall with heavy breaths, as she watches me, waiting to see what I am going to do.

"Everything, Hadley. That's what I'm going to do to you. Fucking everything."

Removing my pants and my boxers, I take my cock into my hand and stroke it slowly, as she watches me with rapt attention, while licking her lips. I climb over her and she speaks seductively.

"Fuck me, Massimo."

I shake my head at her.

"Oh no, little lamb. You have tormented me for days, so now it's your turn. I will take my time having you. By the time I sink inside your pussy, you'll be begging for my cock."

Thrusting her hips up, pushing her pussy against my cock, she moans my name again, knowing damn well what she's doing to me. Ripping apart her lingerie, I brush my thumb over her nipple piercings, one and then the other.

I run my hands between her tits, dragging my fingers down the center of her chest.

"When you were twelve years old, I told you I would one day own you, and now I do. My pretty little lamb, only I dictate when you will come. Or if."

She digs her fingers into the mattress, as I run mine from her throat to her collarbone, and slowly to her shoulder.

I replace my fingers with my mouth and tongue, and a whimper escapes from her throat, that turns into a yelp when I bite the side of her tit, before it morphs back into a whimper, when I lick where I bit.

"Maybe, next time, you'll tell me what you need, instead of torturing both of us."

Moving down her body, I swipe my tongue over one nipple and then the other, before slowly trailing kisses down her abdomen. The marks are still there, although much lighter than they were, but still serve as a reminder of what happened. I'm fighting to ignore the need to shove my cock inside her, and replace the last one that was there. The only reason I'm not doing it is because it wasn't her choice. I will not punish her for something she has not chosen.

Pushing her legs back, unable to control myself, I push my face to her pussy and inhale.

Fuck.

I would happily drown in her if I could. Her scent is all her, and I allow it to invade my senses, and take over, as I will it to my memory. The fear that something could happen to take her from me is visceral, and always present.

"I'm sorry. Please, I need your cock inside me."

Glancing up at her, I arch a brow, before my lips turn up into a smirk.

"If you need me to fuck you so badly, you better behave, and drench my face, baby."

Sliding my tongue up her center, from opening to clit, she grabs onto my hair and bucks, her hips already trying to ride my face. So goddamn needy and perfect. I bite down on her clit, and she tightens her grip on my hair, as she swears at me until I lick, taking away the sting. Running my tongue back down her center, I push it inside her pussy, and her hands move to my shoulders, digging into my skin as she sits up slightly, watching me.

"Please, Massimo," she sobs, snapping my eyes to hers, as I realize she's crying.

"Why are you crying, baby?"

Hadley squeezes her eyes shut tight, and I allow it, because I just want to fucking know what the hell is going on.

"Until you're inside me, he's the last man that fucked me. I need it in the past, Massimo. I'm sorry for playing with you, but I thought it would speed it up, not prolong it. Please. I'm begging you to replace the memory with a new one."

I get onto the bed, and sit with my back against the headboard.

"Come here, and sit on my cock."

Hadley crawls up the bed toward me, looking sexy as fuck, and causing my cock to weep more for her. She straddles my thighs, and I hold my cock for her, as she sinks down on it, both of us gasping when she's seated fully.

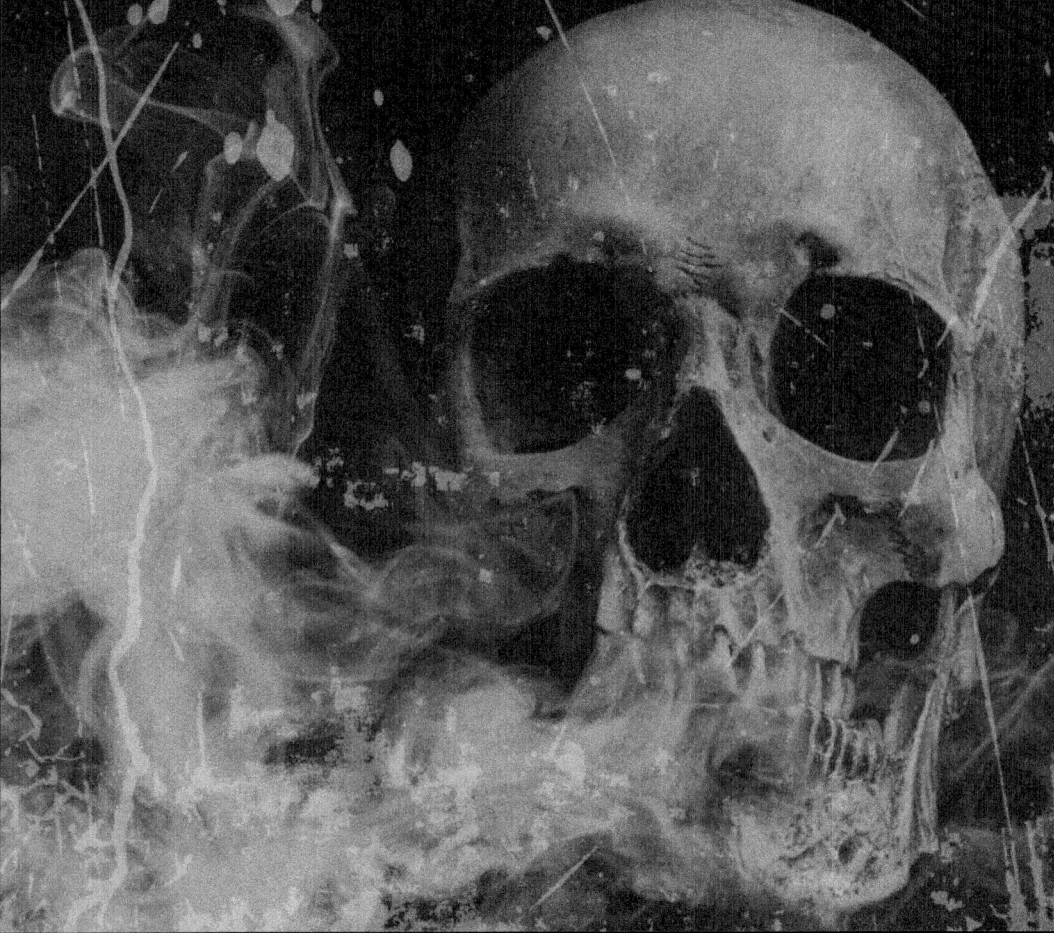

I take her face in my hands, pull her head close to mine, and kiss her, as I wrap my arms around her back, holding her close to me, while she moves up and down on my length. My tongue slides against hers, and she gives back as good as she gets, like she's fighting me for dominance.

When our mouths separate, the drunk gaze in her eyes is fucking beautiful, as she lays her head on my shoulder, her breath on my neck as she gasps, "Massimo, I love you."

'I know' is not an appropriate response, so I say nothing, and pretend I didn't hear her.

She glides up and down my cock effortlessly, until her pussy squeezes me like a vise, her orgasm shattering her, while mine is stolen from me before I have a chance to hold back, so I can fuck her longer. I fill her completely, and she moans as I spasm inside her.

"Thank you," she whispers against my neck.

Chapter Fifty-Five

HADLEY

Six Weeks Later...

Six unreturned I love yous, and I've reached my breaking point. I'm nothing to Massimo, other than a pussy to fuck, and I'm done. I deserve better than this, don't I? I think I do, but maybe he's right, when he says he isn't capable of feelings that deep. I've become friendly with the other wives, even being added to their brat chat on *Facebook*, but they have something Massimo and I don't have. And I crave it.

I storm to the kitchen, where I find Massimo sipping his coffee, while his fingers fly over the keyboard on his phone.

"Love me, or let me go," I blurt out, immediately getting his attention.

"What?"

"Do I deserve a loveless life, Massimo? Is that what you think? I'm not worthy?"

He rises from his chair and walks over to me, with a confused expression on his handsome face.

"What's happening?"

I clench my fists at my sides to stop myself from touching him, because I've learned I have little willpower once Massimo's body becomes involved.

"Love me, or let me go," I say, in a voice barely above a whisper.

His response, while expected, cracks my chest wide open.

"You want a man that will love you, and I can't be that for you. Do you deserve that? You fucking deserve everything, baby."

Tears roll down my cheeks, as he stares at me with an anguished expression on his face.

"You owe me this, Massimo. You fucking owe me this!" I muster a scream.

He goes to touch me, but instantly withdraws his hands, setting them in fists at his sides. His eyes stay on mine, and the intensity threatens to burn me from the inside out, as he speaks low.

"I know I do, but what you're asking of me is impossible. I know how to hurt, but I have no capacity for love."

Hanging my head down in defeat, I shake my head in disappointment, and say, "Then let me go."

"If this is what you want, go. As you know, your car is outside. Open the door, walk through it, and drive out of my life. If you no longer want this, you may go."

I hold my purse tight, like it's a bulletproof vest, as what feels like bullets penetrate my chest. Turning away from him, I walk to the door, put my hand on the door handle, and speak without turning toward him before I leave.

"You are worthy of love, Massimo, and capable of it. Maybe I'm not the woman that can bring that out of you, but I see your heart. It's beautiful, although reserved for few. Massimo Bonetti, I have loved you since I was a girl. Even when I tried to hate you, I still loved you. I think I always will. My only regret is that I am not enough. Goodbye, Massimo."

I turn the doorknob, and open the door to the sun shining bright, a complete contradiction to the storm brewing inside my heart.

Fortress around Massimo's heart: 1

Hadley: 0

Chapter Fifty-Six
PSYCHO

I rub the same damn spot on my chest that has me wondering if a heart attack is around the corner for me. Walking to the door, Hadley stands beside her car, keys in hand, and I'm assaulted by memories of everything her. I'm still reeling from her saying she isn't enough. If anything, I'm not enough, but she's goddamn perfect.

There's a deep desire to let her be happy. As the ache in my chest worsens, I know that's not possible. I can't let her go.

I call Sean, my guard at the gate.

"Do not open those fucking gates. I don't care what she says, or how much she pleads. If you open them, it won't end well for you."

I don't bother with his response before I end the call. Switching my coffee for whiskey, I pour two fingers, drink it, and wait. One hour and twelve minutes later, the front door opens, as I fight the smile on my face. Hadley storms over to me, the halo around her irises more prominent than usual. Her fists are clenched, as she stares at me with something that looks like hatred, even though I know otherwise.

"Fucking asshole!" She screams, as she continues her best angry stare. It's pretty fucking convincing. I lean my head over, looking behind her.

"What are you looking at?"

I chuckle low, as I admit, "You came tearing in here with so much hostility, I was checking for fire behind your pretty little ass."

Placing her hands on her hips, she throws one hip out with such fucking attitude, and it's goddamn adorable.

"Seriously, Massimo? You think this is funny?"

Slowly, I drag my gaze from her feet up her body, trailing every delicious inch, taking it all in, before landing back on her eyes.

"I think it's funny you thought I'd let you go."

I keep to myself that I tried letting her walk away, and physically felt unwell. My obsession is out of control, but it's too late to fix that now.

She raises her fists, and I grab her wrists, not wanting her to get hurt, which is exactly what's going to happen, if she punches me in the chest.

"Why, Massimo, why?"

I give her the only truth I know, as I yank her to my chest, and hold her tight in my grip.

"I don't know what the fuck it's called, little lamb, but it hurts when you're not near me. My chest constricts, and I can't fucking breathe. I'll never be the man you deserve. I'm not going to marry you, and give you fucking babies. Don't you think I know you are worth more than I can give you? It's not because you're not enough. *I'm* not enough. I can't fucking let you go. I'm far too selfish of a bastard to live without you."

Pulling back, she gazes at me with unshed tears in her eyes, as she places her hand on my chest, right over my heart.

"You love me, Massimo."

Hanging my head in defeat, I admit it, because running from it has gotten me nowhere.

"Yeah, maybe I do, baby. I just hope this is enough."

She runs her fingers over my cheek, stroking through my beard, before taking her hand to my chin, and lifting my head back.

"It is. I don't need everything else, Massimo. Only you."

Grabbing her ass, I pull her onto my lap so she straddles me, and she wraps her arms around my neck, running her fingers through the hair at the nape of my neck. I groan lightly as she leans down to kiss me.

Her soft lips on mine, as she sucks my tongue into her mouth, make me want her mouth on every inch of my skin, but that will have to wait. I lift her with me as I rise from the chair, and head to our bedroom. Setting her on her feet, I lick my lips while I gaze at my girl.

Mine.

"Get undressed while I get set up."

She flashes me a 'what the fuck' look, but does as I told her to. Hadley undresses, while watching me hook the chains to the headboard, and if she questions it, she doesn't say a word. Once she's naked, she climbs on the bed and stays silent, while I cuff her wrists to the headboard, and attach her legs to the spreader bar.

"What?" she says, causing me to chuckle.

"Spreader bar. If you spread wider, it'll lock you in place, and I can help if you don't."

I yank on the bar, and she gasps as her cheeks blush beautifully. My gaze drops between her legs, and I groan at the sight of her pussy on display for me, spread, and waiting for me.

Her eyes continue to follow me, as I move to my dresser and remove her vibrator.

"Oh my God."

Standing at the foot of the bed, I take a moment to drink in her beauty.

"Fucking stunning."

She looks like a filthy angel lying on our bed, arms restrained, legs wide open, hair splayed around her shoulders, and eyes on me, waiting for me to make her come undone. Fisting my shirt, I remove it and toss it behind me, as Hadley stares at me like her mouth is watering. I fucking love the way she gazes at me with hunger.

Lifting her head to get a better look at me, she watches as I remove my pants and boxers.

"Fuck," she moans, when I take my cock into my hand, and stroke it for her.

I turn as if I'm going to leave, with a smile she can't see.

"I'll be back. I'm hungry."

"I swear to God, Massimo. I'll fucking stab you."

Glancing over my shoulder, I raise an eyebrow and chuckle.

"That'll be a little difficult, baby, in your current predicament."

Going back over to her, I climb between her legs and blow on her clit, and she moans loudly.

"I was kidding, little lamb. This pretty pussy is the only thing I want to eat."

"It's not pretty," she bites, and I run two fingers up her slit.

"This one is, Hadley. Fucking beautiful. So pink for me, I know it's throbbing, and so fucking drenched."

I flick the knife piercing in her hood as she yelps.

"This jewelry, which is a symbol that you're mine, only makes it more stunning. So fucking pretty," I say, as I flick my tongue over her needy clit. Hadley yanks on the chains, as I put my lips around her clit and suck hard.

"Massimo," she cries, in a breathy moan that has my dick ready to burst.

Grabbing the vibrator, I push it inside her pussy and turn it on, while I continue licking and sucking her clit.

I slowly fuck her with the toy, as she writhes for me, and I know she needs more, but I don't give it to her, because she needs to learn to put a voice to her desires.

"Do you know why I have you bound like this, little lamb?"

I look up at her wide eyes, and she groans pathetically.

"Because you're sadistic."

I chuckle softly, and admit, "Maybe a little, but that's not why. There is nothing you can do to control your body. It's all mine, to do what I want to it. You have only one way to get what you need, by telling me what that is. I suggest you start using your voice to tell me, or this could go on all fucking day."

I fuck her slower and, yes, I know she wants it faster, but I want her to tell me, in her words, what the fuck she wants, instead of leaving it up to me. Hadley didn't have good sexual experiences prior to me. That piece of shit she married didn't give a fuck about her pleasure, but I do.

"Hadley," I growl.

"I want it harder, Massimo. I want you to fuck me hard, with your cock. Not a piece of plastic."

Climbing onto my knees, I fuck her hard with the vibrator, and watch, as it slides in and out of her pussy. I know she wants my cock, and she'll get it, but fuck, this is for me.

"So beautiful, baby, you're dripping for me."

Withdrawing the toy, I move forward, grab onto the spreader bar, and line my cock up with her pussy, slamming into her as she yelps from the intrusion.

"You said you wanted it hard, and that's what you're getting."

I jackhammer her as she whimpers for me, and I watch her pretty pierced tits moving with every thrust.

"Fuck!" she yells, as she shatters for me, back arching off the bed. The way she trembles with her orgasm is intoxicating.

"Good girl. Fucking beautiful."

I pick up my pace and fuck her even harder, my breaths harsh, as I chase my own climax. This woman drives me crazy, and her pussy wrapped around my cock is like heaven.

Chapter Fifty-Seven

HADLEY

Massimo spent the entire day fucking me, and I'm hoping it makes him sleep well, because what I have planned tonight will only get accomplished if he's sleeping. I know I won't get the entire job done, but half is enough for me. Last night while he was in the shower, I went to the basement and got the supplies, so I'm ready, and as his breathing evens out, I smile.

Time for a little payback, Massimo.

Slipping out of bed as quietly as possible, I open the drawer to the night-stand, grabbing the jewelry and needle. I lower myself onto the side of the bed, where Massimo sleeps soundly. He hisses when I swipe the alcohol over his nipple, but he doesn't wake up. Holding his nipple firmly, I push the prepared needle through. Much to my surprise he doesn't wake up, I don't know how, but he's still as a board, so I do the same thing to his other nipple. The adrenaline is coursing through my veins, because when he wakes up and sees this, I'm probably going to be in trouble. I smile to myself at the thought. It'll be worth it. He deserves this. Maybe next time he'll think twice, before doing something to me without asking first.

Reaching over to the table, I place the needles there, along with the alcohol packets. In one swift movement, Massimo grabs my wrists, and I'm underneath him, as he stares at me with a heated gaze.

His eyes darken to the shade of coal, my hands pinned to the mattress beside my head, and my heart is pounding so hard I think I hear it in my eardrums.

"Did you enjoy yourself, little lamb?" He says in a deep, low, threatening tone. I open my mouth to answer, but the words get trapped in my throat. I shake my head no in response, as his lips lift into a smirk.

"You made me bleed… now lick it up."

Finally, I find my voice and say, "I don't want you to get an infection."

Massimo narrows his gaze and growls.

"We play dangerously, baby. I'll take my chances. Fucking lick. Now."

Lifting my head, as much as I can, I swipe my tongue across one of his nipples as he groans, not with pain, but pure desire.

"What do you think your punishment should be, Hadley?"

Narrowing my gaze at him, I all but yell.

"You've got to be fucking kidding me, Massimo? Did I punish you when you pierced me without consent?"

"You will be punished," he repeats.

My eyes widen as my entire body tenses, and he doesn't miss it. Shaking his head, his gaze penetrates mine, with a potency that sends shivers down my spine.

"No, baby. No belt. I will hurt you, because I like it, and so do you, but I'll never do what he did to you. I'll never do anything that could result in permanently losing you."

Death. He means he won't kill me, like he who shall not be named tried to. So many fucking times.

Releasing my wrist, he trails his fingers down my arm, to my breast, as he lightly touches the piercing he put there, before pinching my nipple hard, and chuckling when I yelp from the sting.

"Brave little lamb."

"Stupid lamb," I retort.

Massimo shakes his head, with a low chuckle escaping from his throat.

"Brave," he repeats, "You are fucking mesmerizing, little lamb. Few women would have had the nerve to pierce my goddamn nipples while I slept. You knew exactly what you were doing, and

I'm sure you knew there would be consequences, yet, you did it anyway. Stupidity would be doing it, and thinking nothing would happen. Bravery is doing it, knowing full well, there will be repercussions, but seeking your vengeance anyway."

Kneeling with my legs between his, he turns me over to my stomach, leaning over me, and I hear him getting things off the side table. I can't see what he's taking, because I'm face down on the bed, but I already know his knife is one of the things.

I whimper when I feel the metal of his knife, dragging down the center of my back.

He chuckles darkly.

"Relax, baby. That's the spine of the blade."

Lifting me by the hips, until I'm on my knees, I feel him shifting behind me, moving back slightly.

"Tell me, little lamb. Do you have any regrets?"

Do I tell him the truth, or what I think he wants to hear? My silence is more telling than words could ever be.

"The truth, Hadley. Always the fucking truth."

"No," I breathe, as the tension in my body builds, anticipating the cut that I'm sure is coming.

"Mmm," he hums, "Good girl. Always act with intention. Life is too fucking short for regrets, little lamb. Do whatever the fuck you want, but own it."

The knife cuts into the flesh on my ass, and I hiss from the sting, my fingers digging into the sheets. Massimo groans, as he leans down and drags his tongue through my blood, before dipping it into my pussy.

"This is my favorite flavor. I've never tasted anything like it. The mixture of your pussy, and your blood, on my tongue, is fucking heaven."

"Bloodthirsty wolf," I breathe out, as I let the pain and equal pleasure envelop me.

He chuckles darkly against my ass, his breath fanning over my skin, causing me to stifle a moan.

Pressing the knife into my other cheek, he immediately swipes his tongue through the blood there, before he speaks low.

"I am a bloodthirsty wolf, little lamb. You will always be my greatest hunger, that can never be satisfied. I'll always need more."

Massimo drags his cock up and down my slit, increasing my need as well as my breathing. This is what he does to me; he doesn't make me want him, he makes me need him in the most visceral way. And I crave it.

"Now, the pretty little lamb owns the wolf, as he does her. Any man who has ever hurt her will be slaughtered. Your vengeance is now mine. Together we will take the retribution owed to you. It won't be swift justice, it'll be slow. Agonizing."

His words are a promise, to heal what's broken inside me. I'll take what he has offered me, but every day, he heals me. Massimo isn't a sweet man, he never has been, and never will be. I don't need gentle, I only need him.

Slamming into me, he fills me like only he can, and a gasp escapes from my lips as he rails me like he hates me, but I know he doesn't.

He reaches his hand underneath me and lifts me, so I'm riding him, with my back against his front.

Wrapping his hand around my throat, he squeezes lightly, as he continues moving in and out of me at a vicious pace.

"Fuck," he growls into my ear, as my pussy clenches down on his cock, like it wants to keep him inside forever.

He sinks his teeth into my neck, and licks where he bit, turning the sting to pleasure, and it's an apt description of our story. Massimo will bite, and cause pain, but he always takes it away.

Epilogue

PSYCHO

Getting Carlo Bianchi out of prison was an expensive endeavor. As it turns out, paying off every guard working, as well as the warden, takes a lot of fucking cash. Glancing at Hadley perusing my knives makes it all worth it. She wants this, hell, maybe she needs it.

"What about this one?" She asks, pointing to a nine-inch serrated blade.

I tried to give her my favorite knife, but she refused it, not wanting to use it on this piece of shit, since I frequently use it on her. There was no argument from me because, of course, I don't want her thinking of this asshole when she's in bed with me, or any other time. It's one of the biggest reasons we are doing this in one of my warehouses, instead of our home. It's best for her to not have physical recollections of her past, where we will share our life together.

"That one will hurt, but if you don't want him to die fast, you have to be sure to not insert it too deep."

I catch Carlo's wide eyes, as he lays strapped to the table. Stepping over to him, I rip the duct tape from his mouth, grinning at him humorlessly as he yells from the pain, which makes me laugh, because that is nothing close to what he'll experience.

"Time to spill your secrets, Bianchi."

"Fuck you," he spits.

Hadley comes over, having chosen her knife, and slides it down his limp dick.

"Do you know what I did to Jimmy?"

He shakes his head profusely, as tears spring to his eyes, and I stand back to watch the glorious show.

"Fuck. Stop."

Piercing his ball sack, she continues talking, and I fucking love the way she's elevating his fear. Playing with him while she tortures him.

"I torched his dick."

Much to my surprise, his eyes grow wider, and I chuckle at the thought that he hasn't even heard the worst part yet.

"Then I cut it off and fed it to him. I was nice though, and cut it into bite-size pieces, so he didn't choke."

He stares at Hadley like he is seeing her for the first time, and I'd bet money that he has never seen her like this. She was his victim, now she's my violent angel, taking back what belongs to her. It's fucking beautiful.

"What the fuck happened to you?" He asks, as he continues gazing at her with shock plastered in his expression.

She arches a brow, as if mystified that he can possibly not know the answer to that question.

"You did," she says, with no emotion to her voice, I know it's there but, fuck, I'm proud of her for not showing him weakness, not giving him any power to hurt her further.

"I'm sorry," he says, but it doesn't reflect in his eyes. He is sorry as fuck, but not for hurting her, he is sorry he ended up in this position.

She laughs sardonically, as she drags the blade across his abdomen, and he hisses in pain.

"Oh, well, why didn't you say so, Carlo? If you're sorry, that makes up for you beating me, choking me, and killing my son. Doesn't it?"

When she drags the knife down the center of his chest, I warn her, "Go slow, baby. I know you want to make him suffer, but we need answers."

I can't help but put my arm around her waist when she steps back, because my world is not quite fucking right, if I don't have my hands on her.

"Who killed her father, Carlo?"

The bleeding is minimal at this point, but he's clearly pissed, as he flashes me a glare. He doesn't speak to her, but to me.

"Tell that crazy bitch to put the knife down, or I'll take that to my fucking grave."

"Hadley."

Now it's her turning to me with a glare, and I stare back, with the promise in my gaze that she'll get what she deserves. It has taken us months to get to this point, and my girl has been losing patience, but I want her to have the goddamn closure she needs. I also have some concern that if she doesn't find out the truth, somewhere in the back of her mind, she'll think maybe my family did it, and I can't have that standing between us.

"Talk."

"We did. My family, and yes, I was part of it. Everything was orchestrated. Meeting her was planned, killing her father, telling her that the Bonettis did it. Danielle's involvement. Every fucking bit of it. Except Michael. Her getting pregnant was never part of the fucking plan."

"Danielle?" I question, feeling like I've been punched in the gut at the mere mention of her name. Her father is high up in the FBI's Organized Crime division, so she couldn't be involved with this.

"It was all staged. Your father being arrested, and her coming clean about feeding her father information to take you down. It was all to divert your attention. We killed Amici, because my father wanted your weapons business."

Our weapons business, it's always about the fucking guns.

I grip Hadley a little tighter, running my fingers just up her shirt to feel her skin, while the pain in my chest grows as thoughts of my father filter in.

"How was that going to get our weapons business?"

"It showed that he could not be trusted. If he murdered one of his own men with such callousness, caring nothing about his family, it meant everyone should watch their backs with the Bonettis. The plan was to kill her afterward, in the same manner, but then she got pregnant, and my father wanted to use the baby as leverage."

I have never looked into the date when he was arrested, never asked when Michael was born, I never fucking asked any of this shit, but now that it's staring me in the goddamn face, I do.

"Hadley, how old were you when you got pregnant?"

"Fourteen," she whispers, as if she's ashamed, but it's not her that's causing my blood to fucking boil.

"How old were you?"

I know he's older than her, but I'm not one hundred percent sure how much older.

"Twenty-four," he answers, and the bile rises in my throat. She was a goddamn child, and he fucked her. Then he beat her repeatedly, and took her son from her, in the most fucking traumatic way.

"Do your worst, little lamb. I'm going to sit and watch you make him bleed, for everything he has done to you. For your son. Take as much, or as little, time as you want to. This is for you. If you need me, I'll be here, but this is your stage."

I kiss her on the cheek, and whisper in her ear, "I'm so fucking proud of you."

Turning to me, she places her hand on my cheek, feeling my beard beneath her fingertips, then rises to her toes and kisses me softly.

"Thank you, Massimo."

Pressing my palm to her face, I stop her from moving away for a moment.

"Anything for you, little lamb. Fucking *anything* for you."

I kiss her softly, and allow her to pull away. Taking a seat, I watch my girl blossom into the woman she is. Fucking stunning.

She pushes the knife into his shoulder, and drags it through his flesh, and his screams echo off the walls, his back arching off the table as he's wracked with pain. Hadley is calm, collected, and tortures him like she has done it countless times.

Holding the knife in front of his face, she orders him, "Lick."

"I'm not drinking my own fucking blood," he hisses through a clenched jaw.

Tilting her head at it, she speaks softly.

"Yes, Carlo, you will. I'm in control now. What is it you used to say to me? Oh right. You brought this on yourself. This is what you deserve, so fucking take it."

Hearing her, quoting his words back to him, causes me to clench my jaw, as my own murderous rage sets in. I want to jump up and take over, but I can't. This isn't about me, it's about Hadley.

Bianchi licks the knife, and gags at the taste of his blood, so I warn him.

"You vomit, and you will eat it, asshole, so I suggest you swallow."

He swallows, and she cuts into his chest, below the sternum, so he does what they all do, and tries to manipulate her into stopping the torment.

"Please, Hadley, think of Michael. He wouldn't want you to do this."

I watch as my girl snaps, turning from the sweet girl I knew all those years ago, to an unhinged killer. Pulling the knife out of him, her voice comes out raw, and drenched in fucking pain I wish I could take from her.

"How dare you use my son, not your son, *my son,* to save your own skin. You're a pathetic man, Carlo, fucking pathetic. Rot in hell, you disgusting piece of shit."

She raises the knife over him, both of them sobbing for different reasons, and plunges it into his stomach, pulling it out and doing the same thing over again, as he writhes in pain. I count in my head as she viciously stabs her abuser, the killer of her son, and once I get to twenty, I rise to my feet.

285

"Hadley, drop the knife, baby. It's over."

She drops it, the metal clanging on the tiled floor, and collapses in a mess of sobs. Walking over to her, I fall to my knees, pull her into my arms, and hold her tight against my chest.

"I'm sorry," she cries.

Kissing her on the forehead, I encourage her to get it out, because she needs this.

"No apologies, baby. Let it out."

After crying into my chest for several minutes, her sobs subside, and she tilts her head back to stare at me with an expression I don't deserve. Like I'm a goddamn hero, when I'm anything but.

"Thank you, Massimo. I love you."

I swallow hard, as I tell myself I can fucking do this. For her. Knowing something is true, and speaking it, are different things, and my voice comes out raw, the words foreign on my tongue.

"I love you too, little lamb. I love you too."

Twenty-six years ago, I told her she'd be mine one day, because she was too young, and then she disappeared from my life, like a cloud of fucking dust, leaving me wondering if I imagined her. Now she sits in my lap, covered in blood, and while I can't predict the future, I know one thing for sure.

I'm fucking keeping her.

Psycho: After the Ending

Chapter One

Hadley

One Year Later…

After the best year of my goddamn life, I fucked everything up, and there's only one outcome. Losing Massimo. He has given as much as he could, and this will be his breaking point. I stare at the positive pregnancy test in my hand in utter disbelief. I missed one birth control pill, one, and took it the next morning when I realized it, but apparently, that didn't matter. Massimo made himself very clear. He does not want children.

"Hadley!" His voice booms and I panic. Fuck. Glancing around to hide the test, I scurry, because he will come into the bathroom. He doesn't give a shit. I'll get the usual two knocks, and he'll be inside. I shove it behind the flowers, and am grateful that I threw out the box inside the pharmacy bathroom. As predicted, he knocks twice and enters the bathroom.

"Why are you just standing in the bathroom?"

"If you must know, I just finished peeing."

He steps closer to me like the wolf he is, stalking his prey.

"No attitude, Hadley. Not today."

I press my hand to his face and gaze into his eyes, clearly seeing something is off.

"Is something wrong, Massimo? Do you want to talk about it?"

He runs his hands up my arms, until they are cradling the sides of my neck.

"It was a shit fucking day. I don't want to talk, I want to lose myself inside you."

Sliding his hands from my neck up to my face, he holds me in his grip, but it's not the way he holds me that takes my breath away, it's the intense gaze. I don't want to lose this. Leaning his head down, he takes my bottom lip between his teeth, and bites down gently.

"Get undressed. You're taking a shower with me."

Our eyes stay locked on the other's as we both get undressed. Once he drops his boxers to the floor, he's on me, with a growl.

"All fucking day, this is what I thought about."

Massimo slams his lips to mine, and it's not gentle, it's chaotic, aggressive, and needy. His teeth clash against mine, and he licks every inch of my mouth, devouring me, while he sets me on fire. Wrapping his arm around my back, he moves us closer to the shower and, without letting me go, he reaches in and turns the water on. When he's satisfied with the temperature, he pulls me inside with him.

He pushes me up against the wall, his mouth immediately on mine again, his groans mingling with my whimpers, as he slides his hand down my body, dragging his fingers over every inch of skin he can access.

"Fuck, Hadley. Fuck. You drive me insane."

Placing his hands on my hips, he turns me around so I'm facing the wall, and the water splashes over my ass, as he drags his fingers through the moisture on my skin. Kicking my legs apart, he makes quick work of driving his cock inside me, causing me to gasp. Brushing the hair off my neck, he leans down and bites, then licks my neck, while he reaches around, and pinches my nipple until I yelp.

Trailing his hand down my body, he cups my pussy, while moving his cock in and out of me at a leisurely pace. He chuckles softly at my moan, when he circles his middle finger on my clit.

"Something bothering you, baby?" He asks, and I freeze, shaking my head no.

Pinching my clit, he growls in annoyance.

"Don't lie to me."

"I've just been thinking. How firm are you on not having any children?" I ask, and then hold my breath, bracing for the impact.

"Very fucking firm, Hadley. This conversation was done, and over, a year ago. I told you, I don't want kids. It's a non-negotiable for me."

There's my answer. I swallow past the lump in my throat, as he grabs my hips and rails into me.

"Have you been taking your birth control, or do I need to pull out?"

I tell him the truth, mostly.

"I've been taking them. You don't need to pull out."

He pulls out of me and steps away.

"We have had the children conversation, Hadley. I'm not interested in having it again. Over the last year, I have given you more than I ever imagined I'd be capable of. Stop fucking pushing for more. I can't, and won't, do it. I'm sorry you lost your first child, but I can't give you a goddamn replacement."

And then he's gone, leaving me with the shattered pieces of my heart. He's never going to believe this wasn't intentional. Does it even matter? Now, I know for sure, if I have this baby, I will lose him. That thought is suffocating. Did I want more children? I wasn't sure either way, but I always wanted the option. Yet, when Massimo said he did not want any, and wasn't even open to it, I accepted it. I love him, and I would rather have him with no children, than have been with someone else, with children. Massimo can't live with having a child, and I can't live without him. The only consolation is that I have a few months before I'll start showing.

Chapter Two
PSYCHO

I thought she was happy? I thought she was, but now I'm not so sure. I'm not the guy that does that shit. I can order her to not bring it up again, but I can't erase it from her mind. Is this what she thinks about while I'm working? Stalking to my office, I sit behind my desk and fire up my computer. Everything in here makes me think of Hadley. She made jokes about everything being so dark. My desk is black, so is my bar, and my filing cabinets.

Fuck.

I'm furious that she brought this up again. Why now? This whole thing could end up turning full circle. If she comes to me and tells me she wants to leave me, to find someone that can be the man she needs, I won't be able to let her go. It would fucking kill me.

She walks in, and I'm an asshole, so I bark at her.

"Do you actually need something, Hadley?"

Lowering her gaze to the floor, she shakes her head no, and speaks quietly.

"I'm sorry, Massimo. I should not have brought it up, and I promise I won't again. Are you going to eat dinner?"

Turning my attention back to my computer, I say, "No. I lost my goddamn appetite."

"I'm sorry. I-I'm sorry."

Hadley leaves, and again, that spot on my chest starts to ache. She was close with my family when we were kids, and she's even more so now. Hadley is like the missing link for them. Everyone loves her, and I know, without a doubt, if she asks Bones to help her hide from me, he'll do it. They consider her a Bonetti, even though she'll never truly be one. The fear of losing her is never far away.

Three hours later, she comes back, as I'm watching footage from one of our warehouses before I delete it.

"I'm going to bed."

"Alright," I answer in a clipped tone.

She runs off crying and, because I'm such an asshole, I let her.

After working for another hour, my fingers itch to touch her, which I know I don't fucking deserve. I could have simply said nothing had changed, and left it at that. I'm really trying with her, more than I ever fucking have, and right now I feel like it's not enough. Hadley's happiness fucking matters to me, and I'm really beginning to wonder if I can make her happy.

I walk into the bedroom and find her on the pink chaise, one of the many things I've buckled on for her. Never did I think I'd have something pink in my fucking bedroom, yet, here we are. I stare down at her face, her eyes so sad, and it makes my chest ache again.

"Why aren't you in bed?"

Her lashes flutter as she raises her gaze to mine. Hadley wipes the tears from her cheek, and says, "I can't sleep in the bed without you."

Leaning down, I place an arm under her back and the other under her legs, and lift her, carrying her to bed. I set her down, before removing my sweatpants, and getting in beside her. Lying on her side, with her back to me, I stare at her form in her favorite bedtime attire, my t-shirt. I once asked why she wanted to wear my shirts, instead of the expensive lingerie I bought her. She said she preferred my clothing because they smell like me. I don't know how that can be, since they really should smell like our laundry detergent, but I didn't argue. I like her in my clothes.

"Hadley. That's not how you sleep."

Turning to me, she still keeps distance between us.

"I wasn't sure if you wanted... I was giving you space."

I motion for her to come closer to me, and when she does, I pull her in my arms and press my nose to her neck, inhaling her scent.

"I always want you. That does not change."

Reaching under the shirt, I smack her ass.

"Take the shirt off. I don't want to feel cotton, I want your skin."

She sits up, grabs the hem of the shirt, and pulls it over her head, with a smirk on her lips.

"Better?" she asks.

"Better," I agree.

Settling back into my arms, she places her arm around my back, her leg between my thighs, and now I'm happy. This is how I want her. I want her to be content with her life. There is nothing I wouldn't give her, but not this. I was close to my father, but was he a good father? No, he was not. My brother Reaper suffered, due to his choices, and then it was kept a goddamn secret, like he had done something wrong. Secrets were kept, that should've been shared before he died. It wasn't like he didn't know he was short on time. If he was leaving Bones in charge, which he did, why didn't my father tell him about Hadley? Jesus. What a fucking way to find out. That's what my decision boils down to. I would not be a good father. For fuck's sake, they call me Psycho for a good fucking reason. That's not what a kid needs. I don't blame my brothers for making the choices they did, but it's not for me.

Hadley falls asleep, and I kiss her on the head, then close my eyes, trying to do the same.

Chapter Three

HADLEY

Every Saturday, Massimo drops me off for time with the girls. We all take turns on deciding what we are going to do. Last week, Athena had us at a hockey game, but this week it was my choice, which is the only reason I didn't bail. I really don't feel like socializing, but I made such a fuss about wanting to eat at this restaurant, I have to go.

He kisses me goodbye, and I walk onto the patio of La Bella Vita, which Massimo told me is Italian for The Beautiful Life.

Narrowing his gaze at me, he gives me the same lecture I get every week.

"Behave yourself. Do not attempt to lose your guard, Hadley. It's for your safety and my sanity."

Rolling my eyes, I say, "That was eight months ago, Massimo. I won't do it again."

Turning away from him, I walk over to my girls and take a seat beside Bella. Athena and Raina sit across from us.

All three of them have children, and chatter about the different stages of their children. Athena exclaims, "Atlas is sitting up now!"

Atlas is their second child, the cutest little boy, but I try not to hold him, or be around too much because, honestly, it hurts. It makes me wonder what Michael would be doing now. I'm happy for the three women closest to me, but I try to avoid the topic of children as much as possible.

Raina narrows her gaze at me, as she crosses her arms over her chest.

"What gives, Hadley? You've been quiet on the brat chat, and now you're quiet again. What is going on with you?"

I burst into tears as the waiter comes, drops drinks off on the table, then turns and runs, like he has never seen a woman cry in his entire life. Bella reaches over and rubs my back.

"Oh, honey, what's wrong?"

Glancing around, I make sure the guard is not within earshot, and I tell them my secret.

"I'm pregnant."

Athena's eyes widen, as Bella says, "Oh shit," and Raina covers her mouth in horror for me. Yeah, that about sums it up perfectly.

Bella is the first to speak and asks, "What did Psycho say?"

"I haven't told him. I did ask if he was still firm on no children, and that didn't go well. Let's just say he's very firm on no children."

Athena shakes her head, reaches across the table, and takes my hand.

"He will have to deal with it. You didn't get pregnant on your own."

I wipe my tears away when the waiter comes back, not wanting to scare him again, and he sets our salads in front of us.

We eat quietly and Bella breaks the silence.

"What do you want to do?"

I shrug my shoulders, as I stare at my plate of chicken caesar salad.

"I want what I can't have. The child I'm carrying, *and* Massimo."

Athena says, "You need to tell him."

Bella adds, "And soon. You have to give him time to adjust to this news. He is going to freak out, Hadley, you know that. Psycho has surprised us all over the last year, so give him time, and he might surprise us again."

I don't have the faith she does, but she's right, I have to tell him. When I do, I know he's going to melt down, probably like nothing I have ever seen before.

Raina sits back in her chair and says, mostly to herself, I think, "Wow. Psycho is going to be a father."

Raina and Massimo have a difficult relationship. I'm not sure if he'll ever forgive her, for talking to me when I visited her in the hospital, looking for information on his family. It's stupid really, because what I did was far worse, and he's forgiven me. For some reason I can't comprehend, he will not let her off the hook.

We were supposed to go shopping after lunch, but I decide I just don't have it in me.

"I'm sorry, I think I need to skip shopping. Maybe next time."

Raina glares at me, and shakes her head profusely.

"I don't think so, Hadley, next week it's my turn."

I rise from my chair, and they all stand to hug me. Bella squeezes me first, and whispers in my ear.

"It's going to be okay. He is resistant to change, but he'll deal with it, because there won't be a choice other than losing you, and that is something he will not do."

After hugging Raina and Athena, I turn to my guard, nod at him, and follow him to the waiting SUV.

I get in and buckle my seat belt, while he goes to the driver's seat. He gets in and looks at me from the rear-view mirror.

"Where to, ma'am?"

"Home please."

As he drives, I text Massimo.

Me: *Are you at home?*

Massimo: *Yes. Just finishing my workout. Why?*

Me: *I'm on my way, and I need to talk to you about something.*

Massimo: *About?*

Me: *We'll talk when I get home.*

As my guard pulls up to the house, I wish it were a longer drive. The entire way, I tried to think of how to tell him, but then I guess there's really only one way.

I walk into the house and find him in the kitchen, already angry, with a scowl on his face.

"What the fuck is going on?"

Okay, great, I regret giving him advance warning about this conversation. I should have waited for a not so sour mood, but now I have no choice.

"Can we sit down?"

He walks into the large living room, and takes a seat, and I sit across from him on the chair. I'm not afraid of him, but it feels like the better option right now.

"Massimo, I'm sorry, really fucking sorry. I'm pregnant."

He stills, every muscle in his body seems rigid, but he doesn't say a word.

His expression turns from one of shock to heartbreak, and I think I'd prefer a knife plunged into my heart.

"You trapped me," he says with disbelief.

"No. It was not intentional."

He arches an eyebrow. "Yet just last night you asked me if I had changed my mind."

"Obviously, I was already pregnant before that conversation. I did not get pregnant in the last twenty-four hours, and I certainly did not plan it."

Rising from his chair, he levels me with a vicious glare.

"I told you I couldn't do this with you. Nothing has fucking changed."

He runs his hand through his hair, like he might pull it out, as he turns away from me. When he speaks again, I wonder if there is actually a knife in my chest.

"This is why someone only breaks your trust once. You can either trust someone, or you can't. Fuck. I knew better, but that goddamn pussy felt too good. Now look at me. I gotta go. I can't fucking be here in this house with you."

I jump up and scream at him, before he makes it to the door.

"Massimo! Don't leave like this."

He throws over his shoulder.

"Want to know where I'm going, baby mama? To my brother's club, so I can look at the whores I should have stuck with."

Chapter Four

PSYCHO

"Fuck!" I yell out, as I slam my fist on the steering wheel. My mind is reeling as I race toward my brother's club. I need a fucking drink.

A goddamn baby.

I can't do this shit.

She wanted me to love her and, fuck, I do. I gave her a part of me I truly believed didn't exist, but now this is too much. I can't.

Everything is unraveling, like a spool of thread, and I've never felt more out of control, which is dangerous for society as a fucking whole. Am I losing my goddamn mind? I don't know, but I feel my grip, on whatever semblance of sanity I had, quickly slipping away.

I park my car outside *Kages* and head inside, nodding to the doorman, who greets me, and opens the inside door for me. Walking over to my spot I frequented, before Hadley came back into my life, I take a seat.

The waitress is quick with my whiskey, knowing my order by heart. She flashes me a sweet smile after her surprise fades. I have not stepped foot into this club since the night I took my little lamb from the warehouse. Now here I am again, as my entire life spirals out of control.

Control.

When I lose it, I lose my mind. That's not new to me, but this entire situation has my head so fucked up. I sit watching the women dance while I sip my drink. Welcoming the burn in my throat, I close my eyes, and think of Hadley. The need to touch her causes my fingers to twitch, and I groan inwardly. When shit gets bad, I lose myself in her. She's my relief, and now I have nothing.

The punch to my face is sudden, as my eyes open with an instant rage. My brother Kage stands in front of me, with a glare on his face. One I'm ready to wipe out of existence.

"What the fuck are you doing?"

He shakes his head, as if I'm an asshole, when he is the one that just fucking hit me.

"No, Psycho. What the fuck are *you* doing?"

I shrug my shoulders, and take a sip of my drink, as he continues to drill holes into me with his furious gaze.

"Office. Now."

I'm tempted to tell him to go fuck himself. I do not take orders from him, but I go out of pure curiosity. As I follow him, I bark, "Hit me again, and I will hit you back, fucker."

He chuckles as we walk down the long circular hallway, and it only makes me want to drive his head through the wall. Opening the door, he grins. "Ladies first."

Shoving down the urge to punch my brother, I walk through and sit in the black chair, in front of his desk. He walks around and sits behind it.

"Tell me something, Psycho."

I glance up, and stare at him with the same look he's giving me. One of pure disgust.

"Why are you in my fucking club, looking at half naked women, while your girl sits at home, bawling her eyes out?"

I rub at the ache in my chest, as the pain intensifies.

"I didn't know she was crying, and how the fuck do you know?"

Kage chuckles humorlessly.

"You're a fucking idiot. Yes, our girls talk, that's not exactly news. She called Bella crying, and well, you know they all got pulled in after that. Raina came screaming at me about what an asshole you are."

I chuckle, because she's not wrong.

"She's pregnant," I say low, like if I speak too loud, it'll make it true.

"I know, asshole. Let me tell you something about that. She did not get herself pregnant. If you were that worried about her getting pregnant, you should've used a condom, on top of her birth control, or gotten a fucking vasectomy. This is not on her, it's on you. What the fuck are you doing, Psycho? You're destroying everything with her with this little temper tantrum. Did you really tell her you were going to look at the whores you should've stuck with?"

Dragging my hands down my face, I admit it.

"Yeah. I did."

"What did I tell you about regret, asshole?"

"I can't be a fucking father, Kage. This domesticated shit, I don't know how to do it."

Reaching to the small bar beside his desk, he grabs two tumblers, and sets them on the desk. He pours us both two fingers, and slides one to me.

He swirls his drink around, before taking a gulp, and setting it back down.

"Do you think any of us did? You aren't the first Bonetti to freak out about becoming a father, but you are the first to act like this much of a goddamn child."

My brother continues his tirade, as I drink my whiskey.

"You're going to lose her, man. And you're never going to fucking get over that. The baby you created is inside her already. She is having your child, no matter what you do. Hadley already lost one child, and I guarantee you, she's going to cherish this one. If you make her choose between you and this baby, Psycho, you're going to lose. The only thing you need to ask yourself right now is, can you live without her? Is that something you're willing to do? Because..."

He pours us both more whiskey before he continues.

"While you're in my club, acting like a jackass, Hadley is in your house, *packing*."

My chest squeezes, like there's a goddamn vise wrapped around my heart. The panic seizes me, making it hard to get a breath.

Glancing up at my brother, he doesn't speak another word, knowing full well the bomb he just dropped at my feet, and nods, as if to say, 'yeah, that's how bad you fucked up'.

Rising from my seat, I drag a hand down my beard and sigh.

"Where is she going?"

"That, I'm not at liberty to tell you. If she leaves, Psycho, you'll never see her again."

Chapter Five

HADLEY

I pack the last of my things, and text Bones.

Me: Ready.

Bones: On my way.

Setting the letter I wrote Massimo on the bed, I sigh.
I don't want to do this.
Yet, I know I have to, because he has left me no choice. His brother, Reaper, thought I should leave him to 'snap him out of his haze of stupid', but for me it's not about Massimo. It's about our child. After he left, and many tears had fallen, I picked myself up and went into mama mode. Our child deserves better than this, and so do I. I'm not bringing a baby into a house with a father that hates his mere existence. Imagine the damage that comes from a parent hating you, simply because you were born. That's not what I want for my kid, and honestly, I don't want it for Massimo either.

With one last look at the bed we've shared for the last year, I shake my head with regret, as my heart aches with pure anguish.

Throwing my bag over my shoulder, I shake away the devastation, because this isn't about me, or my silly heart. I'm going to be a mother. Again. Another chance to love a child as I did Michael, but this time not let anything, or anyone, take him from me. Placing my hand on my stomach, I whisper to my child.

"This is for you, little one. We're going to be okay."

I hear the front door and freeze momentarily, until I hold my head high, and approach the entryway. Breathing a sigh of relief, I hold my hand over my chest, and say, "Bones."

"Come on, Little Psycho."

As he takes my bag from my shoulder, I swipe at a tear, and follow behind him.

"Can you just call me Hadley?"

He turns to me with a nod, before looking back at his Range Rover, and I take in a shuddered breath as I slip through the open door. Glancing back at Massimo's house, I silently say goodbye one last time.

We pull away from the house, and he glances at me in the rearview mirror.

"Are you doing okay?"

"No," I answer honestly, because this fucking hurts.

"When he shows up at my house looking for you, how do you want me to handle it? Do you want to see him?"

Shaking my head no, I admit, "No. I can't see him. I can't trust myself to do the right thing."

He nods in understanding.

"I'm sorry for putting you in the middle of this, Bones. He's your brother, and it's not right."

Bones is silent for a beat, as he turns the corner.

"You didn't. Look, Psycho is difficult, he always has been, but this is not fucking right. If he isn't going to take care of his woman and child, I will. I promise you, you'll never worry about financial shit. I've always considered you my annoying little sister. This doesn't change that. I know my brother, Hadley. He's going to figure shit out, and show up at my door. The moment he realizes you're gone, he will be there, probably ready to cut my throat."

"It'll be too late," I whisper, "He went to a glorified strip club, to fuck some random woman, while I was at home, crying, pregnant with his child. I have forgiven Massimo for a lot of things, but not this. It's time I choose me."

He pulls in front of his house, and helps me out, with my bag on his shoulder.

"We have a little apartment for you. It's really a bedroom, but it has a private bathroom, and a small kitchen. You're welcome to the rest of the house, but that way, if you want to be alone, you can be. Athena is stocking it, so you have everything you need."

He hands me a cell phone as we walk up to the house, and I question him.

"What's this for?"

Chuckling, he says, "He's going to track your phone. This will buy some time, while he figures out where you went. Take your sim card out, and turn yours off."

He opens the door, steps aside for me to walk through and, when I do, Athena charges for me, wrapping me into a crushing hug.

"I'm sorry," she says, and I swallow past the lump in my throat, returning her hug.

Looping her arm in mine, we walk together, with Bones following behind us, as she takes me upstairs and to a large bedroom. I glance around, taking in the light blue walls, and cream-colored carpet. There's a king-sized bed, with a nightstand beside it, a dresser on the other side of the room, and the small kitchen he mentioned, on the far side. Athena points to the little half wall beside the bed.

"The bathroom is over there."

I nod slowly.

"Thank you for this."

Bones addresses Athena.

"Come on, Butterfly. Let her get settled."

They leave, and I look around the room, telling myself I should unpack, but instead, I grab Massimo's t-shirt. Putting it on, I climb into bed, and do the only thing I seem to be capable of right now.

Cry.

Chapter Six

PSYCHO

I open the front door, not even bothering to close it behind me, as I race through the house, shouting her name.

"Hadley!"

No response.

I move through the bottom floor to the top, and march straight to the bedroom.

"Hadley," I croak, as I spot a note on the bed.

"It's too late," I say to no one, as I pick it up, stare at the tear-stained paper, and fall to the bed.

Dear Massimo,

I was only twelve years old when I admitted to myself I loved you, for the first time. It was probably just a wild crush at the time, but now, I love you with everything I have. That's why this is so difficult.

I do know this is scary for you, but this isn't about us. Not anymore. I'm bringing our child into this world, and nothing matters more than that. Not even you. This is it for me, please, don't try to find me. Don't make this harder than it already is. I sincerely hope you enjoyed fucking the 'whores' you should have stuck with. If you change your mind about things, it's too late. We cannot come back from this. You always say you have a black heart, which I don't believe, but now mine is the darkest shade of black. It's self-made, because this is the only way I can go on without you. I have to harden myself, as if I'm made of stone. Like you.

You're free now. I hope you find whatever it is you want in life. Thank you for gifting me my child. I will love him or her enough for both of us. I will not bother you with support, visitation, or anything else. What you fractured cannot be fixed. This is a clean break.

Goodbye Massimo.

Hadley

I bring the paper to my face, needing to smell her, but there's no scent of her, only the fucking smell of paper. She left me. Hadley is gone.

It seems to take a long fucking time for that simple realization to dawn on me. My head pounds, along with my heart, as I get up and, with one swipe of my arm, throw everything off the dresser. Everything Hadley. Her moisturizer that she didn't take with her. The earrings I gave her six months ago. The books. Only one thing remains. The one photograph Bella took of us, at their house, from last summer.

She was in my arms laughing, looking up at me like I was the most beautiful sunrise. Her eyes lit up with adoration, her smile only for me. When she realized the way I was looking at her, my name fell from her lips in such a sweet way. It sounded like a plea for this to never end, but now it has.

"This is why you can't have nice things, brother."

I turn to find Kage standing behind me, with a smirk on his face.

Clenching my fists at my sides, I hang my head down, and admit what he already knows.

"She's gone."

"I gathered," he says.

Holding up the note, I say, "She thinks I fucked someone at your club."

He shrugs his shoulders, like I brought this all on myself, and I fucking know that, but it doesn't erase the ache.

"I have to find her. Tell me where she is, Kage."

"I can't do that. That's not why I'm here. I came to make sure you are okay, but I can't help you with Hadley. I told you at the club if you didn't get home before she was gone, it'd be too late, and you'd never find her, and here we are. Let her live her life."

That's not fucking happening. I will never let her go. This is not over, not by a fucking long shot.

I walk past Kage, and ignore him, as he yells, "Where are you going?"

She is closest to Bella, so that's my guess, and where I'll start. My knife is in my sheath, my gun in my holster, and I'll use both of them if I have to. When I find her, I'm dragging her back, whether she's happy about it or not.

I leave Kage standing in my house, utterly not giving a fuck what he does, and get to my car, to go find my girl.

Pulling up to Reaper's house, I slam my car into park, and exit, intent on storming into his house, when he appears on the front porch.

He shakes his head at me with disgust.

"She's not here."

I tighten my fists at my sides, blood boiling in my veins, as I begin feeling like the butt of some fucked up family joke. I'm not fucking laughing.

"I'm coming in. I'll search your entire house, Nico. I am not leaving without her."

Arching an eyebrow at me, he waves his hand toward the door.

"First, it's Reaper. And you are leaving without her, because she isn't here, fucking idiot."

Walking inside, I find Bella staring at me wide eyed, as I start to look for Hadley, while screaming her name. I'm on the verge of breaking, and Bella knows me far too well, so I know she sees it.

"Oh, Psycho," she says, with a sad tone to her voice that pisses me off.

"Fucking don't."

I continue to the bedrooms, with Bella on my heels.

"Have you even thought this through? Say you find her, what are you going to do?"

"Nope," I respond, as I move from one bedroom to the other.

Grabbing my arm, she says, "What are you going to do?"

I shrug out of her grip. "Bring her home, where she belongs."

She shakes her head, with a sad smile on her face.

"They aren't going to let you do that. This is a different situation now, Psycho. They see her as a little sister, and that baby is their niece or nephew. Your brothers are not going to allow you to kidnap her for a second time."

"She's mine," I shout.

Crossing her arms over her chest, she glares at me.

"Do not take that tone with me, Massimo. She was yours. Now she's not. That was your doing. So I think you better plan for all the ways you're going to grovel, before you find her. If you find her. This over the top caveman bullshit isn't going to fly. Did you fuck a woman at Kage's club?"

I shake my head with disgust, that this is what everyone in my family thinks of me.

"Of course I didn't."

Letting out a long, exasperated sigh, she says, "She thinks you did. I'm so fucking mad at you, Psycho. My best friend is crying her eyes out, because you led her to believe that, after you walked away from her."

Chapter Seven

PSYCHO

How did I end up here?

She told me she was pregnant with my child, and I lost it. Exploded, and said words that–

Fuck.

Words cannot be unsaid. They are out there, and then etched into your soul for eternity. I did what I fucking do best. I pushed her away, and hurt her in a way I never have. Jesus, I was going to sell her, and yet, I know this is somehow the worst thing I've ever done to her.

She is my sunrise and sunset.

My air.

Fire and water.

Everything.

Nothing makes sense without her. It's a redundant routine, an empty existence, under a sky without a fucking sun.

Pretty words might have saved things, before I left her crying. Not now. I'm a desperate man, and that means desperate measures, that might change everything. Not just with Hadley. Today is the day that the Bonetti family might be down to three brothers, instead of four. This is not how I wanted to do things. My brothers want to turn into the enemy, and keep her from me, so they leave no goddamn choice. Psycho is here to do what he does best.

Creating a bloodbath.

I park down the street, and walk around to the east entrance, knowing the code to get in. Letting myself in through the gate, I head straight for the guard directly in front of me, his back turned as he tosses down a cigarette.

"Eduardo, that's a nasty habit," I say, as I reach around him and press my knife to his throat.

"Relax. I don't want to hurt you, but I will. We're going to walk calmly to the door."

"Psycho?" he questions, not being able to see me, but I know my deep tone gives me away.

"Correct. Don't do anything stupid, and you won't get hurt."

I'm sure his mind is racing, as he realizes one of the Bonetti brothers is essentially threatening to kill him. He's Bones' most trusted guard, and this will get the attention I want. If my brother refuses to let me see her, Eduardo will pay the price. Nobody will keep me from her.

We walk into the side of the house, Eduardo's breaths heavy, footsteps slow, and I spot my brother sitting with his wife, as if all is great in his world. It causes me to hiss.

"Where is she, Bones?"

He looks up at me, and does a double take, while Athena gasps in absolute horror.

Good. I want them to know the stakes.

As predicted, he's quick to remove his wife from this situation.

"Butterfly. Upstairs. Now."

He rises from his spot, as Athena shakes her head at me in disappointment, and heads upstairs.

"What the fuck are you doing, Psycho?"

"Where is she? I want to talk to Hadley. If you refuse me, I'll slash Eduardo's throat, right where we stand."

My brother stands staring at me, his eyes displaying the dark fury I know well, but I can promise you, mine are darker.

"If Hadley is hiding from you, she doesn't want to see you. Let it go."

Tilting my head to get a better look at his face, I chuckle humorlessly, as I press the knife a little more into Eduardo's skin without cutting it, but I want my brother to know I'm getting closer, and that I will do it.

"If it were Athena, you'd let her go?"

He jerks his jaw up, with a smug expression that makes me want to pound the shit out of him, but I hold my ground.

"We are different, you and I, brother. I wanted her to get pregnant. It was not an accident."

I narrow my gaze at him, Eduardo's breathing getting heavier, as I get more agitated.

"You wanted a fucking heir. It had nothing to do with wanting to be a father."

Low blow, I know, because honestly, Bones is a great father.

"I just want to talk to her."

"Psycho," he grits through a clenched jaw, "If you kill anyone in my house, you will not be welcome here to talk to anyone."

"Massimo, what are you doing?" Hadley gasps, and I turn to the stairs and find her, trembling, staring at me with something that looks like disgust.

"Let him go," she pleads, and I stand still, taking her in.

Fuck, she's so beautiful, and it does not escape me that she's wearing my t-shirt.

"Hadley."

Holding up her hand, telling me to stop, she nearly growls at me.

"Let him go, and then we'll talk. Not a second before then."

I move the knife away from his throat, and he gets away from me quickly, pressing his hand to his skin, as if he needs to check for blood.

Bones says, "Go home for the night, Eduardo. Tell Garcia he's on your patrol for the night."

Hadley steps closer to me, but still keeps over six feet distance, and I don't like it.

"Why are you here? I think you said everything already."

I step forward, and stop, when she holds her hand up.

"I need you, baby. I want you to come home with me, and we can talk there. I'll listen to everything you have to say."

Placing her hands on her hips, she glares at me, and I spot the disconnect in her face. It's as if her feelings are gone.

"I want. I need. It's always about you, Psycho."

Ignoring the stabbing feeling in my chest, I approach her and, much to my surprise, she doesn't back away, but her glare doesn't lessen either. Placing my hand on the side of her face, I admit, "I fucked up. It's what I do. Give me a chance to make this right."

Placing her hand on her stomach, as if she's reminding herself why she's pushing me away, she whispers, "No. It's over."

Ignoring the punch to the gut, I use the only thing I've got, the baby, and I'm not fucking proud of it. What I am is desperate to not lose her.

"That's my child. Are you going to let me be involved?"

She glances at my brother, now known as her fucking bulldog, and then back to me.

"You want to be?"

"Of course I want to be. I was shocked, and I needed a fucking minute."

"Bones, can we have a minute alone?"

He groans at her request, but eventually relents and disappears, leaving me alone with her.

Her eyes dart between my face and the couch, as she says, "Do you want to sit?"

We both take a seat on the 'L' shaped sofa, and she opens her mouth to speak, but then snaps it closed quickly.

I stroke a finger down her cheek, unable to show the restraint I know I should.

"Talk to me."

"Bones arranged for me to see a doctor tomorrow. They're going to do an ultrasound. You can come if-"

She stops and shakes her head, as if she's annoyed with herself.

"You don't want to do that. I'm so stupid."

Placing my finger on her chin, I lift her head gently, needing her fucking gaze on mine.

"I want to be there."

I'm still really not so fucking sure about being a father. When she left me, reality crashed down on me, and I had to face the facts. I cannot live without Hadley. Maybe I could, but I sure as hell don't want to.

Leaning forward, I rest my forehead against hers, and follow Bella's advice.

"I'm sorry, baby."

She takes in a shuddered breath, and lets it out slowly.

"Did you fuck somebody else, Massimo? I guess it doesn't matter now, but I need to know."

Lifting my head from hers, I stare into her eyes, feeling the power of her gaze, reflecting exactly what she's feeling. I've always loved that about her, but now I fucking hate it. It's heartbreak, and I did that. I put it there.

"No. Jesus, baby. I would never. I don't want anybody but you. I went to the club, had a few drinks, got punched in the fucking face, and left to find you."

Her eyes widen, as she gasps.

"Somebody punched you? Who?"

"A real asshole. Kage."

She giggles then, and it causes my chest to hurt. I'd get punched a hundred more times to hear that again. My heart slams, as realization comes crashing into me, and the ache grows out of control.

I want her to be happy.

"Come home with me, baby. Let me make this right."

She shakes her head no, denying me the one thing I want so badly, but know I don't deserve.

"You can pick me up at nine, if you want to go with me. If you don't show up, that's fine, Bones will make sure I get there."

Bones. Luca. My fucking brother that I can't stand the thought of currently.

"I will be here, Hadley. You won't go through this alone. I was an asshole to you. Baby, I know how much I fucked up, but I'm going to make this right, if you give me a chance."

She nods in understanding.

"I need to get some sleep."

Fuck. Now I have to leave her, which is the last thing I want to do. I could take her against her will, and I'm tempted, but I know if I do that, I'll break things worse than they already are.

Leaning forward, I press my lips to hers gently, and, between soft kisses, I say, "I love you, Hadley, and I swear to you, I'm going to make you love me again."

When she walks me to the door, my heart slams into my ribcage with anguish, as I leave her in my brother's house, while my head screams 'she's mine'.

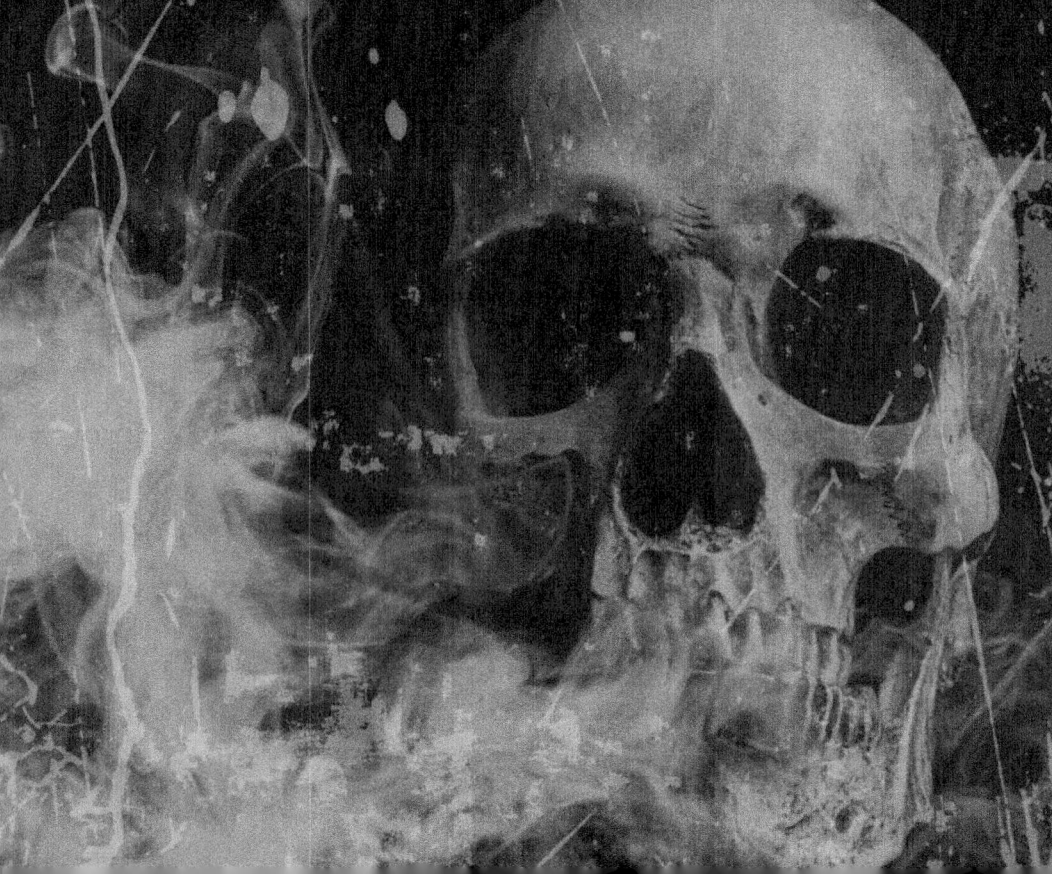

Chapter Eight

HADLEY

"Can I take you out after?" Massimo asks as he drives us to the doctor's office. Am I a little surprised to hear him asking, instead of telling? Far more than a little, but I nod in agreement. I'm trying not to get my hopes up, to prevent myself from getting crushed all over again, but I want to give him the chance, at least. He acted like a complete jackass when I told him I was pregnant, like I knew he would. Massimo doesn't receive information, and think about it, before responding. That's a big part of the reason Bones was made head of the family instead of him. He immediately reacts, making him the most dangerous of the Bonetti brothers. Dangerous not only for others, but also for himself. I may never understand why, but Massimo is convinced he doesn't know how to love, but it's simply not true. While he doesn't say the words frequently, I know he loves me, and I'm convinced he could love our child. If he lets himself, which I'm not convinced he will. There's such a block, like he thinks if he loves too much, he'll lose himself.

He glances over to me as he puts the car in park.

"Thank you."

I stifle a giggle, not wanting to upset him, but him thanking me seems out of character for him. He gets out first, comes around to my side, and opens the door for me. As I stand beside the car, wondering if he's had a personality transplant, he pushes me up against it, and cages me in, with an arm on either side of my head.

Pressing his nose to the side of my neck, he inhales with a growl, his breath on my skin, along with the scratch of his beard, causes a pulsing in my panties I don't need, right before a doctor's appointment.

"I fucking missed you last night, baby."

"I missed you too," I breathe, seconds before he slams his lips to mine, in a kiss so intense I wonder if my soul is on fire. His tongue slides against mine as he tangles his hand in my hair, trying to pull me closer, like he can't get enough of me. With a groan, he pulls back and stares at me, with the same intensity his kiss had.

"You're so fucking beautiful, Hadley. Let's go see what we made."

I giggle as he wraps his arm around my waist, and walks me toward the doctor's office.

"Do you think it's going to be expensive?"

Why I didn't ask about the cost before, I don't know. Bones offered me a job as an attorney for the family, but I haven't accepted yet. I'm waiting to see how things go with Massimo, because I'm afraid working for them, if we aren't together, might be more tension than I'm prepared for.

"It's taken care of, baby."

"Bones?" I question.

He chuckles darkly, clearly not impressed with my assumption.

"You are my girl. That's my baby. I fucking took care of it, just like I'll take care of everything."

I nod my thanks, as we walk through the door, and he takes me to the separate door that takes us to the rooms, and I'm a little confused.

"Massimo, we have to check in."

He chuckles softly as he takes us into examination room three, and lifts me onto the table.

"The Bonettis don't wait, baby."

"Oh," I say, as my mouth forms an 'O' and he groans, making something non-sexual purely erotic.

"Behave."

He arches an eyebrow before shaking his head.

"You stole my line."

We are both laughing when the doctor walks in, pushing a portable ultrasound machine. She stops, and extends her hand to Massimo.

"Mr. Bonetti, good to see you, sir."

After she examines me, and asks me to lift my gown, with a warning about the cold gel, she places the Doppler on my stomach. I flinch, and Massimo stares at me with concern.

"Does it hurt, baby?"

I laugh and say, "No. It's just cold."

"When did you say your last period was?"

"I'm not honestly sure. I lost track of things."

She glances at me, with a weird expression I can't quite identify, and points to the screen.

"Here's your baby."

I stare at the screen in shock. I've been pregnant before, so I know what a baby looks like in early pregnancy, and this is not it, but my shock turns to something else altogether, when I spot Massimo overcome with emotion.

"Holy shit," he gasps.

Rubbing his chest, he speaks low, in a mesmerized voice.

"I'm going to be a father."

It's as if things didn't click for him, until he could see it with his own eyes. He takes my hand in his, pulls it to his lips, and kisses the back of my hand, not taking his gaze from the screen.

"Jesus Christ. I'm such an asshole," he speaks low, so I think he was talking to himself, but I heard him.

With his free hand, he takes his phone out of his pocket, and takes a picture of the screen. The doctor laughs.

"I'll print a picture for you."

She glances between us, and I look at her, waiting for her to say something is wrong. I don't like the growing ache in my belly.

"Is something wrong?" I ask, Massimo looking at me with his brows knitted together, as his own fear sets in.

"Not wrong, no. You're further along than I would've guessed by your size. You're twenty-three weeks, and four days. You have sixteen weeks to go."

My eyes widen as I glance at Massimo, who really needs all the time he can get, to adjust to everything, and he grins. Fucking grins.

"Good. I can't wait for more than that."

He has definitely had a personality transplant, and again he's giving me severe whiplash.

She prints us both a picture, and hands them to us.

"You will need to get prenatal vitamins immediately, and try to eat a healthy diet. Do you want to know the gender, or would you prefer to be surprised?"

Massimo and I share a glance and, with a nod, I say, "Yes, we'd like to know."

The doctor smiles softly, and says, "Congratulations to both of you. It's a boy."

He sighs audibly, but not a sigh of perturbation, but of contentment.

"I have a son."

After she leaves and I get dressed, Massimo sits on the chair beside the desk, and motions for me to come to him. I walk over to him and he pulls me onto his lap.

"I'm so fucking sorry, Hadley. This is not how I want you to remember telling me we're having a child. I can never take back the disgusting things I said. Please tell me I can fix this."

Placing my hands on his face, enjoying the feel of his beard against my fingertips, a tear falls down my cheek, as I stare into his eyes, feeling the weight of the moment.

"Massimo," I breathe, "You already have."

Chapter Nine

PSYCHO

One month later…

"Vincent," she says, while she lays with her head on my lap, as we relax on the sofa, one of my new favorite pastimes. Who knew such mundane shit could be so enjoyable?

I run my fingers through her hair as she gazes up at me, and I say a simple, "No."

"Massimo Jr?" she asks, and I chuckle out another no.

"Naming a baby is hard, they are stuck with it for life."

I remember the words she once said to me.

'People become far too attached to names, and it's insignificant. It's the least important thing about any person.'

I continue my gaze, loving having her on my lap like this, but questioning her words. There's a deep need inside me to know every fucking thought she has. Maybe that's another abnormal thing with me, but I'm obsessed with her. If I could crawl inside her brain, I probably would.

"You said before that names are insignificant."

She rolls her eyes before glaring at me.

"That's different. Sometimes we have to tell ourselves certain things to keep breathing. I had to ditch my identity, and change everything to stay alive. I didn't want to, but I had no choice. I'm hoping that's never the case for our son."

Reaching down, I place my hand on her growing belly, and make a promise I will keep.

"That will never be part of his story. He's a Bonetti, and with that, it practically guarantees an army. Besides, he'll be strong as fuck. What about Kane? It means warrior."

Hadley's lips turn up into a smile, before it turns to a laugh.

"When did you learn names and their meanings?"

Have I spent nights going over baby names while she sleeps? Maybe, but I'll probably never admit it. Out of all my brothers, I was the only one to be this reluctant, in fact, I was furious when I first heard the news, but now I feel different about it. I'm still nervous I'll fuck shit up, and be a bad father, but I'm looking forward to it. I trust that Hadley will make sure I'm not fucking up our kid. I always thought I was a lot like my father, and for a long time I wanted to be, but now that I'm going to be a father, my perspective has changed. The things he allowed to happen to my brother, Reaper, still gnaw at me. My father didn't do those things, but he allowed Frank to live after that shit, hell no. That's not how I would've handled it. If anybody ever dares to try to hurt my son, especially that way, I'll gut them. There won't be any chance of continuing to breathe. Crawling onto my lap, Hadley straddles my legs, and runs her tongue over my bottom lip.

"No more thinking."

"Fuck."

In the last few weeks, Hadley has gotten aggressive sexually, and I love every fucking minute of it. She places her hands on my face, reaching her fingers back and digging her nails into the side of my head, while she takes my bottom lip between her teeth, and bites down. I groan when she grinds her hot pussy over my cock. Placing my hands on the small of her back, she knits her brows together, going for a serious expression.

"Hands off, Mr. Bonetti. Until I give you permission, you know you aren't allowed to touch."

Fuck, I love this game. She fucks with me until I snap, knowing damn well that, when I do, I'll take her, even if she says no. Hadley loves making me feral for her, and she does it often.

I hold up my hands, before placing them at my sides, and watch as she pulls her shirt over her head, and tosses it to the floor.

"Fuck," I groan again, as I spot her big tits spilling from her bra. Pregnancy has several perks, and her pretty tits are one of many.

Reaching her arms behind her, she unsnaps her bra, while her teasing eyes stare into my lust-filled ones. After she gets rid of the bra, she leans down as much as she can with her belly, and runs her tongue up the center of my chest, with a sweet little moan escaping her lips.

Lifting her ass up, she runs her fingers through my hair, pulling at the strands, and putting her tits close enough to my face that I could lick them, if I wasn't committed to her game.

"Such a pretty little lamb," I groan, "eventually you're going to make me lose my mind, and your game will be done."

With a sexy little grin, she admits, "I hope so."

Hadley reaches between her legs, and her hand disappears under her skirt, as she plays with her pussy. I clench my jaw, annoyed that I can't see underneath the fucking fabric. She pulls her hand up, and shows me her fingers, coated in her arousal. This is how I start losing my goddamn mind, her taste drives me wild. And she knows it.

"Say please," she taunts.

"Please, baby. Fuck. Let me taste you."

Pushing her fingers into my mouth, she grinds down on me, while I suck and lick her fingers clean. It's always the same, she knows it's her pussy on my tongue that causes me to lose control.

I grab her with a growl, and flip her onto the couch on her back. Making quick work of unzipping her skirt, I toss it onto the floor. I'm running out of patience, so I rip her panties off her beautiful body, while she complains about them being expensive.

"I don't give a fuck if they were a million dollars."

I move between her legs and inhale her scent. It's changed a bit since she's been pregnant, but fuck, she still smells so good it makes my mouth water.

"If you taunt me with this sweet cunt, baby, I will want it. And when I want it, I'll have it."

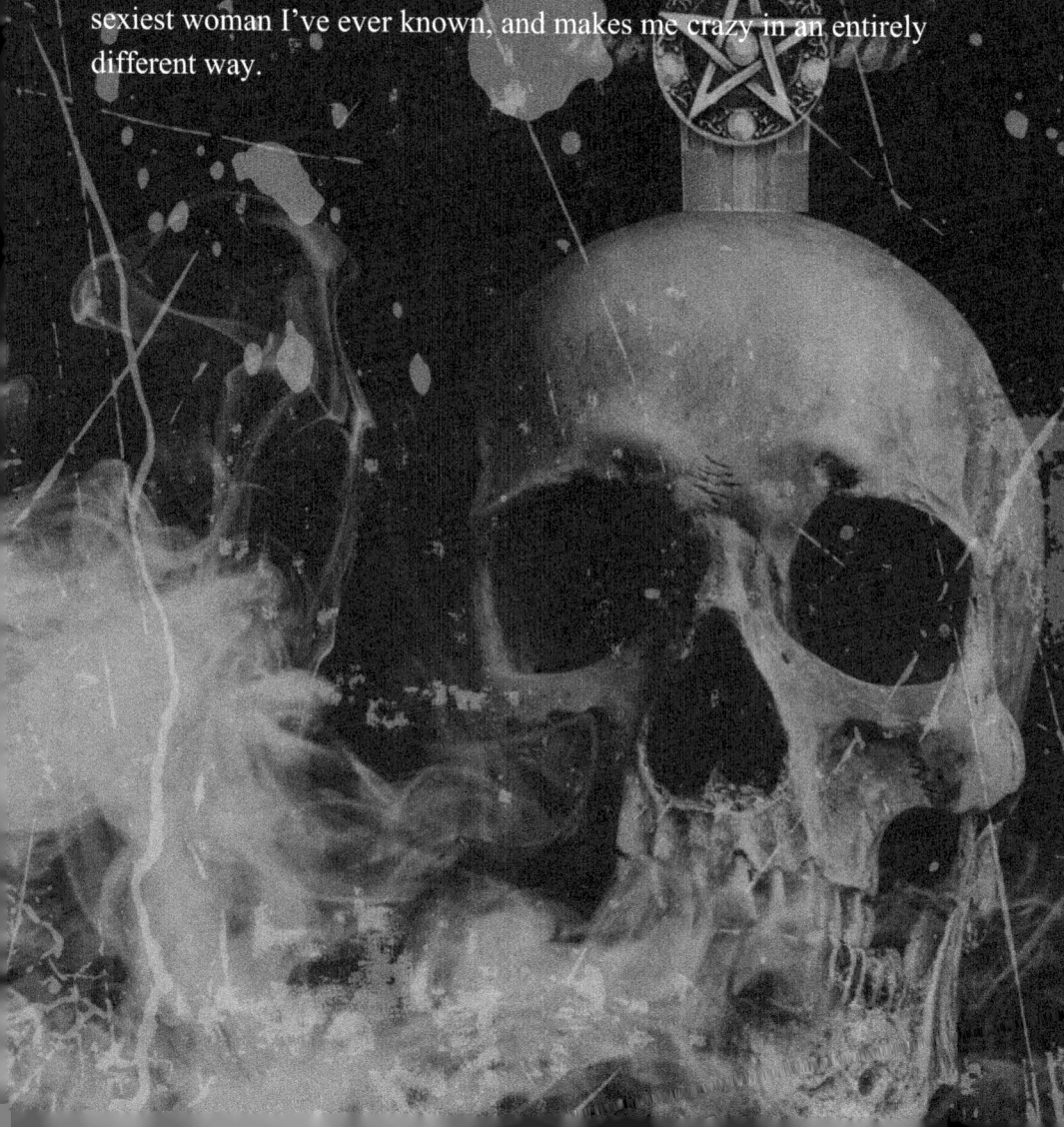

I bury my face in her pussy and lick up her slit, collecting the wetness on my tongue, before swirling it around her clit.

"Massimo," she moans, as she digs her nails into my head, which I love, and the harder she presses into my scalp, the firmer my cock gets.

"Come for me, baby. Drench my face."

I pull her clit between my lips and suck, and, as predicted, she loses control, lifting her hips as she grinds her pussy into my face, and comes undone. I've never been a believer in fate, or that two people were meant to be together. Yet, if any woman was made for me, it's her. The annoying little girl, that drove me insane, is now the sexiest woman I've ever known, and makes me crazy in an entirely different way.

Chapter Ten

HADLEY

The next day…

"Where are we going?"

"To a place," he responds with a smirk.

"Massimo!"

He chuckles and mocks me.

"Hadley!"

Folding my arms over my chest, I huff in mock annoyance, and he laughs again.

"We're almost there. Stop being a brat, or I'll find somewhere to pull over, and spank your ass."

I glance at him with an arched brow, because he knows damn well that only encourages bad behavior with me, but he winks at me, before focusing back on the road.

We stop at a parking lot, and I lose my mind. I know this area, but I haven't been here since I was a kid.

"Massimo?"

We get out of the car, and he pulls me into his arms.

"We were here as kids. Do you remember the way you couldn't behave? And I threatened to tie you up?"

I giggle and nod.

"You were such a jerk."

"I still am, little lamb. That was the first time I saw you and, Jesus, even as kids I knew you were beautiful. And trouble."

I glance in the direction of the lake, then back to him.

"So we're going swimming? I don't even have a bathing suit."

He grabs my hand and starts pulling me toward the lake, pulling my hand to his lips to kiss my knuckles.

"We're getting married, little lamb."

My heart drops.

"What? You don't want to get married. We aren't even engaged."

He stops walking, and turns to me with a serious expression.

"I didn't, but now I do. You are having my child, and there's not a day that will go by that I don't want you by my side, so you should be my wife."

Fighting back the tears threatening to fall, I shake my head, and pull away from him.

"This isn't even about me, is it, Massimo?"

He has, more than once, expressed his concern that if he wasn't around, I might give the baby my last name, instead of his.

I turn back to the car.

"Let's go. I'll sign a fucking legal document guaranteeing he'll have your name, but I'm not getting married like this."

"Hadley!" He snaps, while grabbing my arm, and pulling me back to him.

"I'm fucking this up. Do I want him to have my name? Of course, I do, baby. That's not why we are here. I love you, and refuse to spend one day without you. I want you to be my wife. It's not about our son, it's about us. Our son should be a Bonetti, and so should you. You belong to me, baby, I belong to you. Let's get married."

The tears fall down my cheeks, and I nod, as he wraps his arm around the small of my back, and we walk to the lake.

PSYCHO

We stand in front of the minister, and I honestly can't believe that I'm here. I was sure I'd never get married, or have kids, because I never had any interest in it. Until Hadley. I was honest with her about my reasons. Over the last few weeks, it bothered me that there was a way in which she wasn't mine. Legally. I'll never allow a day to come when she isn't with me. I would have killed Eduardo that night, if it had been necessary. If there comes a time when someone tries to keep her from me, they die. I'm not a bad man because of a traumatic past. I'm bad because I just am. Hadley is the only thing that keeps me somewhat sane.

We said our basic vows, nothing fancy like my brother's, but I'm okay with it. A radiant smile crosses her face, after the minister says I can kiss her. Scooping her into my arms, I whisper in her ear, "I love you, Hadley, but you should prepare yourself. I intend to fuck my wife tonight like I don't."

AKNOWLEDGEMENTS

Thank you for reading Psycho. I hope you enjoyed Massimo and Hadley's story.

This book went through many changes through the writing process. Thank you to my amazing alpha team for helping me get through it. Crystal, Panda, Heather, Nikki, DiDi, and Grace, thank you for always being there to read my words. Your feedback means the world to me.

To my Influencer, Street, and ARC team: Thank you from the bottom of my heart. I see everything you do for me and I appreciate it. So many of you have embraced the Bonetti Brothers in a way I never expected. Thank you for loving them almost as much as I do.

To my PA: Grace Farnsworth aka The Warden. Thank you for coordinating my insane level of chaos. I appreciate you.

To my Editor: Thank you for making sure no comma was left out. I love you to death and appreciate you taking such good care of my babies.

To my Cover Designer/Formatter RedFox Book Design: Thank you for always caring about my vision and providing me with covers I am proud to display. You work endlessly until I say I love it, and that means a lot to me.

To my Patreon community: Thank you for your love and support.

ALSO BY CHELLE ROSE:

Forbidden Desires Series

1. *Mercy www.books2read.com/chellerosemercy*
2. *Finding Mercy www.books2read.com/chellerosefinding-mercy*
3. *Liam and Mercy www.books2read.com/LiamandMercy*
4. *Xander's Secret https://books2read.com/Xanderssecret*

Dark Desires Series

1. *Unholy www.books2read.com/chelleroseunholy*
2. *Unhinged www.books2read.com/chelleroseunhinged*
3. *Unchained www.books2read.com/chelleroseunchained*
4. *Undone www.books2read.com/chelleroseundone*
5. *An Unhinged Wedding www.books2read.com/unhingedwedding*

Men of Mayhem Series

1. *De Luca: The Devil* www.books2read.com/delucathedevil
2. *De Luca: The Saint* www.books2read.com/delucasaint
3. *De Luca: The Sinister Game* www.books2read.com/sinistergame
4. De Luca: The Dalia Effect www.books2read.com/thedaliaeffect

Den of Sin Duet

1. *Zade www.books2read.com/zade*
2. *Sin www.books2read.com/sin-chellerose*

Bonetti Brothers Series

Printed in Dunstable, United Kingdom

68187916R00190